THE USE OF THE CREATIVE THERAPIES
WITH SEXUAL ABUSE SURVIVORS

THE USE OF THE CREATIVE THERAPIES WITH SEXUAL ABUSE SURVIVORS

Edited by

STEPHANIE L. BROOKE, Ph.D., NCC

CHARLES C THOMAS • PUBLISHER, LTD.
Springfield • Illinois • U.S.A.

Published and Distributed Throughout the World by

CHARLES C THOMAS • PUBLISHER, LTD.
2600 South First Street
Springfield, Illinois 62704

© 2007 by CHARLES C THOMAS • PUBLISHER, LTD.

ISBN 13 978-0-398-07701-3 (hard)   ISBN 10 0-398-07701-0 (hard)
ISBN 13 978-0-398-07702-0 (paper) ISBN 10 0-398-07702-9 (paper)

Library of Congress Catalog Card Number: 2006044669

With THOMAS BOOKS *careful attention is given to all details of manufacturing
and design. It is the Publisher's desire to present books that are satisfactory as to their
physical qualities and artistic possibilities and appropriate for their particular use.*
THOMAS BOOKS *will be true to those laws of quality that assure a good name
and good will.*

Printed in the United States of America
UB-R-3

Library of Congress Cataloging-in-Publication Data

The use of the creative therapies with sexual abuse survivors / edited by Stephanie L.
    Brooke.
      p. cm.
  Includes bibliographical references (p.).
  ISBN 0-398-07701-0 -- ISBN 0-398-07702-9 (pbk.)
   1. Adult child sexual abuse victims--Rehabilitation 2. Art therapy. 3. Play therapy.
  4. Dance therapy. 5   Music therapy. 6. Drama--Therapeutic use. I. Brooke,
  Stephanie L.

  RC569.5.A28U74 2006
  616.89'1656--dc22   200644669

CONTRIBUTORS

Sally Bailey, MFA, MSW, RDT/BCT

Brian L. Bethel, M.A., PCC, LCDC

Sandra L. Curtis, Ph.D., MT-BC, MTA

Linda M. Dunne, M.A.

Claire Edwards, ATR

Loretta Gallo-Lopez, M.A., RPT-S, RDT-BCT

Noreen M. Glover-Graf, Rh.D., C.R.C

Maria C. Gonsalves, M.A., MT

Craig Haen, M.A., RDT, CGP

Gisèle C.T. Harrison, MSW

Kate Hudgins, Ph.D.

Toshiko Kobayashi, M.A., ATR, LCAT

Kristen Larson, Ph.D., LPC

E. Magdalena LaVerdiere, Ph.D.

Charles E. Myers, M.A., LPC, LMHC, NCC, NCSC, RPT

Kevin O'Connor, Ph.D., RPT-S

Joan Phillips, Ph.D., LMFT, LPC, ATR-BC

Janice Samoray, Ph.D., LMHC, LLP, ATR-BC, CFS, CSS

Yehudit Silverman, M.A., DTR, RDT

Dee Spring, Ph.D., ATR-BC, MFCC

Grace E. Valentine, Ph.D., ADTR, DTRL, LPC

PREFACE

Inspired by Brooke's (1997) work, *The Use of the Creative Therapies with Sexual Abuse Survivors* is a comprehensive volume that examines the use of art, play, dance, music, and drama to treat trauma related to sexual abuse. The author's primary purpose is to examine treatment approaches which cover the broad spectrum of creative art therapies. The collection of chapters is written by renowned, well-credentialed, and professional creative art therapists in the areas of art, play, dance, music, and drama. In addition, the chapters are complimented with photographs of client art work, diagrams, and tables. The reader is provided with a snapshot on how these various creative therapies are used to treat male and female survivors of sexual abuse, as well as children, teens, and adults. This informative book will be of special interest to educators, students, therapists, and creative art therapists working with traumatized survivors of sexual abuse.

CONTENTS

THE USE OF THE CREATIVE THERAPIES
WITH SEXUAL ABUSE SURVIVORS

Chapter 1

THE MEDICINE WHEEL APPROACH TO THERAPY

Stephanie L. Brooke

INTRODUCTION

Sexual abuse has a pervasive impact on the developing child (Lubit et al., 2003), family, schools, communities, and society as a whole. This type of trauma can result in Post Traumatic Stress Disorder (Agaibi & Wilson, 2005) as well as post traumatic guilt and shame (Wilson, Drozdek, & Turkovic, 2006). I became interested in sexual abuse and art therapy when I was completing an internship at Wiley Preschool Program for emotionally disturbed children in Bethlehem, PA. I was in the undergraduate clinical/counseling program at Moravian College. I was reading books on art therapy with children at the time. I began to experiment with my 4-year-old clients by having them draw pictures. I remember a boy, I'll call him George, who was sexually abused by his father. Over and over, he drew trains, talked about trains, perseverated on trains. His coco brown skin in contrast to his pale green eyes made him a striking child, but his expression was empty, lacking emotion. I remember how sad I felt when the social worker told me that George would never lead a normal life due to his pervasive abuse issues. Another child, a little girl I'll call Alisha, was sexually abused by her mother's boyfriend. In a repeating pattern, she would draw herself next to her mother. She would end each drawing by taking a black crayon and blacking out the face of her mother. Alisha had strong anger feelings toward her mother. This undergraduate experience would later lead to my curiosity about graphic indicators of sexual abuse. I focused on this in my second book, *Art therapy with sexual abuse survivors*. I will recap that research here (Brooke, 1997).

GRAPHIC INDICATORS OF SEXUAL ABUSE

There has been little research which has focused on graphic indicators of sexual abuse. However, numerous observations have been made by art therapists, psychotherapists, and other mental health practitioners. "The use of art expression has allowed us to explore our hypothesis that sexually exploited children may produce predictable themes and images through their art and that substantiation of this hypothesis might aid greatly in the identification and treatment of victims" (Carozza & Hiersteiner, 1982, p. 167). This section will concentrate on common images in the drawings of child and adult survivors of sexual abuse. Although the intent is to identify possible victims of abuse, the significance of indicators is questioned by some practitioners, primarily due to the fact that identification of indicators is based on case studies rather than research studies. Additionally, many of the observations were made by non-art therapists. Identification of graphic indicators is in the beginning stages. Common images have emerged in the literature. The value of identifying common images is that drawings may aid in the disclosure of sexual abuse (Burgess, 1988; Kelley, 1985).

HUMAN FIGURE DRAWINGS

Human figures drawn by sexual abuse survivors often have recurring themes. Omission of body parts is typical in the artwork of sexual abuse survivors, such as missing hands and feet (Burgess, 1988; Burgess and Hartman, 1993; Chantler, et al., 1993; Jones, 1989; Kelley, 1984; Malchiodi, 1990; Riordan & Verdel, 1991; Sadowski & Loesch, 1993; Sidun & Rosenthal, 1987). Spring (1988) conducted a research study with female, adult survivors and observed fragmented bodies in their art. Some sexually abused clients will portray figures with very detailed emphasis on the face and clothing of the upper portion while neglecting to represent the lower portion of the body (Malchiodi, 1990; Sadowski & Loesch, 1993). This may represent helplessness or lack of support related to the sexual abuse (Klepsch & Logie, 1982; Sadowski & Loesch, 1993) and denial of the sexual self (Brooke, 1997; Malchiodi, 1990). For those survivors who do not draw the lower portion, Spring (1993) observed that this may be a fear of acknowledging the weapon of sexual abuse if it was the penis. Spring stated that this depends on the identification of the figure, whether it represents the self or the perpetrator. I have noticed that the focus for some survivors is on intellect rather than affect, which associated with the body; therefore, some tend to draw only portraits (Brooke, 1997). Malchiodi (1990) attributed the lack of torso to denying the sexual areas of the body.

We can, therefore, surmise that the absent torsos were not the result of cognitive limitations. Alice's omission is clearly related to her sexual victimization and points to her use of denial. She uses this primitive defense mechanism in an attempt to keep unconscious the painful experience to which she was subjected. (Kaufman & Wohl, 1992, p. 55)

Some researchers have noted that the absence of body parts indicated denial (Carozza & Hiersteiner, 1982; Levick, 1983). Separation of trunk may also reveal sexual abuse (Kaufman & Wohl, 1992). Generally, drawings by survivors depict poorly integrated figures (Chantler et al., 1993; DiLeo, 1983; Hibbard & Hartman, 1990; Stember, 1980).

According to Kelley (1984), a registered nurse working with children, shading of the figure suggests preoccupation, fixation, and anxiety. Signs of anxiety in children can take other forms according to Briggs and Lehmann (1989): omissions, distortions, heavy lines, turned down mouth, raised arms, and arms turned inward. Kelley (1984) found that sexually abused children shade the genital and chest areas of figures.

Explicit depiction of genitals by children has been used as an indicator of abuse by some clinicians (Burgess, 1988; Faller, 1988; Hagood, 1993; Hibbard & Hartman, 1990; Hibbard et al., 1987; Kelley, 1984; Miller et al., 1987; Yates, et al., 1985). "It must be cautioned that, although the presence of genitalia in a child's drawing should alert one to consider the possibility of sexual abuse, it does not prove it, just as the absence of genitalia does not exclude abuse" (Hibbard et al., 1987, p. 129). Exaggeration or minimalization of sexual features were also widespread in children's art products (Chantler et al., 1993; Dufrene, 1994; Cohen-Liebman, 1995; Riordan & Verdel, 1991; Yates, et al., 1985). Sexual connotations in children's art work can take other forms such as depicting figures wearing sexy clothing or make-up, or with long eye-lashes that conveys seductiveness (Howard & Jakab, 1968; Malchiodi, 1990). On the other hand, some children may avoid sexualization, thus, creating figures with ambiguous sexuality (Faller, 1988; Kelley, 1984). With male survivors whose perpetrator was also male, I have observed that gender confusion or questions about sexual identity surface in their art work. Additionally, I have found that facial features sometimes have female connotations for some male survivors (Brooke, 1997).

Other themes include the lack of a mouth, which may relate the the secrecy surrounding the abuse; this was observed in the art of children and adolescents (Briggs & Lehmann, 1985; Sidun & Rosenthal, 1987). Huge circular mouths are often drawn by children when oral sex was involved (Briggs & Lehmann, 1985). Spring (1993) felt that the circular mouth may be related to the silent scream. Riordan and Verdel (1991) found both the emphasis on the mouth and the omission of the mouth in the work of child survivors. Drachnik (1994) noted that some sexually abused children have drawn protruding tongues in their art; yet, this graphic indicator has not been empirically validated.

Spring (1988) found that sexually abused adults were more likely to draw eyes. Her research study utilized 225 drawings and included a control group. The survivors included two groups: fifteen rape victims and fifteen women who experienced multiple sexual abuse incidents. All thirty women were diagnosed with Post Traumatic Stress Disorder. Their drawings were compared to a control group of fifteen women who did not experience sexual abuse or other life threatening events or illnesses. Spring (1988) associated the disembodied eye, highly stylized eye, or tearful eye to guilt within the context of sexual abuse. Earlier literature in the field revealed an association between eyes and sexuality or sexual abuse (Dax, 1953; Garrett & Ireland, 1979; Hammer, 1978; Howard & Jakab, 1969; Nederlander, 1977; Stember, 1980).

Low self-concept may be a characteristic of sexual abuse survivors. One way low self-concept was graphically portrayed was by representing the self as a small figure. DiLeo (1983) supported the view that small figures drawn at or near the lower edge of the paper indicated feelings of inadequacy, insecurity, and even depression. Hibbard and Hartman (1990) reported that sexually abused children will draw tiny figures more often that nonabused children, which they credited to shyness or withdrawal.

Kaufman and Wohl (1992) observed that some sexual abuse survivors will often shade hair heavily, possibly revealing difficulty controlling impulses. Although other others have not made mention of this fact, Kaufman and Wohl (1992) related thinning hair at the top of the head to possible sexual abuse.

Clown images sometimes characterized the work of child survivors (Burgess & Holmstrom, 1979; Hagood, 1993; Stember, 1980). "This concealment device often appears among severely traumatized female victims who are maintaining a facade of smiling exuberance" (Kelley, 1984, p. 424). Although abused girls depict more clown images, sexually abused boys also depict concealment through football helmets, sport equipment, or other protective gear. Kaufman and Wohl (1992) found that abused girls were significantly identified more often than abused boys using human figure drawings.

Chase (1987) examined human figure drawings of thirty-four female incest survivors, ranging in age from five to sixteen, with a matched sample of twenty-six emotionally disturbed subjects and thirty-four subjects with no history of sexual abuse or emotional disturbance. When compared with the emotionally disturbed subjects, sexually abused children significantly drew more hands omitted, fingers omitted, clothing omitted, and presence of phallic like objects. When compared to nonabused children, sexually abused subjects significantly drew large circular eyes, mouth emphasized, long neck, arms omitted, hands omitted, fingers omitted, clothing omitted, and presence of phallic-like objects.

FAMILY DRAWINGS

The Kinetic Family Drawing (KFD) has revealed several common themes in the artwork of sexual abuse survivors. Kaufman and Wohl (1992) found that the KFD significantly identified male and female survivors of sexual abuse. Goodwin (1982) reported evidence of isolation, role reversals, and encapsulation in the KFD's of child survivors. Cohen and Phelps (1985) discovered that the child will often omit self from the KFD. In my work with adult survivors, omission of self was especially common if the person was struggling to remember aspects of the traumatic situation (Brooke, 1995). Burgess and Hartman (1993) found that the KFD may reveal family conflicts. Isolation, barriers, encapsulation, and sexual themes were also portrayed in the KFD's of children and adolescents (German, 1986; Johnston, 1970). Encapsulation and compartmentalization were repetitive features in KFD's of sexually abused children (Kaufman & Wohl, 1992). "The omission of the trunk and appendages in these family members is important since these are instruments of power with which to manipulate or be manipulated" (Wohl & Kaufman, 1985, p. 74).

Goodwin (1982) used the KFD when evaluating possible sexual abuse survivors. Although she implemented a series of drawings in the evaluation, only the KFD will be discussed. She examined nineteen female children who were suspected sexual abuse survivors. Goodwin (1982) found evidence of isolation, compartmentalization, and role reversals in the drawings of sexual abuse survivors. Additionally, she observed that these children drew themselves larger than their mother.

Chase (1987) compared the KFD's of twenty-seven female incest survivors, ranging in ages from five to sixteen, with a matched sample of thirty-seven emotionally disturbed children and thirty-seven subjects with no history of sexual abuse or emotional disturbance. When compared to the emotionally disturbed sample, incest survivors significantly drew encapsulated figures. When compared to the nonabused sample, survivors significantly depicted nurturance of self and mother.

Kaplan (1991) examined the drawings of fifty-one males and fifty-four females ranging in age from seven to fourteen years. Thirty-five children were sexually abused, thirty-five emotionally disturbed, and thirty-five were "normal" children. Three objective raters identified the presence of designated graphic features in the drawings. The two most significant indicators were the *family engaged in sexual activity* and *family engaged in intimate activity*.

Hackbarth (1991) and colleagues found that the KFD significantly differentiated between abused and nonabused children. Thirty children, ranging in age from six to thirteen years, classified as sexually abused by the Department of Human Services, were compared to thirty unidentified children in a public school district. They ranged in age from six to eleven years. The subjects were matched with those in the experimental group: twenty-five girls and five boys (twenty-six were white and four were black). Mothers also completed the KFD. Using the Like to Live in Family (LLIF) rating procedure (Burns, 1987), five counselors scored the KFDs on desirability of family life. Sexually abused children drew significantly less desirable family situations compared to their mothers. Mothers of sexually abused children drew significantly less desirable family settings than did mothers of unidentified children. Mothers and their unidentified children did not significantly differ in their KFDs. "The KFD shows enough promise as an evaluation tool in the area of sexual abuse that elementary counselors may want to consider this instrument for inclusion in their repertoire of assessment skills" (Hackbarth et al., 1991, p. 260).

HOUSE DRAWINGS

Some clinicians have discovered that red houses are sometimes drawn by child survivors (Cohen & Phelps, 1985; Hagood, 1994; Silvercloud, 1982). Also, children who were sexually abused tend to omit bedrooms or if bedrooms are present, indicate bizarre sleeping arrangements or lack of privacy (Goodwin, 1982). One window treated differently on a house or crossed out windows may be possible indicators of childhood sexual abuse, as observed by some clinicians (Cohen & Phelps, 1985; Hagood, 1994; Kaufman & Wohl, 1992; Silvercloud, 1982). The inclusion of circles, in general, was also another possible indicator (Sidun & Rosenthal, 1987). According to Horovitz (1996), red curtains and/or doors were depicted in the drawings of child and adolescent survivors.

TREE DRAWINGS

Kaufman and Wohl (1992) conducted a pilot study with fifty-four children: eighteen identified survivors of sexual abuse, eighteen children from a mental health organization, and eighteen children randomly drawn from the community. They discovered that tree drawings significantly identified male survivors of sexual abuse as compared to females. "The later may be clinically valid when we understand that the tree, as a growing vegetative form, may at some level relate to the 'growing' shape of the erect penis and that the injury to a male's sense of his virility may be unconsciously connected to the tree" (Kaufman & Wohl, 1992, p. 34). Additionally, Kaufman and Wohl observed that younger children, four to six years, were significantly identified using the tree portion of the HTP as compared to older children, seven to ten years. Generally, the separation of the trunk from the crown, dead trees, and absence of leaves characterized the tree drawings of abused children. In my work with adult sexual abuse survivors, I found that many drew slanted trees (Brooke, 1995), suggesting lack of stability.

HEART IMAGES

Jones (1989) noted that survivors tend to draw encapsulated hearts. According to Malchiodi (1990), sexually abused girls will use heart images in their artwork. This may take the form of the traditional stereotyped heart images or using hearts in shapes on clothing, lips, or hair (Malchiodi, 1990). "A suffering child is perhaps instinctively drawn to the sacrificial heart. The sacrifice of the innocent may be an archetypal memory of children" (Kidd & Wix, 1996, p. 110).

When working with a group of sexual abuse survivors, heart images were commonly depicted (Brooke, 1995). Some survivors often depict broken hearts, which includes wedges as the dividing line, an image that Spring (1993) found when working with adult survivors. Jones (1989) found the predominate use of hearts revealed that "something important is missing in their (children's) lives and that they wish this element could be present" (p. 180). Kaufman and Wohl (1992) reported that heart images reflected feelings of being exposed and vulnerable. Sagar (in Case & Dalley,1990) discussed the case of Fay, a six-year-old sexually abused girl, who made a clay figure that was given a heart transplant. It was important for her to do this before the patient died. "The heart, generally recognized as the seat of feelings, or the generator of feelings, if damaged or absent, would feel like death emotionally" (Sagar in Case & Dalley, 1990, p. 111). A heart image is the focal point for a drawing in Chapter four of this book.

ADDITIONAL DRAWING CHARACTERISTICS

The depiction of inclement weather may be indicative of childhood abuse (Manning, 1987; Miller et al., 1987; Stember, 1980) and depression. These pictures will often contain images of darkened skies and sun, heavy shading, and rain (Burgess, 1988). I have related turbulent weather to the perception of the environment as threatening. Clouds, particularly over human figures, have been associated with sexual abuse (Kaufman & Wohl, 1992). Movement, such as strong wind, was indicative of loss of control (Manning, 1987):

"It has been observed that children who are in trouble frequently produce more moving art than children who are well behaved. Particularly during periods when the struggle for control is intense, art often becomes meager, overly pious, or saccharin, or the child loses interest" (Kramer, 1971, p. 152). Favorite weather drawings made by child survivors have revealed insecurity and isolation of affect (Burgess & Hartman, 1993). Generally, drawings by child survivors will show kinetic activity such as scribbling, dots, and violent themes (Jones, 1989).

Another possible indicator of childhood sexual abuse was enclosure or encapsulation of figures (Cohen & Phelps, 1985; Stember, 1978). Malchiodi (1990) defined encapsulation as anything in which the child has visually enclosed herself such a house, a car, or a tree. DiLeo (1983) suggested that encapsulation expressed feelings of isolation and lack of communication. Floating images and lack of a ground line may reveal a chaotic social environment and an attempt to compensate (Carozza & Hiersteiner, 1982). Spring (1993) related floating images, such as balloons, to dissociation.

On a more abstract level, circles and wedges were often represented in the art of sexually abused people (Dufrene, 1994; Cohen-Liebman, 1995; Malchiodi, 1990; Sidun & Rosenthal, 1987; Spring, 1993). Spring (1993, 1988) found that for adult survivors, wedges symbolized feelings of being threatened in the past as well as the present.

Color has also been related to the identification of sexual abuse survivors. Malchiodi (1990) noted that survivors tend to use complementary colors, such as red and green, which make it difficult to look at a drawing for any length of time. Additionally, black and red common colors used by sexual abuse survivors (Brooke, 1997; Cohen & Phelps, 1985; Spring, 1978, 1993). I can remember the first time that I led an art therapy group for sexual abuse survivors. As we were beginning the first exercise, group members complained that there was not enough dark colors, particularly black.

SUMMARY

Given that sexual abuse is difficult to talk about, particularly for child survivors, mental health practitioners are focusing on additional measures for identifying possible victims, such as graphic indicators of abuse. "Sexually abused children use art materials symbolically to express feelings of being full of mess inside, of being messed-up, and of trying to find some way to control and handle the mess or poison" (Sagar, in Case & Dalley, 1990, p. 108). Art therapy provides a visual dialogue to communicate feelings without relying on words.

Common themes have been noted in the literature: Drawing tiny figures, omission of body parts, encapsulated figures, hearts, circles, wedges, eyes, and drawings which show kinetic activity. The debate about sexual abuse indicators stems from the fact that a majority of the literature focuses on clinical observations of case studies. Also, some clinicians were not art therapists. There has been only one empirical research study (Spring, 1988). A few studies cited in this chapter did conduct research that will begin to establish validity for some graphic indicators of sexual abuse (Chase, 1987; Cohen & Phelps, 1985; Hackbarth et al., 1991; Kaplan, 1991; Kaufman & Wohl, 1992; Spring, 1988). Although the identification of graphic indicators is only in the beginning stages, the use of drawings with sexual abuse survivors is still recommended over other measurement approaches (Bybee, 1987).

Clinicians should be aware of the "normal" stages of artistic development (Malchiodi, 1994). It is beyond the scope of this text to discuss stages of artistic development. When I conduct art therapy diagnostic assessments, I use Lowenfeld and Brittain's (1987) stages of development for a comparison. Additional sources include Kellogg (1969) and Gardner (1980).

It is important to stress that therapists should not determine abuse from one drawing. It is my opinion that a battery of assessments should be used when sexual abuse is suspected. Using several evaluations, Burgess (1988) found sexually abused children differed significantly from nonabused children as far as shading, omission of body parts, and sexualization of figures. Given that many assessments have weaknesses, especially in the areas of reliability and validity, a battery would provide more information and allow for the emergence of themes that yield clinical information (Brooke, 1996, 2004).

MEDICINE WHEEL

Although my research focused on artistic indicators of sexual abuse, similar indicators can also be viewed in the other creative therapies: play, movement/dance, music, and drama therapies. You will see some of the above mentioned indicators in the art work presented in this book. The cover of this text is in the shape of a medicine wheel – bringing art, play, movement/dance, music, and drama therapies together as a medicinal approach to promoting the healing of sexual abuse survivors. Together, these creative energies can be channeled to work with a population devastated by the effects of sexual misconduct and abuse. This medicine wheel is an outward expression of the inner dialogue that ensues through the use of the creative therapies. In a sense, this medicinal wheel acts as a mirror, allowing us to view the reflection of the survivors, specifically, their dialogue, expressed through the use of the creative arts. Each of these therapies is connected with the others. You will see that some chapters combine one or more of the creative therapies as an approach to working with sexual abuse survivors. This medicinal wheel provides us with a vision of where the client/survivor is, and in which areas he or she needs to develop in order to realize and fulfill his or her potential.

This book brings together several of the creative therapies as an approach to working with survivors of sexual abuse as the medicine wheel, which is often known as the circle of life. The chapters are written by experts in their respective fields, with outstanding credentials and contributions to the field of creative arts. Chapters one through eight cover art therapy, with special chapters on Phototherapy and Origami. The Origami chapter does not deal directly with sexual abuse survivors, but does deal with the issue of trauma. The exercises can be applied to other populations of children who experience trauma, such as sexual abuse survivors. Chapters nine through twelve delineate play therapy approaches with sexual abuse survivors. Chapter thirteen explores move-ment/dance therapy with survivors of sexual abuse. Chapters fourteen through sixteen are the music therapy sections. Chapters seventeen through nineteen represent the drama therapy section, with chapter seventeen combining drama and play therapy with a population of male survivors of sexual abuse. Chapter twenty outlines the Therapeutic Spiral Model as an method for working with survivors. This chapter uses the image of the medicine shield to bring together mind, body, heart, and soul. Chapters twenty-one and twenty-two elaborate on ethical considerations and supervision issues when working with this pop-ulation. The medicine wheel is thought to be the key to understanding the uni-verse and as a way that individuals achieve wholeness (Roberts et al., 1998). This book represents the different directions in the creative therapies field and brings them into a circle, a complete and wholistic approach to therapy. "The wheel represents the life cycle of human beings, an interconnectness and cir-cular progression that signifies growth and change in each direction (Roberts et al., 1998, p. 137). The creative therapies respresented in this book achieve harmony in their approach to promoting healing of sexual abuse survivors.

REFERENCES

Agaibi, C.E., & Wilson, J.P. (2005). Trauma, PTSD, and resilience: A review of the literature. *Trauma, Violence, & Abuse, 6*(3), 195–216.

Briggs, F. & Lehmann, K. (1989). Significance of children's drawings in cases of sexual abuse. *Early Child Development and Care, 47*, 131–147.

Brooke, S.L. (1995). Art therapy: An approach to working with sexual abuse survivors. *The Arts in Psychotherapy, 22*(5), 447–466.

Brooke, S.L. (1996). *Tools of the trade: A therapist's guide to art therapy assessments.* Springfield, IL: Charles C Thomas, Publisher, Ltd.

Brooke, S.L. (1997). *Art therapy with sexual abuse survivors.* Springfield, IL: Charles C Thomas, Publisher, Ltd.

Brooke, S.L. (2004). *Tools of the trade: A therapist's guide to art therapy assessments.* 2nd ed. Spring-field, IL: Charles C Thomas, Publisher, Ltd.

Burgess, E.J. (1988). Sexually abused children and their drawings. *Archives of Psychiatric Nursing, 2*(2), 65–73.

Burgess, A.W., & Hartman, C.R. (1993). Children's drawings. *Child Abuse & Neglect, 17*, 161–168.

Burgess, A.W., & Holmstrom, L.L. (1979). *Rape: Crisis and recovery*. Bowie, Maryland: Robert J. Brady Co.

Burns, R.C. (1987). *Kinetic-House-Tree-Person-Drawings: An interpretive manual*. New York: Brunner/Mazel Publishers.

Bybee, D. (1987). *Measurement issues in child sexual abuse*. Paper presented at the Biennial Meeting for the Society for Research in Child Development. Baltimore, MD, April 23–26.

Carozza, P.M., & Heirsteiner, C.L. (1982). Young female incest victims in treatment: Stages of growth seen with a group art therapy model. *Clinical Social Work Journal, 10*(3),165–175.

Case, C., & Dalley, T. (1990). *Working with children in art therapy*. New York: Travistock/Routledge.

Chantler, L., Pelco, L., & Mertin, P. (1993). The psychological evaluation of child sexual abuse using the Louisville Behavior Checklist and Human Figure Drawing. *Child Abuse & Neglect, 17*, 271–279.

Chase, D.A. (1987). An analysis of human figure and kinetic family drawings of sexually abused children and adolescents. *Dissertation Abstracts International, 48*(2), 338.

Cohen, F.W. & Phelps, R.E. (1985). Incest markers in children's art work. *Arts in Psychotherapy, 12*, 265–284.

Cohen-Liebman, M.S. (1995). Drawings as judiciary aids in child sexual abuse litigation: A composite list of indicators. *The Arts in Psychotherapy, 22*(5), 475–483.

Dax, C.E. (1953). *Experimental studies in psychiatric art*. London, England: Faber & Faber, Limited.

DiLeo, J.H. (1983). *Interpreting children's drawings*. New York: Brunner/Mazel.

Drachnik, C. (1994). The tongue as a graphic symbol of sexual abuse. *Art Therapy: Journal of American Art Therapy Association, 11*(1), 58–61.

Dufrene, P. (1994). Art therapy and the sexually abused child. *Art Education*, 6–11.

Faller, K. (1988). *Child sexual abuse: An interdisciplinary manual for diagnosis case management and treatment*. New York: Columbia University Press.

Gardner, H. (1980). *Artful scribbles: The significance of children's drawings*. New York: Basic Books.

Garrett, C., & Ireland, M. (1979). A therapeutic art session with rape victims. *American Journal of Art Therapy, 18*, 103–106.

German, D. (1986). *The female adolescent incest victim: Personality, self-esteem, and family orientation*. Unpublished doctoral dissertation, Andrews University.

Goodwin, J. (1982). Use of drawings in evaluating children who may be incest victims. *Children and Youth Services Review, 4*, 269–278.

Hackbarth, S.G., Murphy, H.D., & McQuary, J.P. (1991). Identifying sexually abused children by using Kinetic Family Drawings. *Elementary School Guidance & Counseling, 25*, 225–260.

Hagood, M.M. (1994). Diagnosis or dilemma: Drawings of sexually abused children. *Art Therapy: Journal of the American Art Therapy Association, 11*(1), 37–42.

Hammer, E. (1978). *The Clinical Application of Projective Drawings*. Springfield, IL: Charles C Thomas, Publisher, Ltd.

Hibbard, R.A., & Hartman, G.L.(1990). Emotional indicators in human figure drawings of sexually victimized and nonabused children. *Journal of Clinical Psychology, 46*(2), 211–219.

Hibbard, R.A., Roghmann, K., & Hoekelman, R.A.(1987). Genitalia in children's drawings: An association with sexual abuse. *Pediatrics, 79*(1), 129–137.

Horovitz, E. (1996). Personal interview with the Director of Art Therapy at Hillside Children's Center. May 15, 1996.

Howard, M.C., & Jakab, I. (1968). *Psychiatry and art: Volume 2, 8th International Colloquium Psychopathology of Expression*. New York: Basel.

Johnston, M.S.K. (1979). The sexually mistreated child: Diagnostic evaluation. *Child Abuse & Neglect, 3*, 943–951.

Jones, L.A. (1989). Hearts wish. *Early Child Development and Care, 42*, 175–182.

Kaplan, B.J. (1991). Graphic indicators of sexual abuse in drawings of sexually abused, emotionally disturbed children, and nondisturbed children: Child sexual abuse. *Dissertation Abstracts International, 52*(2), 1065.

Kaufman, B., & Wohl, A. (1992). *Casualties of childhood: A developmental perspective on sexual abuse using projective drawings.* New York: Brunner/Mazel.

Kelley, S.J. (1984). The use of art therapy with sexually abused children. *Journal of Psychosocial Nursing, 22*(12), 12–18.

Kelley, S.J. (1985). Drawings: Critical communications for sexually abused children. *Pediatric Nursing, 11.*

Kellogg, R. (1969). *Analyzing children's art.* Mountain View, CA: Hayfield Publishing Company.

Kidd, J., & Wix, L. (1996). Images of the heart: Archetypal imagery in the therapeutic artwork. *Art Therapy: Journal of the American Art Therapy Association, 13*(2), 108–113.

Klepsch, M., & Logie, L. (1982). *Children draw and tell: An introduction to the projective uses of children's human figure drawings.* New York: Brunner/Mazel.

Kramer, E. (1971). *Art as therapy with children.* New York: Schocken Books.

Levick, M. (1983). *They could not talk and so they drew.* Springfield, IL: Charles C Thomas Publisher, Ltd.

Lowenfeld, V., & Brittain, W.L. (1987). *Creative and mental growth.* 8th ed. New York: Macmillan.

Lubit, R., Lovine, D., DeFranscisci, L., & Spencer, E. (2003). Impact of trauma on children. *Journal of Psychiatry Practice, 9*(2), 128–138.

Malchiodi, C.A.(1987). *Comparative study of the DAP and the Life Size Body Drawing in the assessment of child abuse.* Proceedings of the 18th Annual Conference of the American Art Therapy Association. Mundelein, IL: AATA, Inc.

Malchiodi, C.A. (1990). *Breaking the silence: Art therapy with children from violent homes.* New York: Brunner/Mazel.

Malchiodi, C.A. (1994). *Using drawings in the assessment of children from violent homes.* Speech presented at the National Children's Mental Health Conference, Jacksonville, FL.

Manning, T.M. (1987). Aggression depicted in abused children's drawings. *Arts in Psychotherapy, 14*, 15–24.

Miller, T.W., Veltkamp, L.J., & Janson, D. (1987). Projective measures in the clinical evaluation of sexually abused children. *Child Psychiatry and Human Development, 18*(1), 47–57.

Nederlander, C. (1977). The use of graphic expression in the modification of sexual behavior. *American Journal of Art Therapy, 16*, 61–77.

Riordan, R.J., and Verdel, A.C. (1991). Evidence of sexual abuse in children's art products. *The School Counselor, 39*, 116–121.

Roberts, R.L., Harper, Tuttle-Eagal Bull, D., & Heideman-Provost, L.M. (1998). The Native American medicine wheel and individual Psychology: Common themes. *Journal of Individual Psychology, 54*(1), 135–146.

Sadowski, P.M., & Loesch, L.C. (1993). Using children's drawings to detect potential child sexual abuse. *Elementary School Guidance & Counseling, 28*, 115–123.

Sidun, N.M., & Rosenthal, R.H. (1987). Graphic indicators of sexual abuse in Draw-A-Person tests of psychiatrically hospitalized adolescents. *The Arts in Psychotherapy, 14*, 25–33.

Silvercloud, B. (1982). *Using art to express the unspeakable: A tool for intervention and therapy with the sexually abused.* The proceedings of the Thirteen-the Annual Conference of the American Art Therapy Association, Philadelphia.

Spring, D. (1978). Jane, case of a rape victim rehabilitated by art therapy. In *Imagery: Its many dimensions and applications.* New York: Plenum Press.

Spring, D. (1988). Sexual abuse and post-traumatic stress reflected in artistic symbolic language. Author, 1–157.

Spring, D. (1993). *Shattered Images: The phenomenological language of sexual trauma.* Chicago, IL: Magnolia Press.

Stember, C.J. (1980). Art therapy: A new use in the diagnosis and treatment of sexually abused children. In *U.S. Department of Health and Human Services, Sexual Abuse of Children Selected Readings* (pp 59–63).Washington, DC, US Government Printing Office.

Wilson, J.P., Drozdek, B., & Turkovic, S. (2006). Post-traumatic shame and guilt. *Trauma, Violence, and Abuse, 7*(2), 122–141.

Wohl, A., & Kaufman, B. (1985). *Silent screams and hidden cries: An interpretation of artwork by children from violent homes.* New York: Brunner Mazel.

Yates, A., Beutler, L.E., & Crago, M. (1985). Drawings by child victims of incest. *Child Abuse and Neglect, 9*, 183–189.

BIOGRAPHICAL STATEMENT

Stephanie L. Brooke has her M.S. degree in Community Agency Counseling, a Ph.D. in Organizational Psychology, and Certification in Art Therapy. She is a Nationally Certified Counselor. Dr. Brooke has written three books on art therapy, edited on the creative therapies, and published several professional, peer-reviewed journal articles. Dr. Brooke is the Vice Chairperson for <u>ARIA</u> (Awareness of Rape and Incest Through Art) and serves on the advisory board of Safe Girls Strong Girls. Additionally, Dr. Brooke is on the editorial board for PSYCCritiques for the Journal of Contemporary Psychology and the International Journal of Teaching and Learning in Higher Education. Dr. Brooke belongs to the American Psychological Association, the American Art Therapy Association, the American Play Therapy Association, the American Counseling Association, the International Society of Teaching and Learning, and the New York Mental Health Counselors' Association. She is editing her next book on the use of creative therapies with people suffering from eating disorders. Dr. Brooke is the chief consultant for the first International C.A.T. Conference in Tokyo, Japan 2006.

You can contact Dr. Brooke through her website: http://www.StephanieLBrooke.com

Chapter 2

SEXUAL TRAUMA: CONFLICT RESOLUTION

Dee Spring

INTRODUCTION

Reoccurring and psychologically damaging criminal sexual acts upon a child within a family setting are unfathomable. A sexual assault by an unknown assailant either in an individual's home or other environment is incomprehensible. Following the traumatic event, victims are left to come to terms with the consequences of the acts and related post-effects. Years may be required for them to resolve the specific conflicts associated with the traumatic experience. This chapter will discuss the importance of conflict resolution during treatment of adults who have experienced traumatic sexual abuse in their lifetime.

SPECIFIC POPULATION

An "incident-specific population, bound together by a category of experience," is created when sexual crimes are committed (Spring, 1993, 2001, 2003, 2004). Within this population exists the need to deny and the will to proclaim. This incident-specific population is not confined to age, gender, or culture, as post-effects are generalized across all boundaries. What is different are legal definitions of sexual abuse across boundaries. Perception is shaped by cultural beliefs, therefore, treatment settings and treatment models are influenced by variances in perception contained within cultural environments.

Response to sexual abuse-assault is shaped by individual perception, ethnocultural aspects, perspective and beliefs, age, family history, coping ability, prior mental health before a traumatic incident, the type of incident experienced, and individual support systems (Pebbles-Kleiger & Zerbe, 1998). Response can be complicated by physical injury, severe or not. Regardless of circumstances, threat (verbal or implied) is a major factor, followed by fear, anxiety, and guilt. In addition, response is linked to sensory and physical reaction, circumstances of the event, significance of the traumatic incident, and environmental context. Response also includes a general disbelief about the existence of cruel people who are capable of malicious intent to harm innocent people.

Although survivors want to tell what happened and to identify their attackers, fear and guilt may be too overwhelming. Fear about maintaining silence and secrecy may be so powerful, survivors cannot tolerate any thought of additional harm, implied or verbalized, by an attacker during the traumatic incident. Moreover, guilt over being forced to participate in obscene or unimaginable acts may carry such shame as to negate reporting.

Complexity of post-effects caused by sexual abuse trauma is an assemblage of definitive symptoms contained within a comprehensive cluster. This cluster is an admixture of impulses, emotions, and perceptions related to the category of experience. Although the cluster may remain pre-conscious for the victim, it strongly influences attitudes and behavior (Dickinson, deGuy, Dickinson & Camdib, 1998). Complexity of sexual abuse trauma requires knowledge and observation to understand the elaborately interrelated elements defined as post-effects. These elements suggest a perplexing entanglement of history, experience, current events, and dysfunctional cognition leading to conflict and emotional chaos. Post-effects contain references and associations to situational elements, individual rationale for behavior adapted to circumstances, and sabotaging efforts attached to survivors' view of themselves. These components are commonly laced together in complicated, often disorganized fashion (Miller, 2000). In terms of trauma synthesis, conflict has distinct application to the secrecy components of "intimate trauma", and its impact on individual self-worth (Spring, 2001).

RATIONALE

Sexual abuse-assault, with its traumatic consequences, often of lifetime duration, is a worldwide social problem surrounded by political issues. The social problem crosses cultural boundaries, but within each culture the perception of what constitutes sexual abuse is diverse. Each type of sexual abuse is associated with unique characteristics, classification of offenders, and the definition of acts considered to be criminal in nature.

When looking at the scope of sexual abuse-assault as a social problem, not only is there necessity for ongoing education of the general public, but more so for students and educators in the social sciences, and all mental health workers. When therapeutic interventions include the use of creative process, there is more likelihood of uncovering undisclosed, unresolved sexual trauma due to neurological connections activated during creative endeavors. When adults are processing sexual abuse incidents, sensory connections and pre-conscious material may be symbolically represented in drawings initiated by kinesthetic-optical movement.

CREATIVE APPROACH

Regardless of the type of creative approach used in treatment to drive trauma integration, in order to be effective, the approach must be grounded in and based on a theoretical model to address traumatic post-effects. The approach must address the three critical factors necessary to process trauma. "These factors are emotional engagement with traumatic memory, organization of trauma, and correction of dysfunctional cognition following traumatic events. . ." (Spring, 2004, p. 200).

Whether survivors are male or female, child, adolescent, or adult, they go through certain phases of adaptation. There is a basic response to trauma, regardless of the circumstance or type of event. Acute Response immediately follows all traumatic events and includes shock (crisis), stabilization, normalization, reorganization, acceptance, and resuming daily life (Figure 2.1). If symptoms linger, or do not sufficiently subside, then a chronic condition develops. This condition is defined as Post-Traumatic Stress Disorder (PTSD) and is not considered routine adaptation to traumatic experience (Brunello et al., 2001) (Figure 2.2). This condition does not happen immediately, but develops over time and is relevant to adults molested as children, or those who experience rape. Lingering symptoms may cause survivors to develop two realities: a "Private Reality," based on traumatic memories and images, and a skillfully crafted "Public Appearance" to disguise symptomatology (Spring, 2001, 2003). The disguised internal chaos may only come alive in isolation. A survivor's energy may be corrupted by focusing on maintaining an appropriate appearance for others while constantly managing the secrecy of the internal reality. The maintenance of the two realities manifests innumerable conflicts.

CONFLICT RESOLUTION

Although the core of PTSD is anxiety, the core of trauma treatment is resolving conflict to find a reasonable middle ground and balance perspective. Conflicts are repetitive and emerge throughout treatment, as layers of emotional damage are peeled away and integrative psychophysiological processes are repaired. Some conflicts may result from triggering of past traumatic experience,

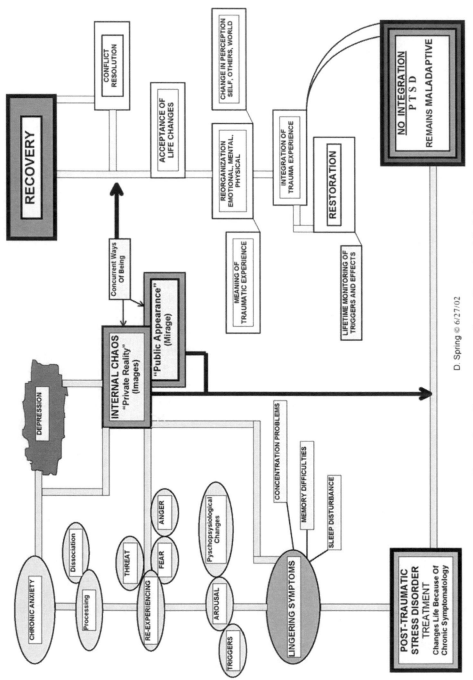

Figure 2.1. Post-traumatic Stress Disorder Model

which results in panic and anxiety. At the time triggers are detonated, these may seem alien to, or disconnected from, the current event. Logically, the situation may be entirely different, but due to information transfer traveling on neural pathways, the current event may trigger a sensory trace to prior traumata. Discovering similarities and parallels is a key function. It is fundamental to recognize conflict in the present and define it in order to trace it to the past, link it, point out the parallel, and resolve it within the current situation. Resolving conflict can only occur in the present. The focus is on connecting current conflicts to the past, so similarities and differences can be articulated, then assimilated. The connections begin a stream of consciousness leading to restoration, Figure 2.2.

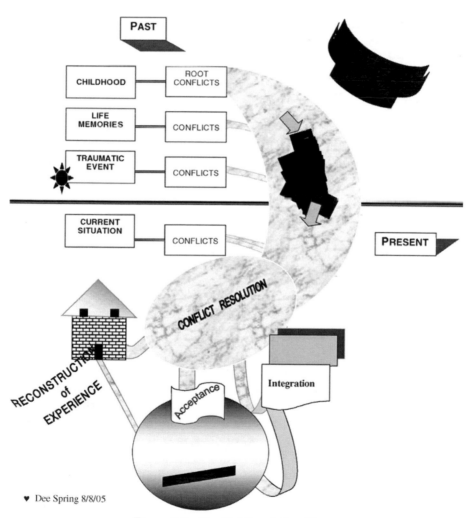

Figure 2.2. Conflict Resolution Flow

Distortions, illusions, and safety maneuvers are interrelated and linked to conflicts. Correction and rearrangement of the links are necessary to form an accurate perception of traumatic experience. A childhood view of a traumatic event may be different from the view held in adulthood. However, when trauma is not resolved and corrections are not made, the survivor may continue to function from the position of state-dependent learning acquired during the original traumatic incident. The adult may retain juvenile perceptions and immature behavior when attempting to resolve conflict. Perceptions may be based on illusions cultivated during abusive situations. An example might be the fantasy of a magical rescue and the development of an imagined rescuer (Spring, 2001).

In childhood, root conflicts are established. These relate to self, others, the world, and environmental circumstances. Basic conflicts affect conceptual and perceptual aptitudes. Additional conflicts later evolve from relationships and other situations. Current life situations (e.g., changing jobs, buying a home, retirement) may provoke conflicts, but these are usually temporary and more easily managed. At times, these situations can become severe enough to connect pre-existing traumatic material to some aspect of the current situation, and exacerbate anxiety to cause irrational perceptions to form in the present.

Conflict involves ideas about fight, flight or freeze impulses, similar to impulses experienced at the onset of trauma. Knowing how these impulses operate when attempting to resolve a current conflict is essential to manage trauma triggers. Attempts to resolve conflicts may bring about face-to-face confrontations and revitalize suppressed anger. When engaging with an adversary in a face-to-face situation, survivors need to learn how to focus on a single issue, or at least, one issue at a time, listening without interrupting, attacking or defending until facts are known. Learning to leave a situation before anger escalates, and learning to use words to diminish tension are acknowledged as standard methods to manage such situations.

Resolving conflict can be confusing for survivors. Some believe they deserve nothing because they are "bad." At times, anger pushes them to be demanding because they believe they are entitled to compensation for their suffering, an illusion of personal justice. Survivors can be conflicted on a continuum from believing they deserve nothing, to believing they are entitled to anything they can obtain. They may also seek instant gratification as compensation for years of suffering. Survivors may find it difficult to assimilate the importance of resolving conflict while learning to compromise as a means to enhance self-worth. Grasping the concept of giving up something to get something, and not seeing this as a loss of integrity can be daunting. Effectively managing conflict is learning to be assertive by stating what is wanted rather than being aggressive or demanding.

Conflicts related to intimate trauma are attached in various ways to distortions about intimacy in relationships including: threat (real, implied, or imagined);

perception of helplessness and control; parent issues often directed at the mother; fear of abandonment; and the use of the word love when it is associated with abuse. These issues emerge on different levels throughout "Stages of Restoration" (Spring, 1993, 2001). It is the ability of both survivor and therapist to stay on track and remain focused on conflicts through the tedious process of repetition occurring on each level of the restoration stages. Consistency in finding the middle ground within *either-or* situations and acquired attitudes is vital when working on conflicts. Conflict resolution eventually leads to synthesis of the multiple facets of traumatic experience. Perceiving and practicing new behaviors related to root conflicts can be a distressing, protracted process for adult survivors.

When traumatic incidents occur, basic views and concepts may be debased or fractured, causing fragmentation to continue into the present. Survivors of intimate trauma share three primary conflicts: love vs. hate, good vs. bad, and life vs. death. Hence, a major portion of trauma treatment is devoted to confronting root conflicts established in childhood, which became amended or changed along the road to adulthood. These conflicts are naturally compounded by history and current events. Conflicts generalized to this incident-specific population embody shame, guilt, threat, rage, rejection, abandonment, sexuality, and feelings of worthlessness. When no opportunity exists to engage with those responsible for abuse, frustration and anger are magnified. Consequently, resolution becomes a one-sided affair wherein the survivor, alone, must come to terms with the problem. When this occurs, the therapist becomes a guide to assist the survivor. Although survivors may describe this as a lonely journey, the calming effects of resolution plus the exuberance of finding a middle ground can be rewarding as insight is gained, and personal strength is acquired.

CONFLICT DRAWINGS

The aim of conflict drawings is a means for survivors to discover comfortable resolutions, and alter perception to form a balanced perspective. The task focuses on finding a symbolic middle ground through visualizing how to connect opposites to form a new image. The externalization of conflictual material comprises the struggles experienced in treatment, as well as collateral parts of traumatic post-effects such as ongoing relationship problems. Titles of conflict drawings should address specific conflicts associated with sexual trauma. Directives such as Good vs. Bad, Love vs. Hate, and Shame vs. Pride, address confusion within the layering of memories and a plethora of struggles experienced by this population. These conflicts are pertinent to sexual abuse survivors, and precisely linked to treatment issues. As choices are exercised and decisions are made, noticeable differences in the way survivors begin to manage their lives are observed. Completed drawings give the therapist an enormous amount of information about how the survivor thinks and manages life outside the therapy room.

At first, conflict drawings are unsettling to survivors, because no words exist to automatically produce an accordant image. Directives are intended to be cognitive and provoke exploration of situations wherein vital information resides. Directives are designed to use creative intelligence to address sensory memory through cognitive application, and to address "unsymbolized material" (Brown, Scheflin, & Hammond, 1998). Sensory material is more readily expressed through color and shape than definitive forms. Color in drawings is important to gauge emotional intensity and compare visual narratives with clinical observations. In addition, directives explicitly related to conflicts attached to post-effects, may prompt a visual mapping of a specific situation wherein thoughts and sensations, attached to a precursory situation, act in concert with the current conflict, causing difficulty in the present. This procedure makes the best use of art as cognitive activity and creative process as the conveyance for uniting sensory knowledge, symbolizing the unsymbolized, and re-associating fragmented psychophysiological function.

A dynamic way to work on conflict resolution is using conflict drawings as homework. This procedure affords the survivor unlimited time to think about the opposite sides of the conflict and ponder ways to design a middle ground. Once the directive is given, the brain instantly begins its search for connections to solve the problem. Survivors must be comfortable with the middle ground they design, and be able to make it work in accordance with their perception of the conflict. Due to the limitation of this chapter, the complete procedure for using conflict drawings with survivors can be found in Spring (1993, pp. 241–243).

Large drawing paper is folded into three equal parts to establish boundaries and bring attention to the equality of opposing sides of each conflict. Connecting or blending the opposites in the middle is the function. The survivor begins the process by drawing opposing elements of the conflict on either side, leaving the middle blank. The next step is imagining how opposing sides of the conflict might function as a co-mingled image in the middle. The task is visualizing how connections in the middle space might create a reasonable fusion, suitable balance, or realistic concession. When the drawing is completed, it is used to illustrate the verbal dialogue associated with the survivor's thoughts, and how the thoughts influenced the construction of the middle ground.

The drawing task stimulates both brain hemispheres, connects implicit and explicit memory (image and language), engages natural dissociative processes, and results in a symbolic language to explain sensory connections which words alone cannot describe. The task incorporates kinesthetic movement (motion of connective tissue), visual perception, creative intelligence, cognition, affect, and linguistic narrative. The task exercises integrative processes, develops problem solving skills, improves concentration, and begins to repair disorganized cognition and fragmented personality. Chapman, Morabito, Ladakakos, Schreler and Knudson (2001) discuss drawing intervention related to trauma resolution.

> [The intervention] . . . utilizes the integrative capacity of the brain by accessing the traumatic sensations and memories in a manner that is consistent with the current understanding of the transmission of experience to language (Horowitz, 1970; van der Kolk, 1994). By activating both right and left hemisphere activity along with both visual and verbal neural pathways, therapeutic potential is maximized as the brain creates a visual, nonverbal narrative that is translated to a coherent linguistic narrative. Coherent narratives require the participation of both right and left hemispheres and are created through hemispheric integration (Siegel, 1999). The drawings, or kinesthetic activity, activate the limbic system, the center for emotional and perceptual process. (p. 102)

Although externalizing conflict is a struggle for survivors, it begins the process of developing the concept of a middle, to move away from developed either-or attitudes and acquisition of rigid defense stances for emotional protection. This procedure assists survivors in gaining insight into trauma-triggering in the present, and brings conflicts in current situations to the forefront for making connections to lingering, unresolved conflicts. Becoming cognizant of the connection of conflicts to trauma-triggering is fundamental for survivors to accept life changes and make sense out of experience.

The use of conflict drawings promotes positive changes. Accepting perceptual changes is similar to accepting the occurrence of sexual abuse as real and cannot be removed from individual experience. Acceptance is linked to working through long-standing conflicts impinging on current conflicts. At first, acceptance is often at a deeper level of awareness, not yet consciously accessible, assimilated, or actualized.

As survivors make sense out of experience, the ability to accept changes caused by a traumatic event becomes easier. Acceptance is linked to reflection, insight, understanding post-effects, and changes accrued since the event. Acceptance is also about integrating trauma as a bad memory, but not one that continues to produce unstable functioning in the present.

RESULT OF USING CONFLICT DRAWINGS

Using drawings for conflict resolution is about visually changing thought patterns through art-making, and understanding how stress initiates reenactment behaviors. Survivors need to be educated to recognize how traumatic events change their lives, and how post-effects overwhelm their ability to adapt in an effective manner. When survivors are unable to negotiate post-effects, the consequence is remaining fixated on the trauma rather than making the necessary adjustments to return to, or develop adequate levels of functioning.

Going through the process of reorganization means correcting cognitive distortions, connecting emotional intensity of the past to current events to be able to work through the intensity in the present. The process includes learning to identify the physiological elements of trauma response to comprehend anxiety, feeling threatened, fear of imagined danger, and seeing the self as damaged goods. This can be a slow, intricate part of therapy resembling a roller coaster ride. As reorganization occurs in the survivor's Private Reality, reorganization of external physical space is detected. One clue might be survivors' references to cleaning closets. Reorganizing things is often a metaphor symbolizing the changing perspective, reorganizing unproductive or negative behavior patterns, and rearranging autobiographical material in a logical order to more adequately accommodate a new dimension of emotional space.

CHANGE IN PERCEPTION

As reorganization proceeds through conflict resolution, numerous changes are evident. Changes tend to stir energy, provide a sense of achievement to elevate self-esteem, and spark a desire to share accomplishments. A sense of pride develops to erode shame. From the small task of cleaning closets, the will to tackle a larger project emerges. The first step can be monumental for a survivor who has struggled for years with chronic PTSD.

As survivors change the perception of a "bad self" to a self who can accomplish, rather than continue to mourn, the perception of others changes. Some changes are directly related to the relationship with a knowledgeable therapist who supports the survivor through all the awfulness of reconstructing experience (Spring, 2005). Identification with a therapist whom the survivor has learned to trust and feel safe with is the most important factor in moving out of chronic PTSD (Herman, 1992; Miller, 2000; Spring, 2001; van der Kolk, 1987; Waites, 1997).

FINDING MEANING IN TRAUMATIC EXPERIENCE

In order to come to terms with trauma, what the traumatic event means to the survivor and what it continues to represent is an essential factor. Meaning is about the definition of trauma conceived by the person who experienced it, not what it means to the therapist, society, the courts, or other family members.

This private realization takes into account the situation, the circumstances, the offender, the acts, the aftermath, and lifetime consequences.

Survivors reach a point when they want to stop hiding. There comes a moment of surrender. They no longer want to defend the abuse; they become weary of taking responsibility for what belongs to the offender. Survivors may signal the arrival at this point by a statement such as, "I'm sick and tired of feeling sick and tired." This is a cue related to perceptual change and points to meaning coalescing with experience due to recovering and processing *layers of memories* (Spring, 2001, 2003). As offered by Waites (1997) and Brown et al. (1998), reconstructing experience is not simply about gathering information about the past, but involves clarity about what has been unclear, or what has been avoided when trying to come to terms with experience.

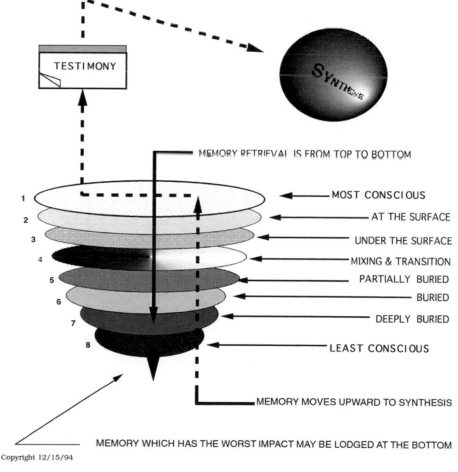

Copyright 12/15/94

Figure 2.3. Concept of Memory Layering and Progression to Synthesis

Finding meaning relates to uncovering and recalling traumatic events. Working through this painful process leads to transforming the meaning (Waites, 1997; van der Kolk, 1987). One positive is the inheritance and development of an "intuitive capacity," as an internal warning system (Spring, 2001, 2003). Brunnello, et al. (2001) discusses the idea of cognitive therapy which aims ". . . to educate the survivor to identify negative thoughts and underlying assumptions to identify logical errors, therein, and to explore more constructive realistic alternatives . . . to modify the meaning attributed to memories . . . thereby overcoming guilt and self-recrimination. . ." (p. 7). Without finding meaning and "illuminating guilt" restoration is more difficult (Rothschild, 2000).

INTEGRATION OF TRAUMATIC EXPERIENCE

Although integration of traumatic experience is a complicated process, in its most fundamental meaning, integration coherently links history to current events. Integration is a unification process to explicate how past traumatic history connects to, and impacts on the current life of survivors. The past will not change, but perception of the past can be changed in the present.

> The integration phase of trauma treatment can be subdivided into two subphases: (1) *memory integration*, and (2) *representational integration*. The first pertains to the integration of the previously dissociated fragments of narrative memory for trauma into a coherent memory and its integration within the consciously available autobiographical memory system (reversal of primary dissociation). . . . The latter subphase pertains to the integration of dissociated representational fragments, e.g., the abuser self and failed protector self. . . (Brown, et al., p. 481).

Herman (1992) outlines symptomatology directly related to traumatic experience that subsequently becomes directly involved in the process of synthesizing traumatic effects. Symptoms must be addressed and overcome, or at a bare minimal, managed by the survivor.

> The many symptoms of post-traumatic disorder fall into three main categories. These are called "hyperarousal," "intrusion," and "constriction." Hyperarousal reflects the persistent expectation of danger; intrusion reflects the indelible imprint of the traumatic moment; constriction reflects the numbing response of surrender. (p. 35)

Therapeutic work must focus on assisting survivors to differentiate what is the past (the then); what is the present (the now); and to concurrently identify similarities and differences. The process is one of comparing and contrasting situations, response in the past to response in the present. Survivors must be reminded what is being experienced in the moment is a memory, not the same event happening in the present. Safety exists in the moment; the past abuse is over.

This method of working with survivors' conflict can be powerful because it addresses and exposes highly sensitive information and personal issues. Timing, when introducing the work, is a crucial factor. The most advantageous time is between the middle and end of treatment. There are several critical cautions. The concept is not applicable to children or adolescents. It is also not applicable to anyone still trapped in an abusive family environment such as domestic violence, or where spousal rape continues to occur. In addition, it is not applicable to any type of group work. The procedure is solely intended for adults in ongoing, consistent private treatment.

CONCLUSION

Conflict resolution is the foundation for restoration. To resolve conflict means editing the trauma narrative, amelioration of distortions, and mapping chronological history to put it in proper order. Restoration means identifying what spells danger in the present, hooks into past danger, but currently feels the same. Conflict resolution includes recognizing intrusive images, understanding memories are attached to the past, and learning how to cognitively manage trauma images in the moment to prevent emotional chaos. Finally, conflict resolution leading to restoration means survivors no longer have to remain numb to ward off emotional or physical pain; they are free to express feelings and tell their story without fear of the offender's threats coming true. They survived the worst; the past traumatic experience is over, and a future exists.

REFERENCES

Brown, D., Scheflin, A., and Hammond, D.C. (1998). *Memory, trauma treatment, and the law.* New York: Norton.

Brunnello, B., Davidson, R. T., Deahl, M., Kessler, R. C., Mendlewicz, J., Recagnib, G., Shalev, A. V., and Zohar, J. (2001). Posttraumatic stress disorder: Diagnosis and epidemiology, comorbidity and social consequences, biology and treatment. *Neuropsychobiology, 43*(3). Online, Retrieved 1/14/2001, www.karger.com/journals/nps

Chapman, L, Morabito, D., Ladakakos, D., Schreler, H., and Knudson, M. (2001). The effectiveness of art therapy interventions in reducing post traumatic stress disorder (PTSD) symptoms in pediatric trauma patients. *Art Therapy: Journal of the American Art Therapy Association, 16*(2), 100–104.

Dickinson, L. M., deGuy, F.V., Dickinson, W. P., and Camdib, L. (1998). Complex post-traumatic stress disorder, evidence from the primary care setting. *General Hospital Psychiatry, 20*(4), 214–224.

Herman, J. (1992). *Trauma and recovery*. New York: Basic Books.

Miller, J. L. (2000, November). Post-traumatic stress disorder in primary care practice. *Journal of the American Academy of Nurse Practitioners, 12*(11), 475–482.

Pebbles-Kleiger, M., & Zerbe. K. (1998). Office management of post-traumatic stress disorder, a clinician's guide to a pervasive problem. *Postgraduate Medicine, 103*(5), 181–195.

Rothschild, B. (2000). *The body remembers*. New York: Norton.

Spring, D. (1993). *Shattered images: Phenomenological language of sexual trauma*. Chicago: Magnolia Street Publishers.

Spring, D. (2001). *Image and mirage: Art therapy with dissociative clients*. Springfield, IL: Charles C Thomas Publisher, Ltd.

Spring, D. (2003). Specific Trauma: Sexual Abuse. *In Continuing Medical Education, 98*(1), 53–98. Sacramento, CA: CME Resource.

Spring, D. (2004). Thirty-year study links neuroscience, specific trauma, PTSD, image conversion, and language translation. *Art Therapy: Journal of the American Art Therapy Association, 21*(4), 200–209.

Spring, D. (2005, manuscript in preparation). Reconstruction of experience. In D. Spring (ed.). *Art in treatment: Transatlantic Dialogue*. Springfield, IL: Charles C Thomas Publisher, Ltd.

van der Kolk., B. (1987). *Psychological trauma*. Washington, DC. American Psychiatric Press.

Waites, E. (1997). *Memory quest*. New York: Norton.

BIOGRAPHICAL STATEMENT

For three decades, **Dr. Dee Spring** specialized in the treatment of PTSD and adults who experienced sexual abuse trauma in their lifetime. Her career has included empirical research on this population, university teaching, international presentations, and a list of publications. She is Past President of the California Society for Trauma and Dissociation, Past Treasurer of the American Art Therapy Association, and has received numerous awards for contributions to the field.

Dr. Dee Spring
147 Shelley Circle
Ventura, CA 93003

Phone: 805-650-1558
E-mail: deespring@msn.com

Chapter 3

TOO YOUNG TO TELL: GROUP ART THERAPY AND PRESCHOOL AGED VICTIMS OF CHILD SEXUAL ABUSE

JOAN PHILLIPS

INTRODUCTION

Allegations of sexual abuse of preschoolers is a particularly problematic arena for all therapists. Due to the age of the child, their verbal reports are rarely clear and often do not result in court action or legal consequences for the alleged perpetrator. Instead, the child's situation is often modified for safety in some way, and services are offered almost in a preventive mode because the abuse is hard for authorities to verify or prosecute. This does not mean the abuse did not occur and child safety issues are paramount. The creative arts therapist has a unique role to play with this population, considering their developmental and expressive needs. Given the ambiguous yet troubling nature of allegations of sexual abuse of a preschooler, forms of intervention must be developed that are developmentally appropriate, not harmful, and show some benefit for the child. In a piloted and now long continuing program at a local nonprofit sexual abuse treatment agency, art therapy has consistently provided the avenue for such an intervention.

SEXUAL ABUSE REPORTING CHANGES

Reporting of child sexual abuse began an alarming rise in the early to mid 1980s and peaked in the 1990s. Since that time, it has undergone a steady decline – one which is not yet explained in the literature. Theories about the decline center primarily on either the optimistic view that such cases are indeed on the decline, or that systemic reporting and labeling changes have changed

31

the way the data is appearing (Jones & Finklehor, 2001). For example, it is possible that overburdened child welfare systems may have moved to a prioritizing system that puts sexual abuse lower on the response chain since often there is no physical evidence or visible immediate threat of harm — especially if the offender vacates the home. Reporting statistics often reflect only substantiated cases, and in the case of preschoolers, substantiating allegations is a difficult if not sometimes impossible task.

CREATIVE THERAPIES WITH THIS POPULATION

Work with preschoolers is a messy and multi-disciplinary task. A creative arts therapist should be grounded in child development and this includes psychological, social, and art development. One major difficulty in working with preschoolers is that their language and expressive development is not sufficiently mature to allow law enforcement or child welfare professionals to rely upon the child's verbal report in documenting sexual abuse. Thus, the role of other expressive mediums becomes very important. That said, there must be a constant caution not to take a solely interpretive stance toward the art because research is only fledgling in this area and there are no clear or wide reaching studies supporting "visual indicators" of sexual abuse. Attempts to study the markers or indicators of abuse in drawings have been pilot studies at best and with very small samples (Cohen & Phelps, 1985; Kelly, 1984; Sidun & Rosenthal, 1987). Case studies have yielded some sense of the unique and helpful role art therapy can play in treatment but this is not to be confused with the use of art to diagnose or identify abuse (Malchiodi, 1990; Peake, 1987; Stember, 1978). The clearest indicator is the child's direct depiction of an abusive encounter, and even these must be seen in developmental and social contexts. Malchiodi (1990), in a thorough review of the existing literature on assessing child sexual abuse through art productions, concludes "Although there may be some common graphic indicators in the drawings of children who have been sexually abused, it is difficult to generalize about how this is typified in the art expressions of this population," adding ". . . how the trauma of sexual abuse is expressed visually in the art production cannot be generalized easily or concisely" (p. 143).

Art therapy has a small but well established basis in treating sexual abuse overall. The literature of sexual abuse is sometimes subsumed into discussions of treatment of trauma in general (Johnson 1987; Malchiodi, 1990). In the 1980s, work by Stember (1980) and Naitove (1982) was published, opening up the inclusion of art therapy in team treatment of sexual abuse. Naitove (1982) addresses several creative modalities. Following that, the work of other art therapists working with sexual abuse has been chronicled in the literature

(Brooke, 1995; Brooke, 1997; Dufrene, 1994; Malchiodi, 1990; Malchiodi, 1998; Murphy, 2001; Rubin, 2005; Spring, 1993). However, few have written about work specifically with preschoolers, although the few reports available are positive in terms of the utility of art therapy with this population (Klorer, 2000; Proulx, 2002). Malchiodi (1990) does a good job of laying the groundwork for working with trauma overall, with child sexual abuse as one of the major traumas creative arts therapists must be trained to deal with. Murphy (2001) sums up much of the literature in affirming the value of art therapy with this population and proposes again an open, unstructured use of art combined with some more cognitively-based work. This balance seems to be emerging as a viable treatment protocol, especially for the younger victim of sexual abuse.

In designing a program that will work, there are few studies to refer to in the literature. Most describe services to latency or school-aged children and beyond, or discuss only individual and not group treatment (Berman, 1990; Carozza & Hiersteiner, 1982; Pifalo, 2002). There are a few reports of group therapy which includes art therapy in a multi-modal approach, and when combined with some structure and a more directive or cognitive-based approach these methods have proved useful (Brooke, 1995; Brooke, 1997; Deblinger, 2001; Morris, 1994; Rasmussen, 1995). However, the use of groups with very young children does provide a workable format despite some biases among therapists otherwise. For example, Rubin (2005) describes how even with developmentally delayed preschoolers expressive art therapy holds potential as ". . . these tiny tots of limited intellect were able to choose and to initiate independent artwork in a variety of media . . . some revealed unknown abilities to concentrate and to organize themselves" (pp. 271–272). For this reason, the program and techniques described in this chapter provide a template for consideration and some grounding to begin work using creative therapies, and more particularly art therapy, with these victims in a skilled, ethical, and caring manner.

PRESCHOOLERS

Preschool generally refers to children ages three to five but can extend up to ages six to seven depending on the maturity of the child. This age is described in the developmental literature as a very active and changing population – as development occurs, children develop language and understanding at widely varying rates. In general, this population can be described as very egocentric, having rudimentary language and abstracting skills, if any, and very kinesthically as well as visually expressive (Lowenfeld & Brittain, 1987; Piaget & Inhelder, 1969). The stage of art development evidenced by most preschoolers is described as pre-schematic (Lowenfeld & Brittain, 1987) and in

Piagetian terms as pre-operational (Piaget & Inhelder, 1969). Being in a very "pre" stage of life, young children are often seen as not yet ready for any kind of therapy as well – given the fluidity of thought and understanding as well as symbolization and imagery they evidence. It is a flexible and changing landscape. However, in considering the development of the two to seven-year-old child and their understanding of trauma, Klorer (2000) states:

> With the beginnings of language and thought development comes a capacity for remembrance of trauma, both with words and through evocative memory and the ability to construct a mental image of the trauma. Memory can be represented through signs and symbols. (p. 87)

Group therapy with very young children is sometimes seen as impossible due to the perception that such young children are incapable of abstraction or non ego-centric mutual activities. However, young children who have been sexually abused do suffer behavioral and emotional reactions to the event in many instances and can benefit from treatment (Borkin & Frank, 1986; Gomez-Schwartz et al., 1985; Haizlip et al., 1975).

PILOT PROGRAM

In the mid 1980s, during the peak of the reporting boom, there existed a need for an intervention that addressed the ambiguity and the need for treatment. The program described here, initially piloted in 1987, is designed for preschoolers where child sexual abuse has been reported to the proper authorities and may or may not have been legally substantiated. Indeed, most of the cases were found "inconclusive" but services were recommended. Thus, the child has already been interviewed by the child welfare authorities and, in some cases, the matter will be pursued further, but in many not. A recent study (Cohen & Mannarino, 1996) parallels the design of this program as described here:

> The present study has several implications for clinical practice. The first relates to the importance of specifically addressing the sexual abuse experience in treating this population. In the current legal climate, there is much controversy over the role therapists should play in encouraging children to directly discuss their abusive experiences. Many therapists are becoming hesitant to encourage this direct discussion, particularly with very young children, as they fear they will be accused of inappropriately reinforcing or even "suggesting" these experiences to their patients. The present study lends support to the view that, in young children who have already reported sexual abuse and have had some form of independent validation of that report, therapy that directly addresses sexual abuse-related issues is more effective at reducing symptomatology than therapy in which the child is not required to (and frequently does not) directly discuss the abusive experience. (Cohen & Mannarino, 1996, p. 47)

Referrals into the group described here were reported cases but not always substantiated ones, so the focus in the groups was on two issues: (1) supported expression and (2) prevention of further harm or abuse. The treatment approach was psychoeducational/cognitive behavioral and utilized art therapy as the main delivery method. Initially, the program was conceived and proposed as a pilot grant program through funds from VOCA (Victims of Crime Assistance) a funding source available in some states for the treatment or development of programs for victims of crime. Based upon the allegations of abuse and the reporting done to the child welfare system, this program fits into that funding umbrella. Research on effective treatments was, and remains, very minimal, so the therapists developed a pragmatic approach grounded in the best practices of the day as learned at workshops and through readings as well as clinical experience. The program was initially conceived by this author, an art therapist and counselor, and was adapted and developed further over the years by Karleen Daugherty, MSW, a licensed clinical social worker. The knowledge of child development and age appropriate art therapy was a major conceptual framework for this program. This link to the clinical world and emerging paradigms is essential in developing programs so that they do not exist in a professional vacuum. Without interdisciplinary roots, many programs will die, or at worst, not reach children at their expressive and developmental level.

This preschool group program functioned as a weekly group art therapy experience and children were placed into group after an initial intake and assessment finding that they were appropriate for the group (i.e., they had an alleged case of child sexual abuse and were preschoolers able to attend weekly). [For specific group goals and activities see Appendix.] The group met for one hour weekly and over a 12-week period addressed many issues relevant to child sexual abuse. Initial sessions had a focus on gaining trust, learning to express appropriately, and sharing information. The middle phase of group focused on identifying and expressing feelings, prevention issues such as telling adults and having no secrets, and dealing with feelings of confusion or anger. The latter part of group addressed safety and prevention further, identifying safe adults, and general self-confidence and developmental enhancement. An evolving curriculum of activities, art directives, experiential activities and therapeutic discussions developed. These were constantly adapted to the make-up and needs of any particular group.

In addition, the structure of the group included a snack and general play interwoven into the more theme-focused activities. This was to maintain the metaphor that there was nothing wrong with the children – after all, they were mistreated – this does not mean there is something wrong with them inherently. Any secondary psychological problems were addressed, but not as some intrinsic flaw in the child. This is an important distinction. Just because a child is sexually abused, or alleges it, they are not damaged goods and thus do not require being seen as a victim. Especially at a preschool age, children do not necessarily perceive or experience the shame that an older child might. "The preschooler has not yet internalized society's views about incest and so experiences less guilt that the older child. A greater trauma is likely to be the ensuing disruption of the family, given the preschooler's emotional and physical dependence on her parents" (Schetcky & Green, 1988, p. 67). Sexually abused preschoolers are more prone to confusion and overstimulation and subsequent behavioral problems associated with those feelings. Thus, it appears that many sexually abused preschool children do show noticeable behavioral and emotional problems, but they may not fall into any particular diagnostic category (Cohen & Mannarino, 1996).

In the few studies published in the sexual abuse literature over the years, what is sometimes referred to as a structured cognitively-based approach appears most effective. Most studies which cite successful programs mention the use of group therapy and typically include some play and art activities (Cohen and Mannarino, 1996; Nurcombe et al., 2000). Art therapists have worked with young victims in groups and generally report that a combination of a supportive and expressive environment along with a strong cognitive component is possibly the best way to address sexual abuse issues in treatment (Buckland & Murphy, 2001; Malchiodi, 1990; Proulx, 2002; Rubin, 2005).

VARIABLES TO CONSIDER

The first variable to consider in establishing a group is the therapist's training and experience, in particular, the creative therapist's training and experience in working with sexual abuse. Personal qualities in the therapist are important, such as a high tolerance for messiness, flexibility, and love of children. In addition, it is important to consider the number of children to include in the group – one rule of thumb is one child per hand. Given the impulsive nature of most preschoolers and the safety issues – it is important that a therapist can literally contain the children – by holding hands as needed to prevent running, hurting others or inappropriate behavior that might negatively impact the other group members. One example of a behavior that sometimes occurs in a group and must be immediately limited is that of a preschooler pulling down their pants – either out of a feeling of stimulation as they talk or out of a desire to show something they are talking about – young children sometimes exhibit this behavior. Adequate therapist supervision and control limits this sort of impulsive acting-out. While this behavior is not necessarily negative in the context of a young child's behavior, the impact on the other group members informs the therapist to limit such displays.

Materials and setting are also important variables, as in all creative therapies; there is the minimal nonnegotiable requirement of a safe, clean, and comfortable setting. Safety for this population will mean containment and also privacy, so there will be no fears of parents listening in or of being punished for exhibiting or expressing thoughts and feelings and behaviors around sexual and abusive issues.

Art therapy as a primary mode of treatment is based in the idea that trauma (at any age but particularly in the pre-verbal or youngest years) is often encoded into a person's brain or thinking in terms of sensory and nonverbal elements. In addition, therapy which uses such multi-sensory modes will be more effective at facilitating thinking and talking about abuse than use of strictly verbal or traditional therapies (Bowers, 1992). Also, the use of group therapy as outlined above is established as helpful in regard to reducing the isolation a victim may feel and in spreading out the emotional intensity into a wider group, thus offering some relief. (Haizlip et al., 1975; Malchiodi, 1990; Murphy, 2001).

Messy media such as paint and clay have a place in this group, despite the logistical issues it raises in terms of clean-up and stress on the therapist and environment. Almost every individual and group scenario at almost any age will contain some component of messiness as a metaphor for the large mess that sexual abuse is and becomes for a child – even post-disclosure (Murphy, 2001). Working with very young children is, in any context, a messy endeavor, but a clinically valuable one. From a psychodynamic view, it can be seen as a way for the child to unconsciously represent messy feelings and internal chaos. From a cognitive view, mess-making can present a problem solving and self-control opportunity. From whatever label or theory you want to attach to it, the phenomenon of mess-making is essential and one that art therapists, indeed creative therapists, have real strengths and skills to share. In preschool sexual abuse treatment, the children sometimes make free-choice sculptures, used the clay for pounding or manipulating without a focus on production, or create animals or people to play out scenarios for discussion in group. The modeling materials offer a unique tactilely stimulating media that must be used with caution due to its nature; however, children respond well to it and enjoy it. They may regress, which for a preschooler is not a leap, and require even more help to remain within appropriate bounds and not throw or eat the clay when they have the impulse to do so.

PREVENTION

One important area covered in the group described here is one of prevention curricula. Given the ambiguous nature of preschool allegations and substantiation, every group must take as one key goal that of providing prevention training of sorts. This is by no means placing the emphasis on the child as responsible for preventing abuse. It is more about building confidence and an ability to understand and speak about sexual abuse with caregiving adults. One component of this semi-structured group art therapy format is the inclusion of prevention and personal safety materials. For example, the group will be taught basic "stop, go, tell" concepts and identify who they see as safe adults in their environment to whom they would go with any uncomfortable or problematic feelings or events. As stated by Klorer (2000):

> The primary issues in psychological education at this stage are ones of safety. Children should be able to identify kinds of good touch and kinds of bad touch. Children should be able to identify who they can go to and tell if they feel unsafe. Children should be able to repeat simple safety rules. (p. 91)

Thus, children in group might draw, sculpt, sing, dance, play, or otherwise work experientially and actively around such themes – drawing "who is safe" and "who you would tell" are standards that bear some repeating. Use of human figure drawings and family drawings help explore these areas, as do use of toys and pretend play.

Another technique used in this program and also described in the literature is one of using manuals or exercises from curricula. A description of one program in Australia specifically mentions the inclusion of positive imagery, journal writing, and structured activities (Cohen & Mannarino, 1996). A now out-of-print workbook called the St. Sach's Playbook (Akron YWCA Rape Crisis Center, 1984) contained many valuable drawing and play activities. One exercise in particular has proved useful to many preschool participants is the use of a pre-drawn childlike human figure – cartoon-like but anatomically correct, and asking children to place bandaids on the part of the body where they don't like to be touched or touch hurts, and stars on the parts where they do enjoy touching. This can be used to discuss and demonstrate what parts of the body are considered "private" and also to help children verbalize or clarify their reports of abuse. The use of a pre-drawn human figure facilitates accurate discussion of the body parts they are referring to, since their human figure drawings at this age will not be sufficiently detailed (usually) to accommodate such discussion or clarity. Even in unsubstantiated abuse, this technique is a noninvasive way to just teach prevention skills and ownership of the body. Klorer (2000), in speaking about treatment of any kind with the preschool aged child – not limited only to sexual abuse situations – states: "In terms of therapy, psychological education aimed at teaching the child new responses is appropriate at this stage" (p. 90). For the sexually abused child, "*you decide who touches where*" is the message. One preschool-aged boy, anally abused by a male, used this activity by turning over the sheet of the little boy's figure and placing his bandaids on the back side – concretely expressing the exact location of his abuse. Some young victims place both a star and a bandaid on some private area – indicating that the abuse was both painful and pleasurable – as is often the case, leaving them with ambiguous feelings both psychologically and physically.

CONCLUSION

The program described here, while utilizing many media and modalities including movement, imagery and art, and play, is based primarily on art therapy principles. However, the underlying link between all creative therapies makes this a generalizable program if the key components remain in terms of content, developmental appropriateness, and structure. Based upon a review of the literature, preschool-aged victims of child sexual abuse remain an underserved population and uniquely suited to the interventions of creative arts therapists. This chapter outlines work with very young children and offers a concrete model for creative arts therapists to consider and to adapt to their settings and needs. Additionally, allied and interdisciplinary professionals may want to seriously consider the inclusion both in team treatment and in utilization of therapists – an art therapist or creative arts therapist well trained in child development and sexual trauma issues. Preschoolers are neither "too young to tell" nor unable to benefit when given appropriate venues in which to work.

APPENDIX – SESSION PLANS

[This format evolved over ten years of working with preschoolers in group settings in a sexual abuse treatment agency and was piloted by Joan Phillips, ATR-BC and further developed and refined by Karleen Daugherty, LCSW.]

This is a twelve week format of hourly group sessions. Co-therapists were always used, given the need for close supervision of this age group. Art therapy interns sometimes provided co-therapy. Group time included a small snack and the children assisted in serving and cleaning up for the snack, which aids in group cohesion, feelings of being "fed", and structure that reduces anxiety overall. The description below is very abridged and many of the activities described or mentioned are in the general literature of both creative therapies and child therapy. They were adapted to this age range. Over time, therapeutic books and games come in and out of availability or print, and thus therapists are encouraged to use whatever is currently available for this age range and to maintain a repertoire of activites and resources that they are constantly updating. Parallel and at the same time as this group, a parents group met with a different therapist and the parents were provided with educational and developmental information, as well as a place to process their own feelings about the alleged abuse.

Weeks 1–2

GOAL: Establish a safe place

OBJECTIVES: develop trust in the group and the group processes, establish group norms, develop rapport, reduce sense of isolation through group, begin to identify feelings in a safe way

ACTIVITIES:
- group creates a welcome banner to hang in the group roon
- use of animal puppets and animal drawings
- draw or choose the animal that you feel like
- family and self drawings and telling about yourself and family
- looking at feelings faces and identifying and naming feelings

Weeks 3–5

GOAL: Self-disclosure

OBJECTIVES: clearly establish goal of group in addressing inappropriate sexual touching or contact, assess level of trauma and allow expression, identify different types of touch, identify safe and caregiving adults to go to for help

ACTIVITIES:
- use of books about "good touch-bad touch" – read to group, follow with free art and discussion
- identifying body parts through human figure drawings, pre-drawn outlines of bodies to color and point out places on, free art around themes of body
- mental imagery exercises to envision telling an adult or asking for help

Weeks 6–8

GOAL: Regression (allowing it and supporting it)

OBJECTIVES: encourage child to express feelings about the abuse and abuser, support the lowering of defenses so child may fully express themselves, listen to and process memories, develop symbolic expression of memories and events, all with supportive safe environment of group

ACTIVITIES:
- use of clay for aggressive impulses or feelings
- painting, experiencing some messy and loose media that mirrors feelings at times
- draw a monster or acting out monster fairy tales (metaphoric enactment of abuse)
- draw or create a monster and then put him in a cage

Weeks 9–10

GOAL: Reconstruction

OBJECTIVES: re-establish useful defenses, further develop coping skills emotionally, work on healthy body image, develop self-nurturance versus self-stimulation

ACTIVITIES:
- age appropriate sex education
- body tracing/outline colored in with positive things about self; lie down on large paper and a trusted adult leader outlines the body with a marker on the paper then child fills in with colors or collage materials and it can be hung as is or cut out and displayed that way – in the group room
- relaxation exercises – mental imagery and systematic relaxation

Weeks 11–12

GOAL: Termination

OBJECTIVES: review and summarize educational components of group (safety/sex education), relapse prevention – identification of safe adult and coping strategies, enhance sense of self- mastery and confidence

ACTIVITIES:
- drawings about good touch
- creation of artwork to take home – free choice but designed to garner positive feedback and enhance confidence
- movement exercises to enhance sense of body ownership – "my body is my own" examples include two children mirroring each others movement, being allowed to direct someone elses movement, etc.
- final session with certificates of completion and a celebratory atmosphere

REFERENCES

Akron YWCA Rape Crisis Center. (1984). *St. Sach's playbook: a program to help stop sexual abuse of children.* Akron, OH: Akron YWCA.

Berman, P. (1990). Group therapy techniques for sexually abused preteen girls. *Child Welfare, 69*(3), 239–252.

Borkin, J., & Frank, L. (1986). Sexual abuse prevention for preschoolers: a pilot program. *Child Welfare, 65*(1), 75–81.

Bowers, J. (1992). Therapy through art: Facilitating treatment of sexual abuse. *Journal of Psychosocial Nursing and Mental Health Services, 30*(6), 15–24.

Brooke, S. L. (1995). Art therapy: An approach to working with sexual abuse survivors. *The Arts in Psychotherapy, 22*(5), 447–466.

Brooke, S. L. (1997). *Art therapy with sexual abuse survivors.* Springfield, IL: Charles C Thomas Publisher, Ltd.

Brooke, S. L. (2004). Tools of the trade: A therapist's guide to art therapy assessments. Springfield, IL: Charles C Thomas Publisher, Ltd.

Buckland, R., & Murphy, J. (2001). Jumping over it: group therapy with young girls. In *Art therapy with young survivors of sexual abuse: lost for words.* Ed. Murphy, J. pp. 143–166. Taylor & Francis Publishers: Philadelphia, PA.

Carozza, P., & Heristeiner, C. (1982). Young female incest victims in treatment; Stages of growth seen with a group art therapy model. *Clinical Social Work, 10*(3), 165–175.

Cohen, F., & R. Phelps. (1985) Incest markers in children's artwork. T*he Arts in Psychotherapy, 12*(4), 265–283.

Cohen, J., & Mannarino, P. (1996). A treatment outcome study for sexually abused preschool children: initial findings *Journal of the American Academy of Child and Adolescent Psychiatry, 35*(1), 42–50. retrieved online 10-19-05.

Deblinger, E., Stauffer, L., & Steer, R. (2001). Comparative efficacies of supportive and cognitive behavioral group therapies for young children who have been sexually abused and their nonoffending mothers. *Child Maltreatment, 6*(4), 332–344.

Dufrene, P. (1994). Art therapy and the sexually abused child. *Art Education, 47*(6) 6–11.

Gomez-Schwartz, B., Horowitz, J., Sauzier, M. (1985). Severity of emotional distress among sexually abused preschool, school-age, and adolescent children. *Hospital and Community Psychiatry, 36*(5), 503–508.

Haizlip, T., McCree, C., & Corder, B. (1975). Issues in developing psychotherapy groups for preschool children in outpatient clinics. *American Journal of Psychiatry, 132*(10), 1061–1063.

Johnson, D. (1987). The role of the creative arts therapies in the diagnosis and treatment of psychological trauma. *The Arts in Psychotherapy, 14*(1), 7–13.

Jones, L., & Finklehor, D. (2001). *The decline in child sexual abuse cases.* In U.S. Department of Justice, Juvenile justice bulletin, January 2001.

Kelley, S. (1984). The use of art therapy with sexually abused children. *Journal of Psychosocial Nursing, 22*(12), 12–18.

Klorer, P. G. (2000). *Expressive therapy with troubled children.* Northvale, NJ: Jason Aronson, Inc.

Lowenfeld, V., & Brittain, W. (1987). *Creative and mental growth.* New York: Macmillan.

Malchiodi, C. (1990). *Breaking the silence: art therapy with children from violent homes* (2nd ed.). New York: Brunner-Routledge.

Malchiodi, C. (1998). *Understanding children's drawings.* New York: Guilford.

Morris, P., (1994). Superkids: short-term group therapy for children with abusive backgrounds. *Journal of Child and Adolescent Psychiatric Nursing, 7*(1), 25–31.

Murphy, J. (2001). *Art therapy with young survivors of sexual abuse: lost for words.* Philadelphia: Taylor & Francis Publishers.

Naitove, C. (1982). Arts therapy with sexually abused children. In S. Sgroi (Ed.), *Handbook of clinical intervention in child sexual abuse.* Lexington, MA: Lexington Books.

Nurcombe, B., Wooding, S.,Marrington, P., Bickman, L., & Roberts, G. (2000). Child sexual abuse II: treatment. *Australian and NewZealand Journal of Psychiatry, 34,* 92–97.

Peake, B. (1987). A child's odyssey toward wholeness through art therapy. *The Arts in Psychotherapy, 14*(1), 41–58.

Piaget, J., & Inhelder, B. (1969). *The psychology of the child.* New York: Basic Books.

Pifalo, T. (2002). Pulling out the thorns: Art therapy with sexually abuse children and adolescents. *Art Therapy : Journal of the American Art Therapy Association, 19*(1), 12–22.

Proulx, L. (2002). Strengthening ties, parent-child-dyad: Group art therapy with toddlers and their parents. *American Journal of Art Therapy, 40,* 238–258.

Rasmussen, L. (1995). Focused play therapy and non-directive play therapy: Can they be integrated? *Journal of Child Sexual Abuse, 4*(1), 1–20.

Rubin, J. (2005). *Child art therapy: 25th anniversary edition.* New York: John Wiley & Sons.

Schetky, D., & Green, A. (1988). *Child sexual abuse: A handbook for health care and legal professionals.* New York: Brunner Mazel.

Sidun, N., & Rosenthal, R. (1987). Graphic indicators of sexual abuse in draw-a-person tests of psychiatrically hospitalized adolescents. *The Arts in Psychotherapy, 14*(1), 25–33.

Spring, D. (1993). *Shattered images: Phenomenological language of sexual trauma.* Chicago: Magnolia Street Publishers.

Stember, C. (1978). Change in maladaptive growth of abused girl through art therapy. *Art Psychotherapy, 5*(2), 99–109.

Stember, C. (1980). Art therapy: a new use in the diagnosis and treatment of sexually abused children. In K. McFarlane (Ed.), *Sexual abuse of children: selected readings*. National Center of Child Abuse and Neglect: U.S. Government Publications.

Wohl, A., & Kaufman, B. (1985). *Silent screams and hidden cries*. New York: Brunner Mazel.

BIOGRAPHICAL STATEMENT

Joan Phillips, Ph.D., LMFT,LPC, ATR-BC is in private practice in Norman, Oklahoma and teaches at the University of Oklahoma. She has trained therapists locally, nationally, and internationally in the areas of abuse and trauma, family art therapy, child and adolescent therapy and art therapy, and professional ethics and issues. She has served on the board of directors for both the American Art Therapy Association and the Art Therapy Credentials Board. Joan does mixed media art and is a published poet.

Chapter 4

ART AS WITNESS, ART AS EVIDENCE: A COLLABORATIVE INVESTIGATION INTO ART THERAPY WITH ADULT SURVIVORS OF CHILDHOOD SEXUAL ABUSE

CLAIRE EDWARDS

INTRODUCTION

Many authors have argued that art therapy is an effective medium for working through sexual abuse issues (Brooke, 1995, 1997; Hagood, 2000; Murphy, 2001; Tanaka, Kakuyama and Takada Urhausen, 2003). Since the majority of sexual abuse survivors are female, with possibly as many as one in three women having been sexually abused (Herman 2001), an awareness of gender and power issues is crucial in working with survivors of childhood sexual abuse. It is interesting that a feminist approach to art therapy has not been frequently articulated in relation to this client population. Feminist art therapy addresses issues of power and control, which are critical issues in the treatment of sexual abuse (Herman, 2001).

In this chapter, which is illustrated with a case study narrative, I will outline the particular advantages of using art as a therapeutic tool in the treatment of women who have been sexually abused as children. In addition, a feminist approach to art therapy is demonstrated, both in relation to the treatment of sexual abuse, and also through the methodology of a collaborative case study narrative. This narrative serves to empower the client, and to be inclusive of her voice alongside the voice of the art therapist. Nonspecific factors, which are beneficial to the therapeutic process, are also considered. Although many of the principles discussed can be applied to working with other populations, in this instance, I am specifically concerned with addressing art therapy for women who have experienced childhood sexual abuse.

CREATIVE APPROACH

Art therapy is an extremely beneficial tool for processing trauma, including sexual abuse (Brooke, 1997; Cohen, Barnes, & Rankin, 1995; Hagood, 2000; Murphy, 2001) for a number of reasons. The particular visual and concrete nature of image-making may have unique qualities to offer adult survivors. Memories of childhood sexual abuse, which are stored either as somatic (body) sensations or visual images, rather than explicit verbal memories, (van der Kolk & Fisler, 1995) may surface during art therapy activities, or be triggered by viewing the artwork of others. Through art-making, trauma can be expressed nonverbally, providing an alternative avenue to verbal therapy, when speaking about it is too difficult or may exacerbate the existing trauma. Images may serve as a container for negative and self-harming behaviours. Art produced in art therapy may be seen as providing evidence of abuse, especially when conscious, explicit memories are limited or nonexistent. Art-making can assist in examining the psychological, and behavioural consequences of abuse, and in exploring issues such as safety, personal strengths, and future goals. The case study presented concerns a client, "Aviva" (not her real name), who identified herself as an artist. Her healing process included the use of art to make public statements about traumatic memories. I argue that traumatic images may be viewed as "witness" to the abuse, in making it visible and known to others. This process may be intrinsically therapeutic, but it is distinct from the concept of art-making in therapy, which is essentially a private activity that takes place within the context of a supportive relationship.

In addition to discussing the particular elements of art therapy that are beneficial, I also address factors which are nonspecific to art therapy, but which I will suggest are particularly pertinent in working with women who have experienced sexual abuse. These include: working within a feminist therapeutic framework (Hogan, 1997); the use of client-based outcome measures (Duncan, Miller, & Sparks, 2004); the adoption of an inclusive, collaborative approach to case study narrative (Redstone, 2004); the importance of establishing clear therapeutic boundaries, and negotiating issues of sexuality and intimacy within the therapeutic frame (Schaverien, 1995).

Feminist Art Therapy

Burt (1996) and Joyce (1997) have highlighted the dearth of feminist analysis within the art therapy literature, given the fact that most art therapists are women, and that other forms of psychotherapy have embraced feminist approaches more willingly. Whilst arguing that feminist therapy is "a philosophical approach . . . rather than a prescription of techniques" (p. 90), Joyce

(1997) outlines her model for feminist art therapy, which includes the following principles:

- Awareness of issues of power, racism, and gender
- Strengths and skill-building focus
- Rejection of sex-role stereotyping
- Working with the client's goals
- Using explicit methods

These factors are particularly relevant to art therapy with clients who have experienced sexual abuse. Sexual assault is an abuse of power, and the art therapist must be careful not to replicate the abuse. Awareness of power in the therapeutic relationship can assist the therapist to empower the client and give her back a sense of control. The therapist needs to be aware of relevant cultural issues, for example in relation to sexuality or ethnicity, in order to avoid stereotyping her client (Addison, 2003). By focusing on the client's strengths and goals, and by adopting an open, transparent approach, in which the client is given information about the rationale for the approach taken, the therapist helps to make therapy safe for the client. These principles were utilised in the case study, as will be demonstrated in this chapter.

CLIENT DIRECTED OUTCOME MEASURES

The therapy process may be further assisted by the use of client-directed outcome measures (Duncan, Miller & Sparks, 2004). These measures are based on scaling questions completed at the beginning and end of each therapy session, which enable clinical progress to be monitored, and provide ongoing feedback to the therapist about the client's experience of therapy. Use of these measures gives clients the message that their feedback is encouraged, and assists them to be reflective about the therapy process. The outcome measures indicate directly to the therapist whether the therapy is effective and meeting the client's needs.

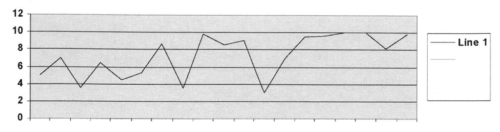

Chart 1: Aviva's Self Rating

Chart 1 demonstrates Aviva's self rating of her progress in the final phase of therapy, over a period of fifteen months, using Duncan and colleagues (2004) outcome measure. Ten represents the maximum possible score and denotes a total sense of well-being, whereas zero represents a total lack of well-being. Scores were taken in each session, initially fortnightly, and then monthly as the sessions became less frequent. Aviva's overall improvement is clearly demonstrated. Recent scores are high (between eight and ten) and show much less extreme fluctuations in mood.

As with a feminist approach, it should be clear that the use of such outcome measures are beneficial with women who have experienced sexual abuse, since it gives clients the opportunity to comment on their experience of therapy, and honours their theory of change (Duncan et al., 2004). This gives them a voice and demonstrates that their view is valued.

COLLABORATIVE APPROACH TO CASE STUDY NARRATIVE

It is becoming more commonplace for art therapists to include the voices of their clients in addition to their art work in their case studies. These voices may take the form of direct quotes or reported speech, which are incorporated by the art therapist as she constructs her case study narrative. An example of this approach is Makin (2000), who includes clients' journal extracts in her description of art therapy with women with eating disorders. The extracts provide a commentary on the clients' art work from their own perspective. Brooke (1995, 1997) also includes clients' journal extracts describing their artwork. It is more unusual to involve clients directly in the writing process. Liebmann (1997) describes the process of writing about a self-help art therapy group for new parents using a collaborative approach: "To fit in with the ethos of the group, I did not want to write just from my perspective, but to find a way of enabling the women to put their point of view. In this way, the chapter would be part of the life of the group and the project, rather than something external to it" (p. 201). Liebmann (1997) cites new paradigm research methods that view participants as co-researchers rather than subjects as being more aligned with the empowerment model of this group (p. 201).

This chapter was written using a collaborative approach, by involving the client, Aviva, in the writing process, and by actively seeking her commentary as an additional voice in the case study narrative. This was at times difficult to negotiate, since Aviva was still in the final stages of therapy, and therefore the need for clear boundaries was paramount. However, despite the difficulties, Aviva's voice was included in the narrative. The collaboration itself enabled the therapeutic relationship, including the process of art-making, to be examined in greater depth.

In writing this chapter, I wrote a draft, then sent it to Aviva, who commented on it and suggested changes, as well as writing her own narrative. This process occurred several times. Whilst I was the primary author, Aviva has had an influential role in deciding what to include, what terminology to use, and what she wanted to say. Writing about her experience, and reading what I had written, helped her to start telling other people her story, which is perhaps the most therapeutic outcome of this collaboration for her.

> Through the process of being consulted about my experiences, I really felt like I had something very valuable to contribute to the chapter; that I was not the subject of the writing, but an important part of making the chapter a richer read. Also, it gave me a vehicle to discuss my story more openly.

> Just as visual art can be used to discuss painful experiences, I was able to use the chapter as a diversion and indirectly discuss my story. . . . It has been incredibly liberating to have collaborative input into my story getting out there.

Davis Halifax (1997) suggests that utilising multiple perspectives, as opposed to the therapist's view alone, results in a more empowering experience for the client: "This kind of therapy suggests that people entering a supportive, collaborative, empowered, therapeutic relationship will carry that experience with them into their world" (p. 51).

Collaborative case study writing to this degree may not be suitable for all clients, but Aviva was at a point in therapy where she was able to step to one side and reflect on the therapeutic process; otherwise, this level of collaboration would not have been attempted. Hopefully this example will encourage other therapists to consider ways of including their clients' perspectives in their clinical writing.

CASE STUDY

This case study describes the use of art therapy as a therapeutic medium with a woman, Aviva, who had experienced childhood sexual abuse. Therapy took place in the context of private practice, and focused on issues of crisis management, safety, self-esteem, relationships, and sexual intimacy. The case study will include examples of Aviva's art work as well as her own narrative, which are included in italics.

Aviva is a 35-year-old visual/community artist, with significant symptoms of post traumatic stress disorder (P.T.S.D.) as a result of being sexually abused by her father on many occasions. Post traumatic stress disorder is a diagnostic term used to describe the cluster of symptoms commonly experienced by trauma survivors. These symptoms can include: flashbacks, panic attacks, nightmares, depression, and anxiety.

Aviva's abuse started when she was an infant (pre-verbal) and continued until she was a teenager. As an older child, Aviva also experienced sexual assault and rape by other perpetrators. Aviva grew up in a small country town in Australia. She has a younger brother and sister. Her parents, separated when Aviva was in grade ten, have both remarried.

Aviva did not remember any incidents of childhood sexual abuse until commencing art therapy. In fact, she did not remember much about her childhood at all, a phenomena known as global memory impairment (van der Kolk & Fisler, 1995), which is consistent with early childhood trauma. Aviva suffered chronic bouts of depression, and had a history of self-harm and eating issues, including anorexia. She was unable to maintain healthy boundaries with either of her parents. She frequently experienced feelings of extreme self-hatred. This took the form of believing that her body was contaminated and that potential sexual partners would find her physically repulsive. Although able to establish supportive friendships, Aviva had an extreme fear of sexual intimacy, describing herself as *"independent to the point of isolation."* Aviva experienced physical problems including severe premenstrual syndrome (P.M.S.), which describes a group of physiological and emotional symptoms commonly experienced by women in the week or two before their menstrual period. These symptoms can include bloating and irritability, depression, and anxiety. Aviva also experienced an inhibited sexual response, which was an undoubtedly an outcome of her abuse. She was not on any form of medication.

In spite of her childhood abuse, Aviva had developed a strong coping façade in the form of an outgoing, bubbly personality, a self-deprecating sense of humour, and huge compassion for others. During the period I have known her, she has commenced her visual arts degree, has a large group of friends, and has worked for some time as a talented community artist.

Aviva's involvement with art therapy started when she participated in an introductory art therapy course. These courses are intended for people who are interested in training as art therapists or who wish for a variety of reasons to learn about art therapy. In one art-making activity, Aviva had a strong, unexpected emotional reaction. The activity was to make a self-box collage. The purpose of this activity is to enable the client to use the three-dimensional form of a box to make a piece of artwork which is a statement of self and identity. For example, the self-box can be used to express visually what the client chooses to show to others on the outside of the box, and what she chooses to keep private on the inside of the box. The use of collage can be a relatively nonthreatening medium for individuals who, unlike Aviva, are not confident about using art materials. I have found this activity to be very useful for severely traumatised clients, who often have a fragile sense of identity.

Perhaps not surprisingly, images of boxes and walls often resonate with issues of self-disclosure and containment (Farrell-Kirk, 2001). In Aviva's case, the activity had triggered either a visual memory or physical sensation of sexual abuse, which had previously been repressed. Aviva spoke to me about this memory and we agreed she would come to see me individually to explore this further.

Aviva engaged in individual art therapy, which she continued weekly for three months. During this period, Aviva was starting to experience flashbacks and was in a state of emotional crisis much of the time, as she started to get in touch with previously repressed material. She used art in most sessions, and together we explored issues of establishing safety, seeking support, and developing helpful coping strategies. For example, in attempting to imagine a place of safety, Aviva identified her bedroom in the shared house that she lived in as the only place where she felt safe (Figure 4.1).

Figure 4.1. "A Safe Place"

She drew an image of her bedroom, and some of the items she needed to have with her in order to feel safe. These included food in a bowl (so she did not have to leave her room), her art materials, her quilt to hide under in bed, the closed door, and a sign which read "no noise." Aviva used this image to describe how she would retreat into her room when she was having flashbacks. She was thus starting to identify and utilise coping strategies for these experiences.

When she was at home, during this critical stage of her recovery, Aviva was able to use her art at home to avoid urges to self-harm, by attacking a piece of her own artwork with a razor rather than cutting herself, as in the image "Living well is the best revenge" (Figure 4.2).

Figure 4.2. "Living Well Is the Best Revenge"

The title comes from Dolan's self-help manual, *Beyond Survival* (2000), from which I had given Aviva excerpts to read. In this image, Aviva cut the middle of the paper many times with a razor and surrounded these cuts with some of her questions, such as "Will they love me if they see my pain?," "How do I live well?" and "Where is it safe?" This image seemed to have a cathartic effect and helped her avoid self-harming.

Like many survivors of sexual abuse, Aviva was struggling with developing clear boundaries in relationships (Hagood, 2000; Herman, 2001). She had been unable to stop contact with her father, which she knew she needed to do to feel safe. She was having ongoing contact with an ex-partner, which was also problematic. Aviva found it difficult to be assertive with this woman, and to end both these relationships: "Through artwork and discussion I was able to understand how I wanted my relationship with her and others in my life to be, and how to make it a reality that I could have relationships that were a supportive and a healthy experience for me."

After about three months, Aviva went on holiday and did not return to art therapy for another three months, when she came back for a single session. At this time, she was *"losing faith in the process of art therapy,"* as she was feeling stuck in the crisis stage characterised by flashbacks and overwhelming emotions and was frustrated with her lack of progress.

Aviva returned to art therapy a year and a half later. In the initial session of the final phase of art therapy, Aviva talked about her fears of becoming known as 'a client' on the local art therapy scene, since she wished to train in art therapy after completion of her visual art degree. Hence, she had been reticent about seeing an art therapist who could be involved in her future education. This issue was discussed and the boundaries around the sessions were clearly stated. We were now able to negotiate a more open, grounded approach to the art therapy sessions, based on clear boundaries, transparency, and client-directed goals. Having moved on from the crisis-driven earlier stage of recovery, Aviva's goal was to continue to use art therapy to explore her capacity for intimate relationships.

In the image "Dance around Intimacy" (Figure 4.3), Aviva identified and drew five stages of her usual response patterns when other women showed an

Figure 4.3. "Dance around Intimacy"

interest in her sexually. These were: (1) Being grabbed at by many hands; (2) Seeming indifferent; (3) Confusion; (4) Fear (when someone breaks though the indifference); and (5) Retreat/rejection/avoidance. Aviva recognised that whereas she used to get to stage three, she was now able to get to stage five, although this was still not the outcome she hoped for. She wanted to stop "running away" from intimacy and sexual relationships, although she was still struggling with feelings of being repulsive and unworthy. The initial experience of being "grabbed at" was strongly evocative of her abuse, and made more explicit the link between her early experiences and these current difficulties. Creating and processing these images helped her to understand her reticence to progress through these stages in order to establish a truly rewarding relationship: "I explored, through images of myself, how I was feeling in different stages of a relationship. I was able to see when certain behaviours trigger emotions in me and find ways to make myself safe through this."

Aviva was now making art outside the sessions rather than in the sessions, partly as a way of getting the most out of the time available, and partly because she found this less confronting:

> Bringing in the artwork to the sessions enabled me to explore my emotions in a private space with no one around. I found it hard to express the really scary stuff while someone was in the room. Then I could feel the emotions that went along with the image or memory rather than keeping a brave face. I found this a really healing experience where I had the freedom to cry or cut up the paper without worrying about my impact on others around me. Also, I really enjoyed sitting at a comfortable couch rather than at the table; it gave me more personal space and freedom to move.

Aviva was producing a series of images that were visual expressions of flashbacks of her experiences of sexual abuse. She brought the images to discuss with me, and would leave some of them with me to store in her art folder — usually the ones she felt to be the most distressing. Some representational images were part of a montage which Aviva was building as "evidence" of her abuse, in an attempt to construct a visual narrative of childhood events, whilst others were more symbolic representations. In "Bait" (Figure 4.4) Aviva depicted a small pink heart hanging from the end of a green thread, which is attached to a circular green ring.

She described this image as follows: "I was being dangled like bait in front of the community . . . dangling there to be toyed with like a fish toy with bait on a fishing line."

She also spoke about the feeling of "going into a void," represented by circular whirlpool-like lines beneath the heart. The void could be understood in a number of ways: it may have related to the dissociation she experienced whilst being abused; it may also have represented her lack of childhood memories,

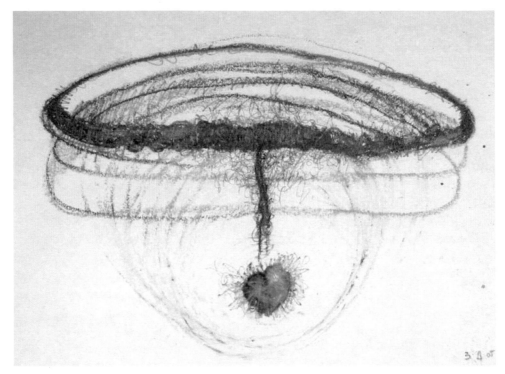

Figure 4.4. "Bait"

as well as her sense of hopelessness that resulted from the abuse. This image was an example of a symbolic representation of sexual abuse and powerlessness, which carried a high level of emotional energy.

At this time, Aviva has not finished art therapy but is in the final stages. Apart from the occasional difficulty, life seems much better for her now. She is in a supportive, intimate relationship and is learning to accept being loved and desired. She is emotionally stable, she has been able to persist with her visual art degree as well as continuing to work as a community artist. She has a supportive circle of friends and is developing a good relationship with her mother, whilst breaking contact with her father. She still has times when she feels sad or angry about her ongoing physical and emotional struggles with the legacy of abuse.

> *The last three years have been devoted to healing. Although issues still arise for me, I have tapped into my inner resources to find ways to manage the situation. I am currently in the first sexual relationship where I feel very safe, loved and cared for. I also have strong and supportive friendships around me with the people I call my family.*

But she can also recognise the gains she has made, and feels optimistic about the future.

DISCUSSION

Client as Artist: Art as Witness

Aviva wished to explore ways of using her art both publicly and privately to express trauma in a safe manner, both in her own therapy and as an inspiration to other sexual abuse survivors. Her healing process also involved being exposed to the artwork of other women who had experienced sexual abuse, which sometimes triggered flashbacks and memories of her own abuse, as in the following account of an art exhibition she visited:

It was an amazing and important artwork. I felt saddened by the story . . . the last panel . . . related to an experience that I hadn't remembered until then. I saw a very clear visual image of a moment in time and I was able to place another puzzle piece into my story. I drew a picture of the visual flashback, and this created another piece to the montage of memories I was drawing as evidence of my experiences. Later that week I had a physical flashback, which gave me an insight into another repressed memory.

Although I spent a while afterwards dealing with shock and sadness, eventually I was glad that I had more evidence to validate my story.

This use of *art as witness to the abuse* is perhaps a relatively safe way of making sexual abuse public without directly using words. The impact of this visual material on other survivors can be confronting but, according to Aviva, ultimately therapeutic:

It was not just other survivors, not just women from my community, but also movies which depicted scenes about sexual abuse or rape, which affected me. I don't really see this as a downside, more as something I need to find skills to manage. I know I spent a bit of time wishing I wouldn't remember anymore, but now after the storm has died down, I'm glad that I remember more, and that it comes slowly.

Boundary Issues: Art Therapy as Containment

Boundary issues, such as establishing trust and safety, are paramount in all therapeutic encounters with women who have been sexually abused. Given Aviva's experience of incest, which is about extreme physical and emotional boundary violation within the family, these issues were very pertinent to her situation. I spent a lot of time clarifying the boundaries around individual art therapy with Aviva in order to ensure confidentiality for her across the spectrum of situations in which we might come into contact, such as at university, or art therapy conferences, for example. The local art therapy scene mirrored Aviva's social scene, which involved a group of women whom she identified as her "family." This family included women who were dealing with similar issues to Aviva, which created dilemmas for Aviva around self-disclosure to others, with the risk of either overwhelming or re-traumatising them by triggering their own memories. As a heterosexual therapist outside this group, I was able to offer her a sense of safety, through being removed from her immediate social circle.

> I do like to see heterosexual therapists because I'm unlikely to run into them in my community. I've never had a crush on a therapist before but I've heard that it happens, so it seems safer to see a heterosexual therapist.

Loureiro De Oliviera (2003) notes that the therapist's sexual orientation "is a difficult issue and there has been very little written about it" (p. 145). He argues that therapists are more comfortable analysing their clients rather than examining themselves. Schaverien (1995) also acknowledges that the implications for transference and countertransference issues in relation to heterosexual art therapists working with clients with diverse sexualities have not been fully explored. Addison (2003) has written on the need for heterosexual therapists to be aware of, and open to learning about, cultures surrounding diverse sexualities.

Aviva's primary goal in art therapy was to examine her sexual response and fear of rejection and the impact these phenomena had upon her intimate relationships, which were a direct result of her sexual abuse. Discussion about intimate sexual issues is potentially difficult and frightening for clients, particularly those who have experienced sexual abuse, as their issues can easily be triggered by the conversation. Therapists need to indicate to clients that it is safe for these discussions to take place, and that the therapist can "handle" the material. Aviva tested my resilience by introducing traumatic material gradually and noticing my reactions.

The use of artwork to explore sexual and relationship issues was helpful, in that it deflected attention onto the images, and away from more confronting face-to-face discussions; as well as allowing Aviva to decide what was discussed, and to determine the pace of the discussion. By taking control of the process (which is congruent with a feminist, client-centred approach), she felt safe to discuss these issues with me. The use of art therapy enabled these discussions to occur more readily, as it frequently provided an indirect route for talking about sexual issues (see e.g., Figures 4.3 and 4.4).

CONCLUSION

This chapter has highlighted aspects of a feminist, client-centred approach to art therapy with survivors of childhood sexual abuse. It has demonstrated how art therapy can be conducted within a feminist framework which emphasises open, transparent, client-directed work. The role of art in the treatment of women who have experienced sexual abuse has been illustrated. The case study highlights a number of pertinent issues, such as: client as artist; client as potential future art therapist; the importance of boundaries, and negotiating issues of sexuality and trust. It also provides reflection on the nature of sexual trauma, and the ways in which the therapeutic framework within which art therapy and other creative therapies take place can provide a supportive and empowering context for change.

REFERENCES

Addison, D. (2003). Art therapy with gay, lesbian, bisexual and transgendered clients. In Hogan, S. (2003). *Gender issues in art therapy.* London and Philadelpia: Jessica Kingsley.

Brooke, S. L. (1995). Art therapy: An approach to working with sexual abuse survivors. *The arts in psychotherapy, 22*(5), 447–466.

Brooke, S. L. (1997). *Art therapy with sexual abuse survivors.* New York: Charles Thomas.

Burt H. (1996). Beyond practice: A post modern feminist perspective on art therapy research. *Art Therapy Journal of AATA, 13*(1), 12–19.

Cohen, B. M., Barnes, M. M., & Rankin, A. B. (1995). *Managing traumatic stress through art: Drawing from the center.* Baltimore: Sidran.

Davis Halifax, N.V. (1997). Feminist art psychotherapy: Contributions from feminist theory and contemporary art practice. *American Journal of Art Therapy, 36*(2), 49–55.

Dolan, Y. (2000). *Beyond survival: Living well is the best revenge.* London: B.T.

Duncan, B., Miller, S., & Sparks, J. (2004). *The heroic client: A revolutionary way to improve effectiveness through client-directed, outcome-informed therapy.* San Francisco: Jossey Bass.

Farrell-Kirk, R. (2001). Secrets, symbols, synthesis, and safety: The role of boxes in art therapy. *American Journal of Art Therapy 39*(3), 88–92.

Hagood, M. M. (2000). *The use of art therapy in counselling child and adult survivors of sexual abuse.* London and Philadelphia: Jessica Kingsley.

Herman, J. L. (2001). *Trauma and recovery: From domestic abuse to political terror.* London: Pandora.

Hogan, S. (1997). *Feminist approaches to art therapy.* London: Routledge.

Joyce, S. (1997). Feminist perspective art therapy. In S. Hogan (Ed.), *Feminist approaches to art therapy.* London: Routledge.

Liebmann, M. (1997). Art therapy and empowerment in a women's self-help project. in Hogan (Ed.), *Feminist approaches to art therapy.* London: Routledge

Loureiro De Oliveira, J.B. (2003) A Mediterranean perspective on the art therapist's sexual orientation. In Hogan, S. (Ed.), *Gender issues in art therapy.* Philadelpia, PA: Jessica Kingsley.

Makin, S. (2000). *More than just a meal: The art of eating disorders.* Philadelphia, PA: Jessica Kingsley.

Malchiodi, C. (Ed.). (2003). *Handbook of art therapy.* London and New York: Guilford.

Murphy, J. (Ed.). (2001). *Art therapy with young survivors of sexual abuse: Lost for words.* Philadelphia, PA: Brunner-Routledge; Taylor and Francis.

Redstone, A. (2004). Researching people's experience of narrative therapy. *The International Journal of Narrative Therapy and Community Work, 2,* 57–62.

Rothschild, B. (2000). *The body remembers: The psychophysiology of trauma and trauma treatment.* New York: Norton.

Rothschild, B. (2003). *The body remembers casebook: Unifying methods and models in the treatment of trauma and PTSD.* New York: Norton.

Schaverien, J. (1995). *Desire and the female therapist: Engendered gazes in psychotherapy and art ther-*

apy. London and New York: Routledge.

Tanaka, M., Kakuyama, T. & Takada Urhausen, M. (2003). Drawing and storytelling as psychotherapy with children. In Malchiodi, C. (Ed.), *Handbook of art therapy.* London and New York: Guilford.

van der Kolk, B., & Fisler, R. (1995). Dissociation and the fragmentary nature of traumatic memories: Overview and exploratory study. *Journal of Traumatic Stress, 8,* 505–536.

BIOGRAPHICAL STATEMENT

Claire Edwards, BA (hons), P.G. Dip. Art Therapy, MA (hons) Art Therapy (to be conferred in April 2006 University of Western Sydney) trained as an art therapist in London in the 1980s. She has previously worked with adults in mental health, and alcohol and drug rehabilitation, and as a child and family worker in a child protection service. Claire is currently employed part-time as an art therapist in a hospital-based child and youth mental health service. She also lectures on the Masters in Mental Health (Art Therapy) program at the University of Queensland, Brisbane, Australia, and is in private practice. She has a Masters of Art Therapy (Hons), in which she explored the topic of a feminist approach to art therapy and eating issues, from the University of Western Sydney.

Chapter 5

ART AS AN INITIAL APPROACH TO THE TREATMENT OF SEXUAL TRAUMA

SALLY BAILEY

SEXUAL TRAUMA AND THE BRAIN

I am a drama therapist who could not function properly without art, music, movement, and poetry. All of the other art modalities intersect with drama, prepare for it, enhance it, empower it, develop it, and release it. I have found this to be particularly true when working with clients who are recovering from sexual traumas of all kinds.

Because sexual trauma runs so deep and creates so much overwhelming shame and confusion within the survivor, addressing the emotional wounds caused by the manifestations of sexual abuse requires the choice of therapeutic methods which can create emotional distance and a safe container. Survivors of sexual trauma are not just resisting when they avoid dealing with their issues, or when say they cannot access their emotions because they feel numb. They are not just overreacting when they lash out in anger, experience flashbacks, or display other emotional outbursts in or outside of the therapy session. Their behavior is a direct result of the biological changes that have occurred in their brains in response to their traumatic experience.

Studies reveal that trauma material is not encoded in the brain's long-term memory system in meaningful narrative form as nontraumatic experiences are, but is dissociated into somatic sensations, undifferentiated, free floating affective states, and visual images that can break through to consciousness in nightmares and flashbacks (van der Kolk et al., 1996; van der Kolk, 2002). This is experienced as threatening and overwhelming, as if the trauma were happening all over again in the present moment, not as a past event (van der Kolk et al., 1996; van der Kolk, 2002). An immediate lack of emotional distance is created the minute the survivor starts accessing their past trauma, whether triggered by chance in everyday life or on purpose in therapy.

Words are inaccessible when the brain is in a traumatized state. Brain scans reveal that while remembering trauma, survivors' right hemispheres, where negative emotions are processed, become active and Broca's area in the left hemisphere, where words are processed, shuts down (van der Kolk, 2002). This literally leaves trauma survivors in a speechless condition. Bessel van der Kolk, one of the world's foremost authorities on traumatic stress reactions, says, "When people get close to re-experiencing their trauma, they get so upset that they can no longer speak. . . . Fundamentally, words can't integrate the disorganized sensations and action patterns that form the core imprint of the trauma." (cited in Wylie, 2004, pp. 34–35). As a result, he currently advocates nonverbal therapeutic approaches to trauma material (Wylie, 2004; van der Kolk, 2002).

VISUAL IMAGES TO ART TO WORDS

If clients do not have access to words, it makes sense that the subject of the trauma is best broached through images. Likewise, if clients feel mentally, physically, and emotionally overwhelmed when approaching traumatic memories, it makes sense that a less embodied, more distanced therapeutic modality be used. Art therapy is often a better initial approach to identify and express an experience that was horrific beyond words and somatic in origin. The visual images which have been preserved in unconscious, nonverbal memory can serve as the tools to bring the unconscious to light. The resulting art work acts as a safe, distanced container that can hold the feeling and the memory of the experience for the client.

Putting the trauma into words so it can be understood, translating those words into metaphors, and integrating the meaning that is created back into one's life history is necessary for healing. Humans are narrative-making creatures and we cannot integrate an experience into our mental schema and emotional make-up until we can make sense of it for ourselves within a worded story of our life (Dayton, 1994, 1997, 2000; Herman, 1992; van der Kolk et al., 1996). The art work, because it physically exists, can capture the essence of the image and feeling in a way that does not feel overwhelming. It can then be returned to in future therapy sessions as a resource for putting the experience into words and creating metaphors. The therapist can say, "Tell me about this" or "Tell me more." What often begins as a description of the object turns into an explanation of what it means at a symbolic level or a narrative of the traumatic experience itself. Therapeutic work can move into the other distancing containers of movement, music, drama, or poetry later when the client has been able to get past the hurdle of acknowledging the traumatic experience to the self and to witnesses (therapist alone or therapist and group) and has moved a little further into the healing process. At all points, the client can feel in control because she made the image herself, she is able to step back from it to observe it, and she uses her own words to describe what it means to her.

SEXUAL TRAUMA AND ADDICTION

While I was working with recovering drug addicts at Second Genesis in Washington, DC, a long-term residential substance abuse treatment center, I found that the vast majority of my clients, both male and female, had at some point in time, experienced multiple sexual traumas. van der Kolk (2002) states that about one-third of traumatized people eventually turn to alcohol or drugs to relieve themselves from the emotional symptoms caused by their trauma. I discovered as I listened to my clients' stories that many were survivors of childhood/adolescent incest or rape and almost all of them had prostituted themselves during their addiction in order to procure drugs. If you need to get high and you did not have any money, sooner or later, you ended up prostituting yourself formally for money or informally as a barter for drugs. It was hardest for the men to admit to this, since most of them identified as heterosexuals but had engaged in homosexual acts. The vast majority of potential customers interested in buying sex on the street were men who were looking for either heterosexual encounters or homosexual encounters. While everyone felt shame about their street behavior after they got sober, the heterosexual men had real difficulty coming to terms with their prostitution experiences as it was cognitively dissonant with their life-long internalized beliefs about their sexual preference. African-American males had the most problem as their community is traditionally macho and homophobic.

Additionally, addicts who ended up imprisoned had often endured rape while incarcerated, sometimes gang rapes by other inmates or sexual alliances forged with one particular inmate to gain protection from gang rapes. This set up existed in male and female prisons. Although protection through sexual alliances was a practical matter of survival behind bars, it was still experienced as extremely shameful and traumatizing, particularly for males.

On one hand, if residents did not admit to their past sexual traumas, especially those incurred while they were active addicts, treatment staff did not feel they were fully addressing the goal of Phase one of the program (Accepting the Need to Change) or Steps four and five of the twelve Steps of AA/NA (Narcotics Anonymous, 1988):

Step four: We made a searching and fearless moral inventory of ourselves.
Step five: We admitted to God, to ourselves, and to another human being the exact nature of our wrongs.

On the other hand, residents were not supposed to focus on healing from their sexual traumas while in drug treatment because the philosophy of the therapeutic model required that they focus on recovery from their drug addictions first. The idea behind this focus makes sense at first glance. Residents were in treatment primarily for their addiction, so that was what the therapeutic contract identified and prioritized. Overseeing government agencies and managed care organizations that pay for treatment like to see very specifically identified goals and objectives on treatment plans that refer directly back to the identified treatment issue they are funding. Many staff members were recovering addicts themselves who had earned their certification in addictions counseling, but were not trained in dealing with sexual trauma. Many of them were still young in their own recovery from substance abuse and had not yet addressed their own sexual trauma issues. When I brought up the need to deal with abuse issues in our treatment team meetings, I was told focusing on them would take away from addiction issues and we hardly had enough time to work through them. The official word from above was that healing from sexual traumas or any other traumatic experiences prior to or concurrent with addiction were supposed to wait until the recovering addicts had been clean and sober for a minimum of a year, otherwise their sobriety was at risk.

However, this caused a very big Catch-22. One of the major reasons these clients had become addicts in the first place was to numb the emotional pain caused by their sexual (and other) traumas. Stopping the drugs meant not just struggling with the symptoms of withdrawal and the cravings created by their physical and psychological addiction, it also meant that with sobriety the old feelings from the trauma that had been numbed away for so long started to come back.

Many residents were not able to handle learning to live without drugs, developing the social and emotional skills they had not practiced for years while "on the street," holding at bay all the feelings of guilt and shame for their addictive behavior (cheating, lying, stealing, neglecting children and spouses, betraying friends and family) while doing drugs and handling the feelings generated by their unresolved traumas. It was too overwhelming. Second Genesis had a very high success rate as far as drug treatment programs went (33%), but many people absconded and relapsed before they ever finished the program and I have always believed that some of them left in order to medicate their trauma symptoms, not because they could not resist drug cravings.

CASE EXAMPLE: THE BOX SELF-PORTRAIT WITH CAMILLE

For the first eight years I worked at Second Genesis, I was the itinerant drama therapist who traveled between the six residential facilities running a weekly drama therapy group in each. Later, I worked full-time as a primary therapist and drama therapist at Melwood House, the facility for women addicts and their children. Throughout these years, other primary therapists came to me to share that they had difficulty getting their clients to deal with essential issues in individual sessions; some clients resisted talking in group sessions about anything beyond the obvious — "I had a drug problem." I found that I did not have difficulty getting drama group members to open up about issues or to talk in my drama group because through basic games and improvisations they began to feel very safe with each other and with me. Usually about the fifth or sixth session, I would bring in an art exercise which we used to facilitate NA Steps four and five, the "searching and fearless moral inventory." I called this the Box Self-Portrait. This exercise creates a literal and metaphorical container for clients' issues in concrete three-dimensions. It illuminates for them the emotional dichotomy that exists for them as addicts and survivors: projecting a false identity to the world on the outside while hiding their real thoughts and feelings inside. Denial is a big issue in addiction and must be addressed before addicts can begin to get honest and deal openly with their issues. Dissociation is a big issue in trauma and must be broken through before the trauma can be consciously accessed and addressed. Exploring their feelings through the Box Self-Portrait helped reveal what was happening on the inside while also validating the existence of their outside defenses. In a sense, they could have their cake and eat it, too, because they were able to acknowledge their defenses and what those defenses were protecting.

I bought three different sizes/shapes of boxes from a local bakery supply store and brought in an array of art supplies: Magic Markers, crayons, construction paper, tissue paper, pipe cleaners, colored cellophane, scissors, tape, and glue. Each person picked a box that best represented them (a big rectangular box, a flat pie box, or a medium square box). They were to decorate the outside with colors, shapes, pictures, and symbols (no words, unless they were involved in a symbol — like a STOP sign) to express all the qualities, emotions, behaviors, and personality traits — good *and* bad — that they show to others. They decorated the inside with colors, shapes, pictures, and symbols to express all the qualities, emotions, behaviors, and personality traits — good *and* bad — that they experience on the inside, but which they may or may not show to others. I always had to say "good *and* bad" or I would only get one or the other, depending on how the person was feeling about himself that day. A talent for drawing was not necessary in order to make the box very effective and striking, because there were the options of cutting out paper, coloring designs, making three-dimensional objects to put inside or outside, or even cutting the box itself.

Drama group was two hours long. After a check in and a physical warm-up, the group members typically spent an hour creating their Box Self-Portraits.

Then we went around the circle and shared them. Each person got to describe what the symbols on the box and inside the box meant.

What was inside the box was hidden from view as long as the box was closed, but when the box was opened, it would become visible for the whole group to view. This often caused some anxiety for people who were willing to express what was happening on the inside as long as nobody ever saw it. My response to their questions about this while they were working was, "The rule for this exercise is you have to show us whatever you put in the box, but then you can close the box back up after you show us. If you don't want to show us something, don't put it in the box." This was enough of a reassurance of safety for group members to move forward. I never had anyone refuse to open their box and share it with the group, partly because there was a great deal of pride generated in making this kind of self-portrait and partly because of the level of trust we had generated by that time in the series of sessions. While I'm sure there were plenty of unhappy experiences and ugly feelings that did not get put in boxes, no one avoided including at least some of their uncomfortable inside parts. If nothing else, I could always count on getting a depiction of the person's drug of choice!

The sharing time was often the first time many had ever expressed either their abuse or the emotions they felt about it. One of the most dramatic examples of this was Camille, whose earliest memory at the age of 3 was of her older brother sexually abusing her, a practice he kept up the entire time they were growing up. When, as a teenager, Camille finally disclosed the abuse to her mother, she was not believed. Camille had to wait until her brother graduated high school and went out on his own for the daily abuse to stop. By that time she had such a low self concept and lack of physical and emotional boundaries that she continued to allow herself to be used sexually by every man who came her way. In groups and individual sessions at the beginning of her treatment, she insisted that she wasn't angry about anything, that she was, quite on the contrary, very happy and optimistic. Her rationale for this happy state of mind was that she had made it into treatment and was in the process of turning her life around.

It was not until she made her Box Self-Portrait that she felt safe enough to express the truth. The outside of her box had a bright happy sun on it with flowers growing and birds flying in the air, but the inside of the box she had filled with a three dimensional sculpture of red, orange, and black tissue paper in the form of an erupting volcano. Underneath the volcano, drawn very small in faint crayon was a little girl, hidden, helpless, and trapped beneath it all.

Color is an important element in art therapy, as it symbolizes emotions. Some color symbolism is culturally derived. For example, in Western countries white symbolizes purity which is why brides wear white, but in many Asian countries, white symbolizes death and is the color worn by mourners.

Some use of color is based on nature: fire is red, grass is green. Other uses are very personal emotional symbols, such as a client associating lavender with love because her loving mother always wore that color. Due to different associative experiences, one person may associate a color with one quality or emotion, while another associates the same color with something very contrasting. For example, someone who loves being near and in water might associate blue with relaxation and happiness while another might associate it with sadness and another might connect it with fear. Some art therapists subscribe to the belief that certain colors always represent certain emotions, but I was trained in the psychocybernetic model of art therapy (Nucho, 1987), so I believe in asking clients to interpret their work to me, rather than putting my own symbolism on their images. This, I think, works well with trauma survivors because a large part of their therapeutic task in recovery is to make meaning of their own experience (Dayton, 1997, 2000; Herman, 1992; van der Kolk et al., 1996).

Camille reported that the red, orange, and black symbolized a volcano, its molten lava, and fire which, in turn, symbolized her rage. She was relieved to finally be able to express what she was feeling in (what she considered) an indirect way. In her mind, she had not actually *said*, "I'm angry," but she was able to *acknowledge* the unacceptable emotion. Anger had not been an emotion that was allowed expression in her home at any time in her past or present.

Anger, like all emotions, is a survival signal that tells us when we are in potential danger and we need take action to protect ourselves from being violated (Bilodeau, 1992; Tavris, 1982.) However, anger is usually not expressed openly by survivors to their abusers or to their families, sometimes not even to themselves. Expression of it during or after the trauma could have put them in danger at the hands of their abuser. In case of incest, where there are family bonds and emotional connection at stake, expressing anger could put the survivor at risk of losing the love of the abuser to whom she still feels a loving connection. Instead, survivor anger tends to be turned inward against the self, leading to depression, self harm, or suicide attempts (Dayton, 1997, 2000; Herman, 1992). If trauma occurs repeatedly over a long period of time, the survivor can develop learned helplessness, a belief that action is useless and the only choice is to accept the abuse passively (Dayton, 2000).

Whenever Camille had expressed her anger in the years after she revealed her brother's abuse, her mother and father had accused her of trying to hurt them and rejected her. After Camille made the volcano, she began to be able to talk about her family dynamics and to understand how her parents had been implicitly involved in the abuse by turning a blind eye to her situation. She began to acknowledge *all* the emotions – positive and negative – that she was experiencing on a daily basis. She went back to working through *The Courage to Heal* (Bass & Davis, 1988), a self-help book for survivors of sexual trauma, which she had tried unsuccessfully to work on during her addiction. Later in treatment, I had her write a fairy tale about the little girl under the volcano and explore how she got there and how she finally got out. Camille also began attending a weekly sexual survivors' support group outside of the facility.

I was called on the carpet for allowing Camille to work on her sexual abuse issues so directly. The facility director said, "Residents aren't ready to deal with sexual trauma while they are in treatment." But I knew that if I didn't help her deal with it while she was in a residential facility, where there was lots of support – staff members and other residents to whom she could go to 24 hours a day – that once she moved out and the old feelings of guilt and shame returned, she would start smoking crack again in order to deal with the feelings.

Other residents also used the Box Self-Portrait to symbolize traumatic experiences in acceptable and safe ways. Using images instead of words, they felt as if they were being extremely honest and direct, while also being covert and indirect. They enjoyed being able to feel proud and sneaky at the same time. As addicts, they put a great deal of energy into rationalizing, hiding behind words, and manipulating meaning for others and themselves through language. Graphic images bypassed their practiced verbal abilities and gave them an "out" for being honest since it was a wordless medium. It was simultaneously less real and more real, in part because it was an unfamiliar way of communicating, but also because it created a safe distance and communicated viscerally, as opposed to intellectually, through color, shape, and image. Great pride was taken in sharing images and then revealing their meaning through words. For many, it was their first truly honest attempt at a moral inventory they had undertaken.

CASE EXAMPLE TWO:
DRAWING AND MASK MAKING WITH GENA

At the time I was working at Mellwood House, the entire residential treatment program lasted six months and each drama therapy group was about three months long. Phase one: Accepting the Need to Change was one month. Phase two: Working on Recovery and Relapse Prevention was three months. Residents were usually assigned to drama therapy group in this phase. Phase three: Re-entry was two months. Then the women returned for after-care meetings one evening a week for several months.

Gena, one client on my caseload, waited until she was in her sixth month before she revealed that she had been a victim of incest as a teenager. Throughout her time in treatment, she had been compliant, but evasive. I knew there was something going on inside, but she wouldn't let anyone in. She was what we at Second Genesis called a "people pleaser," willing to work hard and do anything asked of her, to the point of denying her own needs, in hopes that others would like her. She had difficulty disciplining her children because that meant confronting them and saying "no!" She agreed with whatever others said and never put forth her own opinion, to avoid confrontation and controversy. In essence, she compromised her own needs, wants, and desires in order to fulfill those of others, in hopes that they would protect her; however, what happened instead was that she was used by them and then abandoned. She would not set limits on the negative behaviors that others performed in her presence and would "go along" in order not to make waves. This had the potential of jeopardizing her recovery, because if she got involved with the wrong crowd once she was out on her own, chances were she would end up relapsing because she could not say no. "People pleasing" is a survival behavior that develops in chemically dependent and abusive families. It works, but at great cost to the self-efficacy of the "people pleaser."

In the early months, Gena would do anything to avoid individual sessions with me, because – as it turned out – she was afraid she would reveal her traumatic secret and I would not like her anymore. She would always say, "I'm OK. I don't want to bother you," and would go on an errand or work down in the child care center. I would have to seek her out and tell her again and again that she was not bothering me; she deserved her individual session; furthermore, she was required to have one. Finally, the week before she was ready to move out, in her individual session, she was talking about how even though she was getting ready to leave, she did not feel ready because she still felt uncomfortable. She said she could not describe it in words, but she felt it in her body. I asked her where this uncomfortable feeling was and she pointed to her chest. Then, I asked if she could maybe draw for me what it felt like. She quickly drew a little round ball with many spikes sticking out of it. It looked to me like an explosive mine. I asked her to tell me about it and suddenly she was telling me the story about how her mother and father had died when she was about eleven and she had to go live with her grandmother and grandfather. A year or so later her grandmother died. Her grandfather started "using her for his sexual needs." And her uncle who lived with them found out. Instead of rescuing her, he demanded that his father share her with him. She seriously considered running away, but she did not know how she would survive on her own, so she stayed. And began hating herself. And doing drugs to numb the pain. None of this history was in her intake interview, nor had she breathed a word of it in any groups she had participated in the last six months!

When I asked, "Why didn't you tell me about this *before*?" her response was, "I have never told *anyone* before and I thought if I told you, you would think badly of me." I immediately reassured her that it was not her fault, that she did nothing to deserve this treatment, and, of course, I did not think badly of her! She was immensely relieved.

I knew that having just revealed this horrible secret, leaving treatment would be experienced by her as a rejection. In truth, her revelation was quite literally a cry for help. I told her I thought we needed to bring this information to the attention of the director and the rest of the therapeutic team because maybe now was not the right time for her to move out, maybe she needed some more time in the facility to work on this important issue. She agreed. I requested that she be demoted to Phase 1 so she could start treatment over. My reasoning to staff was that she was only now finally able to be honest and could begin addressing her addiction issues. Luckily, the rest of the staff agreed with me and she was able to stay for another six months.

Never a verbal person, art remained the best way for Gena to express how she felt, how she thought, and how she could change. One of the most powerful pieces she made during that time was a plaster of Paris life mask that expressed exactly how her history of abuse fueled her people-pleasing behavior. Again, the outside/inside metaphor helped her express the conflict between her feelings and her behavior. The outside of the mask was painted with images of love – a large heart covering her mouth showed she only said loving and pleasant words to others and another heart on her forehead showed how she only thought positive thoughts about others. But on the inside of the mask, the heart over her forehead was broken and the whole bottom of her face was covered with prison bars which held back the words she *really* wanted to say: No! No! No! No! No!

Figure 5.1. Inside of Mask

Figure 5.2. Outside of Mask

When asked what the two faces would say if the mask could come alive, she wrote:

FRONT
I'm looked on as
The one who's always happy,
Smiling,
Always caring,
Always sharing,
Always willing to do whatever
For whoever.

BACK
But what I'm really feeling is
Frustration,
Angry,
Guilty,
Because what I really want to say is
"NO, NO, NO,
PLEASE NOT NOW!"
But I'm afraid I might hurt your feelings.

Six months later Gena was truly ready to move out with her children and begin to try to live life on life's terms. She had matured a great deal, and while she still struggled with "people-pleasing," she had begun to be able to hold herself and others accountable for their actions.

My experience suggests that traversing the bridge of healing involves careful movement from unspeakable wound to image to languaged story, in order to unlock and release the trauma that is trapped in the heart and mind of a survivor. A journey that happens too quickly or which covers too much distance at once can cause re-traumatization or can scare the client into being unwilling to make the journey at all. Art, as a more primal expression than language, but a less embodied one than movement, can be a valuable tool, particularly in allowing the client an initial way of expressing what seems to be inexpressible.

APPENDIX

Sample of Therapy Plans for Drama Therapy Group at Melwood House

Session One: Introduction
Physical Warm-up
Name Game
Individual introductions to group and pantomime something you like to do
Mirrors

Session Two: Games
Check in (Identify an emotion)
Physical Warm-up
The Winds are Blowing
Partner Pantomimes
What Are You Doing?

Session Three: Nonverbal Communication
Mind-Reading
Physical Warm-up
Come-Go-Stay
Identify Personal Space
Making an Entrance
Tone of voice/Open Scenes

Session Four: Personal Inventory
Check in (what color are you?)
Stretch and write your names in the air
Make Self-Portrait boxes and share

Session Five: Setting Goals
Check in (what animal do you feel like?)
Pass the imaginary object and change it
Emotion statues (drama game)
Past-Present-Future Self Portrait Statues (drama game)

Session Six: Mask Making
Check in
Physical Warm-up
Make plaster of Paris Life Masks

Session Seven: Mask Making
Check in
Physical Warm-up
Design and begin painting masks

Session Eight: Mask Making and Exploration
Check in
Physical Warm-up
Finish painting masks
Writing: Imagine what the inside and the outside of the mask would say to you if it came alive. Write it down.

Session Nine: Performance and Closure
Check in
Physical Warm-up
Practice performing mask pieces
Perform mask pieces for invited audience
Graduation from Drama Group

REFERENCES

Bass, E. and Davis, L. (1988). *The courage to heal.* New York: HarperCollins Publisher, Inc.

Bilodeau, L. (1992). *The anger workbook.* Minneapolis, MN: CompCare Publishers.

Dayton, T. (1994). *The drama within: Psychodrama and experiential therapy.* Deerfield Beach, FL: Health Communications, Inc.

Dayton, T. (1997). *Heartwounds: The impact of unresolved trauma and grief on relationships.* Deerfield Beach, FL: Health Communications, Inc.

Dayton, T. (2000). *Trauma and addiction: Ending the cycle of pain through emotional literacy.* Deerfield Beach, FL: Health Communications, Inc.

Herman, J. (1992). *Trauma and recovery.* NY: Basic Books.

Narcotics Anonymous (1988). *Narcotics Anonymous.* Van Nuys, CA: World Service Office, Inc.

Nucho, A. (1987). *The psychocybernetic model of art therapy.* Springfield, IL: Charles C Thomas Publisher, Ltd.

Tavris, C. (1982). *Anger: The misunderstood emotion.* New York: Simon & Schuster.

van der Kolk, B. (2002). In terror's grip: Healing the ravages of trauma. *Cerebrum, 4*(1), 34–50.

van der Kolk, B., McFarlane, A.C., and Weisaeth, L., (Eds). (1996). *Traumatic stress: The effects of overwhelming experience on mind, body, and society.* New York: Guilford Press.

Wylie, M.S. (2004). The limits of talk. *Psychotherapy Networker, 6*(1), 30–41, 67.

BIOGRAPHICAL STATEMENT

Sally Bailey, MFA, MSW, RDT/BCT is director of the drama therapy program at Kansas State University, Manhattan, KS, a site for alternative training in drama therapy. She is a recent past president of the National Association for Drama Therapy and the author of two books: *Wings to fly: Bringing theatre arts to students with special needs* (1993) and *Dreams to sign* (2002).

Chapter 6

SEXUAL TRAUMA – IMPACT ON MARITAL COMMUNICATIONS

Janice Samoray

INTRODUCTION

In the chapters of this book and elsewhere in current research, one finds strong evidence to suggest that art therapy is a highly effective intervention strategy in the treatment of sexual abuse survivors. Most often, art therapy is used to treat the short- and long-term aftereffects of sexual abuse directly. However, the case study below finds art therapy to be a highly productive treatment option for survivors of sexual abuse, even when other issues are being addressed in counseling. Specifically, art therapy is shown to be a productive intervention when the survivor is experiencing difficulty in an intimate relationship. In fact, the study shows that the survivor, his or her partner, and the couple as a unit all benefit tremendously from the nonverbal communication that takes place through art experientials.

The case study under consideration here demonstrates both how sexual abuse impedes the ability of survivors to communicate, and how art therapy has the potential to make inroads in communication where other types of therapy have not proven as effective. The stated purpose of the study was to use group counseling to help relieve communication issues experienced by two intimate couples. In the course of treatment, however, a history of premarital sexual abuse was disclosed by one partner in each couple. One implication of these disclosures (which had not surfaced through other types of therapy) is that they provide evidential support for the case that art therapy is a particularly appropriate and effective method of treatment for survivors of sexual abuse. A second, broader implication of the study is that the survivors' experiences of sexual abuse perpetually informed their verbal communications, resulting in communication difficulties with their partners and other individuals in their lives. After sexual abuse was identified as a root cause of verbal communication difficulties, participants were able to employ nonverbal communication tactics to communicate more productively.

CASE STUDY

The research for this chapter focused on heterosexual couples in the process of divorce. As defined by Everett (1987), divorce comprises the following four stages: recognition, discussion, action, and post-dissolution. The process of divorce begins with the internal recognition, by one or both members of the couple, of dissatisfaction with the marriage. That initial stage is followed by the outward expression of dissatisfaction, which results in discussion between the couple and with others. The action stage follows the discussion stage, and the final stage of divorce, post-dissolution, begins once the partners accept that the marriage will end (Everett, 1987).

The couples involved in this study were in the action stage of divorce, which is the point after which one member of the couple has initiated action to secure a legal dissolution of the marriage. The action stage, along with the post-dissolution stage, is typically very difficult because of a high degree of ambivalence between marital partners who remain attached while simultaneously trying to separate. Clear and accurate communication is of the utmost importance during the action stage, yet participants in this study cited communication difficulties as a key source of conflict. A history of sexual abuse was not a criterion for participation in this research, although childhood sexual abuse was identified as a root cause of communication issues in the course of the study.

Two couples participated in the research. Ben and Paula, a middle-class African-American couple from the city of Detroit, had been married 22 years. At the time of the study, Ben was 44 years old and Paula was 40 years old. Brad and Megan, a Caucasian couple from a metropolitan Detroit suburb, had been married 10 years. Brad was 44 years old and Megan was 34 years old at the time of the study. Neither couple had children together, nor had they children under the age of 18. For confidentiality purposes, the participants' names have been changed. Close facsimiles of the experientials produced in session are shown in Figures 6.1 through 6.5.

Criteria that were considered essential for this study were (a) that the participating couples were in the action period of the divorce process (as mentioned above), (b) that both partners participated equally in the study, (c) that both partners consistently attended each session, (d) that both partners participated fully in the art experientials and other data-gathering strategies, and (e) that both partners were willing and able to articulate their experiences in the form of verbal descriptions in a group setting. Both couples were offered the opportunity and self-selected to participate in this research as a result of the Start-Making-It-Livable-For-Everyone (SMILE) Program. Now in its second decade, the SMILE Program currently services divorcing parents in Oakland County, Michigan through a mandatory, court-ordered, single group session, the purpose of which is to educate participants on strategies for healthy adjustment during divorce. At the time this research was conducted, SMILE was a voluntary program open to all area couples in the process of divorce, with or without children living at home. Participation in the study cited here was offered to roughly twenty couples attending the SMILE Program; twelve accepted, but did not consistently attend or participate fully in the sessions, while the others declined.

The research program that provides the data for this chapter consisted of six weeks of bi-weekly, three-hour therapy sessions. Over that period, the sessions were divided into three main themes: increase of awareness; assessment and modification of problematic communication patterns; and closure accompanied by steps toward post-dissolution adjustment. Art therapy experientials were the primary method used to generate data, although written questionnaires and verbal exchanges also were used in each of the three phases of the study. The participants actively assumed the role of co-researchers by investigating, reflecting upon, and verbally and visually describing their marital relationships. The therapist and all members of the group jointly analyzed participants' visual communications, which were expressed through art experientials. The experientials at times affirmed, and at times contradicted, verbal and written messages – both those messages expressed in session, as well as messages expressed more generally in the marital relationships. Reflecting upon the consistencies and inconsistencies between messages expressed in different communicative modes enabled participants to pinpoint key sources of miscommunication and facilitated the overall understanding of family dynamics.

Specific art experientials were employed and particular communicative issues were addressed each week. Week One focused on each participant's perception of the partner's communications and his or her own communications. As might be expected, the experientials revealed that all participants were feeling various levels of dissatisfaction, ambivalence, conflict, depression and anxiety. However, these feelings were not being communicated between partners with full honesty, accuracy and understanding.

Week Two required of each participant three drawings of self with family-of-origin engaged in activity. The drawings were created chronologically and first depicted childhood, then adolescence, and finally, young adulthood. The purpose of this drawing series was to contextualize participants' present situations within their life cycles in order to help them better to cope with current crises. The experientials facilitated revelations regarding family patterns and early-life traumas, which in turn began to open communication and inspire sympathy and empathy between spouses. Through the drawing series, participants were able literally to see their own and each others' origins, and to understand how their individual histories had impacted upon their interspousal communications.

A drawing series centered on relationship milestones was the focus of Week Three. Participants drew five chronological pictures depicting first date, wedding day, first anniversary, and two other landmark anniversaries (either fifth and tenth, or tenth and twentieth). Through the drawing series, wide discrepancies between communicational intent and communicational impact were identified and determined to be caused largely by previously undisclosed family-of-origin secrets. The revelations of this session, although highly distressing at the onset, did ultimately facilitate further insight and heighten awareness of the importance of communication as a whole.

Week Four involved two projects: a drawing and a collage. For the drawing, participants were directed to create self-portraits to give to their spouses. After the portraits were exchanged, spouses were directed to modify the portraits so as to adjust one quality each perceived as negative in his or her spouse. Therefore, the focus of the drawing experiential was negative spousal attributes; in contrast, the focus of the collage was positive spousal characteristics. Each participant was directed to identify three positive qualities in his or her spouse, choose three different materials to symbolize these qualities, and create a 'medal of honor' for the spouse (a collage pin). After the pins were completed, each participant formally presented the pin to his or her spouse.

Like Week Four, Week Five entailed two projects – in this case, the projects shared the theme of collaboration. The expressed purpose of the session was for spouses to work together to build better communication, thereby building a stronger relationship. The first project was a joint drawing that began with each spouse marking a single line, and ostensibly was intended to grow into a fully integrated picture. The second project asked couples to build an environment together using wooden blocks. The couples made progress toward improved communications as a result of the clear communication breakdowns that came to the fore during these collaborative projects.

The focus of Week Six was a review of the art experientials from Weeks One through Five. Participants compared their artwork across weeks to identify themes, as well as to look for progress with respect to improved communications. They discerned and reflected upon similarities and differences in their individual perceptions of the major occurrences in their relationships.

The most surprising, intriguing, and perhaps relevant aspect of this study was the methodical emergence, through the art experientials, of devastating family-of-origin secrets previously unknown to the spouses. This revelatory atmosphere was created at the outset: in the course of Week One, both Megan and Paula disclosed a history of childhood sexual abuse previously unbeknownst to Brad and Ben. Figure 6.1, drawn by Megan during the first week of therapy, shows Brad turning his back on her. Megan indicated in session that this gesture causes her to feel "closed-out, lonely and distant" from him. Though Megan did not disclose her childhood sexual abuse until later in the research program, she revealed then that her perpetrator made the same movement of turning his back after every sexual encounter. Also during Week One, Paula's drawing (Figure 6.1) indicates "problems in the bedroom," which she, like Megan, did not connect to her sexually abusive past until later in the study.

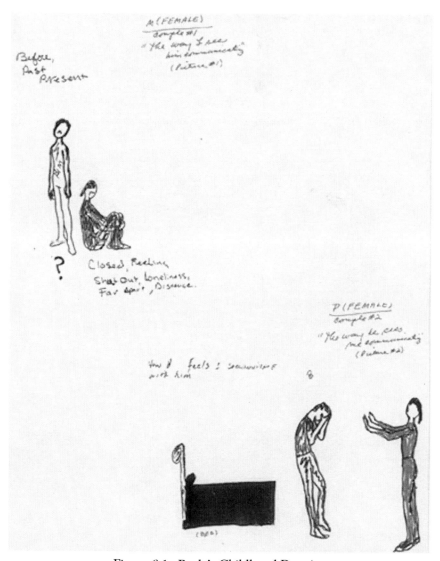

Figure 6.1. Paula's Childhood Drawing

During the second week of the study, Megan and Paula disclosed teen pregnancies that resulted from sexual abuse (both, coincidentally, at age sixteen). This shared experience initiated a bond between them that grew throughout the study. The trust between Megan and Paula empowered the women to a higher level of openness and self-disclosure as the sessions progressed.

Figure 6.2, Megan's depiction of her childhood, shows her with her family at a Sunday afternoon fish fry. Though the picture appears to depict a happy family picnic, Megan revealed verbally that she had been abused by her stepfather from age seven, and also expressed feelings of detachment and anger toward her mother for failing to stop the abuse. Sgroi (1981) notes that many mothers of incest victims are "psychologically absent," and goes on to explain, "[O]ne of the characteristics of the "psychologically absent" mothers of incest victims is to fail to protect by failing to limit inappropriate behavior between their husbands and their children" (p. 193). Megan clearly felt that psychological absence, and the tree she drew between herself and her mother (Figure 6.2) must be viewed as a visual expression of the emotional space between them.

Figure 6.2. Megan's Childhood Drawing

Paula's childhood drawing (Figure 6.1), contains only the word "nothing," though she, Megan, Brad and Ben were given the same directive. Paula's descriptive narrative of her early childhood sheds light on her art: Paula's father was unknown to her and, though she knew her mother, she was raised by her grandparents. She revealed that she had been sexually abused by several of her mother's male friends, as well as "some relatives," in her childhood and adolescence. Visually and verbally, Paula expressed feelings of total abandonment at age five, and described herself as, "having nothing – *being nothing.*" Clearly, Paula's depiction of early childhood demonstrates trauma and struggle on several fronts, showing scars from sexual abuse, abandonment issues, and an underdeveloped sense of self. In contrast, Megan's painful childhood memories derive more directly from her sexual abuse.

In her narrative on adolescence, Megan shared with the group that her drawing depicted herself, crying, with her sister upstairs (Figure 6.3). Her mother, downstairs, had forgotten her sixteenth birthday. Paula's drawing of adolescence (Figure 6.3) shows her with her grandparents inside their house. In her verbal narrative, Paula explained that the figures outside the house are those of her siblings who lived with her mother; their facial features correlate positively with her perceived degree of closeness to them. In her narrative, Paula did not refer to the small figure in the house until she was asked directly whom the figure represented. She then disclosed that it represented her infant daughter, who was born out of wedlock when Paula was sixteen years old. Paula's grandparents raised her daughter, just as they had raised her.

In light of their growing bond, Paula's revelation encouraged Megan to disclose that she, too, had given birth to a daughter at age sixteen. The "sister" depicted in Figure 6.3 was actually this child, whom she had been forced by her mother to give up for adoption. Megan specifically cited Paula's narrative as the impetus for her disclosure. Not surprisingly, both Ben and Brad were overwhelmed and taken aback by Megan's and Paula's disclosures. Ben expressed shock and hurt that, after having been married to Paula for twenty-two years, only through the artwork in session did he learn about her abuse. He asked Paula, "Why couldn't you trust me enough to tell me this years ago?" Brad's reaction was similar, but both Megan and Paula cited shame, fear, guilt and anger as the forces stifling disclosure.

The third week of the study brought the revelation for both couples that core marital problems stemmed from reactions formed in youth as a result of the women's sexual abuse. The decline in each couple's marriage can be seen, explicitly, in the drawing series from Week Three. Megan's drawings show that she felt ambivalence toward her relationship with Brad as early as their wedding day. In her verbal narrative, Megan indicated that she felt "shut out" by Brad on their wedding night. Brad then admitted to the group that he had turned his back on her and fallen asleep after sex. On some level of consciousness,

Figure 6.3. Megan's and Paula's Adolescent Drawings

that motion triggered in Megan the memory of her childhood abuse by her stepfather. Megan explained, "Seeing this big, round back turned on me after getting what he wanted was just like my stepfather all over again." Brad replied that he now understood her anger, but had not on their wedding night. He stated, "Now I can see why she was so mad at me on our wedding night, but I wouldn't have gotten mad back if I had known that this happened to her." Ben supported Brad's position, asserting that he, too, would have adjusted his behavior, had he known more about the sexual abuse in Paula's past.

With the participants still raw from the emotional intensity of the prior week, Week Four focused on further exploring the ways in which behaviors that triggered memories of childhood sexual abuse crippled the marital relationships. In discussing what participants would change about their spouses, Megan asserted that Brad's recent body language caused her to feel as though she were, "being re-violated." Furthermore, Brad's heavy drinking – sporadic throughout their marriage – brought to mind for Megan the inebriated state of her perpetrator during the many instances of sexual abuse in her childhood. Paula empathized with Megan, citing the specific behaviors exhibited by Ben that triggered her memories of abuse. Both men expressed ignorance of the communicational impact of the perceived offensive behaviors, as well as concern and sympathy for their wives' past traumas. The session ended on a solemn but caring note, and it was remarked by the group that the presentation of the medals had a ceremonial feel reminiscent of the recitation of their wedding vows.

The experientials of Week Five demonstrated the discrepancies between participants' verbal and nonverbal communications and underscored some of the problematic marital patterns in which the couples engaged. For example, although couples were directed to create integrated drawings together, the group specifically noted the lack of integration in each of their drawings. They further noted significant divergence between the titles of the drawings, such as "The Family House" and "The Love Nest," and the messages communicated visually by the images. Both Megan and Paula superimposed boundaries over their husbands' drawings (Figures 6.4 and 6.5), indicating a desire to

Figure 6.4. The Family House

Figure 6.5. The Love Nest

take control of their marital relationships. The participants admitted that the titles, initial narratives and other verbal communications associated with the drawings conveyed "expected" messages, while the drawings themselves expressed "actual" feelings. This reaction is typical of art therapy experientials – because picture-making is a less familiar mode of expression than talking, over-rehearsed assumptions often are undercut by this approach to communication. Additionally, "words often fail to convey the entire experience. . . . If words were sufficient, the art experience would be unnecessary. It is because art taps into reservoirs of being that are not necessarily verbally articulable that it is of significant communicative import" (Wadeson, 1995).

As the study came to a close in Week Six, the burden of blame was lifted from participants' shoulders. All participants, particularly Ben and Brad, voiced appreciation for the insight they had gained with regard to their spouses' childhoods. Ben and Brad continued to express sympathy and concern for their wives' childhood traumas, and all participants emphatically acknowledged the profound impact of Megan's and Paula's sexual abuse on their marital relationships and communications. Each participant took away new self-knowledge as a result of the art therapy. Megan stated, "My sexual abuse affected me much more than I ever realized." Brad demonstrated a clearer understanding of Megan's responses, stating, "When I turned my back on [Megan] in bed, it reminded her of her abusive stepfather, so she was really angry at him, and not me." Paula admitted, "I've been in denial about my childhood abuses forever, and that's the primary source of my anger – not Ben." In turn, Ben acknowledged that Paula's distance was a result of "the many abuses and rejections she suffered as a child," rather than being "a protection against me." All participants underscored the definitive role the art experientials had played in bringing these concealed issues to the foreground. Each participant used the word "see" in describing his or her therapeutic experiences during the study.

Based on the findings of this study, it appears that art therapy is exceptionally effective in helping to resolve communication difficulties between intimate couples where sexual abuse is, or may be, one deeply-rooted source of the conflict. However, the limitations of the study are important to address: first, the actual test population consisted of only two couples (although five of the other ten couples who initially joined the study did cite childhood sexual abuse as "an issue"). Future research in this area should include a larger test population. In addition, the limited time frame and high intensity of the study (six hours per week for six weeks) expedited the therapeutic process. In a more long-term, less intense program, participants' focus may expand from childhood sexual abuse to a wider array of marital issues. Finally, though the individuals involved in this study came from varying backgrounds, they shared many traits. Both couples lived in the same metropolitan region, neither couple was raising children, the couples were roughly the same age and divorcing at the same time, and both couples had been recruited from the SMILE Program, showing a natural affinity for therapeutic intervention (though none of the participants were familiar with art therapy before participating in the study). Future research should introduce greater diversity into the sample population. Nonetheless, the insight gained over the course of the study – particularly with regard to memories and disclosures of sexual abuse – facilitated the creation of new, more positive modes of communication between the participating couples.

Overall, this case study strongly suggests that art therapy can help couples in intimate relationships reconcile communication problems; further research is clearly merited. In the interim, therapists treating intimate couples with communication issues – particularly where a history of sexual abuse is known or suspected – should consider referring the couple to a trained, licensed art therapist.

CONCLUSION

In the study discussed above, childhood sexual abuse was determined to be the source of the couples' marital relationship issues. These marital troubles had become so distressing that the couples had begun the process of divorce, yet it was not until the study that the root cause of the problems was identified as childhood sexual abuse. Correspondingly, the theme of sexual abuse became so dominant in the sessions that it superseded the original intent of the study, which was to address general interspousal communication.

This surprising phenomenon can best be understood by considering the important ways in which nonverbal communication compliments, rather than displaces, verbal communication. A misperceived or under-perceived verbal message may be illuminated by a concrete visual. Verbal messages may convey distorted perceptions formed and retained from the abusive event(s). Artwork helps to differentiate between past and present, as Paula demonstrated when she explained that analyzing her experientials helped her to realize that the abuse, not Ben, was the source of her anger. Thus survivors of sexual abuse can mature in their communicative function beyond the moment of violation.

Art therapy and other creative therapies developed to meet a need that was not met by more traditional therapies. Where trauma runs deep, such as in the cases of childhood sexual abuse survivors, sometimes only nonverbal communication will reveal and begin to heal the trauma. Though this observation is not unfamiliar to therapists working with sexually abused clients, art therapy remains underutilized. This and other research indicates that art therapy is a powerful intervention with widespread application, and the time has come to put the research into practice.

REFERENCES

Everett, Craig A. (1987). *Divorce process: A handbook for clinicians.* New York: Haworth Press, 3–4.
Sgroi, S. (1982). *Handbook of clinical intervention in child sexual abuse.* New York: Simon & Schuster Inc.
Wadeson, H. (1995). *The dynamics of art psychotherapy.* New York: John Wiley and Sons Inc.

BIOGRAPHICAL STATEMENT

Janice Samoray, Ph.D., is a clinical psychologist specializing in traumatology and art therapy. Her career has included both empirical research and clinical work with survivors of victims of homicide, sexual abuse, combat and natural disasters. She is an educator, a consultant and has authored work on the healing effects of creative expression in reducing the symptoms of compassion fatigue. Dr. Samoray regularly conducts workshops and presentations on a regional and national level.

Chapter 7

THE THERAPEUTIC USE OF PHOTOGRAPHY FOR SEXUAL ABUSE SURVIVORS

Noreen M. Glover-Graf

INTRODUCTION

The intent of this chapter is to discuss the therapeutic use of photography for the purpose of addressing sexual abuse. By definition, phototherapy is described as the use of photography in a therapeutic setting, under the direction of a trained therapist, to reduce or relieve painful psychological symptoms, as a method of facilitating growth and change (Stewart, 1979) and to promote healing and self-awareness (Martin, 2001). Photography used in therapy is not about counselor interpretation of client images, rather, it is a communication tool that allows the counselor and the client to better understand and explore issues. Therefore, no specialized training or certification in photography is necessary (Hammond & Gantt, 1998; Weiser, 1984) for counselors and clients to take advantage of the benefits offered by phototherapy.

Historically, the first recorded use of photography for therapeutic purposes was in 1850 in a psychiatric hospital. In the 1940s, photography of servicemen in New York gave rise to the establishment of an organization in which volunteers taught photography to disabled veterans as a form of recreational therapy. Soon thereafter, volunteers became aware of the unanticipated, co-occurring psychological benefits that included increased positive coping and self-expression. This led to an extension of the use of phototherapy to other persons with disabilities including those with physical and mental disabilities. By the 1980s, an edited text entitled *Photo Therapy and Mental Health* (Krauss & Fryrear, 1983) provided examples of practice among professionals. Professional conferences and a quarterly journal added to the credibility of phototherapy, which was increasingly being used to provide treatment for a variety of mental health issues and disabilities related concerns for persons with developmental disabilities, AIDS, visual, and hearing impairments (Perchick, 1992; Weiser, 1993).

In an extensive review of the phototherapy literature, Fryrear (1980) categorized the therapeutic use of photography into eleven classifications that addressed: emotional states, verbal behaviors, modeling behaviors, confrontation, skill mastery, socialization acquisition, creative expression, nonverbal communication, documentation of change, diagnostic support, and experience prolongation. While limited in number, current examples of the use of photography have continued to appear in the literature for use both with children and adults in order to address issues of rapport building, emotional expression, memory exploration, grief and anger processing, self-understanding, gender and relationship issues, substance abuse, and resolution of past life events (Bach, 2001; Damarre, 2001; Glover-Graf & Miller, 2005; Kahane, 2001; Koretsky, 2001). Empirical studies of the efficacy of phototherapy are essentially absent from the literature, however, Glover-Graf and Miller (2005) recently used qualitative and quantitative research methods to examine the efficacy of a twelve week group intervention that focused on the topics of trust, honesty, self-worth, power, and abuse. Following treatment, the majority of participants showed post-test increases in self-esteem.

As interest in the use of photography in therapy has expanded, distinctions in terminology have appeared in the literature. A fundamental distinction lies in the use of the terms "therapeutic photography" and "phototherapy." Unfortunately, the terms have been used interchangeably in the literature and among practitioners. Weiser coined the term "Phototherapy" to describe the process of using photographs within the context of therapy with a trained therapist in a formal session. However, when photography is produced by a person wishing to explore some aspect of themselves, it is more aptly termed "Therapeutic Photography" (Weiser, 1993).

THEORY AND COUNSELING APPROACH

Using and creating visual images in counseling has largely been the realm of art therapists. While the use of photography is similar in some ways, there are also theoretical differences in the process of creating art and of taking photographs that deserves consideration. Berger (1980) stated, "Painting [or other art processes] is the art of arrangement" (p. 291) and of a careful construction of images to portray a visual message. Photography differs in that it "is the result of the photographer's decision that it is worth recording. . . .

The language of photography is the language of events" (p. 293). Photography is interpreted as a factual recording of events that have occurred or are currently transpiring. For the photographer, this is visual proof of the reality of an event. The truth of photographs is rarely challenged. By contrast, artwork is considered subjective and viewed as individual interpretations rather than realities. Thus, using photography in therapy is intended to be a photographic representation of an individual's reality. In this way, photography seems particularly appropriate for persons in treatment for sexual abuse who may benefit from confronting, processing, and validating the reality of their lives.

Few models have been developed to assist the process of using photography in therapy, rather there has been emphasis upon the use of good counseling skills to facilitate the processing of photographs. Hedges (1972) used photo therapy with children in order to increase self-esteem. He described the basic counseling skills as essential to the use of photo therapy and described the process as having three basic phases: (1) establishing a good rapport through warmth and acceptance; (2) coming to sessions without pre-conceived notions; and (3) focusing on the participant as central when discussing photographs. In her book, *PhotoTherapy Techniques*, Weiser (1993) detailed five techniques for working with photographs in therapy, which include the use of photographs taken of the client, taken by the client, self-portraits, biographical photographs, and a projective technique.

TREATMENT BENEFITS

Several treatment benefits have been noted for persons who participate in phototherapy. In general, photography is generally less intimidating than the process of making art (Merrill & Andersen, 1993). It allows for a nonverbal starting point, and may assist in the breakdown of rationalizations, denial, and other defense mechanisms (Weiser, 1993). The therapy is exploratory rather than confrontive and can be used to empower the client because it is self-directed and allows for choices in content and in expression. For the client, phototherapy offers an opportunity for exploration of the self in terms of thoughts, feelings, emotions, and resulting behaviors. When the client, through photography, allows herself and the therapist to "see" the feelings as reflected in the photograph they reach greater understanding of the client and come to share more fully the client's internal world. Graf (2002) suggested that photography be used as a method of "treatment initiation and exploration for substance abuse clients who have a history of sexual abuse" (p. 201) and reviewed the rationale, advantages, current applications, and practitioner concerns associated with the use of photography as a therapeutic tool.

PHOTOGRAPHY AS A THERAPEUTIC TOOL
FOR SEXUAL ABUSE

For several reasons, the initial treatment of sexual abuse issues may be assisted though the use of client-produced photography rather than traditional talk therapy alone. These include resistance to talk therapy due to a lack of trust, denial of the impact of sexual abuse, stigmatization, secrecy, and a lack of previous verbal translations on the part of the client. A lack of trust on the client's part makes treatment progress slow and arduous and can interfere with the establishment of a therapeutic alliance (Bollerud, 1990). As trust begins to develop, talking about abuse may invoke stress and it may be difficult for clients to initiate verbalizations. Due to the stigma associated with sexual abuse, the client may never have previously talked about or processed the abuse. It may be impossible to recall words to describe the experience or the associated feelings because they may have avoided thinking in words about the abuse. The memories may be stored in whole or part as visual images, sounds, and tactile sensations (Glover, 1999). The intent of using phototherapy is to begin moving the client toward healing through recognition of feelings and behaviors through visualization, exploration and verbal clarification.

Herman (1992) states that disempowerment and disconnection are the primary manifestations of abuse and suggests healing must focus on empowerment and establishing connections with others. Photography is empowering because it is client-initiated and produced. It also offers a level of safety to the client because clients and counselors can focus the therapeutic talk around the photograph itself, rather then the client. For example, a client might state, "The person in the picture is angry or hurt" rather than "I am angry or hurt." This distancing provides emotional safety, similar to the use of puppets in play therapy, because it re-directs the focus outside of the self to an external representation of the self, allowing a greater sense of protection until trust is further developed. Photographs become individual, personal expressions that can give testament to the experience of abuse even without words, or until words are joined with the images.

LONG-TERM AFFECTS OF SEXUAL ABUSE

This chapter is geared toward adults who have been sexually abused as children and/or as adults. To understand the needs of this population, it is essential to understand the numerous potential effects of sexual abuse in order to provide comprehensive treatment. The long-term effects of untreated or unresolved sexual abuse include: negative feelings, interpersonal problems, and destructive behaviors. (Courtois, 1988; Gordy, 1983; Kondora, 1993; Sheldon, 1988).

Negative self-perceptions include: chronic anger, phobias, feelings of shame, feelings of guilt, a perceived powerlessness, and worthlessness, and are strongly related to interpersonal and destructive behavior problems. Interpersonal problems may involve: isolation from others, a lack of personal boundaries, lack of trust in others, and an inability to sustain relationships, and re-victimization. Adults who have histories of sexual abuse may be currently in abusive relationships, and adults with histories of abuse may also be perpetrators of abuse toward others. Negative or destructive behavior may include: eating disorders, sleep disorders, anxiety attacks, self-injury, sexual promiscuity, and substance abuse (Courtois, 1988; Gordy, 1983; Kondora, 1993; Sheldon, 1988). Additionally, some of the most common forms of self injury may occur among clients with a history of sexual abuse. These include: self-mutilation through cutting and burning (including "branding" with heated objects), picking at skin or wounds, hair-pulling, self-hitting with objects, and multiple piercing or tattooing.

COUNSELING APPLICATION

Because "the recovery process does not theoretically require women to focus on deficits" (Veysey et. al., 2004, p. 28.) phototherapy can take a "present day, wellness approach" that has a recovery focus which is here-and-now or future focused. The use of photography for treatment of sexual abuse does not require a counselor-imposed, re-living of the past abuse. Focus can be placed upon attainment of positive coping skills and feelings of self-worth while addressing the negative feelings, interpersonal problems, and destructive behaviors. For example, Glover-Graf and Miller (2005) assigned clients to photograph *Healing from abuse that others have caused to me*, and *Healing from abuse which I have caused to others*. Clients were asked to take photographs of these topics as they were related to their present life and as they hoped to see them in themselves in the future. This is consistent with present-focused treatment that is intended to reduce stress and modify behaviors by focusing on current life circumstances, without re-experiencing past trauma (Spiegel et al., 2004).

The following five-step model is suggested for use with clients who have a history of sexual abuse. However, before beginning to use photography in therapy, some initial training may be necessary in the use of camera equipment and in gaining understanding of using photographs to represent emotions or events. Instructions on how to operate the camera depend largely upon the type of camera used. Introduction to the process of using cameras to represent how a client feels should begin with recognition of basic emotions in photographs. This may be accomplished through examining magazine photos or photograph albums. Beginning simply, a photograph of a woman smiling might be said to represent the emotion of happiness. Other photos may then be reviewed and discussed in terms of the possible emotions that they might convey (a lone tree field might suggest loneliness or independence or emotional strength to participants). It is important to stress the multiplicity of potential reactions to photos and the validity of each response. It is also beneficial to discuss metaphors in order to assist clients to begin to think visually. For example, the counselor might ask the client to complete a list of open-ended string responses such as: "As tired as a _____, a funny as a _____, as hungry as a _____."

Once clients begin to process visual images as they relate to emotions, clients may receive specific thematic assignments that reflect symptoms which result from a history of sexual abuse. The five step model includes: (1) thematic presentation, (2) client decision-making, (3) client photography, (4) client written processing, and (5) client/counselor verbal processing.

1. *Counselor Presentation:* At the conclusion of a group session, the counselor presents a particular thematic photography assignment (these issues are presented briefly at the beginning of this paper and include a variety of negative feelings, destructive behaviors, and interpersonal problems). The assignment is due at the beginning of the next group session and clients are instructed to take several photographs that represent how they feel about the topic. The counselor may also provide the client with a list of questions for use in step four at this time.

2. *Client Decision-making:* The client decides upon what to photograph that will address the theme presented in step one. How a client responds will be a personal reaction to and interpretation of the theme. Clients may be encouraged to think through what they wish to photograph before taking shots, however, Hedges (1972) believes that this is not necessary because clients will unconsciously think through the issues and photograph the theme with little advance conceptualization.

3. *Client Photography:* The client engages in the physical act of recording a visual image. After printing or viewing the photographs, the client selects photos which are representations of the issue being explored. Clients are free to manipulate the environment and stage a photograph, or find an environment that emulates their feelings. Choosing the most representative photo(s) to bring to the counseling session is completed based upon feelings and thoughts about the photos in relation to the assigned theme. As sessions progress, clients may be encouraged to manipulate the photographs in a variety of ways in order to create their most accurate visual representation of the theme.

4. *Client Processing – Written:* Before meeting for the session, the client explores through writing how a particular issue impacts their life and how a positive change might feel. In this step, clients are provided with written questions related to the assigned theme such as: What about this photo reminds

you of the theme (e.g., shame)? What do you like most about this photo? This step further assists in the process of verbal translation of feelings and clarification of thoughts, and ideally is completed prior to the next meeting and brought in for discussion. However, based upon the clients' cognitive and motivational level, this step may be completed at the beginning of the sessions, after step five, or eliminated altogether.

5. *Client processing – Verbal:* The client verbalizes thoughts about the photographs selected to a group or individual counselor and is further facilitated in cognitive and emotional processing by using primarily open-ended questions such as: "Tell me about the photograph."; "Does it express exactly what you want it to?"; "If you could change it in some way, how would you?" It is the actual verbalization and making known to others which begins to dissolve secrecy and allows for interaction with others to help further clarify feelings and thoughts. The product itself is not the focus, rather it is the individual's assigned meaning. The product is important because it "makes the internal self visible to oneself and to others . . . it is helpful to take time to assimilate and reflect. . . . This reflective process is often what leads to new insights and self-discoveries." (Merrill & Andersen, 1993, p. 113)

GENERAL GUIDELINES

The logistics of having clients take photographs, have them printed, and answer questions, in order to be prepared for session the following week, can present organizational challenges for the client, which may require modification according to client motivation and readiness. However, the availability of one-hour processing and the immediacy of working with digital photographs have served to decrease the logistical and time concerns.

As with the use of any counseling technique, individualization and modification are necessary according to individual and group needs. The following guidelines outline some of the practical implementation and procedures for using photo therapy with clients in either individual sessions or group session. It is suggested the treatment last at least ten weeks. While practical application of this modality is relatively simple, the following must serve as only as guidelines in a process that will be determined largely by the response of the group or individual.

SELECTING TOPICS

Topic selection for photography can be done in several ways through: (1) addressing symptoms that are frequently common to sexual abuse victims, (2) evaluation of client needs in the intake process, (3) client selection, or (4) information gleaned from standardized tests such as the Trauma Inventory Scale (TSI; Briere, 1995), the Multi-Dimensional Self-Esteem Scale (MSEI; O'Brien, & Epstein, 1988). The client selection method generally requires a high level of client insight and established group dynamics and is not recommended for new groups or individuals who have not previously dealt with issues of sexual abuse. Using a common symptom method, examples of topics might include for example: My Self-Portrait, Dealing with Stigmatization, Honesty with Myself and Others, Trust in Self and Others, Overcoming Anger (Shame, Guilt), Healing from Abuse from Others, Healing from Abuse to Myself or Others, and Relationships and Commitments.

THE USE OF SELF-PORTRAITS

One distinctive aspect of photo therapy that adds an additional dimension of individualization and personalization is the use of self-portrait photography. These can be used to confront and explore the self-image, for values clarification, introspection, to explore self-image, and to document change (Hogan, 1981; Weiser 1984). A counselor-selected theme related to self-worth might be photographed with the incorporation of self-images. Beginning and ending the individual or group sessions with self-portraits might also serve to document participant changes. Self-portraits may be literal or representative. Figure 7.1 provides an example of a self-portrait which contains a self-image. When this photograph was processed with the client, feelings of low self-esteem emerged. This photograph was later compared to photographs of positive self-images.

Figure 7.1. Self Portrait

PHOTOGRAPHS THAT REPRESENT ABUSE

Because it can be statistically assumed that persons who have been abused may also be perpetrators against themselves and others, the topics of exploration must permit clients to express the full extent of abuse. If the therapist chooses only to ask about victimization, they may hear only about the victimization. And, clients may be given the message that they are only permitted to discuss the portion of abuse that is acceptable to the therapist. At the same time, therapists need to be aware, and make clients fully aware, of their duty to report current abuse of children and the elderly as well as suicidal and homicidal intent.

There are also practical, legal, and ethical issues associated with the taking of the photos and display of photographs of abuse. Clients must be instructed never to make an environmental manipulation that could result in harm to themselves or others, and therapists may wish to disallow images of perpetrators and photographs that in anyway glorify self-abuse or other-abuse.

Photographs of the themes: *Healing from harm or abuse which others have caused to me,* or *Healing from harm or abuse which I have caused to self or others* are frequently among the most revealing and provocative. Using open-ended questions. the counselor can solicit information and feelings which the client wishes to further process and share. Examples of photographs that depict this theme are provided below. When the photograph in Figure 7.2 was discussed with the client, she revealed that the cuts in the tree reminded her of her own self-cutting.

Figure 7.2. Self Abuse

MANIPULATION OF PHOTOGRAPHS

Some authors have suggested the use of instant photography (Fryrear & Corbit, 1992; Zwick, 1978). This may limit photography manipulation, but is perhaps the simplest and most convenient choice. Digital photography offers the benefits of photographic manipulation but requires additional resources, is a more expensive alternative and requires further training and equipment. Using either of these options, or traditional photography, photographic manipulation can occur in a number of inexpensive ways including adding pen or crayon marks, cutting and pasting, addition of other images from magazines, etc.

Several additional options are available for digital photographic manipulation but it should be understood that manipulations of photographs should occur in order to more clearly represent client expression and not to demonstrate technical proficiency. Simple manipulations can include color changes available in the edit mode of most software programs. This generally allows clients to choose from a spectrum of available colors. While it is recommended that phototherapy initially use black and white photograph in order to focus on content rather than color, selection of color can be used to help convey the mood or emotion that the client intends to convey. Figure 7.3

Figure 7.3. Color Change

Figure 7.4. Skewed Image

demonstrates how a change in color affected a red tulip. Images can also be stretched or skewed resulting in desired distortions of images. The skewed image in Figure 7.4 above was intended by the photographer to represent her struggle with bulimia.

Other helpful manipulations such as reversal of images (Figure 7.5), negative images (Figures 7.6 and 7.7), and combinations of images through cutting

Figure 7.5. Reversal of Images

Figure 7.6. Negative Black and White Image

and pasting (Figure 7.8) can also be used to assist the client to create a visual representation and to more thoroughly explore their feelings and thoughts related to sexual abuse. The addition of words to photographs can also assist in creating powerful personal statements.

Figure 7.7. Negative Color Image

Figure 7.8. Cutting and Pasting Portions of the Photograph and Adding Words

ETHICAL CONCERNS

It goes without saying that only counselors trained in sexual abuse treatment should be counseling victims of sexual abuse or using photography for this purpose. Hammond and Gantt (1998) examined the ethics of using artwork and treatment and cautioned that it could trigger highly emotional responses. While a similar study has not been conducted to examine the use of photography in treatment, caution should be used to follow their recommendation that verbal exploration of visual images take place at the client's pace.

Also, group disclosures of any specifics of past sexual abuse should be previously planned with the counselor and individually processed after groups. Clients who experience distress at anytime should be assessed for suicidal ideation, self-abuse, and dysfunctional behavior relapse potential. At the close of groups, all clients should be assessed for the need for continued treatment.

As a sense of closure is important in all counseling, the planning of a group show that celebrates the process and the products may be desirable and also serve as a time of reflection and assessment of the process. Group shows should be limited to therapists and participants due to issues of confidentiality, or participants may mutually create a list of approved invited guests. Photographs should be treated as any other confidential materials and remain ideally in the control of the client and not become part of the client's record

(Hammond & Gantt, 1988). Finally, the process and outcome of groups should be continually assessed by the participants and therapist to determine the most effective use of this treatment technique.

CONCLUSION

The need for effective treatment for sexual abuse is apparent. Due to the dysfunction that may result from nontreatment, counselors may wish to consider a more inclusive treatment program. For several reasons, initial treatment of sexual abuse issues may be better addressed though the incorporation of phototherapy rather than traditional talk therapy alone. These include strong defense mechanisms, a lack of trust, and a lack of previous verbal translations on the part of the client. Phototherapy has a unique ability to bypass defense mechanisms and to reveal emotions. It provides for empowerment opportunities to clients who have previously felt powerless. Furthermore, it affords levels of safety through self-direction and interpretation. This chapter presents the history, theory, and rationale of phototherapy use. In addition, guidelines specific for the use of phototherapy with clients who have a history of sexual abuse are presented along with photographic representations . A wellness component that encourages healing through exploration of positive feelings and coping skills is also incorporated into the healing process. Practical issues related to camera education, optional software manipulation choices, treatment initiation, group format and processing, topic presentation, and ethical considerations were presented.

Note: The photographs presented are intended as representations only and do not imply that the persons depicted or the photographers have a history of sexual abuse. Written consent has been obtain for these reproductions.

REFERENCES

Bach, H. (2001). The place of the photograph in visual narrative research. *Afterimage, 29*(3), 7.

Berger, J. (1980). Understanding a photograph. In A. Trachtenberg (Ed.), *Classic essays in photography*. New Haven, CN: Leety's Island Books.

Bollerud, K. (1990). A model for the treatment of trauma-related syndromes among chemically dependent inpatient women. *Journal of Substance Abuse Treatment, 7*(2), 83–87.

Briere, J. (1995). *Trauma Symptom Inventory professional manual.* Odessa, FL: Psychological Assessment Resources.

Courtois, C. A. (1988). *Healing the incest wound.* New York: W. W. Norton & Co.

Damarre, L (2001). Photography: Traveling beyond categories. *Afterimage, 29,* p.6

Fryrear, J. L. (1980). A selective nonevaluative review of research on photo therapy. *Photo Therapy Quarterly, 1,* 7–9.

Fryrear, J. L, & Corbit, I. E. (1992). *Photo art therapy.* Springfield, IL: Charles C Thomas Publisher, Ltd.

Glover, N. M. (1999). Play therapy and art therapy for persons who are in treatment for substance abuse and have a history of incest victimization. *Journal of Substance Abuse Treatment, 16,* 281–287.

Glover-Graf, N. M., & Miller, E. (2005). The use of phototherapy in group treatment for persons who are chemically dependent. *Rehabilitation Counseling Bulletin, 43*(3).

Gordy, P. L. (1983). Group work that supports adult victims of childhood incest. *Social Casework, 64,* 300–307.

Graf, N. M. (2002). Photography as a therapeutic tool for substance abuse clients who have a history of sexual abuse. *Counselling and Psychotherapy Research, 2,* 201–207.

Hammond, L. C., & Gantt, L. (1998). Using art in counseling: Ethical considerations. *Journal of Counseling and Development, 76,* 271–276.

Hedges, R. E. (1972). Photography & self-concept. *Audiovisual Instruction, 17*(5), 26–28.

Herman, J. L. (1992). *Trauma and recovery: The Aftermath of Violence – from Domestic Abuse to Political Terror.* New York: Basic Books.

Hogan, P. T. (1981). Phototherapy in the educational setting. *Arts in Psychotherapy, 8*(3), 193–199.

Kahane, L. (2001). If this picture could talk. . . . *Afterimage, 29*(3), 5.

Kondora, L. L. (1993). A Heideggerian hermeneutical analysis of survivors of incest. *IMAGE: Journal of Nursing Scholarship, 25,* 11–16.

Koretsky, P. (2001). Using photography in a therapeutic setting with seniors. *Afterimage, 29*(3), 8.

Krauss, D. A., & Fryrear, J. L. (1983). *Photo Therapy in Mental Health.* Springfield, IL: Charles C Thomas Publisher, Ltd.

Martin, R. (2001). The performative body: Phototherapy and re-enactment. *Afterimage, 29*(3), 17–20.

Merrill, C., & Andersen, S. (1993). Person-Centered expressive therapy: An outcome study. In D. Brazier (Ed.), *Beyond Carl Rogers* (pp. 109–128). London: Constable Publishers.

O'Brien, E. J., & Epstein, S. (1988). *The Multidimensional Self-Esteem Inventory Professional Manual.* Lutz, FL: Psychological Assessment Resources, Inc.

Perchick, M. (1992). Rehabilitation through photography: The power of photography as physical & emotional therapy – contribution of Josephine U. Herrick's volunteer service photographers organization to teaching photography to wounded World War II servicemen. *PSA Journal, December,* 13–15.

Sheldon, H. (1988). Childhood sexual abuse in adult female psychotherapy referrals. *British Journal of Psychiatry, 152,* 107–111.

Spiegel, D., Classen, C., Thurston, E., & Butler, L. (2004). Trauma-focused versus present-focused models of group therapy for women sexually abused in childhood. In L. J. Koenig (Ed.), *From child sexual abuse to adult sexual risk: Trauma, revictimization, and intervention.* Washington, DC: American Psychological Association.

Stewart, D. (1979). Photo therapy: Theory & practice. *Art Psychotherapy, 6,* 41–46.

Veysey, B. M., Anderson, R., Lewis, L., Mueller, M., & Stenius, V. M. K. (2004). Integration of alcohol and other drug, trauma and mental health services: An experiment in rural services integration in Franklin County, MA. *Alcoholism Treatment Quarterly, 22*(3/4), 19–39.

Weiser, J. (1984). Phototherapy: Becoming visually literate about oneself or, Phototherapy??? What's Phototherapy? *Phototherapy, 4,* 2–7.

Weiser, J. (1993). *PhotoTherapy Techniques.* San Francisco: Jossey-Bass.

Zwick, D. S. (1978). Photography as a tool toward increased awareness of the aging self. *Art Psychotherapy, 5,* 135–141.

BIOGRAPHICAL STATEMENT

Noreen M. Glover-Graf, Ph.D., C.R.C., is an Associate Professor in the Department of Rehabilitation at the University of Texas-Pan American. She received her doctorate in Rehabilitation Counseling from the Rehabilitation Institute at Southern Illinois University. Her main research interests are directed at creating clinical applications for the treatment of sexual abuse and the resulting traumas including dissociation, substance abuse, and self-abuse.

Chapter 8

USE OF ORIGAMI FOR CHILDREN WITH TRAUMATIC EXPERIENCES

Toshiko Kobayashi

INTRODUCTION

This paper introduces a part of the developing theory and practice of Enrichment Origami Art Therapy in relation to trauma and children, following the 9/11 incident. Enrichment Origami Art therapy is a therapeutic use of folding paper that I have been formulating in the course of studying art therapy and my life experiences as an artist organizing art workshops and art exhibitions in Japan and in other countries.

One of the main focuses of this chapter is a potential of creative processes of Origami as a therapeutic tool in educational, communal, and family settings. Next, I will examine its possibility as an expressive activity beyond cultural confinement. At the end, several practical ideas and applications of therapeutic use of Origami will be introduced alongside the group and individual case samples. These Origami projects are easily adapted to the children of different developmental stages and their individual needs. With children at risk, Origami will be used as a safe and nonthreatening modality.

Origami itself can be nontherapeutic and has many disadvantages as compared to other traditional art media. In order to use Origami in a therapeutic manner, it requires certain precautions. For this reason, some points of concerns and limitations are brought to attention.

Recently, Origami has been incorporated in advertisement, seen as window displays, appeared in math textbooks, on TV shows, and movies. It seems more and more people all over the world are folding paper nowadays and Origami has become increasingly popular.

Six years ago, I moved to New York City and started to advocate the use of Origami in a therapeutic manner when I began studying art therapy in New

York. I became a member of Origami USA (OUSA) and British Origami Society (BOS) to learn how people in the U.S. enjoy Origami. OUSA is one of the largest Origami societies in the world and has more than 2000 members in 49 states and 19 countries. There are local groups in cities all over the United States and Canada (http://www.origami-usa.org/membership.htm). BOS has over 700 members all over the world (http://www.britishorigami.org.uk). Both organizations publish periodicals and host international conventions every year. People are actively involved in folding paper, building communities, and coordinating convention meetings of different purposes and objectives. Without question, there are many small and large groups and individuals engaged in Origami enthusiastically in Europe, including Eastern Europe and Russia, North and South America, Australia, not just East Asia but South and Central Asia, as well as some of African countries.

After I joined two prominent English-speaking Origami groups, I realized the similarities and differences of how people look at Origami as a creative activity. I learned an alternative cultural adaptation of Origami in Western world. Simultaneously, I noticed the gap of perception of Origami among Origami enthusiasts and general public. The gap between people who know and who do not know Origami is enormous. I wanted to try to do something to bridge the gap, so I started to fold Origami in public spaces. With this intention, I folded paper in public, such as while I am waiting on the line for my turn, on transportation, and at parties. Also, in order to gain experiences of public reaction to Origami, I pre-folded Origami models to give to those who are interested in keeping them. It helped me develop relationships as a stranger in an enormous city, in addition to bringing relaxation to my stressful life as an international student.

Those experiences with people in public spaces and with clients at my internship placements as an art therapy student provided me some of concrete evidence, which helped me formulating the idea of Enrichment Origami Art Therapy in addition to my previous Origami experiences. Those ideas were not so clear and not yet ready to be expressed at that time. So my quest to articulate the potential of Origami as a tool of art therapy was full of adventures and trial-and-error. I cannot forget these instances of witnessing happy smiles on children's faces after holding an Origami model in their hands on a busy subway car and while waiting in a long line at a post office.

In this chapter, discussions are limited to the specific area of childhood trauma of physical and emotional difficulties that prevent them from performing age appropriately in their daily life, at home and school and other communal settings. The origin and severity of trauma is not easy to articulate in certain situations when working in public settings, and the treatments required are sensitive when dealing with children experiencing suspected traumatic event(s) in domestic environments.

My limitation of this area is that I do not have any working experience with children with trauma caused by a disaster, natural or otherwise. Whereas, I am acquainted with those who have been exposed to man-maid terrors and adversities. These are the cases that I am familiar in a discourse of social phenomenon. Some of the therapeutic aspects of Origami are based on historical implications and shared cultural ambiances.

Alongside my study on Origami phenomenon in New York, I realized that these therapeutic aspects come from not only Japanese and Asian traditions but also Western cultural heritages. Another important therapeutic aspect of Origami is physical and psychological effect of the act of folding paper, which allows us to use the left and right spheres of our brains at the same time (Shumakor, 2000). Emotional and psychological outcomes of engaging in folding processes are deeply related to physical consequences on our body, especially for young people who are in a stage of development of their mind and body in terms of brain functions.

Origami as a ubiquitous tool of art therapy is included in this discussion following a unique culture of New York City where people live together in cultural diversity. In terms of cultural differences, I would like to add my experiences working with children in Palestine, who were attending rehabilitation programs due to their mental and physical disadvantages with severe trauma caused by the catastrophic situation of the region.

How to work with a group of children not sharing cultural uniformity is also a prevalent issue in our profession, since cultural issues are one of the most important concerns of art. Especially when we use Origami as a tool of art therapy, cultural concern is unavoidable in relation to the therapist's own cultural backgrounds.

WHAT IS ORIGAMI?

Since the phenomenon of Origami has been spread into a wide-ranging area of our social fabric in recent years, it is necessary to clarify what Origami is in order to understand its efficacies and to explore potentials of its therapeutic use (Kobayashi, 2004). All over the world, there are many Origami folders who have noticed the therapeutic quality of Origami: Ho (2001), a social worker and mental health clinician in Perth, Australia; and Chang (1995), a psychiatrist in New York City, talked about their experiences of using Origami with young patients. The main purpose of this chapter is to share my point of view in order for the reader to develop a personal, unique way of using Origami and adapting it into creative arts therapies techniques based on the culturein which they are applied. What I present here is a part of my understanding that convinced me Origami can be therapeutic.

DEFINITION OF ORIGAMI

As Smith (1995) described, recent attempts to define Origami have prompted reconsideration of the problem as one in which the individual's view of Origami itself constitutes a definition. By showing the individual's view as a graphic profile, one can see how much common ground there is amongst folders. This seems a more fruitful approach than trying to supply an authoritative definition in answer to the overwhelming movement of discussion on what is Origami.

Smith (1995) also elaborates his idea of Origami and explains it as a pure form of human activity under constraints. A square piece of paper that represents a pure form that is the base for Origami and he distinguishes eight folding methods as follows.

1. *Shaping.* – the outline of the paper is varied.
2. *Slitting.* – cuts are used.
3. *Supporting.* – additional materials are used to hold or change the shape of the final model.
4. *Multilayers.* – two or more sheets of material are folded together; in the final model the separate layers are used to create special effects.
5. *Multi Sheets.* – the model consists of two or more separate sheets, which are each folded and then brought together for the final model.
6. *Lengthening.* – the qquare is "stretched" in one direction, that is it becomes a rectangle and so on.
7. *Decorating.* – the square is textured or patterned either before or after the creation of the model.
8. *Modeling.* – this applies to three-dimensional techniques.

Smith's (1995) eight ways of distinguishing Origami elaborate the fundamental potentials of Origami as a tool of art therapy in general. Smith's main purpose for these definitions is solely seeking a pure form of Origami, and he has an established "Pure Land" theory of Origami. This defines Origami beautifully in terms of a creative activity that has flexibility for freedom of expression. I believe these are the important fundamental characteristics of Origami in art therapy. These points will be indicated by numbers later at the project description section.

HISTORY OF ORIGAMI

Origami has been appreciated widely as a recreational and educational activity for centuries. Origami is popular not only in the U.S. but all over the world, including Japan, the country of origin of the word "Origami" (Lister,

1995). At the same time, using a conventional material, paper, as a creative medium became popular under the influence of the contemporary art movement. This drew attention toward Origami and brought recognition to Origami as an art form, which became increasingly popular and recognized by more and more people. The widening viewpoints of how to look at art such as Langer (1957) allows the potential for Origami to be considered as an art form and it has been brought into people's lives in many different fashions, paralleling the appearance of paper in human history. Origami is a form of paper culture that is conceptualized as "folding paper," which became popular and elaborately developed in Japan, yet it is a phenomenon beyond time, places, and people (Lister, 1975). Origami has had importance in every aspect of life, influencing religious symbols, ceremonial goods, ritualistic offerings, gift-wrapping, apparel, toys, games, containers that hold a variety of everyday items, and art forms (Kobayashi, 1998; Lister, 1995; Okamura, 1999; Smith, 1995; Temko, 1986). These help us to realize how Origami has been naturally incorporated into our daily life with meaningfulness.

There are many different views and discussions of when and how Origami started. One of the possibilities is to trace the origin of Origami in Japan somewhere between the fourteenth to sixteenth centuries CE. It seems that the simplest form of folding paper could have been started as a part of religious ceremonies and ritualistic offerings conducted in everyday life in Japan (Miyashita, 1994). A written document called "Verses on 71 Craft Men" published in 1500 includes a women selling a folder made from paper (Okamura, 1999). Naturally, this custom was closely related to the development of papermaking, which was imported from China in the first century CE and spread all over Japan very quickly. One of the reasons for this rapid development was due to Japan's natural resources, such as paper mulberry and ample clean water for papermaking. Japanese cultures that admire craftsmanship encouraged people to create paper and promoted competition. Paper was used for keeping governmental documents, for copying religious manuscripts, and as blankets, clothing, and gift-wrapping. People started to look for paper of better quality and variety. Buddhism played an important role, too. Shotoku, a crown prince, ordered the production of scrolls of Dharanis, which were woodcut prints of Buddha's teachings at the time of Asuka period (sixth to early seventh century CE). This accelerated the development of paper manufacturing. Paper was considered as valuable as silk and gold, and became one of the important products used for tributes (Narita, 1980).

There are only a few written documents in Japan describing how the paper was folded and used before the Edo period, C.E. 1603 to 1868, (Okamura, 1999). Even during the Edo period, most of the documents we find are within images of Ukiyoe, woodcut print, style and a few written records of personal diagrams. This suggests that the prominent characteristics of Origami as a part of everyday custom and tradition was handed down from one generation to the next. In other words, Origami was a tradition taught in daily life by elderly family or household members to younger generations by way of demonstrations, one of the most rudimentary and concrete manners of handing down a cultural heritage.

I would like to emphasize the fact that the culture of folding paper emerged all over the world wherever papermaking was introduced and became popular. This includes China, as the country of origin of paper invention, Korea, and South East Asia. Through the Silk Road to West Asian countries, the knowledge traveled down to the South and the West. Today, there are many Origami folders in Australia, Argentina, Denmark, France, Germany, Israel, Italy, Netherlands, Russia, the U.K., the U.S.A. and many more. Using paper folding in ritualistic ceremonies is commonly found in Asian countries such as Korea and China (Temko, 1986). It is still popular to organize spiritual festivals where people create colorful ceremonial paper offerings and decoration such as hats, flowers, and other symbols in Korea as well as in Japan (Oru, 1993).

It was not surprising that German educator Friedrich Froebel (CE 1782–1852) included paper folding in his educational method for his young students (Liebschner, 1992; Lister, 1975). Froebel's influence has been seen greatly not only in the development of European paper folding but also in Japanese Origami after the Meiji period (CE 1868–1912). Froebel's method and philosophy of education was integrated into the Japanese educational system for children by a Japanese educator who studied in Germany. Japanese government believed in following the advanced Western philosophy of education thought to be indispensable at that time (Kobayashi, 1998; Okamura, 1995).

When we focus on the development of Origami in the U.S., Lillian Oppenheimer is the most prominent contributor (Temko, 1986). She started the Origami Center in New York in 1958, which developed into the Friends of Origami, which became the Origami USA of today. It is impossible to mention the wide acceptance of Origami in the U.S. without mentioning the name of Lillian Oppenheimer. Her enthusiasm for paper folding and the use of the Japanese word "Origami" influenced the worldwide trend of developing Origami into the unique entity it is today. Lillian Oppenheimer was pivotal in enabling Origami enthusiasts and societies around the world to connect beyond borders.

The British Origami Society was established shortly after Oppenheimer's visit to London in 1967 (Lister, 1975). This society took an important role at the beginning of the 1990s in organizing and advocating a Conference of Origami in Education and Therapy (COET). The second conference was held in New York in 1995 and the third in 2004. Today, there are more and more people who have access to Origami information given by such Origami societies all over the world. In addition, Origami folders have recently started to exchange information by conducting conventions, formal and informal workshops, as well as communicating through the Internet. It is overwhelmingly interesting to look for Origami-related websites all over the world today.

ENRICHMENT ORIGAMI ART THERAPY

The basic principle of Enrichment Origami Art Therapy is based on the Symbolic Formation and its Meaning through the Process (Wilson, 2001) of folding Origami. This is an interactive experience occuring between clients and therapists during the process of folding paper as Object Relationships (Balint, 1968), and the possession of product in our hand at the end of folding paper as a Transitional Object (Winnicott, 1986).

The underlying Asian philosophies explain that Origami can be a therapeutic tool as well as an application for treatment based on cultural heritage. Enrichment Origami Art Therapy (Kobayashi, 2004) workshops that have been organized by Kobayashi in New York since 2002 are based on the following therapeutic components formulated in her theory.

These components of Origami can be discussed from different angles. One of them is following the Smith's definition of Origami, which he distinguished in eight different components.

The other angle is to look at the Origami activity through historical aspects and its manners that have been accepted by many people beyond language and cultural differences. When we try to trace back the history of Origami, it seems there is no doubt it started as a ritualistic offering. It then developed into ceremonial and daily custom, which has gone in new directions and expanded as pastime activities, entertainment, and educational tools. All components are profoundly related to our everyday life and have become a shared phenomenon for Origami folders. Recent developments of Origami as an artistic form and as a scientific research subject are natural consequences of its historical evolution. Origami is a creative activity, which is relational, of interest in daily life, and meaningful as a ritualistic offering.

The scientific study of what Origami does to the brain is at the beginning of exploration (Shumakov, 2000) for understanding what Origami is from the scientific perspective. Overall, four major therapeutic components of the theory of enrichment Origami art therapy are:

1. Physical stimulation to the brain – Good Health
2. Supportive Relationships – Intrinsic need of good family and friends
3. Creativity – Self Satisfaction
4. Safe and practical use in daily life – Physical safety and quality of life

These four points will be discussed again at the Trauma and Origami section. The next section focuses on my ten tips for Enrichment Origami Art Therapy (Kobayashi, 2002).

TIPS FOR THE ENRICHMENT ORIGAMI ART THERAPY

For a practical application, there are tips for successful Origami therapy sessions. Some of the tips are common precaution for art therapy sessions in general. The first and most important, as an art therapist utilizing Origami as a modality, you need to be familiar with and feel comfortable with the modality. Understanding the creative processes of Origami and anticipating possible destructive components that might occur, not just physical but psychological aspects of what might be going on with your clients is critical. As I pointed out in the three major principles of the theory of Enrichment Origami Art Therapy in previous section, each step of folding paper is deeply related to the client/therapist relationship. Without a knowledge of what is being folded and a forgiving capacity of "to do" and "not to do," it will not be easy to expect a constructive outcome of the therapy session.

Tips:

1. Ample Materials: Make sure that there are more than enough materials and no need to worry about misuse or extravagance. It is OK to try as many times as one may wish.
2. Memorize the folding steps by heart: Be knowledgeable about the sequences of folding instructions of models that you are going to introduce.
3. Clear Simple Instruction: Use simple language with the same movements for the same words, and repete instructions in clear manner.
4. Interpersonal learning atmosphere: Create a good working alliance among the group members. Participants have a potential to become an instructor that fosters a strong student-to-student relationship.
5. Be aware of individual needs: Anticipate the needs of each child, following the specific age appropriate developmental guidelines in relation to the group dynamics.
6. Consider physical limitations: Recognize individual problems, such as visual, auditory, and motor coordination problems based on participants' needs, as Origami requires dexterity, spatial awareness, and problem solving ability that have nothing to do with conventional age appropriate developmental stage.
7. Constellation of Hope: Keep the level of mood up by initiating attraction, curiosity, motivation, and continuation for the next session as a group.
8. Be Flexible and well prepared: Be ready for unexpected reactions from participants. Be well prepared for mistakes and misunderstandings of the given instructions for folding.
9. Be aware of the potential of obsessive quality: Origami is not immune from the characteristics of individual and repetitive creativity.

10. Be aware of the potential of becoming a trigger of trauma: Origami is an activity using a material, which is fragile and vulnerable, which be associated with traumatic events.

TRAUMA AND ORIGAMI

Why it is useful to use Origami with children who are suffering from traumatic experiences? How is it different from other art media? Further research is anticipated. I learned, from my experiences facilitating Origami art therapy to children with severe trauma, some of the mechanism that seem to be working well. Traumatized children may feel uncertain about the future and anxious about events that are out of their control. Traumatic experiences create fear and uncertainty about the future. Children may be afraid of something new, feel insecure, and become vulnerable as a result. Trauma affects each child differently, and they all have an individual and unique way of dealing with stressful situations. Building resilience – the ability to adapt well to overwhelming situations – can help children manage stress and feelings of anxiety and uncertainty. However, being resilient does not mean that children will not experience difficulty or distress. Emotional pain and sadness are common after suffering major trauma. It involves behaviors, problem solving skills and actions that can be learned over time. Origami has potential of involving behaviors, problem solving skills and positive actions to build resilience cognitively as well as emotionally. The following table contrasts the basic needs and Origami in relation to the nature of trauma.

Table 8.1. Needs, Trauma, and Advantages of Origami		
Basic Human Needs	*Nature of Trauma*	*Advantages of Origami*
Well Being	Overwhelming information	Structure
Good Relationships	Helplessness	Building trust
Self Satisfaction	Hopelessness	Physical and Emotional Accomplishment
Physical Safety	Physical danger and discomfort	Safe and nonthreatening activity

However, in order to prevent traumatized people from falling into vicious cycles of trauma again and again, the nature of trauma needs consideration alongside the therapeutic processes.

> *The perpetrator has emotion and will*
> *The victim transfers emotions and wills to the next generations*
> *The victim becomes another perpetrator*
> *Psychology of the chain of human beings continues*

The following is a recommended application of origami art therapy.

APPLICATION OF ENRICHMENT ORIGAMI ART THERAPY

1) Individual Origami Collage Project

"My Favorite Ice Cream Cone" *(Smith's eight ways: 1, 3, & 7)*
Setting: Individual or a small group
Aims for session: Emotional support for basic needs
Number of sessions: one session
Duration of session: thirty minutes
Number of participants: one to six children
Members of the group: pre-kindergarten to second grade elementary school students
Materials: Origami paper (6 in. by 6 in.), construction paper, glue, oil pastels

"My House" *(Smith's eight ways: 1, 3, & 7)*
Setting: Individual or a small group
Aims for session: Looking into the representation of "My House"
Number of sessions: one session
Duration of session: thirty minutes
Number of participants: one to six children
Members of the group: pre-kindergarten to second grade elementary school
Materials: Origami paper (6 in. by 6 in.), construction paper, glue, oil pastels

"My Flower" *(Smith's eight ways: 1, 3, 4, 7 & 8)*
Setting: Individual or a small group
Aims for session: Symbolic presentation of oneself
Number of sessions: one session
Duration of session: thirty minutes
Number of participants: one to six children
Members of the group: pre-kindergarten to third grade elementary school students
Materials: Origami paper in different colors (6 in. by 6 in.), construction paper, glue, coloring materials, scissors

Individual Origami with Playful Activity

"My Flapping Bird" *(Smith's eight ways: 1, 7, & 8)*
Setting: Individual or a small group
Aims for session: Emotional support for traumatic incidents
Number of sessions: one session
Duration of session: thirty minutes
Number of participants: one to six children
Members of the group: pre-kindergarten to third grade elementary school students
Materials: Origami paper (6 in. by 6 in.), coloring materials

"My Jumping Frog" *(Smith's eight ways: 1, 3, & 7)*
Setting: Individual or a small group
Aims for session: Emotional support for traumatic incidents
Number of sessions: one session
Duration of session: thirty minutes
Number of participants: one to six children
Members of the group: second to sixth grade elementary school students
Materials: Origami paper (6 in. by 6 in.), coloring materials

Individual Origami with Symbolic Meaning

"Color My Boxes" *(Smith's eight ways: 1, 5, & 7)*
Setting: Individual or a small group
Aims for session: Creating a Safe Container for Feelings
Number of sessions: one session
Duration of session: forty minutes
Number of participants: one to six children
Members of the group: third to sixth grade elementary school students
Materials: two sheets of rectangle paper for top and bottom of a box (such as copying paper, but construction paper is not suitable), coloring materials

"My Wreath, Our Frame" *(Smith's eight ways: 1, 3, 5, & 7)*
Setting: Individual or a small group
Aims for session: Creating a structured containment
Number of sessions: one session
Duration of session: forty minutes
Number of participants: one to six children
Members of the group: fifth to ninth grade elementary school students
Materials: eight sheets of square Origami paper for each garland, coloring materials

Communal Origami Project

"My Village, Our Village" *(Smith's eight ways: 1, 3, & 7) (Figure 8.1)*
Setting: Group
Aims for session: Emotional support for a group of people sharing similar experiences
Number of sessions: one session
Duration of session: thirty to forty-five minutes
Number of participants: ten to twenty children
Members of the group: Children of all ages
Materials: Origami paper (6 in. by 6 in.), coloring materials

Figure 8.1. "My House, My Village"

"Butterfly at Our Windowsill" *(Smith's eight ways: 1, 3, 7, & 8)*
Setting: Group
Aims for session: Emotional support for a group of people sharing similar experiences
Number of sessions: one session
Duration of session: thirty to forty-five minutes
Number of participants: ten to twenty children
Members of the group: Children of all ages
Materials: Origami paper (6 in. by 6 in.), coloring materials

"My Flower, Our Bouquet" *(Smith's eight ways: 1, 2, 3, 4, 7, & 8)*
Setting: Group
Aims for session: Emotional support for a group of people sharing similar experiences
Number of sessions: one session
Duration of session: forty-five minutes
Numbers of participants: ten to twenty children
Members of the group: third to ninth Grade elementary school students
Materials: 6 in. by 6 in. Origami paper for a flower, 3 in. by 3 in. Origami paper for a leaf, coloring materials, Scissors, Glue, Tape, Pipe Cleaners, A container for flowers

5) Decorative Origami Project

"Where we live? Where we are going?" *(Smith's eight ways: 1, 2, 3, 4, 7, & 8)*
(Figure 8.3)
Setting: Closed group
Aims for session: Emotional support for traumatic incidents
Number of sessions: six sessions (Once a week)
Duration of session: forty-five minutes
Number of participants: six to eight children
Members of the group: third to sixth grade elementary school students age eight to twelve
Materials: Origami paper, coloring materials, scissors, glue, tape, large paper

This mural project took place at an after school program in the lower east-side of Manhattan as a part of Friday club activities. This club was designed for third to sixth grade students to experience well-structured free expression art therapy in a closed group. Due to the need for intervention after the 9/11 event, it was designed as a part of ordinary club activities and students were asked to sign up voluntarily. Considering the diversity of the cultures and backgrounds of the community of the part of the Manhattan where the school is located, extra care was needed for structuring the sessions. Many of the students who live in this neighborhood are recent immigrants from different parts of the world, living next to former immigrant families with mixed ethnicities. It was conducted as a closed group.

As Origami was new to the most of the students, the group started with in-troductory individual work, which later developed into a group mural work. The theme was "Where we live and where we want to be" after the universal event of 9/11. It took a whole semester to complete, starting with introducing Origami from scratch. One of the children transformed an Origami human figure into fireman wearing a red hat in front of the twin tower image. Another child added stick figures. People seemed happier in the other part of the picture.

> *Stay in metaphor*
> *Structure gives safe environment*
> *following ritual provide a feeling of belonging.*
> *Symbolic representation requires active perception in the process of creativity.*

"Flower Garland" *(Smith's eight ways: 1, 2, 4, 7, & 8) (Figure 8.2)*
Setting: Group
Aims for session: Crisis intervention for children in need of structured cohesiveness
Number of sessions: two to three sessions
Duration of session: forty-five minutes each, once a week
Numbers of participants: six to eight children
Members of the group: second to sixth grade elementary school students
Materials: Origami paper (6 in. by 6 in.), Scissors, Stick Glue, Coloring Materials

Figure 8.2. "My Flower Garland"

Figure 8.3. "Sailing for the Future"

FAMILY ORIGAMI ART THERAPY

Finally, I would like to draw attention to the importance of family art therapy. I did not have space to talk about how I use Origami in cross-generational settings, such as parent-child, family with siblings, and extended family, including close friends collective assemblies. Human beings are collective animals that have great difficulty living alone and feeling lonely. It is more so with children, as they need to be accepted and included in the society in which they belong. They need to be able to form a feeling of connectedness and to be positive that they are treated with respect. I found Origami to be a useful tool in this purpose, which is the natural outcome of Origami itself. Its history tells us why Origami has existed for so many years in Japan, as well as many parts of the world.

"Origami Wish Tree" *(Smith's eight ways: 1, 2, 3, 4, 5, 6, 7, & 8)*
Setting: Family
Aims for session: Family in crisis
Number of sessions: two to three sessions
Duration of session: thirty to forty-five minutes
Number of participants: two to four children and adults
Members of the group: Children of all ages and parents/care givers
Materials: Origami paper of different kinds, coloring materials, tape, scissors, a tree twig from an old tree or picture of tree twigs

* This project is suitable for a group of children of all ages up to 18 who share similar issues that need intervention.

"Community Holiday Tree" *(Smith's eight ways: 1, 2, 3, 4, 5, 6, 7, & 8)*
(Figure 8.4)
Setting: Family
Aims for session: Origami as a bridge between family members in crisis
Number of sessions: two to three sessions
Duration of session: thirty to forty-five minutes
Number of participants: two to four children and adults
Members of the group: Children of all ages and parents/care givers
Materials: Origami paper of different kinds, coloring materials, glue, string, one hole puncher, scissors

* This project is suitable for a communal setting where people need crisis intervention.

Figure 8.4. "Community Holiday Tree"

CONCLUSION

Facilitating an effective art therapy treatment for children with traumatic experiences is not an easy task. It is not easy for children to start expressing themselves freely in front of the therapist by any creative means and/or by speech. The role of Origami is to support the child's feeble ego to become steady and to encourage them to start expressing themselves in their own manner, behaviorally, verbally, and creatively. As I mentioned before, the nature of trauma is that the overwhelming unprocessed information gives the child feelings of hopelessness and helplessness, and they become unable to trust anyone to secure physical and psychological safety.

Origami is a simple and straightforward activity using a piece of paper, which has a lot of constraints and physical structure. Touching a piece of Origami paper is, first of all, grounding. Secondly, it gives a child a chance to feel that the paper is totally under his or her control. Being in charge of a piece of paper and making changes to it is, metaphorically, a firm ground to start with. Thirdly, following instruction is a passive mode with structure but the act of folding is, on the contrary, an active mode. The positive experience of giving effect to a piece of paper is an experience of being a master of the paper and controlling one's body and mind, installing hope. Finally, through following the instruction of an Origami art therapist, the child starts rebuilding positive relationships.

Even for those children who are not ready to verbalize experiences, Origami allows the child to stay in metaphor. While the structure of Origami gives a safe environment, following ritual provides a feeling of belonging and acceptance by the others. Symbolic representation of Origami allows perception to become active and activates the child's brain functions. Interpersonal learning without words enables children to process unspoken anxiety and stress within a group setting, which is fulfilling.

In conclusion, I would like to repeat the following efficacies of Origami:

Healing Process of Origami

- Healing process that stands on human relationship
- Rebuilding trust
- Reconciling through creativity
- Recognize differences and the ubiquity
- Sharing nature
- Potential of situational/relational healing process
- Paper Folding – "Origami" – as a universal tool of therapy

There must be more research before more people are convinced that Origami works. As an art therapist, I can attest that it works without doubt.

REFERENCES

Balint, M. (1968). *Basic fault.* Illinois: Northwestern University Press

Chang, T. (1995). Using Origami as a psychotherapeutic tool. *COET '95* (pp. 81–86). New York: Origami USA.

Ho, G. (2001). *Advantages of using origami in therapy.* Retrieved January 1, 2003 from http://www.go.to/origami.

Kobayashi, T. (1998). Peace in Palestine '98 Art Workshop. *Al-Sahha, 27,* 5–7. Tokyo: Japan Palestine Medical Association.

Kobayashi, T. (2002). *Role of "Origami" in art therapy with elderly people from Korea.* Submitted in partial fulfillment of the requirements of the degree of Master of Arts in Art Therapy at School of Education, New York University.

Kobayashi, T. (2004). *Enrichment Origami art therapy with the people at lower eastside.* Care Study #4 Tokyo: Index Press.

Langer, S. (1957). *Problems of art.* New York: Charles Scribner's Sons.

Liebschner, J. (1992). The life of Friedrich Froebel and his main philosophical ideas. *COET '91* pp. 3–15). Birmingham: British Origami Society.

Lister, D. (1975). *The history of paper folding in Britain.* Birmingham: British Origami Society.

Lister, D. (1995). Some observations on the history of Origami. *COET '95* (pp. 5–17). New York: Origami USA.

Miyashita, A. (1994). Origami: one hundred years. *Oru, 7,* 71–72. Tokyo: Sojyusha.

Narita, K. (1980). *Life of Ts'ai Lung and Japanese paper-making.* Tokyo: The Paper Museum.

Okamura, M. (1995). Literature study of Origami: Origami during Meiji era. *Oru, 9,* 76–80. Tokyo: Sojyusha.

Okamura, M. (1999). The stream of Origami. In *Oru-Kokoro.* Oru; History of Origami (pp. 4–15). Tatsuno: History Museum of Tatsuno.

Oru. (1993). The beat of Korean Sharmanism. *Oru, 1,* 114–120. Tokyo: Sojyusha.

Shumakov, K. Y. (2000). *Left brain and right brain.* December 10, 2001, from http://www.oriland.com/lcrning/.

Smith, J. (1992). Proceedings of the Conference of Origami on Education and Therapy '91 (Ed.), Birmingham, UK: British Origami Society.

Smith, J. (1995). Opening address to COET '95. *COET '95* (pp. 5–17). New York: Origami USA.

Temko, F. (1986). *Paper pandas and jumping frogs.* San Francisco: China Books.

Wilson, L. (2001). *Symbolism and art therapy.* In Approaches to Art Therapy. New York: Brunner-Routledge.

Winnicott, D. W. (1986). Transitional Objects and Transitional Phenomena. In P. Buckley (Ed.), *Essential Papers on Object Relations.* New York: New York University Press.

FURTHER RESOURCES

Origami Club: http://www.origami-club.com
Brian Cox: http://www.whimsical-workshop.mb.ca
George Ho: http://www.geocities.com/paper_folding/index.html

BIOGRAPHICAL STATEMENT

Toshiko Kobayashi, MA, ATR, LCAT earned her Art Therapy master's degree at New York University in 2002. She has been practicing as an art therapist in New York, and currently she is working for a New York State psychiatric hospital as a full-time art therapist for Project Liberty after 9/11. She advocates "Enrichment Origami Art Therapy," which was a part of her motivation of studying art therapy following her long career as a contemporary artist, organizing art exhibitions and art workshops in Japan. She has been lecturing and facilitating Origami workshops in the U.S., U.K., Middle East, and Japan as well as exhibiting her art works in several countries.

Chapter 9

HEALING THROUGH PLAY:
AN OVERVIEW OF PLAY THERAPY WITH
SEXUALLY ABUSED CHILDREN

CHARLES EDWIN MYERS

INTRODUCTION

The sexual abuse of children is a difficult topic to discuss. It is even more difficult to acknowledge that this abuse occurs every day to children of all ages. In 2001, more than 903,000 children in the United States were substantiated victims of abuse and neglect. Of this number, almost ninety thousand, or 9.6%, were victims of sexual abuse (U.S. Department of Health and Human Services, Administration on Children, Youth, and Families, 2001). Other studies suggest that even more children suffer abuse and neglect than is ever reported to child protective services agencies. A survey of 1,712 college students revealed a seventeen percent rate of occurrence of sexual abuse before age eighteen (Epstein and Bottoms, 1998). Many victims of child abuse and neglect are very young. In 2001, about twenty-eight percent of child maltreatment victims were under the age of three (U.S. Department of Health and Human Services, 2001). The prevalence of child sexual abuse is widespread and includes ten to fourteen percent of American households (MacFarlane and Waterman, 1986).

Sexual abuse is among the most potentially damaging sources of emotional distress in young children (Gallo-Lopez, 2000). Young children who have been sexually abused experience a monstrous invasion of their whole being (Cattanach, 1992). Sexual abuse, one of most familiar forms of trauma today, can be grossly disturbing; or it can appear to be "loving," "gentle," and "subtle." As such, the victim may not recognize the abuse as something fearsome or even wrong; yet, it can be extraordinarily traumatizing (Donovan and McIntyre, 1990). Sexual abuse robs children of their childhood and creates a loss of

trust, feelings of guilt, and self-abusive behavior. It can lead to antisocial behavior, depression, identity confusion, loss of self-esteem, and other serious
emotional problems. It can also lead to difficulty with intimate relationships
later in life. Because of their self-referent and egocentric nature, children tend
to believe all experiences happen to them, for them, by them, and because of
them. Trauma can affect all levels of a child's development, including intel-
lectual development, physical health, emotional functioning, academic
achievements, and social skills. Children subjected to sexual abuse experience
trauma that profoundly damages their lives and overwhelms their usual coping
abilities to such an extent that they need therapeutic help to recover (Cattanach, 1992).

The effects of child sexual abuse encompass a multitude of symptoms. The
sexually abused child feels betrayed, tricked, fearful, vulnerable, ashamed, and
different from other children (Cattanach, 1992). They experience great emotional upset, depression, fear, anxiety, anger, shame, and guilt (Damon, Todd,
and MacFarlane, 1987; Finkelhor, 1986; Kaufman and Wohl, 1992; McMahon, 1992). These children often have poor self-image, relate badly to others,
and often experience and express feelings of hostility (Finkelhor, 1986; Hall-
Marley and Damon, 1993; Martin and Beezley, 1977). Separation and abandonment are difficult, strongly-felt issues for sexually abused children
(Cattanach, 1992; Damon et al., 1987). These children frequently experience
feelings of confusion and loss and are often hypervigilant (Cattanach, 1992;
Martin and Beezley, 1977; White and Allers, 1994). Sexually abused children
experience difficulties in school such as a lack of concentration, poor attention, and declining school performance, as well as delinquent behaviors such
as opposition defiance, negative and uncooperative attitudes, and running
away (Finkelhor, 1986; Hall, 1997; Martin and Beezley, 1977). Sexually
abused children may exhibit inappropriate sexualized behaviors (Finkelhor,
1986) and have sexual identity problems (Kaufman and Wohl, 1992).

Most sexually abused children struggle with issues of trust and betrayal
(Cattanach, 1992; Knell, 1993; Kaufman and Wohl, 1992). When a known and
trusted person sexually abuses children, the betrayal of their relationship is
very great (Knell, 1993). Abuse by a parent has a profound impact on the relationship with that parent. There is pain, confusion, and fear of the abuse
itself; there is the unimaginable experience of having both the source of
danger and the source of protection in one person. Most terrifying of all is the
fear of loss of the relationship, a loss children often believe is likely to happen
if they try to protect themselves from being abused by a parent. Trust in the
nonabusing parent is affected as well, because he or she has been unable to
protect the child, and because the abusing parent often deliberately isolated
the child from the other parent by insisting that the child keeps their relationship a secret. If the nonabusing parent does not believe the child when she

dares to reveal the secret, or, believing, insists that she forgive the abusive parent, the child's trust in the nonabusing parent is again undermined (Jernberg and Booth, 1999). The child feels abandoned, unsure what adults want from them, often making connections with others by sexual signals and not knowing any other way of making friends (Cattanach, 1992).

Sexual abuse forces children to experience behavior for which they are developmentally or emotionally unprepared (Perez, 1987). Sexually abused children often develop an excessive and abnormal interest in sex, an interest frequently expressed in precocious sexual activity (Gil, 1991). Sexualized behaviors include adherence to personal boundaries, exhibitionism, gender role behavior, self-stimulation, voyeuristic behavior, sexual anxiety, sexual interest, sexual intrusiveness, and sexual knowledge (Friedrich, Fisher, Broughton, Houston, and Shafran, 1998). Pathological sexual behaviors in children are distinguishable from developmentally appropriate sexual behavior play by examining the dimension of intensity. Sexual behavior considered inappropriate can include persistent public masturbation that causes pain or irritation, touching or asking to touch another's genitals, excessive interest in sexual matters, and sexualized behavior imitative of adult sexual relationships. Another characteristic of many sexualized children is a disinhibition of masturbatory behavior. A child who has not been sexualized will abruptly stop masturbating when someone enters the room; sexually abused children, possibly having learned the sexual behavior from another person, may continue to masturbate (Berkliner, Manaois, and Monastersky, 1986).

There is no single, universally applied definition of child sexual abuse. Yet, all offenses that involve sexually touching a child, as well as nontouching offenses and sexual exploitation, are just as harmful and devastating to a child's well-being. Denial and repression are the primary defenses of young children (Damon et al., 1987). Sexually abused children usually enter into therapy presenting a wide variety of problems (Brooke, 1997; Hall, 1997).

Finkelhor (1984, 1986) developed a four-factor conceptual model for understanding the traumagenic dynamics occurring in sexual abuse. These factors are traumatic sexualization, stigmatization, powerlessness, and betrayal. In traumatic sexualization, the child has suffered sexual trauma affecting the child's developing sexuality and perception of and attitude toward sexual activity. Children may feel dirty or suffer from a conditioned fear of sexuality or become inappropriately sexualized. Therapy may help to restore the child's capacity to feel and to express and cope with feelings of anger, fear, disgust, and sadness, enabling the eventual development of normal relationships of mutual sharing and care. In stigmatization, a child develops a negative view of self, feeling "different," and develops negative ways of communicating with others. Therapy may restore the child's feeling one is normal. Children develop feelings of powerlessness from having physical and emotional boundaries violated, and from having lost what little control they have over their bodies and their lives. Therapy may increase the child's feelings of control to a level appropriate for his or her age and stage of development. Children experience a deep sense of betrayal as the source of nurturing and the source of pain reside in the same person. Therapy may restore the child's trust in people (Finkelhor and Browne, 1985).

IMPORTANCE OF PLAY

The importance of play in the lives of children is evident in its pervasiveness in childhood. The United Nations' proclamation of play as a universal and inalienable right of childhood emphasizes the importance of play to the development and wholeness of children. Play is the singular central activity of childhood (Landreth, 2002) and is the means by which children come to understand the world around them and their place within that world (Jennings, 1999). Children learn to respect themselves, to control their feelings responsibly, and to be creative in confronting problems. Play helps children explore their inner world and express their true self, which are full of needs, as well as wishes and wants. Play represents the child's attempt to organize one's experiences and personal world, and provides a means through which conflicts can be resolved and feelings can be communicated (Landreth, 2002). Through play, children can imagine other possibilities and ways of being. These imaginings develop their capacity to be creative in confronting problems and finding solutions. Play has a reality of its own as an activity in which children explore their identity in relation to others (Cattanach, 1992).

Play and activity are a child's natural medium of communication (Ginott, 1959; Landreth, 2002) and are the young child's primary mode of emotional expression (Hall, 1997). Through play, children communicate what they cannot in words. Through toys, children express emotions about their self-perceptions, others, and significant events they have experienced (Ater, 2001). Play is the most natural and healing process in childhood. Children have the capacity to find recreation and to self-cure in the activity of play (Erickson, 1963). Play is particularly useful with abused children as they are more likely in general to express their innermost feelings and fantasies much more readily through play than verbalization (Mann and McDermott, 1983). The recognition of the importance of children's play is paramount. The value of play to children and to the therapeutic process with children is crucial (Caplan and Caplan, 1974).

Play is the child's symbolic language of self-expression. Developmentally, children lack the cognitive and verbal facilities to express what they feel, and emotionally are unable to speak of and focus on the intensity of what they feel in a manner adequately expressible in a verbal exchange (Landreth, 2002). Piaget (1962) stated that play bridges the gap between concrete experience and abstract thought. The symbolic function of play is tremendously important in the manner children communicate. Children use symbolic play to create their own special worlds, set in their own time and space, aside from "ordinary" life. Children have a clear understanding of the boundaries of play and signal their intention to begin and to end play in ways that keeps the boundaries clear (Cattanach, 1992). Play, as a meaning of self-expression, is an opportunity for a child to "play out" feelings and problems as an adult might "talk out" difficulties (Mader, 2000). Landreth (2002) stated, "Children's play can be more fully appreciated when recognized as their natural medium of communication. Children express themselves more fully and more directly through self-initiated spontaneous play than they do verbally because they are more comfortable with play. For children to 'play out' their experiences and feelings is the most natural dynamic and self-healing process in which children can engage" (p.14).

PLAY THERAPY

It is important for a therapist to consider the developmental levels of the child when considering what approach to use. Since children behave and think differently from adults, the approach to working with them must reflect this (Webb, 2002). Play is a natural treatment vehicle for young children, allowing them to externalize trauma and to work it through at their own pace (Allan and Lawton-Speert, 1989b). Play therapy is a primary, and usually the most appropriate, intervention for children. It is a therapeutic approach based on the understanding that play is the child's natural medium of self-expression (Homeyer, 1999). Play therapy ingeniously undertakes the hard work of child psychotherapy in the appealing guise of play. Play therapy has adapted its methods to accommodate the world of childhood, using the medium of play as the means of communicating symbolically with the child (Webb, 2002).

Child therapists have been using play therapy with children since the 1920's, when Anna Freud (1946) used games and toys as a way to build a relationship with her child patients. Another child analyst, Melanie Klein (1932), used the child's play as the basis for interpretations to the child. Other play therapy pioneers include David Levy (1938), who helped the child recreate a traumatic event through a structured play format; Fredrick Allen (1942), Clark Moustakas (1959), and Virginia Axline (1947), all emphasized the child's natural growth process as key to helping the child individuate and develop basic self-esteem (positive regard). Achievement of these goals in play therapy occurs through recognition of the child's feelings as expressed in the play and through the therapist's belief in the child's strengths and potential for growth and change (Webb, 2002).

The purpose of play therapy is to help children, using the medium of play in the context of a therapeutic relationship. Play therapy incorporates the unique meaning of play to children and the importance of understanding the symbolism of the child's play language (Webb, 1991). Therapists who understand the importance of play in the lives of children, and that children naturally communicate through play, are well on their way to understanding the world of children. Conversely, therapists who employ adult-style talk counseling with children send a very clear message to child clients: "I am unwilling to enter your world of communication; therefore if this process is gong to work, you have to leave that world and come into my adult world, which includes my level of thinking and communication" (Sweeney and Homeyer, 1999). The responsible therapist goes to the child's level and communicates with children through the medium with which they are comfortable (Landreth, 2002).

RATIONALE FOR PLAY THERAPY

Adult therapy depends heavily on the formal operations of Piagetian development (Sweeney, 1997). Adult communication is by its nature abstract and sophisticated, whereas the communication of children is concrete and simple. The nature of child's play and play therapy are both fundamentally preoperational. Play and language are essentially relative opposites as they are contrasting forms of representation. When a therapist insists that a child cognitively verbalize, the child in essence must translate their thoughts into the therapist's accepted medium of communication of talk. Play and fantasy do not carry this limitation. Children can create without the restriction of making their creation verbally understandable. Therefore, children and play do not lend themselves to operationalism, as they are in fact preoperational. The therapist must approach and understand children from a developmental perspective (Landreth, 2002).

Through play, the therapist is able to develop a sense of understanding between the child and therapist quickly and smoothly (Kottman, 2001). The therapist's willingness and ability to "speak" in the child's language conveys a respect for the child that the child may have never experienced previously. By watching how the child plays, the toys chosen, and when the child switches from one activity to another, the therapist is able to enter and learn much of the child's world.

One of the jobs of the play therapist is to provide opportunities for children to prove to themselves that they have the potential to be successful. Play assists children in learning about themselves and the world around them (Landreth, 1987). Engaging children through play therapy allows the children to tell their stories and provides the therapist the opportunity to understand the child's phenomenological world (Axline, 1969; Ginott, 1959; Landreth, 2002; Moustakas, 1953; Mullen, 2002). By engaging in the process of play, children attempt to reduce overwhelming events into manageable situations through symbolic representation, thereby creating an opportunity for self-expression (Johnston, 1997). Through the use of symbolic materials, play permits the child the necessary therapeutic distancing from the trauma of sexual abuse (Mann and McDermott, 1983). Play therapy provides the child a safe and protected space where one can enact, ingest, and assimilate trauma slowly over time. The child divides overwhelming experiences and emotions into small quantities and handles them through play. The child can now be active in the relationship to expressing feelings and mastering the environment through play (Allan and Lawton-Speert, 1989b).

CHILD-CENTERED PLAY THERAPY

Child-centered play therapy opens the door into the language of the child (Mader, 2000). The child-centered play therapy philosophy considers play essential to the healthy development of children. Play gives concrete form and expression to a child's inner world. A child is able to give meaningful expression to emotionally significant experiences through play. A major function of play is the transformation of what may be unmanageable in reality to manageable situations through symbolic representation providing children with opportunities for learning to cope by engaging in self-directed exploration (Landreth, 2002).

Child-centered play therapy is a philosophy resulting in attitudes and behaviors for living one's life in relationships with children. It is both a basic philosophy and an attitude of deep and abiding belief in the child's ability to be constructively self-directing (Landreth and Sweeney, 1997). The child-centered play therapist believes deeply in and trusts explicitly the inner person of the child. The play therapist's objective is to relate to the child in ways that will release the child's inner directional, constructive, forward-moving, creative, and self-healing power. When children experience this philosophical belief within the playroom, they are empowered and their developmental capabilities are released for self-exploration and self-discovery, resulting in constructive change (Landreth and Sweeney, 1997).

Axline (1969) clarified the nature of the interaction between the therapist and child in the child-centered approach in her eight basic principles that serve as a guide for therapeutic contact with the child (Landreth, 2002):

1. The therapist is genuinely interested in the child and develops a warm, caring relationship.
2. The therapist experiences unqualified acceptance of the child and does not wish that the child were different in some way.
3. The therapist creates a feeling of safety and permissiveness in the relationship so the child feels free to explore and express self completely.
4. The therapist is always sensitive to the child's feelings and gently reflects those feelings in such a manner that the child develops self-understanding.
5. The therapist believes deeply in the child's capacity to act responsibly, unwaveringly respects the child's ability to solve personal problems and allows the child to do so.
6. The therapist trusts the child's inner direction, allows the child to lead in all areas of the relationship and resists any urge to direct the child's play or conversation.
7. The therapist appreciates the gradual nature of the therapeutic process and does not attempt to hurry the process.
8. The therapist establishes only those therapeutic limits that help the child accept personal and appropriate relationship responsibility.

PLAY THERAPY AND SEXUAL ABUSE

The treatment of sexually abused children is difficult and complex. These children have experienced a violation of trust and a wide range of abuse in terms of severity, frequency, age of onset, nature of relationship to perpetrator, and whether the abuse was characterized by violent rape at one end of the spectrum to "gentle" seduction at the other end (Allan and Lawton-Speert, 1989a). Therapy with the sexually abused child must address both the short- and long-term needs of the child. Short-term needs center primarily on the fear about initial disclosure and its effects on the child and the rest of the family if the abuser is a family member. The need for these children to develop feelings of safety and protection are crucial. Long-term needs center primarily on growth and healing from the abuse (Hall, 1997).

Play therapy is the primary mode of treatment recommended for child victims of sexual abuse (Bagley and King, 1990; Cockle and Allan, 1996; Damon et al., 1987; Gil, 1991; Jones, 1986; Mann and McDermott, 1983; McDonough and Love, 1987; Orenchuch-Tomiuk, Matthey, and Christensen, 1990). The goal of play therapy with children who have been sexually abused is to help them master the multiple stresses of abuse and neglect and to reduce the present and future negative psychological impact arising from the trauma of sexual abuse. With these children, play is particularly useful as they, even more than children in general, express their innermost feelings and fantasies much more readily through action than verbalization. Sexual abuse is an overwhelming, anxiety-provoking issue for a young child. Play permits the child the necessary therapeutic distancing from the traumatic event by the use of symbolic materials (Ater, 2001; Johnson, 1987; Walker and Bolkovatz, 1988). Play therapists, through the use of play, can address trauma-related issues effectively, while providing sexually abused children a place to feel at ease (Hall, 1997), an emotional space for the repetitive expression of the experience needed by trauma victims (Walker and Bolkovatz, 1988), and a emotionally safe environment for the process of healing to occur (Gallo-Lopez, 2000).

The lives of children are sometimes intruded upon in very traumatic ways and are so often outside their own control. Therapeutic interventions, therefore, should not only be nonintrusive, but also provide high level of safety for children. Play therapy provides children a safe place and a safe environment in which to heal. Through play, children may use metaphors and symbols to represent an abuser or an abusive situation; project intense and frightening emotions onto toys and activity; and sublimate negative emotions towards other people onto toys. Play therapy allows the child to experience in fantasy what they cannot in reality: mastery and control over people and situations (Sweeney and Homeyer, 1999).

Play therapy frees the child to begin to emote freely without the need to translate emotion into verbal expression. Play themes naturally and spontaneously emerge in a cascading display of emotional reactions to the abuse. Simultaneously, the play experience generates a feeling of relief and mastery for the child, promoting healing and growth (Hall, 1997). Play therapy can be an extremely powerful modality, but it is also a complex, subtle, and sophisticated tool. The play therapist needs to possess an in-depth understanding of how children think, interact, communicate, and change – both normally and when traumatized (Donovan and McIntyre, 1990).

Through play therapy, children come to an acceptance of what has happened to them and learn new ways of coping to protect themselves from further abuse (Ater, 2001; Cattanach, 1992). Play provides children with courage, empowering them to heal what is hurting (Homeyer, 1994). Healing can only occur within safe boundaries, this is especially true for sexually abused children who have experienced a traumatic violation of their boundaries. The play therapist provides the child this safety to work through sexual abuse without needing or feeling pressured to verbalize their feelings. In the playroom, the play of sexually abused children will exhibit very different behaviors than nonabused children (Mayer, 1985). Several properties of play allow sexually abused children a sense of safety and distance while working through their trauma (Sweeney, 1997). Children will displace their trauma and conflicts onto the dolls and puppets without even realizing the connection to their own lives. Play provides a safe place for the child to reenact, rehearse, and practice skills needed to strengthen the child, and to prepare one for directly dealing with the traumatic events (James, 1989).

Four basic concepts of play therapy help focus the therapy towards healing the abused child (Cattanach, 1992). Play is central to the child's way of understanding one's world. Play is a developmental process, and in therapy the child moves back and forth along a developmental continuum as a way of discovering individuation and separation. Play is a symbolic process through which the child can experiment with imaginative choices appropriately distanced from the consequences of those choices in "real" life. Finally, play happens in a therapeutic space, where the child's creative life starts and one experiences for the first time the psychological significance of art.

The playroom serves as the child's own personal space. Children often need to express their feelings or communicate about actual or imagined events, which they would never do if they thought anyone, especially a parent, would ever know what they said. For many children the privacy of their space represents the confidentiality of the therapeutic relationship. In the case of sexually abused children, the play therapy room may be the only space in the life of the child, which is consistently safe, secure, and inviolable (Donovan and McIntyre, 1990).

Sexually abused children typically present with play themes of good and bad, submissive and dominant confrontations, overpowering "bad guys," and highly sexualized themes between boys and girls or mommies and daddies. In all these themes, the child is attempting to sort out and make sense of the various confusing images and interactions that have taken place during the incidents of sexual abuse. Play becomes an open road to the child's inner world. Through play, the child can identify the intricacies of the one's pain, and express and release these anxieties and concerns through therapeutic play. This release is usually an empowering and validating experience for the child. While employing the "playing cure," the therapist has an opportunity to observe and monitor the progress of the child's conflicts in vivid and descriptive play themes. The child can work through the trauma in an indirect, less anxiety-evoking fashion. All the stages of healing and resolution are evident in the child's play. As the therapist affirms the play themes, one also affirms a new message to the child – that it is okay to heal, to feel one's personal power, and to assert that power when feeling threatened by others (Hall, 1997).

PLAY THERAPY SKILLS

Play therapists utilize a number of therapeutic skills that communicate to the child four basic messages: I am here, I hear you, I understand, and I care. The basic play therapist skills include (Kottman, 2001): (a) tracking behavior to establish a relationship with the child, (b) restating content to build rapport, (c) reflecting feelings to help the child to feel understood, (d) limit setting, (e) returning responsibility to the child, and (f) dealing with questions. It is important for the therapist to allow the child to decide when to deal with issues. Given a safe therapeutic environment and relationship, children will deal with those issues in the order most important to them (Homeyer, 1999).

A sexually abused child may attempt to act out on the therapist sexual or erotic behaviors they learned from perpetrating adults, because the child feels safe in the playroom or in an unconscious attempt to communicate to the therapist what they have experienced. Limits need to be set on such behaviors. As with many other acting-out behaviors, therapeutic limit setting enables the child to express the behavior and accompanying feelings symbolically and allows the therapist to be an objective but involved participant, thus preserving the professional and ethical therapeutic relationship (Landreth, 2002).

Limit setting is important for sexually abused children (Landreth, 2002). Children do not feel safe, valued, or accepted in a completely permissive relationship (Moustakas, 1959). Limits are a vital and necessary part of relationships. Limits exist in every relationship. An individual is free to grow and develop within the limits of one's own potentialities, talents, and structure. Limits are one aspect of an individual's true experience, an aspect that identifies, characterizes, and distinguishes the dimensions of a therapeutic relationship. Limits provide the form or structure of an immediate relationship. In a therapeutic relationship, limits provide the boundary or structure in which growth can occur. Consistency and predictability help the child to feel safe. The therapist words limits in a way that allows the child to bring oneself under control. All children experience a need to feel understood and accepted. All children experience issues of self-concept maintenance and enhancement, and the child will deal with those issues in one's own unique way. The child determines the content and direction of the play.

POST-TRAUMATIC PLAY

Children often dramatically reveal sexual abuse in pathological patterns of play (Allan and Lawton-Speert, 1989b). Post-traumatic play is a type of play observed in children who have undergone a psychic trauma, such as sexual abuse, so intense that ordinary coping mechanisms and defenses are insufficient to prevent the child from being overwhelmed by pain and anxiety. Some of the characteristics of post-traumatic play include compulsive repetition, unconscious link between play and the trauma, literalness of play with simple defenses, and failure to relieve anxiety (Terr, 1983). When engaged in post-traumatic play, the child is oblivious to the presence of the therapist. The child appears to be disengaged from reality, in a world of one's own, absorbed and mesmerized by one's play (Jones, 1986).

Through post-traumatic play, children can communicate to the therapist how the child perceived the trauma (Marvasti, 1994). Post-traumatic play lacks the metaphorical or symbolic expression and mastery of feelings normally seen in nontraumatized play (Harvey, 1993). Research has shown that traumatized children engage in post-traumatic play that is secret and ritualistic, with a driven quality to it (Terr, 1981). Post-traumatic themes of sexually abused children include abreaction, preservation, aggression, dissociation, nurturance, regression, and sexual play (Ater, 2001).

In abreactive play, sexually abused children need to recreate the trauma that they have survived. When children play out their abusive experience, it will often be literal and repetitive (Gil and Johnson, 1993). Through play, children reenact situations that are important to them in reality. As children repeat these situations, they diminish the power elements and learn actively to control their feelings about the trauma (Gil, 1991). With every new repetition, children gain control and mastery over their situations. Children may change the ending of the abuse in their play by creating hopefulness rather than the helplessness they experienced in reality (Marvasti, 1994). Play therapy provides children the means to deal with small parts of their trauma until the experience becomes more emotionally manageable (Kelly, 1995). The preservation play usually appears as a routine, rigid, and literal. However, it differs from abreactive play in that children are not able to change the ending to create hope. The child is stuck in the hopelessness of one's issues. This play involves a constant, monotonous, and ritualized reenactment of the trauma that sexually abused children have experienced.

With aggressive play, sexually abused children will test limits of the relationship as well as exhibit acting-out behaviors during the play session as their way of working through trust issues with the therapist (Kelly, 1995). Sometimes children's feelings of 'being bad' will show through in the therapy because they feel the abuse is their fault (Cattanach, 1992). Their aggressive play behaviors may somehow relate to their abuse. Children may act aggressively due to an overidentification with the abuser; displacing the hurt and anger they feel towards the abuser onto something else (White and Allers, 1994).

In dissociative play, the sexually abused child is able to deny and avoid the pain of the trauma by mentally escaping. Dissociation involves distancing from one's own thoughts, situations, and emotions. It seems that once play becomes too stressful and emotional, the child disconnects with what is occurring in the here and now (White and Allers, 1994). When dissociating, a child cannot hear, understand, or process what happens in the session (Gil and Johnson, 1993).

Nurturing play is very important for sexually abused children in helping them express their feelings of their lack of nurturing and their need for it.

Sexually abused children might exhibit nurturing behavior by cooking a meal and feeding the therapist, or providing medical care to therapist or a doll. Sexually abused children often exhibit nurturing behaviors toward self and toward the therapist in the playroom. Sexually abused children may exhibit regressive behaviors such as acting in childlike ways that might help them to "escape" from the abuse they experienced (Ater, 2001).

With sexualized play, sexually abused children do not have a sense of appropriate touching and boundaries, oversexualized behavior often occurs in the playroom (Sagar, 1990). Sexualized play behavior is the most commonly observed behavior of sexually abused children (Homeyer, 1994). Three types that maybe expressed during play therapy are abuse-reactive play, reenactment play, and symbolic sexualized play. Working with this sexualized play, the therapist faces the challenge of finding the balance between allowing children free expression of themselves and placing limits on their behavior, so that children will become aware of acceptable ways of expressing their experience (Van de Putte, 1995).

CLINICIAN SELF CARE

Working with sexually abused children is both rewarding and demanding. Due to the compelling nature of this work, therapists may literally consume themselves with the subject, spending many hours reading and attending trainings on child sexual abuse (Gil, 1991). The therapist needs to be aware of one's feelings that arise when working with a sexually abused child. The therapist may find the child's play, words, or experiences so shocking or overwhelming that to cope with these events, the therapist must block out certain feelings or themes (Wilson, Kendrick, and Ryan, 1992). It is crucial for the clinician to set limits on the number of child abuse clients seen overall, cases seen per day and per week, and clients accepted who have the same difficult diagnosis. The therapist is advised to replenish oneself through physical activity, vacations, and frequent changes of environment. In addition, it is important to balance the child abuse work with treatment of other, less urgent problems. Balance is crucial in the prevention of burnout.

CONCLUSION

Through play, children open windows to their inner world, their developmental level of functioning, and their competency abilities (Myers, 2006). Play presents children with a mode for communicating those experiences in their life too difficult or scary for them to face. Sexual abuse is one of the hardest of those areas. Play therapy is a developmentally appropriate and curative approach to helping children victimized by sexual abuse. Issues of sexual abuse are often too difficult for young children to verbalize, but through the healing modality of play, a child can reveal and resolve complex conflicts and intense feelings. Play can help children focus more clearly and reduce the increased anxiety usually found in sexually abused children. The natural elements of play make therapy less threatening and can encourage the child to be more open, less guarded, and more spontaneous. Through the empowering process of play therapy, a child can relieve emotional distress (Griffith, 1997) and replenish the feelings of joy and hope often lost (Hall, 1997) from sexual abuse. Play opens the path to healing for a child.

REFERENCES

Allan, J., & Lawton-Speert, S. (1989a). Sand and water in the treatment of a profoundly sexually abused preschool boy. *Association for Play Therapy Newsletter, 8*(4), 2–3.

Allan, J., & Lawton-Speert, S. (1989b). Play psychotherapy of a profoundly sexually abused boy: A Jungian approach. *The Annual Convention of the American Psychological Association.* New Orleans, LA.

Allen, F. (1942). *Psychotherapy with children.* New York: Norton.

Ater, M. K. (2001). Play therapy behaviors of sexually abused children. In G. L. Landreth (Ed.), *Innovations in play therapy: Issues, process, and special populations* (pp. 119–129). Philadelphia: Brunner-Routledge.

Axline, V. (1969). *Play therapy.* (Rev. Ed.) New York: Ballantine Books. (Original work published 1947).

Bagley, C., & King, K. (1990). *Child sexual abuse: The search for healing.* London: Routledge.

Berkliner, L., Manaois, O., & Monastersky, C. (1986). *Child sexual behavior disturbance: An assessment and treatment model.* Seattle, WA: Harborview Sexual Assault Center.

Brooke, S. L. (1997). *Art therapy with sexual abuse survivors.* Springfield, IL: Charles C Thomas Publisher, Ltd.

Caplan, F., & Caplan, T. (1974). *The power of play.* New York: Anchor Books.

Cattanach, A. (1992). *Play therapy with abused children.* Philadelphia: Jessica Kingsley Publishers.

Cockle, S., & Allan, J. (1996). Nigredo and albedo: From darkness to light in the play therapy of a sexually abused girl. *International Journal of Play Therapy, 5*(1), 31–44.

Damon, L., Todd, J., & MacFarlane, K. (1987). Treatment issues with sexually abused young children. *Child Welfare, 66*(2), 125–137.

Donovan, D. M., & McIntyre, D. (1990). *Healing the hurt child.* New York: Norton.

Epstein, M., & Bottoms, B. (1998). Memories of childhood sexual abuse: A survey of young adults. *Child Abuse & Neglect, 22*(12), 1217–1238.

Erickson, E. H. (1963). *Childhood and society.* New York: W.W. Norton & Company.

Finkelhor, D. (1984). *Child sexual abuse – new theory and research.* New York: Free Press.

Finkelhor, D. (1986). *A sourcebook on child's sexual abuse.* Newbury Park, CA: Sage.

Finkelhor, D. & Browne, A. (1985). The traumatic impact of child sexual abuse: A conceptualization. *American Journal of Orthopsychiatry, 55*, 530–541.

Freud, A. (1946). *The psychoanalytic treatment of children.* London: Imago Press. (Original work published 1926).

Friedrich, W. N., Fisher, J., Broughton, D., Houston, M., & Shafran, C. (1998). Normative sexual behavior in children: a contemporary sample [On-line]. *Pediatrics, 101*(4). Retrieved December 7, 2005 from http://www.Pediatrics.org.

Gallo-Lopez, L. (2000). A creative play therapy approach to the group treatment of young sexually abused children. In H. G. Kaduson, & C. E. Schaefer, (Eds.), Short-term play therapy for children (pp. 269–295). New York: Guilford Press.

Gil, E. (1991). *The healing power of play: Working with abused children.* New York: The Guilford Press.

Gil, E., & Johnson, T. (1993). *Sexualized children: Assessment and treatment of sexualized children and children who molest.* Rockville, MD: Launch Press.

Ginott, H. (1959). Theory and practice of therapeutic intervention in child treatment. *Journal of Consulting Psychology, 23*, 160–166.

Griffith, M. (1997). Empowering techniques of play therapy: A method for working with sexually abused children. *Journal of Mental Health Counseling, 19*(2), 130–142.

Hall, P. E. (1997). Play therapy with sexually abused children. In H. G. Kaduson, D. Cangelosi, & C. Schaefer (Eds.), *The playing cure* (pp. 171–194). Northvale, New Jersey: Jason Aronson Inc.

Hall-Marley, S. E., & Damon, L. (1993). Impact of structured group therapy on young victims of sexual abuse. *Journal of Child and Adolescent Group Therapy, 3*(1), 41–48.

Harvey, S. (1993). Ann: Dynamic play therapy with ritual abuse. In T. Kottman & C. Schaefer (Eds.), *Play therapy in action: A casebook for practitioners* (pp. 371–415). Northvale, New Jersey: Jason Aronson Inc.

Homeyer, L. E. (1999). Group play therapy with sexually abused children. In D. S. Sweeney & L. E. Homeyer (Eds.), *Group play therapy: How to do it, how it works, whom it's best for.* (pp. 299–318). San Francisco: Jossey-Bass Inc.

Homeyer, L. E. (1994). *Play therapy behaviors of sexually abused children.* Unpublished doctoral dissertation, University of North Texas, Denton, TX.

James, B. (1989). *Treating traumatized children: New insights and creative interventions.* Lexington, MA: Lexington Books.

Jennings, S. (1999). *Introduction to developmental play therapy.* London: Jessica Kingsley Publishers.

Jernberg, A. M., & Booth, P. B. (1999). *Theraplay: Helping parents and children build better relationships through attachment-based play.* San Francisco: Jossey-Bass Publishers.

Johnson, B. (1987). The use of drawings in the treatment of child abuse victims. *Association for Play Therapy Newsletter, 6*(2), 1–3.

Johnston, S. S. M. (1997). The use of art and play therapy with victims of sexual abuse: A review of the literature. *Family Therapy, 24*(2), 101–113.

Jones, D. P. H. (1986). Individual psychotherapy for the sexually abused child. *Child Abuse and Neglect, 10*, 377–385.

Kaufman, B., & Wohl, A. (1992). *Casualties of childhood: A developmental perspective on sexual abuse using projective drawings.* New York; Brunner/ Mazel.

Kelly, M. (1995). Play therapy with sexually traumatized children: Factors that promote healing. *Journal of Child Sexual Abuse, 4*(3), 1–9.

Klein, M. (1932). *The psychoanalysis of children.* London: Hogarth Press.

Knell, S. M. (1993). *Cognitive-behavioral play therapy.* Northvale, New Jersey: Jason Aronson Inc.

Kottman, T. (2001). *Play therapy: Basic and beyond.* Alexandria, VI: American Counseling Association.

Landreth, G. L. (1987). Play therapy: Facilitative use of child's play in elementary school counseling. *Elementary School Guidance & Counseling, 21*(4), 253–261.

Landreth, G. L. (2002). *Play therapy: The art of the relationship* (2nd ed.). New York: Brunner-Routledge.

Landreth, D. S., & Sweeney, G. L. (1997). Child-centered play therapy. In K. J. O'Conner & L. M. Braverman (Eds.), *Play therapy theory and practice: A comparative presentation* (pp. 17–45). New York: John Wiley & Sons, Inc.

Levy, D. (1938). Release therapy in young children. *Psychiatry, 1*, 387–389.

MacFarlane, K., & Waterman, J. (1986). *Sexual abuse of children: Evaluation and treatment.* New York: The Guilford Press.

Mader, C. (2000). Child-centered play therapy with disruptive school students. In H. G. Kaduson, & C. E. Schaefer, (Eds.), *Short-term play therapy for children* (pp. 53–68). New York: Guilford Press.

Mann, E., & McDermott, J. F. (1983). Play therapy of child abuse and neglect. In C. E. Schafer & K. J. O'Conner (Eds.), *Handbook of play therapy*, (pp. 283–307). New York: John Wiley & Sons.

Martin, H., & Beezley, P. (1977). Behavioral observations of abused children. *Developmental Medicine and Child Neurology, 19*, 373–387.

Marvasti, J. (1994). Play diagnosis and play therapy with child victims of incest. In K. O'Connor & C. Schaefer (Eds.), *Handbook of play therapy: Vol. 2 Advances and innovations* (pp. 319–348). New York: John Wiley & Sons, Inc.

Mayer, A. (1985). *Sexual abuse: Causes, consequences and treatment of incestuous and pedophilic acts.* Holmes Beach, FL: Learning Publications, Inc.

McDonough, H., & Love, A. J. (1987). The challenge of sexual abuse: Protection and therapy in a child welfare setting. *Child Welfare League of America, 66*, 225–235.

McMahon, L. (1992). *The handbook of play therapy.* London: Tavistock/Routledge.

Moustakas, C. E. (1953). *Children in play therapy: A key to understanding normal and disturbed children.* New York: McGraw-Hill.

Moustakas, C. (1959). *Psychotherapy with children: The living relationship.* New York: Harper & Row.

Mullen, J. A. (2002). How play therapists understand children through stories of abuse and neglect: A qualitative study. *International Journal of Play Therapy, 11*(2), 107–119.

Myers, C. E. (2006). Play therapy assessments. In S. L. Brooke (Ed.), T*he creative arts therapies manual: A guide to the history, theoretical approaches, assessment, and work with special populations of art, play, dance, music, drama, and poetry therapies.* Springfield, IL: Charles C Thomas Publisher, Ltd.

Orenchuk-Tomiuk, N., Matthey, G., & Christensen, C. P. (1990). The resolution model: A comprehensive treatment framework in sexual abuse. *Child Welfare League of America, 59*, 417–431.

Perez, C. L. (1987). A compassion of group play therapy and individual play therapy for sexually abused children. Doctoral dissertation, University of North Colorado. *Dissertation Abstracts International 48*, (12A).

Piaget, J. (1962). *Play, dreams, and imitation in childhood.* New York: Basic Books.

Sagar, C. (1990). Working with cases of child sexual abuse. In C. Case & T. Dalley (Eds.), *Working with children in art therapy* (pp. 89–114). New York: Tavistock/Routledge.

Sweeney, D. (1997). *Counseling children through the world of play.* Wheaton, IL: Tyndale House Publishers, Inc.

Sweeney, D. S., & Homeyer, L. E. (1999). Group play therapy. In D. S. Sweeney & L. E. Homeyer (Eds.), *Group play therapy: How to do it, how it works, whom it's best for* (pp. 3–14). San Francisco: Jossey-Bass Inc.

Terr, L. C. (1983). Play therapy and psychic trauma: A preliminary report. In C. Schaefer & K. O'Conner (Eds.), *Handbook of play therapy* (pp. 308–319). New York: John Wiley & Sons.

Terr, L. (1981). Forbidden games: Post-traumatic child's play. *Journal of American Academic Child Psychiatry, 20*, 741–760.

U.S. Department of Health and Human Services, Administration on Children, Youth, and Families. (2003). *Child Maltreatment 2001.* Washington, DC: U.S. Government Printing Office.

Van de Putte, S. (1995). A paradigm for working with child survivors of sexual abuse who exhibit sexualized behaviors during play therapy. *International Journal of Play Therapy, 4*(1), 27–49.

Walker, L. E. A., & Bolkovatz, M. A. (1988). Play therapy with children who have experienced sexual assault. In Walker, L. E. A. (Ed.), *Handbook on sexual abuse of children: Assessment and treatment issues* (pp. 249–269). New York: Springer Publishing Company.

Webb, N. B. (2002). Play therapy crisis intervention with children. In N. B. Webb (Ed.), *Play therapy with children in crisis: A casebook for practitioners* (pp. 29–48). New York: Guilford Press.

White, J., & Allers, C. T. (1994). Play behaviors of abused children. *Journal of Counseling & Development, 72*, 390–394.

Wilson, K., Kendrick, P., & Ryan, V. (1992). *Play therapy: A nondirective approach for children and adolescents.* London: Baillière Tindell.

BIOGRAPHICAL STATEMENT

Charles E. Myers, M.A., LPC, LMHC, NCC, NCSC, RPT, is a Licensed Professional Counselor in the State of Texas, a Certified School Counselor and Licensed Mental Health Counselor in the State of Florida, a National Certified Counselor, a National Certified School Counselor, and a Registered Play Therapist. Mr. Myers is currently a doctoral student at the University of North Texas specializing in play therapy and works for the Center for Play Therapy. He has presented at the local and state levels on play and filial therapy, sandplay, and elementary counseling. In addition, he has served as a counselor in inner city schools, as well as providing play and filial therapy in a homeless shelter in Tampa and crisis counseling in the hurricane shelters in Dallas. Mr. Myers has also served in leadership roles for a number of professional organizations and currently on the Ethics and Practice Committee of the Association for Play Therapy.

Chapter 10

PLAY THERAPY TECHNIQUES FOR SEXUALLY ABUSED CHILDREN

Brian L. Bethel

INTRODUCTION

Nowhere could I have a greater sense of tragedy than when I consider the consequences young survivors of sexual abuse confront. Although the media frequently reports stories of children who have been sexually victimized, these accounts do not provide an accurate portrayal of the trauma survivors often experience.

For decades the issue of child sexual abuse has been examined in the mental health field. Yet, as the numbers of sexually abused children continue to increase, so does the controversy surrounding the treatment of these young survivors. Although several treatment models have been documented as effective treatment strategies for treating this population, no one approach has been accepted and most research encourages a multi-dimensional approach when treating survivors. Therefore, clinicians continue to explore new treatment approaches for working with this challenging issue.

Despite play therapy being used for a variety of children's mental and emotional problems, relatively little research has examined the effectiveness of its applications with young survivors of sexual abuse. As professionals continue to explore treatment options for survivors of trauma, a growing body of evidence is emerging regarding the use of play therapy for young victims of sexual abuse. This chapter will explore the use of three theories of play therapy with a young survivor of sexual abuse.

It is estimated that up to eighty thousand children are reported each year as victims of sexual abuse (American Academy of Child and Adolescent Psychiatry, Facts for Families, 2005). Additional research has reported that as many as 45% of females and as many as 31% of males are survivors of sexual abuse (Johnston, 1997). However, accurate statistics are difficult to obtain, as it is well suspected that thousands more cases of child sexual abuse go unreported. Hall (1997) discussed the lack of statistical data involving cases that are dismissed, as well as those cases that are never reported to authorities. Similarly, Costos and Landreth (1999) reported that statistical interpretations regarding child sexual abuse are complex, as there are a variety of legal definitions in each state of the country.

OBSTACLES TO TREATMENT

Children who confront issues of sexual victimization often experience a variety of emotional and psychological obstacles. Specifically, children who are survivors of sexual abuse commonly feel betrayed, overwhelmed, and helpless, which may further complicate the child's healing process (Namka, 1995). It has been documented that child survivors of sexual abuse frequently struggle with interpersonal relationships, feelings of insecurity, and social isolation (Middle and Kennerley, 2001). Likewise, Lisak (1994) also cited issues of anger, betrayal, fear, sexuality issues, feelings of helplessness, negative relationships, and isolation as common difficulties that young survivors may encounter.

Traditional models of therapy for child survivors typically focus on the child re-experiencing the trauma. Cognitive Behavior Therapy is commonly cited in literature for treating sexually abused children. This theory offers techniques that promote gradual to more frequent exposure to thoughts or objects that may trigger memories of the traumatic event (Deblinger and Heflin, 1996). Berkliner and Wheeler (1987) discussed the importance of family therapy of support groups as key elements in treating young survivors of sexual abuse. Like these models, most therapeutic approaches require young survivors to recall their traumatic experience or retell their story of the horrific event. These approaches can provide the potential for re-victimization during treatment.

Other challenges commonly encountered when working with child survivors of sexual abuse involve their attachment to the perpetrator. Children who are sexually abused typically know their offender. It is estimated that at least 85% of survivors know their offender (Whetsell-Mitchell, 1995). Young survivors frequently have ambivalent feelings regarding the perpetrator and the impact of the traumatic event(s). Child survivors struggle to find a balance between the prior positive experiences with the perpetrator and the feelings of betrayal that have resulted from the abuse. Although young survivors want the abuse to stop, many times these children express loyalty towards the perpetrator.

The legal system can also present obstacles in working with young survivors of sexual abuse. Children who disclose sexual abuse are faced with an unpredictable legal system with lengthy procedures (Gil, 1991; Brooke, 1997). These external forces can often serve to exacerbate symptomology for children through ongoing legal challenges and requirements for children to testify. It is common for survivors to experience an increase in anxiety-related symptoms when legal interventions are repetitive and ongoing.

Working with young victimized children requires skilled professionals who are familiar with the complex issue of sexual abuse. Thompson and Rudolph (2000) reported the treatment of children with a sexual abuse history could be overwhelming for counselors. According to Middle and Kennerley (2001), children who have a history of sexual abuse typically have more difficulty in establishing therapeutic relationships than nonabused children. Gil (1991) also cautioned clinicians regarding potential burnout and encouraged professionals working with abused children to implement appropriate self-care strategies.

RATIONALE FOR PLAY THERAPY

Because of the complexity involved when treating survivors of sexual abuse, creative therapists, educators, and researchers alike are continually exploring innovative approaches for working with survivors. For decades, clinicians have attempted to provide therapeutic interventions to these unique survivors. Yet, as recently as 1999, Costas and Landreth stated that there is no one accepted treatment approach for sexually abused children and encouraged professionals to use a multi-modal approach when working with survivors. Gil, (1991) acknowledged play therapy as the preferred technique when working with young survivors of sexual abuse. Likewise, Hall (1997) reported the use of play therapy as the most valuable technique when treating young children who confront sexual abuse issues. Leading researchers in the field of play therapy have documented the effectiveness of play therapy when working with sexually abused children. Specifically, Landreth, Homeyer, Glover, and Sweeney (1996) cited play therapy as an effective therapeutic approach for working with abused and neglected children.

Play therapy offers a unique approach for working with children. The therapeutic use of play offers young survivors a nonthreatening environment in which children can work to regain some sense of stability. With the specialization of play therapists, play therapy techniques have been popularly implemented in child therapy over the last fifty years (Kauduson, Cangelosi, and Schaefer, 1997). Unlike traditional therapeutic models, play therapy does not require children to cognitively re-visit past traumatic events. Conversely, clinicians can use child-centered play as avenues for children to regain a sense of mastery and control over their environment without necessarily reliving the trauma that they have experienced. It is important for professionals to identify both short-term and long-term goals when working with young survivors of sexual abuse. Interventions that are implemented to address immediate concerns after the disclosure would be identified as short-term goals whereas those techniques that address the healing process itself are more relevant to long-term goals (Hall, 1997).

Children who have been sexually victimized can use play as a means of expression in a safe and nonthreatening environment. It is common for young survivors of sexual abuse to engage in post-traumatic play. Terr (1990), noted that it is common for children with a history of trauma to re-enact the traumatic event via play. Professionals have documented additional themes of good and bad, submissive and dominant interactions, defeating bad guys, as well as sexualized play for children who have been sexually abused (Hall, 1997). Child-centered play therapy, Directive play therapy, and Filial play therapy have been most commonly examined in the literature for working with young survivors of sexual abuse.

CHILD-CENTERED PLAY THERAPY

Child-centered therapy, or nondirective therapy, grew out of the work of Carl Rogers. This model emphasized the philosophy of unconditional positive regard and being present with the child as foundations of the theory (Rogers, 1951). Landreth (1991) identified the term child-centered play therapy using these same standards. Like the work of Rogers, child-centered play therapy focuses on the relationship between the therapist and the child. It is believed that the relationship promotes effective treatment and a sense of mastery for young survivors.

Child survivors of sexual abuse frequently struggle with feelings of safety and insecurity. Cockel and Allan, (1996) indicated that child-centered play therapy is effective for the treatment of sexually abused girls, as it provides a safe atmosphere for child survivors to express themselves freely and be accepted. While safety and acceptance are important, additional therapeutic considerations should be noted. Gil (1991) reported that therapeutic interventions should be nonintrusive, as abuse itself is a violation of the child's boundaries.

DIRECTIVE PLAY THERAPY

Directive play therapy techniques are typically best implemented to address specific concerns related to the abuse a child has experienced. These may include techniques to address fear and anxieties, sexualized behavior, anger, and aggression. In my work with sexually abused children, I have used directive techniques cautiously and for a time-limited portion of therapy.

Using directive play therapy techniques, clinicians introduce specific play activities for a therapeutic goal. Gil (1991) described story-telling techniques, puppet play, and certain board games as directive therapies for children who are survivors of sexual abuse. Namka (1995) discussed cognitive restructuring as a directive technique implemented to dispute irrational beliefs of shame with sexually abused children. Directive role-play exercises can also assist children in addressing conflicts related to the abuse they have experienced (Hall, 1997).

FILIAL PLAY THERAPY

Filial therapy has been described as teaching parents to conduct play sessions in order to strengthen the parent-child relationship (Costas & Landreth, 1999). Guerney (1964) developed filial therapy as a means of treating children with emotional and behavioral difficulties. Similarly, Gil (1994) suggested Filial therapy as a successful intervention for parents of sexually abused children, as it teaches parents appropriate and effective skills to implement when responding to their child(ren).

It has been my experience that parents of child survivors may distance themselves from treatment for a variety of reasons. As Corcoran (2004) noted, parents might experience a variety of emotions when sexual abuse disclosures are made. Specifically, feelings of guilt, shame, and depression may be reasons that parents are not more actively involved or, in some cases, sabotage treatment efforts. It has also been common in my experience; parents have a great deal of anxiety that they may re-traumatize their child by engaging in therapy.

Despite these obstacles, research indicates that children who are sexually abused can greatly benefit from parental involvement. Costas and Landreth (1999) noted that filial therapy could provide the child survivor the opportunity to express their emotions while simultaneously gaining parental support. Corcoran (2004) also reported that parental support following a sexual abuse disclosure is one of the most significant factors that are beneficial for a child's short- and long-term therapeutic issues.

CASE ILLUSTRATION

Katelyn seemed like any other seven-year-old child when I saw her for the first time. Her hair was as golden as sunshine and tiny freckles dotted her fair face. She presented as a somewhat shy child initially, and was very timid to participate in her first counseling session. After introducing myself, Katelyn slowly made her way to my office holding her mother's hand tightly. Nothing in her appearance alone would have ever indicated the type of trauma this young child had experienced.

Katelyn's mother described her daughter as having mood swings and often was easily angered. Additionally, Katelyn had been experiencing nightmares and expressed extreme fears that her biological father would come and take her away. According to her mother, this child would continually check to make sure that the doors were locked and the blinds were pulled in the home. Katelyn's family also reported that this child was exhibiting regressive behaviors and poor social skills. It appeared as though Katelyn's intense fears, frequent mood swings, and the changes in behavior were puzzling to her family.

The initial phase of therapy was designed to address this child's fears and anxieties. After the first session with Katelyn and her mother, it was unclear if she would meet with this clinician individually. However, upon arrival for the second session, Katelyn independently made her way to the playroom. Because of the unknown reasoning behind Katelyn's anxieties, this clinician chose a nondirective play therapy approach. This was also beneficial in developing rapport between the child and clinician.

Kathlyn and her family assisted this clinician in identification of both short- and long-term goals. The family indicated that they would like Katelyn to be able to decrease her frequency of intense fears, mood swings and anger outbursts. These goals were listed as short-term goals for Katelyn. Long-term goals included assisting Katelyn in developing positive coping mechanisms and implementing these skills in real-life situations to maintain control over her mood and environment. Socially age appropriate behavior was also listed as a long-term goal.

Throughout the next several weeks, Katelyn became more actively involved in play therapy. On a weekly basis we proceeded down the hallway to my office with Katelyn eagerly asking, "Are we going to play today?" Through the implementation of play therapy techniques Katelyn and I quickly developed rapport. Initially, Katelyn was encouraged to engage in nondirective play and had free choice of play. This clinician reflected Katelyn's activity through verbal statements, which told this young girl that I was present and could identify with the emotions she displayed in her play activities.

After a few sessions of nondirective play therapy, Katelyn and I began to engage in more directive play therapy techniques. These techniques were intended to specifically address fears that she was experiencing. Lastly, Katelyn's mother was brought into treatment to assist her daughter in reinforcing therapeutic goals as well as serving as additional support.

During a game of "The Evening News," Katelyn drew a picture of her biological father as the top news story of the day and reported her thoughts that her biological father needed to be shot. She then drew several bullet holes in a picture of her father and disclosed that her father had touched her inappropriately. This was the beginning of a lengthy child welfare investigation in which it was suspected that her father had sexually abused Katelyn.

Nondirective play therapy permitted Katelyn the freedom of choice during her play activity. This clinician reflected verbal feedback regarding the child's play and emotions that were displayed throughout Katelyn's play activities. Themes of good and evil were apparent throughout the first session with Katelyn. For example, a superman miniature rescued a family from an evil dragon and ultimately killed the dragon leaving the family to live happily ever after. The intensity of the child's play was reflected back through verbal statements throughout the session. Feedback was provided in an attempt to offer acceptance and support to the child.

Any questions regarding rapport were quickly resolved by the third session when Katelyn demanded that her mother not talk to this clinician so she could have time to play. It was also during this third session that Katelyn found a small toy video camera and made the announcement we were going to be "news people." This became a frequent activity for us to pursue in therapy. For the first time, the child was inviting me into her play activities, which I interpreted as her being secure and trusting of the therapeutic relationship.

Katelyn resumed with "The Evening News" at the fourth session and ultimately made the disclosure of her own sexual abuse. The session began with this child announcing she had a news bulletin and proceeded to report "Daddy Ronny needs shot." Katelyn then drew a picture of her biological father with bullet holes throughout the picture and a yellow stick-like figure protruding from between his legs. Without hesitation Katelyn said, "Daddy Ronny does bad things to me."

Katelyn's disclosure became a transitioning point of therapy. Immediate concerns of safety and coping became paramount. Directive play therapy techniques were implemented in an attempt to assist this child in coping with her fears of her biological father. Safety concerns were noted throughout Katelyn's play activities in which she frequently built walls out of blocks and escape routes for miniatures she was using. Police and ambulances were common toys used in her play, which indicated themes of safety and control. Throughout the next several weeks, Katelyn participated in games that taught personal boundaries and safety planning. Treasure chests and safety boxes were made to reinforce safety plans as well as identifying support persons in Katelyn's life. Over time, Katelyn began to report feeling safe in her home and her nightmares began to decrease.

After safety concerns were addressed, Katelyn's therapy began to focus on anger issues reported by her family. Not unlike other victimized children, Katelyn exhibited a great deal of anger. Mood charts and anger thermometers were introduced to assist this child in gauging her level of anger and mood

Figure 10.1. "Daddy Ronny Needs Shot"

fluctuation. Cautiously, this clinician began to assist this child with recognizing physical cues to her own anger, which often correlated to triggers of the abuse. Once Katelyn began to recognize these triggers, play activities were used to assist her in developing more appropriate techniques for managing her anger.

Themes of guilt and self-blame were observed in Katelyn's play activity. The child's regressive behaviors were indications of her irrational beliefs regarding the abuse. Not only had Katelyn displayed regressive behaviors at home but also she often engaged in regressive play. Throughout the nondirective portion of treatment Katelyn was permitted to use any toys she wanted in the playroom. Themes of caring and nuturance were often exhibited in the child's play.

However, directive play therapy techniques were introduced to assist this child in gaining a sense of mastery and control over her environment. Therapeutic games including The Ungame, The Talking, Feeling, and Doing Game, as well as Feeling Posters were used to address feelings of guilt, shame, and a sense of security. These techniques also provided an avenue for encouraging Katelyn to dispute her irrational ideations. In an attempt to further validate Katelyn's feelings of security, her mother was brought into treatment.

Although Katelyn's mother was informed throughout the treatment process of safety plans and techniques introduced during session, her presence in the room provided additional value. Katelyn's mother began to engage in techniques that this clinician modeled throughout the child's play. Specifically, the child's mother began to reflect the child's feelings as well as the emotions she displayed during play. These responses appeared to strengthen the parent-child bond. Katelyn's mother could respond appropriately to her child's play without analyzing or asking intrusive questions. This allowed Katelyn the freedom to act out her trauma without feeling judged by her mother.

Including Katelyn's mother in treatment provided additional benefit to the therapeutic services. Although Katelyn remained active in therapy for several months, her mother was gaining skills that would further prove beneficial for assisting Katelyn in coping outside of the therapeutic environment. Through her mother's encouragement, Katelyn was empowered in overcoming her traumatic experience.

At the conclusion of Katelyn therapy, this clinician offered her an additional opportunity of playing "The Evening News." Whenever therapy became stagnant, we could frequently revert to this game created by the client to move through difficult topics. However, the last newscast was videotape with Katelyn and her mother doing a special report on helping young children who are survivors of sexual abuse. This provides an example of the insight and mastery this child developed throughout her course of treatment.

CONCLUSION

In conclusion, play therapy offers valuable approaches for working with young survivors of sexual abuse. The three theories of play therapy identified in this chapter are offered to enable clinicians additional creative strategies in working with child survivors of sexual abuse. Play therapy assumes that the child wants and has the ability to gain mastery and control over the trauma they have experienced.

Additionally, child survivors of sexual abuse can use play as an avenue in re-establishing control over their environment without needing to necessarily re-experience the traumatic event. These approaches promote independence and choice for young survivors while also providing coping techniques and supportive networks to the young survivors.

Although working with survivors of sexual abuse can be challenging, it can simultaneously provide professionals with rewards. It is encouraging to know that children can truly become survivors after learning of the tragic and devastating injuries they may endure. Children like Katelyn can adapt to the negative impact of sexual abuse but typically require assistance in supporting their difficult journey.

Clinicians should be continually aware of the potential for burnout and secondary trauma when working with this population. It is important to note that professionals must be cautious when treating this special population and utilize appropriate self-care strategies.

REFERENCES

American Academy of Child & Adolescent Psychiatry Facts for Families. (Updated July 2004). Retrieved July 16, 2005 from http://www.aacap.org/publications/factsfam/sexabuse.htm.

Berkliner, L., & Wheeler, J. R. (1987). Treating the effects of sexual abuse on children. *Journal of Interpersonal Violence, 2,* 415–434.

Brooke, S. L. (1997). *Healing through art: Art therapy with sexual abuse survivors.* Springfield, IL: Charles C Thomas Publishers, Ltd.

Cockel, S., & Allan, J. A. B. (1996). Nigredo and albedo: From darkness to light in the play therapy of sexually abused girl. *International Journal of Play Therapy, 5*(1).

Corcoran, J. (2004). Treatment outcome research with the nonoffending parents of sexually abused children: A Critical Review. *Journal of Child Sexual Abuse 13*(2), 59–84.

Costas, M., & Landreth, G. (1999). Filial therapy with nonoffending parents of children who have been sexually abused. *International Journal of Play Therapy, 8*(1) 44–66.

Deblinger, E., & Heflin, A. (1996). *Treating sexually abused children and their nonoffending parents: A cognitive behavioral approach.* Thousands Okas, CA: Sage Puplications.

Gil, E. (1991). *The healing power of play: Working with abused children.* New York: Guilford Press.

Gil, E. (1994). *Play in family therapy.* NewYork, New York: Guilford Press.

Guerney B. G. (1964). Filial therapy: Description and rationale. *Journal of Consulting Psychology, 28*(4), 303–310.

Hall, P. E. (1997). Play therapy with sexually abused children. In H. G. Kauson, D. Cangelosi, & C.E. Schaefer (Eds.), *The playing cure,* (pp. 173–194). Northvale, NJ: Jason Aronson.

Homeyer, L. E., & Landreth, G. L. (1998). Play therapy behaviors of sexually abused children. *International Journal of Play Therapy, 7*(1), 49–71.

Johnston, S. S. M. (1997). The use of art and play therapy with victims of sexual abuse: A review of literature. *Family Therapy, 24*(2), 101–113.

Kauduson, H. G., Cangelosi, D. & Schaefer C. E. (Eds.). (1997). *The playing cure* (pp. 173–194). Northvale, NJ: Jason Aronson.

Landreth, G. L. (1991). *Play therapy: The art of the relationship.* Muncie, IN: Accelerated Development Inc.

Landreth, G. L., Homeyer, L. E., Glover, G., & Sweeney, D. S. (1996). *Play therapy interventions with children's problems.* Northvale, NJ: Jason Aronson, Inc.

Lisak, D. (1994). The psychological impact of sexual abuse: Content analysis of interviews with male survivors. *Journal of Traumatic Stress, 4*(7), 525–548.

Middle, C., & Kennerley, H. (2001). A grounded theory analysis of the therapeutic relationship with clients sexually abused as children and nonabused clients. *Clinical Psychology and Psychotherapy, 8,* 198–205.

Namka, L. (1995). Shame busting: Incorporating group social skills training, shame release and play therapy with a child who was sexually abused. *International Journal of Play Therapy, 4*(1), 81–98.

Rogers, C. R. (1951) *Client-centered therapy.* Boston: Houghton Mifflin.

Terr, L. (1990). *Too scared to cry: Psychic trauma in childhood.* New York: Harper & Row.

Thompson, C. L., & Rudolph, L. B. (2000). *Counseling children.* New York, New York: Wadsworth Publishing Co.

Whetsell-Mitchell J. (1995). The many faces of child sexual abuse. *Issues in Comprehensive Pediatric Nursing, 18*(4), 299–318.

BIOGRAPHICAL STATEMENT

Brian L. Bethel is a Professional Clinical Counselor (PCC) and a Licensed Chemical Dependency Counselor (LCDC) who specializes in the treatment of abused and neglected children. As the Director of Outpatient Services for a community mental health center in south central Ohio, Mr. Bethel coordinates counseling services in a variety of venues. Mr. Bethel holds a Masters degree in Clinical Counseling as well as a Masters degree in Rehabilitation Counseling from Ohio University. In addition to his regular job duties, Mr. Bethel works as an independent trainer and consultant addressing child and adolescent mental health issues.

Chapter 11

"IT HURTS TOO MUCH." USING PLAY TO LESSEN THE TRAUMA OF SEXUAL ABUSE EARLY IN THERAPY

KEVIN O'CONNOR

INTRODUCTION

One of the most uncomfortable dilemmas faced by therapists who work with children who have undergone traumatic sexual abuse involves deciding when to bring the traumatic content into the play therapy sessions. The vast majority of therapists, particularly those who practice within a child-centered framework, believe children will bring traumatic content into the session themselves when they are ready to and able to do so.

> The therapist has no need to direct or lead the child to a particular topic or activity. The therapist allows the child to lead the way and is content to follow. What is important is not the therapist's wisdom but the wisdom of the child; not the therapist's direction, but the child's direction; not the therapist's solution, but the child's creativity. (Landreth, 2002, p. 108)

They firmly believe it is counter-therapeutic for the therapist to attempt to address the traumatic material earlier in the play therapy process. To do so would mean forcing children to address material with which they are not yet ready to cope and to risk both overwhelming the children and violating their trust in the therapist. As child-centered work is based on the premise the therapist's role is to support the child's inherent drive to self-actualize (Landreth, 2002), this position is entirely consistent with the theoretical model. However, clinical anecdotes reveal that many children can be in therapy a very long time (six months or more) and never venture near content related to their traumatic experience. Slowly, they seem to settle into a pattern of comfort with the therapy and skillful avoidance of any difficult content. If the therapist attempts to introduce the traumatic content at this point the child often becomes angry, feeling as if the long delay was a merely a planned deception on the part of the therapist, thereby escalating the sense of betrayal. Thus, therapists struggle with the decision of how and when to introduce the difficult and painful content that brought the child to therapy in the first place.

As a result of this dilemma, the general consensus among play therapists seems to be that one needs to have some period at the beginning of therapy during which the traumatic content is avoided and the therapeutic relationship solidified. Eliana Gil (1991) suggests, "because physical and sexual abuse are intrusive acts, the clinicians' interventions should be nonintrusive, allowing the child ample physical and emotional space" (p. 59). This stance is certainly confirmed at all of the seminars and workshops I conduct, where at least 95% of play therapists indicate they would spend a considerable number of initial play therapy sessions building trust with children who had experienced traumatic sexual abuse. Is there an alternative that would provide the child with more immediate relief and yet retain a solid theoretical foundation?

ECOSYSTEMIC PLAY THERAPY

The session and technique described in this chapter suggests one possible alternative conceptualization and is grounded in Ecosystemic Play Therapy (EPT) which was first developed in the 1980s. It was gradually refined over the next two decades and the reader is referred to the *Play Therapy Primer,* Second Edition (O'Connor, 2000) and *Play Therapy Treatment Planning and Interventions* (O'Connor and Ammen, 1997) for comprehensive presentations of the model. This brief presentation of EPT was first published in the The Japanese Journal of Psychiatry (O'Connor, 2005) and will give the reader a good summary of the model. EPT is the result of integrating "elements of several existing theories and techniques using cognitive developmental theory as an organizing framework . . . (and) a broadly systemic perspective called ecological or ecosystemic as the filter for determining which elements, of the theories or techniques of play therapy that were reviewed, should be retained or discarded" (O'Connor, 1991, p. vi). The term "ecosystemic" as opposed to "systemic" was used to convey the breadth of the approach as no system is excluded from the model. Further, the model recognizes the unique way children are dependent on, and minimally able to influence, the many systems in which they are embedded. Because of this dependency, ecosystemic play therapists must often be open to intervening more directly in their client's lives in order to affect a positive treatment outcome than would most therapists who work with adults. In fact, children are regularly brought to treatment not for internalized, neurotic sorts of problems but because they are negatively reacting to systemic problems such as crises experienced by their caregivers (medical, employment, marital, etc.), their siblings (medical, school, legal, etc.), their teachers, schools, and communities, to name but a few. The interactions children have with other systems shape their worldview (O'Connor & Ammen, 1997). Their worldview, in turn, affects children's ability to enjoy their lives and to function optimally on a day-to-day basis.

One of the central assumptions underlying EPT is the notion therapists can only be effective when they consistently work from an organized theoretical frame. EPT does not presume that one theoretical model is necessarily better than another. Therapists can be effective working from a psychodynamic, cognitive-behavioral, family-systems or other theory, so long as they use the theory consistently. Doing so allows the play therapist to present their child clients with clear and consistent interventions, both verbal and experiential. Like all good models of psychotherapy, EPT theory incorporates five essential elements: (1) a basic underlying philosophy, (2) a theory of personality, (3) a model of psychopathology, (4) a way of conceptualizing the overarching goal of therapy and, (5) a model of the therapeutic processes that result in achieving the treatment goals.

PHILOSOPHY

Most of psychology is rooted in a western, hard or natural sciences philosophy. The primary assumption of this model is there are right and wrong answers to be found for every question. The answers may change as we come to know more but eventually a *final* right answer can be uncovered. This philosophy tends to push one into black and white thinking and into making value judgments based on perceptions of the "rightness" or "wrongness" of a given behavior or situation. For example, this philosophical position would posit that one could come to a definite and universal conclusion as to whether sexualized contact between an adult and a child is always harmful. While EPT acknowledges the potential value of treatment and research grounded in a natural sciences philosophy, EPT is a theory grounded in phenomenology.

Phenomenology is a subject dependent (Giorgi, 1983) philosophy based on the notion we can never really know how another individual perceives the world, but we can attempt to come to such an understanding by considering the person's life and those experiences the person has had. That is, all knowledge is based on how we perceive the "facts." To give a very simplistic example, how do we know each of us sees the same color when we look at a cherry? All we really know is that whatever it is we see we have been taught to call that color, "red." In fact, colorblind individuals will still say a cherry is red even though their perception of the color is known to be different from that of others. When working with children, this also means trying to understand how their developmental level makes their experiences and worldviews radically different from those of adults.

The ecosystemic play therapist consistently assumes the information provided by each of the people involved in a case is accurate. When two people's stories differ significantly, the ecosystemic play therapist does not assume one or the other is mistaken or lying. Instead, the ecosystemic play therapist begins by assuming each person perceives the situation very differently based on his or her experience and understanding. Parents interpret reality from their developmental perspective and in light of their experience; children do the same. To override either person's experience is to deny its reality and to frustrate them to the point where they are very likely to resist change. Phenomenology serves to guide the strategies used by the play therapist to help client's engage in functional problem solving.

Phenomenologic subject dependency applies to us all. Therapists are not, somehow, magically excluded. How play therapists understand children and their problems will be affected by their own experiences and worldviews. This creates interplay between play therapists' and children's subject dependent perspectives. Therapy becomes a dance in which play therapist and child learn to move between each other's worlds in search of ways to improve the child's life.

The other effect of working within a phenomenologic frame is that one evaluates right and wrong only in context. In discussing the natural science philosophy, the notion of being able to determine the universal impact of sexualized contact between adults and children was mentioned. From a phenomenologic perspective such a determination would be impossible. Each adult's and each child's experience of sexualized contact is unique and occurs in a unique context. The potential negative impact of that contact can only take place in context. Even when evaluating a relatively innocuous behavior, context can make all the difference. Generally, parents who kiss their children goodnight are doing the "right" thing. But, most play therapists would agree that a parent who kisses their child goodnight for the twentieth time because child has fussed and whined for hours about having to go to bed is probably reinforcing a problem behavior rather than giving appropriate nurturance. In neither of these particular situations does the problem have anything to do with the potential sexual nature of a goodnight kiss.

The other philosophy that underlies EPT is humanism, an essential aspect of which is the evaluation of the "rightness" or "wrongness" of human behavior by the impact it has on others. In humanism, there is no external, absolute standard of right or wrong. A behavior is only considered problematic, and therefore the rightful focus of therapy, when it causes harm to the self or others. For example, lying is not inherently wrong. Lying might save a life or it might cause grave harm. To determine if the lie represents pathologic behavior the play therapist must take the impact of the lie into consideration. The ecosystemic play therapist uses a humanistic perspective to make decisions about those behaviors that are to be targeted for change in play therapy.

One of the great advantages to using phenomenology and humanism as the foundations of any model of play therapy is the degree to which these two philosophies lend themselves to work across cultures. By its very nature, phenomenology considers culture to be a very important lens through which people see the world around them. Those of Anglo descent tend to see and evaluate situations from the perspective of their impact on the individual while most Asian and Latin cultures are more likely to consider the impact on the family or community. Phenomenology gives equal weight to both perspectives. Similarly, humanism gives one a relatively neutral way of evaluating the impact of behavior. When a behavior is problematic only because it violates a cultural norm but does not, in fact, cause harm to the child or to others the ecosystemic play therapist will want to seriously question if that behavior should be the target of treatment. This applies irrespective of the culture in which one is practicing.

THEORY OF PERSONALITY

A comprehensive discussion of the personality theory underlying EPT is not possible in this short chapter. Here we will focus on two elements somewhat unique to EPT as opposed to other theories of play therapy. One is the concept of the child's underlying motivation. In EPT children are seen as motivated to get as many of their needs met as possible while avoiding as many consequences as possible. Children's basic needs are conceptualized in a manner consistent with the needs hierarchy developed by Maslow (1970). Even the most seemingly dysfunctional, self-destructive behavior children exhibit is considered to be their best effort to get their needs met. When behavior persists in spite of seemingly overwhelming negative consequences the play therapist must make an extra effort to understand the need the child is striving to have met. For example, many previously abused children persist in being very aggressive even when they face dire consequences. For them, the aggression meets their need for some sense of power and control (safety) over their interactions. Unless the play therapist can help the child find alternative ways of achieving a sense of power and safety, the aggression will persist no matter what sort of punishments are meted out.

In this model, the concept of children behaving badly in order to get "negative attention" does not exist. Children to not engage in problematic behavior with the intention of creating negative interactions with either adults or peers. They do not want to be punished, yelled at or hit. When they behave in ways that trigger such behavior in others, it is most often a poorly executed attempt at control. They enter into power struggles to gain some meager sense of control over their otherwise bleak lives and in their desperation and panic push the control issue so far it results in negative consequences. Unfortunately, the brief sense of power they gained along the way, the sense of not being a passive victim, is usually so reinforcing it will keep the behavior going in spite of the direst consequences.

EPT also maintains an extreme developmental focus. Developmental theory is

> the cornerstone on which the model rests; it is the template against which the child's history will be compared. Deviations or disruptions in the child's progress through it are the basis for formulating the major therapeutic goals and for designing the interventions that will be implemented within the play sessions. Finally it is the yardstick against which the child's progress is measured. (O'Connor, 2000, p. 93)

Children's needs and their ability to get those needs met are conceptualized from a developmental perspective. Finally, helping a child to resume a developmentally appropriate level of functioning in all aspects of his or her life is a goal for all children in EPT.

PSYCHOPATHOLOGY

Ecosystemic Play Therapy psychopathology is conceptualized in a manner consistent with both humanism and with the personality theory just described. Pathology exists when children are unable to get their needs met effectively and/or in ways that do not substantially interfere with the ability of others to get their needs met, that is, appropriately. Essentially, they have been blocked in their attempts to satisfy their basic drives. This blockage is often inextricably linked to a disruption of children's attachment relationships. By the time children are brought to therapy, it is often difficult to tell which came first the failure to get their basic needs met or the disruption of the attachment. These two factors then set off a third, as consistent, inability to get one's needs met and/or disruption of important attachments can interfere with children's developmental progress. The disruption in the child's behavior or pattern of reinforcement or the sheer energy required by children's attempts to cope with life can leave them without the resources necessary to continue to develop normally. Within EPT, true pathology is conceptualized as occurring when a child "repeatedly engages in behavior that does not get his or her needs met and is unable to generate alternative behavior or to engage in effective problem solving" (O'Connor, 1997, p. 240).

Children's ability to get their needs met effectively is always evaluated in a developmental context. The number and sophistication of children's strategies for getting their needs met should increase with age. The appropriateness of a child's behavior is also considered developmentally but the overarching concern is the degree to which the child's behavior interferes with or violates the basic needs of others. For example, the occasional use of physical aggression to get their needs met is expected in toddlers but not in young adults. However, because physical aggression interferes with others' basic safety needs it is always problematic. Thus, developmental considerations provide norms for evaluating behavior while humanism provides a basis for determining the degree of pathology.

Psychopathology is seen as originating from three possible sources. The origins may be individual to the child; the result of some biopsychological obstacles that make it difficult for the child to function effectively irrespective of the environment. Autism, developmental delays and learning disabilities are all examples of individual causes of psychopathology. Second, the causes may be interactional. The child and parent are both essentially functional individuals but when they interact, one or the other fails to get their needs met effectively and/or appropriately. The cause of the problem lies not within one person or the other but somewhere in the interaction between them. Lastly, one or more of the systems in which the child is embedded may cause pathology. The child is functional but a system such as school or a hospital make it difficult for the child to get his or her needs met. In many of the cases treated by play therapists, sources of difficulty can be found at all levels. The child has individual limitations that, in turn, lead to interpersonal problems and negative interactions with one or more systems.

GOAL/CURE

The primary goals of EPT are to:

1. maximize children's ability to get their needs met effectively and in ways that do not interfere with the ability of others to get their needs met,
2. maximize children's attachment to others as a primary way of ensuring they get their needs met in a socialized manner so as to avoid egocentrism and sociopathy and,
3. to return children to a level of functional development consistent with their biologic endowment.

As stated by Vernberg, Routh and Koocher (1992) the aim of therapy is to "help children regain footing on a developmental pathway more likely to lead to adequate adaptation in subsequent periods of life" (p. 73). The goal is to bring the child to a developmental level as close to age appropriate as possible and to even the child's development across domains. The play therapist works to have the child function as well socially as behaviorally or as well socially and behaviorally as academically. This is important because children whose functioning is uneven across domains often garner less support from their environments than do those whose functioning is uniformly low. A child who is clearly behind in all areas evokes sympathy from those who can see the child is clearly in distress. In counterpoint, teachers often see the child who does very well academically but is socially immature as being in need of excessive adult attention and by peers as the 'teacher's pet.' Neither of these views is likely to gain the child much support on a day-to-day basis. Similarly, when an obviously intelligent child is unable to perform academically due to emotional interference, the child is often criticized for not trying hard enough. More even developmental functioning will make it much easier for the child to get his or her needs met in daily life.

Lastly, "play therapists universally recognize that treatment has been successfully completed when the child demonstrates the ability to play with joyous abandon – this is what makes play therapy unique" (O'Connor, 2000, p. 7).

CURATIVE ELEMENTS

There are two elements of the EPT process that are viewed as fostering the resolution of psychopathology. One is the nature of the relationship between the child and the therapist. The other is the ability of the therapist to engage the child in developing problem solving strategies that enable the child to get his or her needs met effectively and appropriately. Simply put, the role of the ecosystemic play therapist is to create a context in which the therapeutic or curative elements of EPT take place. To accomplish this, the therapist provides children with experiences and cognitive/verbal explanations that alter their understanding of their life situation. With this new understanding, they are able to engage in alternative problem solving and to discover more effective and appropriate ways of getting their needs met. The alternative experiences are provided through the context of the relationship between the child and the therapist and through the play. The alternative cognitive/verbal explanations are provided through interpretation and by engaging the child in active, overt problem solving. It is not so much the specific solutions to problems that matter. It is the very process of experiencing something differently or understanding different possibilities for getting their needs met can have a profound positive effect on clients (Elliott, 1984). This is a basis of the solution-focused and constructivist techniques that emphasize helping people change the meanings they attribute to their experiences (e.g., Anderson and Goolishian,

1992; Eron and Lund, 1996). "Therapists need simply to help clients talk differently about their lives and to notice their own successes" (Eron and Lund, 1996, p, 31). With children, not only do they need to talk differently, they also need to experience different meanings through interactive and symbolic play (O'Connor and Ammen, 1997, pp. 11–12).

THE PRACTICE OF EPT

Up until this point, the focus of the discussion has been on the philosophy, theory, and basic assumptions that underlie EPT. We will now turn our attention to a brief discussion of the ways in which these are operationalized in the practice of EPT. One of the most unique things about EPT is that it holds the play therapist fully responsible for both the overall course of the therapy and for the course of each individual play therapy session, as well. Unlike child-centered models of play therapy, it is not the child who leads. It is the play therapist. This does not necessarily mean the play therapist is directive. It does mean the play therapist will provide direction and structure proportional to the child's developmental level. An EPT session with a child whose current developmental functioning is in the toddler range will be very structured and primarily led by the play therapist. This is true irrespective of the child's chronological age. Additionally, the problem solving done in the session will be grounded in activities and experiences as opposed to language and discussion. An EPT session with a child whose developmental functioning is in the late elementary school range will likely be relatively unstructured and the play will be used only to support problem solving that is primarily language based. The ecosystemic play therapist focuses on building a relationship with the child and then bringing his or her wealth of knowledge and life experience to bear in helping the child problem solve ways of getting his or her needs met effectively or appropriately within the supportive frame that relationship provides.

Playroom and Toys. Because the structure and content of EPT sessions can vary so much from one child to the next it is important for the therapy to be conducted in a room that serves as a neutral container for the process. An EPT playroom is rather sparsely decorated with as little permanent furniture as possible. The goal is to create an environment in which the child is more likely to attend to the play therapist than to any aspect of the room or its contents.

Role of the Therapist. One defining element of EPT is the role of the therapist which is defined as having three parts: (1) to establish a supportive relationship with the child; (2) to help the child find new ways of understanding and solving problems; and (3) to regulate the child's level of arousal during the play therapy session. The therapist is seen as being active, but not necessarily directive, in fulfilling all of these roles. When establishing a relationship, the ecosystemic play therapist does not wait for the child to become accustomed to his or her presence and to the sessions but works actively to create an engaging, directly interactive, and playful atmosphere into which the child cannot help but be drawn. Similarly, the ecosystemic play therapist engages children in active problem solving geared toward symptom reduction. And, lastly, the ecosystemic play therapist is constantly alert to the child's level of arousal during the sessions, ready to step in and engage or challenge children who are losing interest (Jernberg and Booth, 1999) or to structure, nurture, soothe, and comfort those who are becoming overstimulated (Jernberg and Booth, 1999). The good therapist is one who can use engaging, challenging, structuring, and nurturing in a manner that is empathically attuned to the child. The better therapist is one who can do all this and be playful at the same time (Jernberg and Booth, 1999). The hope is the child will rapidly come to see the therapist as a highly attuned and protective individual with a clear agenda that includes the child's welfare and happiness. Aside from building the therapeutic relationship and guiding the therapy process, the ecosystemic play therapist has serves as a mediator when conflicts arise between the needs of the child and those of other individuals in the family or systems in which the child is embedded.

Human beings constantly make compromises with respect to their needs as they interact with one another. A mother will give up sleep to care for her sick child. Siblings will share toys. Children will agree to do an unpleasant household chore to please their parents. Children will sit still in school just because the teacher expects it, even if it is developmentally difficult for them to do so. Children and families in play therapy often have a great deal of difficulty finding ways to compromise appropriately. The children no longer comply when they should and the parents may vacillate between making excessive demands and letting things go just to avoid a confrontation. Often the situation has been going on so long everyone seems to have trouble recognizing his or her own, or anyone else's, underlying needs. In the worst cases, the parent and child do not even seem to like each other any more. The parent (or sibling, or teacher, etc.) wants the child to meet his or her needs. However, nothing changes and the resentment grows. The ecosystemic play therapist recognizes the validity of each person's needs and helps them find ways to ensure that each need is met as much as is humanly possible. As people see others' needs can be met without necessarily sacrificing their own needs, each will be willing to move forward and engage in additional problem solving. The child who is afraid of being helpless can learn through play therapy he or she can still feel some sense of control while following a parental directive. Similarly, the parent who finds he or she can set a limit and still engage in a loving interaction through play with his or her child is also more likely to set clear limits. Engaging clients in the better recognition, compromise and gratification of needs is yet another way EPT incorporates culture-specific values into the therapy sessions.

The other key element of Ecosystemic Play Therapy that forms the foundation of this technique is the emphasis placed on the development of a clear, phenomenologically based treatment contract between the child and therapist. Usually, this contract is developed and articulated by the end of the intake and/or pretreatment assessment. In all cases, it would be discussed with the child prior to the actual beginning of the first play therapy session. This is not a contract in the traditional sense, in that it is not usually written out, nor do both parties sign it. This is simply a verbal understanding of what the child stands to gain by participating in therapy. The basis of the contract is always the reduction of some affect or symptom the child experiences as distressing and the replacement of that symptom or negative affect with more happiness and fun. The contract *never* specifies a change to behavior the child does not find personally distressing no matter how much that behavior may distress others. For example, a contract would not specify a child stop hitting others unless the child found some aspect of hitting distressing. Getting the child to stop hitting would be accomplished separately, by advising those in the child's environment to begin engaging in some very serious and consistent limit setting. The treatment contract might then become, "I know you get angry a lot and end up hitting people. Then you get punished and get even angrier. All that time being angry and being punished doesn't leave much time for having fun or being happy. So . . . our job will be to figure out what is making you so mad and see if we can't make it less. We can also work on getting a lot of your 'mads' out in here so you don't want to hit other kids so much. And, we definitely have to practice being happy and having fun because it is hard to have fun and be mad at the same time."

TREATMENT PHASES

Prior to beginning treatment, the ecosystemic play therapist conducts the initial intake session with the caregiver(s) alone. During this first session, the therapist gathers an intensive intake, that includes information on the child's developmental milestones, family system, the medical and legal history of the child and family members, and the caregiver's perception of the child difficulties (O'Connor and Ammen, 1997). The intake is completed during the following session when the therapist meets with the child. It is during this phase that the therapist conducts a mental status exam and gets the child's opinions about how the problem is experienced and how it should be defined (O'Connor and Ammen, 1997). The play therapy itself usually begins in the third session and is based on a comprehensive case formulation derived from the intake information. Consistent with a model described in the Theraplay literature (Jernberg and Booth, 1999) EPT is seen as progressing through five treatment phases: (1) Introduction and Exploration, (2) Tentative Acceptance, (3) Negative Reaction, (4) Growing and Trusting, and (5) Termination.

Introduction and Exploration. During this phase, the child becomes familiar with the therapist, the playroom, materials, and the general format of the sessions. For children with more severe pathology or greater developmental delays, this phase may take some time and may include helping them learn how to play. The establishment of a very specific treatment contract directly with the child at the outset of play therapy may be one of the ways in which EPT most differs from other play therapy models. By the end of the intake with the child, the therapist will present a potential treatment contract that focuses on the child's unmet needs. The therapist will select from those things the child has discussed in the intake the things that seem most distressing to the child and will define the purpose of therapy as trying to minimize these distressing things and maximize the child's enjoyment of life. The contract is never about creating change simply to satisfy others but rather emphasizes change that will concretely improve the child's quality of life. This contract/goal is frequently referenced in sessions with the child over the course of treatment and serves as the measure of treatment efficacy. After all, it would be difficult to say play therapy has been effective because the child changed in ways that satisfied others if the child is still unhappy. A parallel contract with the parents to help them focus on changing the child's problematic behaviors can also be made. When the contracts seem contradictory, it is up to the therapist to help both sides see how mutual problem solving can result in both sides feeling happier and healthier and, best of all, having a better relationship.

Tentative Acceptance. During this phase, children develop an initial positive relationship with the play therapist. They come to believe the therapist really does have their best interests at heart. One sign of the degree to which their acceptance is tentative, is their tendency to be happy to come to sessions so long as any difficult content is avoided.

Negative Reaction. This phase is not often discussed in other play therapy models but seems nearly universal. It is during this phase that children suddenly resist further participation in the play therapy process. They may complain about sessions or refuse to attend. They may attend but be very reluctant to talk or interact with the play therapist. The process that seems to underlie this shift is the stress produced by the growing realization that change is inevitable and uncomfortable. These children are beginning to come to terms with their dysfunctional beliefs and behaviors, and though they may want to change, they fear the unknown and resist it. The play therapist needs to remain firm in pursuing the treatment goals, while providing the child and family with a great deal of support during this phase.

Growing and Trusting. This phase takes up the bulk of the child's play therapy treatment. The therapist engages the child, and/or the caregivers, and/or those in the child's environment in active problem solving to ensure qualitative change. In this context, the phrase "problem solving" does not simply refer to a cognitive, rational exercise. Instead, the term is used more loosely to refer to all efforts at getting the child's needs met consistently and appropriately. An ecosystemic play therapist might help one child to better express emotion so that others respond more appropriately while helping another child develop specific strategies for coping with a bully at school. The problem solving process might be entirely covert in that the therapist is actually doing all of the problem solving and simply helping the child follow along. Or the process might be overt with the therapist training the child in basic problem solving strategies.

The support children receive from the play therapist in the previous phase enables them to risk making changes, and as their life situation actually improves, they embrace the work of play therapy. Children gain insight during this phase, and if sufficient experiential work is done, learn to apply what they have learned in the real world. This is often a good time to begin engaging the parents in treatment if the child has been seen individually up to this point.

As the child learns better problem solving skills the play therapist must work to ensure those newfound skills and behaviors generalize to the child's life outside the playroom. This is most often done by gradually increasing the caretaker's involvement in the session while fading the play therapist's involvement. However, because children are much more dependent on others in their day-to-day lives than are adult clients, ecosystemic play therapists may find themselves more involved with others in the child's environment. This may range from simple consultation or education with teachers to intense advocacy for the child in the legal arena. This ability to move between the world of the playroom and involvement in the child's real world characterizes ecosystemic play therapists, and requires both great skill and the ability to maintain excellent boundaries.

Termination. This phase is difficult for all clients but it tends to be particularly difficult for children as they are likely have formed a genuine attachment to the play therapist in addition to a working alliance. From their perspective, they are being rejected just as their lives have really improved and stabilized.

Termination seems like a punishment for improving and many children regress significantly in the face of it. Three things can make termination easier. First, focusing on the treatment contract throughout the course of therapy can help remind the child that therapy is work; work that will end when the goals are achieved. Second, giving children substantial warning that therapy is coming to an end (at least 4 sessions) and assuring they will be supported throughout the process will give them time to adjust. Lastly, making the last play therapy session a celebration of the child's gains can counter the child's sense of loss and focus on the bright future that lies ahead.

CASE EXAMPLE

In the following case example, the therapist recognized the symptoms of extreme trauma in a new client and determined the child needed immediate symptom relief in order not to present some danger to herself. Based on the two key elements of Ecosystemic Play Therapy just described the therapist designed a very intense cognitive and play intervention for the child's first intake-treatment session. That session and technique are described here.

Case History. Claire was six years old when the janitor repeatedly sexually abused her at her church. These episodes occurred when the children were in a playgroup and the adults were in a Bible study group. Unbeknownst to the teens supervising the children's group, Claire was lured away by the janitor who sexually abused her and then paid her for her "services." Though Claire never disclosed what was happening, the abuse was eventually discovered. The janitor was arrested and the case went to trial. At the trial, Claire became hysterical "because he (the perpetrator) wouldn't stop looking at me" and had to be carried from the courtroom. As she was carried out, the perpetrator said to her, "I will get you for this." Claire was not quite seven years old at the time.

Claire underwent a specialized six week treatment program for sex abuse survivors between the time the abuse was discovered and the time of the trial. She did well in the program and was not referred for further treatment. When she was eight years, old Claire was brought to back therapy by her mother. At that time, Claire had many post-traumatic symptoms. She had auditory hallucinations in which she heard her abuser talking to her. These were so predominant they interfered with her ability to complete her schoolwork. She had visual hallucinations in which she would see her abuser in her room at night. She had difficulty sleeping and had abuse related nightmares. She had become agoraphobic and had trouble going outside of her house and yard unless accompanied by her mother or brother. She had also begun burning herself with cigarettes on her hands and feet in an attempt to keep the hallucinations and emotional pain at bay. The event that caused her mother to bring Claire to therapy was an aborted attempt on Claire's part to cut her wrist with a rusty razor blade she had found. Finally, Claire was adamant she did not want to talk to anyone about her abuse.

It seems important for me to make a side comment to the reader before detailing the content of my initial contact with Claire. It is very difficult to convey voice tone in the written word. Through all of the following, I worked hard to make sure my voice tone was what can best be described as playful. This is tone is somewhat difficult to achieve as one has to take care to be neither sarcastic nor disrespectful. A playful voice tells the listener, "What I am about to say is difficult but it need not be deadly. If we approach it with a sense of lightness and humor, it is less likely to overwhelm us." At the same time, it is important to convey empathy and compassion. It is a matter of finding that balance between sympathy that is not maudlin and humor that is not callus that is the hallmark of playful empathy.

Initial Session. When I went to get Claire from the waiting room, she was down behind a chair hiding. I went over to her and said, "Hi, you must be Claire."

She looked around at the other people in the room and then back at me, "How did you know?"

"Well, your mom told me you didn't want to be here and you didn't want to talk to me. Then I came out here, and you are the only one hiding behind a chair, so I put two and two together and figured you just must be Claire." This got a smile. "As long as you are here, how about at least coming back and seeing my office?" As I said this, I reached out my hand to take Claire's. Note: In retrospect I consider this a technical error. I should not have put it as a question. I should have said, "Since you are here I want to show you my office. That doesn't require you to talk and I have some pretty cool toys. Let's go." This would have conveyed the same message and would have been much clearer and confident on my part. Fortunately, Claire had been so impressed by my detective work she was ready to come to my office anyway.

Once in my office, we both took seats and I began by saying, "I understand from your mom you really don't want to be here, but you absolutely don't want to talk about having been sexually abused." This was said in a very supportive tone, in spite of having introduced the forbidden content in the first sentence.

"No. I hate talking about it. I've had to tell tons of people all about it (social workers, police, doctors, lawyers, etc.) and every time I talk about it, it makes me think about it more. Then I get more scared and feel even worse. I just want to forget about it."

"I sure understand that. You've probably told this story twenty or thirty times, so how about we do something different this time?" Claire looked interested.

"How about I tell you? I know a lot about what happened from all the records and from your mom. I'll tell you about your abuse. But I may not get it all right, so if I make mistakes you jump in and correct me. That way, the only time you have to talk is if I mess up." Claire immediately agreed.

I began to tell Claire her abuse history in as much detail as I could, being relatively graphic. Claire listened intently and began to fill in details and make corrections almost immediately. In about ten to fifteen minutes, we had completed the most detailed version of her abuse history that had been obtained to date, and Claire actually seemed energized as opposed to drained. I sat back and said, "That was really great. We worked well together and you gave me lots of new information. We're done."

Claire looked confused, "You mean we don't have to talk about it any more?"

"Not for now. You told me a lot and now we get to rest and have some fun."

"So we never have to talk about it again? Because I hate talking about it. When I do it makes things worse." Clare said as she wriggled and looked at the ceiling.

"I understand that, but you don't look worse right now."

"No, this was easier because you talked. I don't like to talk about it." Claire replied, sliding all the way down in her chair.

"Well, we can't stop talking about because it will never go away if we do. You have tried not talking about it for two years and it is bigger than it ever was before. Now your abuser talks to you most of the time, you see him at night; he is in your dreams. This 'not talking' thing just doesn't seem to work for you."

"But when I talk about it I have even more dreams." By now Claire was outright whining.

"I understand that, so we need to find a different way of talking. For now, though, let's take a break and just play, because you already did such a great job of talking." At this we engaged in some silly play with some foam balls and some oversized puppets just to burn off a little energy. This also allowed me time to think about how I could frame the concept of catharsis for Claire and operationalize it into something fun, or at least nonthreatening.

At the end of our free play, I again talked to Claire about the fact that avoiding the topic of her sexual abuse history did not seem to be helping her. She again complained that talking about it was just too painful. At this point, I introduced a metaphor saying, "I understand that, so let me ask you a different question. Have you ever had the stomach flu, where you threw up a lot?" Claire nodded yes. "Well, at first you start to feel sick to your stomach and you just concentrate on trying not to throw up because throwing up feels so bad. You say to yourself, 'Don't throw-up. Don't throw-up. Don't throw-up.' until pretty soon you can't think about anything else." Again, Claire was nodding in agreement. "That is kind of where you are. You keep telling yourself not to think or talk about your sex abuse, but now you can hardly think about anything else."

"When you have the flu, you finally throw-up and it feels horrible but . . . when it is over you actually feel better. The problem is, you don't feel better for too long. Then you start to feel bad again, and again you start telling yourself not to throw-up, until that is all you are thinking about. That is sort of like you, too. You have a really horrible nightmare or a really bad day and you spend hours finally talking to your mom and feel better for a little while, only it doesn't last." Claire was totally engaged at this point.

"With the flu, your body keeps making you throw-up whether you want to or not, until you feel better for good. That is what we need to have happen in here. We need to find a way for you to get out all those awful feelings that are making you have bad days and bad nights. It will probably not feel good when the feelings are coming out, just like throwing-up doesn't feel good. But I can promise it will make you feel better every time, and I'm sure if we do it enough, it will make you feel better for good. So . . . instead of not talking about your abuse we're going to 'throw-up' your abuse every time. We are going to get out those bad feelings to make room for good ones, so you can spend less time feeling scared and more time feeling happy. And, once we've done it enough times, I'm thinking the good feelings will take over." By this time, Claire had moved to the edge of her seat and quite wiggly. She seemed anxious, but she also seemed so convinced the idea would work she was eager to get started.

"Since it would be boring to just sit here and talk more, I've invented a silly game to help get the bad thoughts and feelings you have about being sexually abused out. To get started we need to make lots of strips of paper." Claire and I proceeded to tear several sheets of $8\frac{1}{2}$ x 11 inch paper into approximately 2 inch strips until we had about thirty or so. Then I said, "OK, now we need to write something about your sexual abuse that still bothers you onto each strip of paper." Claire sort of slumped at this suggestion. In order to keep it moving, I encouraged her by reminding her many of these had come up while I was relaying her history and I began to quickly generate strips. "I hate it when I can hear *perpetrator* talking to me." "I hate it when I see *perpetrator* in my room at night." "It still bothers me that *perpetrator* gave me money when he abused me." "I hate being scared all the time." I worked as quickly as I could and Claire began adding to the list. In no time at all we had more than twenty separate issues written down.

"OK. Now for the silly game part, we are going to play the Throw-Up Game." Claire was laughing and looking a little anxious now. I pulled the wastebasket in front of her chair and said, "I want to make sure you get all these things out; that you throw them up so you feel better right away. Bend over the wastebasket like you were going to be sick." Claire was laughing nervously but did as she was told. I took one of the paper strips and read what it said out loud then crumbled it up. "Now make some throwing up noises so we can get rid of that thought." Claire leaned over the bucket and made some coughing sounds. "No, you're coughing. You don't get better from coughing. This is serious stuff, so you need to throw-up. Now give me some throw-up sounds." By now Claire was shaking her head at my silliness and laughing, but she did imitate throwing-up. I leaned over her and dropped the crumbled paper into the wastebasket. We continued this ritual of reading, crumpling, making noises, and discarding the papers until all the strips were gone. During the time Claire laughed a great deal.

When all the strips were gone, I got a small paper lunch bag and pulled them out of the trash and placed them in the bag making a comparison to an airsickness bag. Then I said, "Now that you have thrown-up all those bad thoughts and feelings I'll think you'll feel much better for at least a little while. You already seem better. You did a lot of laughing while we were doing all that serious work of getting out bad thoughts and feelings. Today talking about your abuse didn't seem so bad."

Claire responded, "No, it wasn't bad. This was fun and very silly."

"Good. I think you will feel better for at least a little while. But I'm sure we'll have to keep working on getting those feelings out. You have spent a lot of time keeping them in and they won't go away all at once. Just like the flu, the sooner we can get the throwing-up part over with the sooner you will really start to feel better."

At this point it was time to end the session. Claire said she wanted to take home the paper bag with all the strips of paper in it. I said, "That is disgusting. You don't take throw-up home with you. Gross!" Claire checked to make sure I was still at least half-joking with her. "The throw-up stays here. That was the point; to get them out so you'd feel better and have some time without them. Next week we'll look at these things again and see what ones still matter and play the game again, but in the mean time, the throw-up stays here so you can have a rest."

Claire was clearly very happy with the session. I repeatedly complimented her on how much hard work she had done and how much better she seemed to feel. I also assured her we would do both work and play every week until we got the bad feelings out and made room for some happy and silly feelings, and some time for fun. Claire readily agreed to come to the next session and bounded out of the office.

Rationale: In this session I adhered to each of the basic tenets of Ecosystemic Play Therapy while creating a playful, goal-oriented session for the child. Through the activity I established a supportive relationship with Claire. There is no question she left this session with a deep sense of my commitment to helping her reduce her symptoms as quickly as possible. There is also no question she left understanding that play therapy is just that – a real blend of both play and therapy, play and work. The throw-up activity also helped Claire "break set" and find a new way of understanding and solving some of her problems. Prior to this session she had hoped that locking her sexual abuse history away and trying not to think or talk about it would eventually make it fade. This activity helped Claire understand the benefits of releasing her thoughts and feelings as opposed to trying and control them. She also learned that not all conversations about her painful thoughts and feelings needed to be horribly serious and post-traumatic in and of themselves. The activity allowed her to master the expression of her thoughts and feelings instead of having these master her. Lastly, everything I did as a therapist in this session was geared toward regulating Claire's level of arousal. I wanted to be sure she could face content related to her sexual abuse without becoming overwhelmed by it. I also wanted make sure we did not let therapy become just one more situation in which Claire could avoid the material that had been festering inside her for two years. The former would have seriously over-stimulated her while the latter would have left her under-stimulated to the point of believing therapy would serve no useful purpose.

Subsequent Play Therapy Sessions. When Claire returned to therapy a week later, she virtually ran into the office and immediately announced she had not had a single nightmare since our last session. I let her know how thrilled I was that all of her hard work in the first session had paid off so quickly and so well. Claire beamed. We then talked about doing more work so more symptoms might go away. Claire was ready. She quickly said we needed to keep working because her other symptoms were still present but that she was really glad to have gone a week without nightmares. Since the nightmares had been on one of the strips of paper we created for the throw-up activity I suggested we review all the strips and see which ones we most needed to work on. Claire and I sorted the strips into three piles: still a big problem, sort of a problem, and not a problem anymore. There were a couple of strips we decided to throw away, and then we played the throw-up game again with all but one strip. One strip was selected to keep out for discussion and direct problem solving. This became the format for the beginning of the next half dozen or so sessions. It produced a very rapid reduction in Claire's symptoms and fully engaged her in the therapy process. As the need to use the throw-up activity to get sessions started abated, we used it less and less, eventually just engaging in more traditional pretend play and active problem solving.

CONCLUSION

Sexually traumatized children present special challenges for play therapists. These children are often multi-symptomatic and appear very fragile. Additionally, play therapists are faced with overcoming the social taboos regarding discussing sexually charged topics with children. The combination of these challenges with the child centered play therapy guideline that therapists follow, rather than lead, the child in session can combine to result in many therapist's having difficulty knowing when, how or even if to raise their client's sexual abuse content in the course of treatment. The Ecosystemic Play Therapy model presents an alternative strategy in which the therapist and child enter into an explicit treatment contract aimed at reducing the child's symptomatology. In this chapter, an intervention grounded in ecosystemic play therapy theory was presented as an example of how a play therapist might move to address a child's sexual abuse content very early in the course of treatment, so as to help produce rapid symptom reduction and quickly engage the child in the treatment process.

REFERENCES

Anderson, H., & Goolishian, M. A. (1992). The client is the expert: A not-knowing approach to therapy. In K. J. Gergen & S. McNamee (Eds.), *Therapy as a social construction* (pp. 25–39). Newbury Park, CA: Sage.

Elliott, R. (1984). A discovery-oriented approach to significant change events in psychotherapy: interpersonal process recall and comprehensive process analysis. In L. Rice & L. Greenberg (Eds.), *Patterns of change: Intensive analysis of psychotherapy process*. New York: Guilford Press.

Eron, J. B., & Lund, T. W. (1996). *Narrative solutions in brief therapy*. New York: Guilford.

Gil, E. (1991). *The healing power of play: Working with abused children*. New York: Guilford.

Giorgi, A. (1983). Concerning the possibility of phenomenological psychological research. *Journal of Phenomenological Psychology, 14*(2), 129–169.

Jernberg, A., & Booth, P. (1999). *Theraplay: Helping parents and children build better relationships through attachment based play* (second edition). San Francisco: Jossey-Bass.

Landreth, G. (2002). *Play therapy: The art of the relationship* (second edition). New York: Brunner-Routledge.

Maslow, A. (1970). *Motivation and personality*. New York: Harper and Row.

O'Connor, K. J. (1991). *The play therapy primer: An integration of theories and techniques*. New York: Wiley.

O'Connor, K. (2000). *The play therapy primer* (second edition). New York: Wiley.

O'Connor, K. (2005). Ecosystemic Play Therapy. *The Japanese Journal of Psychiatry, 19*(3), 273–284.

O'Connor, K. J., & Ammen, S. (1997). *Play therapy treatment planning and interventions: The ecosystemic model and workbook*. San Diego: Academic Press.

O'Connor, K., & Ammen, S. (1998). *The play therapy treatment planning workbook: An ecosystemic model*. San Diego, CA: Academic Press.

Vernberg, E., Routh, D., & Koocher, G. (1992). The future of psychotherapy with children: Developmental psychotherapy. *Psychotherapy Theory, Research, Practice and Training. Special Issue: The Future of Psychotherapy, 29*(1), pp. 72–80.

O'Connor, K. (1983). The color-your-life technique. In C. Schaefer and K. O'Connor, *Handbook of play therapy, Volume II*, pp. 251–258. New York, Wiley

BIOGRAPHICAL STATEMENT

Kevin O'Connor, Ph.D., RPT-S is a Clinical Psychologist and Professor. He is the Director of the Clinical Psy.D. and Ph.D. Programs and the Coordinator of the Ecosystemic Clinical Child Psychology Emphasis at the California School of Professional Psychology-Fresno of Alliant International University. He is the cofounder and now Director Emeritus of the Association for Play Therapy. He is the author of the *The Play Therapy Primer, Second Edition* and numerous articles on child psychotherapy and professional practice. He is the co-author of *Play Therapy Treatment Planning and Interventions.* He is the co-editor of the *Handbook of Play Therapy, Volumes I & II* and *Play Therapy Theory and Practice.* He regularly presents workshops across the United States and abroad including workshops conducted in the Netherlands, Canada, Israel, Italy, Japan, Korea, Singapore, Kuwait and South Africa. His areas of specialization include: (1) Ecosystemic Play Therapy, (2) treatment planning, (3) Attachment Disorders, (4) the use of interpretation, (5) conducting structured groups, and (6) the treatment of medically ill children. He also maintains a small private practice treating children and adults.

Chapter 12

BEYOND SURVIVAL: PLAY AND CREATIVE THERAPY WITH ADOLESCENTS WHO HAVE BEEN SEXUALLY ABUSED

LORETTA GALLO-LOPEZ

> I feel that adolescence has served its purpose when a person arrives at adulthood with a strong sense of self-esteem, the ability to relate intimately, to communicate congruently, to take responsibility, and to take risks. The end of adolescence is the beginning of adulthood. What wasn't finished then will have to be finished later.
>
> Virginia Satir (1988, p. 324)

INTRODUCTION

Virginia Satir provides us with a view of adolescence as the passageway to adulthood. Completing the tasks of adolescence, such as individuation, autonomy, increased competence, personal identity, sexual maturity, and the development of relationship skills, should, under ideal circumstances, lead to Satir's definition of a "finished" adult. But for adolescents who have been traumatized by sexual abuse, accomplishing normal developmental tasks may not be possible without therapeutic intervention and support. Sexual abuse compromises many of the tasks of adolescence, often keeping an adolescent stuck and unable to move forward developmentally. In order for adolescents to do the developmental work necessary to effectively move them into adulthood, the abuse issues that continue to impact their current level of functioning must be directly addressed.

This chapter aims to provide clinicians with an approach to treatment for sexually abused adolescents that directly addresses abuse issues, while supporting competency, engendering empowerment, and working toward establishing a positive self view.

MOVING BEYOND SURVIVAL

When I first began working with children and adolescents who had been sexually abused, professionals in the field – clinicians, researchers, authors – referred to our clients as "victims." Since that time, the label of "victim" has come to be viewed in a negative way, as something that allows people who have been abused to remain vulnerable and stuck in the victim role. The more hopeful term "survivor," commonly used today, allows those who have been abused to feel empowered and capable of moving forward, while offering an alternative to the victim role. Webster (1995) defines the word "survival" as the continuation of life or existence. As clinicians, our goal should be to help our clients to move even further, beyond survival, to envision a future in which their abuse no longer impacts their ability to create the life they deserve. In order to accomplish this goal, our therapeutic interventions must be purposeful, must be provided within the context of the lives of individual clients, and must directly examine unresolved abuse issues (Gil, 1996). An effective treatment approach will attempt to meet adolescents where they are, as opposed to dragging them kicking and screaming to where the therapist might like them to be. Treatment goals much be individualized based on the needs of each client.

Sexually abused adolescents may present with any number of symptoms, including but not limited to distorted body image, feelings of guilt and shame, a skewed view of sexuality and their own sexual identity, negative self-image, threats to personal safety due to risk-taking behaviors, depression, panic, displaced anger and/or rage, suicidal ideation, and self-injurious behaviors (Browne and Finkelhor, 1986; Finkelhor and Browne, 1986; Gil, 1996). Sexually abused adolescents often feel powerless over their own lives and may act out in an attempt to retrieve some sense of control.

The focus of this chapter is to provide the reader with expressive and play therapy interventions for use in working with adolescents who have been sexually abused. However, there is no set of interventions, techniques, or activities that will be truly effective unless the client and therapist have made a connection. This is true for any therapist and client, but is especially true for therapists working with adolescents. Connecting with an adolescent can be a tricky endeavor. Most adolescents come to therapy at the insistence of someone else, so they may already be somewhat resistant to the process. Some clinicians working with adolescents fall into the trap of taking on the role of the punitive, lecturing authority figure, while others leap to the other extreme, hoping the adolescent will view them as a friend. Obviously neither stance will support the development of an effective therapeutic relationship. Engendering trust is paramount, as is accepting that resistance and rebellion are natural, and possibly necessary, features of adolescence.

Emunah (2005) describes adolescent rebelliousness as a "necessary aspect of the adolescent's dramatically changing self-identity" (p. 109). Adolescents often rebel in an attempt to resist treatment. The resistance often represents a fear of rejection, of being judged, lied to or betrayed. Emunah (2005) describes an approach to treatment that enables the therapist to join with and support the adolescent's resistance, with the goal of engaging the adolescent and minimizing fear and anxiety. Emunah's approach allows adolescents to "behave as they actually feel" (p. 111). She describes a drama therapy session during which a fourteen-year-old client insisted he was not going to get out of his chair or participate in the activity. Emunah playfully instructed the boy to try as hard as he could to stay put in his chair. Additionally, Emunah gently took hold of his arms and attempted to pull him out of his chair into a standing position. As the boy struggled to remain in his chair, his obstinate and hostile posture became one of playful interaction, enabling his therapist to break through the resistance and begin to establish a relationship.

The goals of treatment for adolescent survivors of sexual abuse will vary from client to client. It would be useless, and possibly even harmful, for therapists to follow a rigid treatment protocol that does not necessarily meet the needs of an individual client. Within the treatment process, the abuse will need to be addressed directly in order for positive change to occur. Healing cannot be complete without working to rebuild and repair the wounds caused by the abuse and trauma. Interventions should be incorporated that seek to enhance the adolescent's sense of empowerment, support competency, mastery and the development of a sense of personal power and safety, and improve the way adolescents see themselves in the world.

WHY PLAY THERAPY?

Discussing sexuality issues with an adult, either one-on-one or in a group setting, is likely to be one of the most anxiety-producing experiences imaginable to an adolescent. Yet, this is what we expect of adolescents involved in sexual abuse treatment. Verbal therapy alone does not afford the level of emotional distance that many adolescents need to feel safe and comfortable dealing with emotionally loaded issues. A play therapy approach, utilizing puppets and dollhouse play, sand tray work, role play, mask work, art or other expressive activities, allows adolescents the opportunity to employ projection and various levels of emotional distance to safely address the most difficult issues. Many clinicians may worry that adolescents will be resistant to playing, and view play as too childish or embarrassing. Although the play of adolescents differs from the play of younger children, in that it tends to be more interactive, structured, and reality based (Tysse Breen and Dahlgren Daigneault,

1998), I have found most adolescents quite willing to engage in creative and playful activities. Often an adolescent will spontaneously pick up a toy left out on a table and begin to play while engaged in conversation. Most adolescents cannot resist digging their fingers through the sand tray or rearranging the furniture in the dollhouse. For instance, Danny, an eighteen-year-old male client, would make his way over to the dollhouse during the last few minutes of his therapy sessions and pile the furniture into stacks, or arrange the dollhouse figures in funny or sexual positions. As his treatment progressed he would spend more and more time engaged in what he called "messing with" the dollhouse, eventually engaging the figures in dramas and stories which often mirrored his own experience of abuse and trauma.

Play, when used appropriately and responsibly, can be an incredibly powerful intervention. The symbolic nature of play, especially for adolescents who may be stuck developmentally, supports a deeper level of exploration and self disclosure then would likely be possible through a purely verbal intervention.

The play therapy interventions presented here are just a sampling of the many activities and approaches that have proved useful in meeting the treatment needs of sexually abused adolescents. They can be used in the order in which they appear here, or in any order which best meets the needs of individual clients. Remember to work with, not against, resistance and rebellion, and to encourage clients to "behave as they actually feel" (Emunah, 2005, p. 111).

PLAY THERAPY INTERVENTIONS

Self Portrait. An adolescent's self portrait can reveal much about his or her self view. Self portraits done early in the treatment process, during the first or second session, establish a baseline to measure possible change over the course of treatment (Cockle, 1994). Adolescents can be asked to draw self portraits at varying intervals throughout the treatment process. The portraits can be examined by both the therapist and the client, and changes can be noted and discussed.

Spectrogram. A spectrogram is an intervention based in sociodrama that allows clients to make comparisons between themselves and others, or to identify their own feelings or attributes along a spectrum. In a group of thirteen- to fifteen-year-old girls who had been sexually abused, a spectrogram was used in one of the initial sessions. The focus of the activity was to enable the girls to interact in a playful nonthreatening way and to set the tone for the playful approach of the treatment program. The girls were instructed to line themselves up based on the number of days until their next birthday. In order to accomplish this task, the girls had to communicate with each other and share some nonthreatening personal information. Next, they were asked to place themselves in a line based on the distance they traveled to attend the group. This question required a greater level of trust, in that more personal information was being revealed. The girls had to share information about where they lived, which inevitably led to them sharing information about where they went to school and what grade each girl was in. This simple activity allowed the girls to begin to form relationships.

In individual therapy, a spectrogram can be created using a rope on the floor with each end symbolizing different ends of a spectrum of opinion or feeling, such as love and hate, or none and a lot. The client is then asked to show how she feels about such benign issues as broccoli, chocolate ice cream, a popular band, or math. As treatment progresses, the spectrogram could be used to explore more personal issues, such as the number of friends a client has, the number of schools attended, or the perceived level of competence related to a particular task. Clients who are resistant to movement can create a spectrogram on a dry erase board or a large sheet of drawing paper, and point to or circle the point on the line that represents the given response. This activity comfortably leads to more in-depth conversation, and affords the therapist a playful way to begin to help adolescents explore personal issues.

Today, Yesterday, Tomorrow. Similar to the self portrait, this is an activity that can be done several times throughout the treatment process. The client is given three sheets of paper and is asked to draw herself in the present, then to draw herself as she was ten years ago, and finally to draw herself ten years into the future. The client is then asked to write or speak as herself at each age and to tell about her life. Details should include, where and with whom the client lives, happiest and saddest experiences, wishes, fears, and accomplishments. The narrative allows for the creation of either a reparative or historical self view.

Tamara, a fourteen-year-old, was sexually abused by a day care provider when she was four-years-old and then again by her mother's boyfriend at the age of fourteen. Her mother's drug use had resulted in the family being homeless for periods of time. Tamara remembered being sexual abused when she was four-years-old but could not recall many details. She engaged in the "Today, Yesterday, Tomorrow" drawing activity on two occasions during the time she was in therapy. Tamara enjoyed writing, and wrote long narratives to accompany the drawings. Her first set of drawings were done during one of her initial sessions. In the drawing of herself at twenty-four-years old, she drew herself standing in front of a nondescript gray house. She stood next to a large expensive-looking car. Her mother could be seen in the house peering at Tamara through one of the windows. Her narrative described her favorite activity to be cruising around town in her big new car. She indicated that she lived with and cared for her mother who was "old and sick." Tamara's second set of drawings were done after six months of therapy. Tamara's view of her future was brighter and more hopeful. Her twenty-four-year-old self was pictured in front of colorful house building a snowman. As a child who had lived all of her life in a southern climate, seeing snow had always been one of her dreams. It also signified Tamara's desire to move on and to build her own life and her belief that she was capable of doing so. She reported that she had graduated from college and was working as a writer for a magazine. She indicated that she shared her home with several friends and that together they traveled and spent their free time doing fun things together.

Inner Resources Drawing. Mills (1999), views her creative approach to healing work as a way "to help you to see life's scars as markers of where you have been, not where you are going" (p. 6). Her Inner Resource Drawing activity enables clients to look within themselves for the strength to heal and move forward. The client is first asked to draw the pain, anxiety, or fear that they feel, or to draw a specific problem that is an obstacle in their healing process. The client is then asked to draw a picture of what that pain, anxiety, fear or problem would look like if it were all better. Finally, the client is asked to draw a picture of "the healing bridge" i.e., what would turn picture one into picture two. This activity allows adolescents to feel a sense of control over feelings or events that had previously been viewed as beyond their control. It offers adolescents a broader perspective on problem solving and a means of identifying personal resources that they can access to assist in the healing process and improve overall functioning.

Dollhouse Figures. Dollhouse figures allow adolescents to utilize their childlike qualities to explore issues and experiences through play. The figures can be used within the dollhouse or on the floor or a table. A client should be asked to choose a given number of items, or any amount he or she chooses, from a collection of people figures, animals, environment pieces, and other objects. The client should then be asked to create a story, with or without an assigned theme. In a more directive approach, the client is asked to use the figures and objects to enact the disclosure of their abuse. This approach allows adolescents to begin to discuss their abuse experiences form the perspective of the initial disclosure of the abuse. Questions such as: "how and to whom was the abuse disclosed?" and "what was the initial response of the people in your life?" help to establish a focus and move the adolescent toward deeper exploration of feelings.

Tina, a fourteen-year-old who had been sexually abused by her biological father, used this activity as a means of creating a different response to her disclosure. Tina was not believed or supported by her mother or other family members. Her mother was disabled and was physically, emotionally, and financially dependent on her husband. Tina's father denied the abuse allegations and accused Tina of lying about the abuse and of being a liar in general. As a result, no charges were ever filed against Tina's father. Because the department of children's services could not guarantee her safety, Tina was removed from her family and placed in foster care. In her enactment with the dolls, Tina initially played the events of her disclosure as they had actually happened. After processing her feelings related to her father's denial and her mother's inability to support her, Tina created a new version of her story. In this revised version, Tina's mother believed and supported her daughter and Tina's father admitted to abusing her and asked her forgiveness.

Music. Music has been an integral part of the lives of generations of adolescents. Music is one of the elements that enables adolescents to distinguish themselves from previous generations. It gives them a peer group to connect with, heroes to admire and emulate, and provides a sense of identity. Many adolescents make emotional connections with the music that they listen to, based either on the lyrics or the music itself. Music can be utilized quite effectively in therapy with adolescents. Showing an interest in what is important to adolescents is validating and communicates a respect for their choices.

Ben, a thirteen-year-old who had been sexually abused by his uncle liked to challenge his therapist by asking her to identify song lyrics he would recite to her. A song that he referred to several weeks in a row was by a popular band and told of broken dreams and feeling totally alone. The therapist suggested that she and Ben search for the lyrics on an Internet site. They downloaded the lyrics and read through them and sung the song together. Ben was able use the song to communicate to his therapist how alienated and stigmatized he felt as a result of his sexual abuse and how he isolated himself in response to those feelings. Ben and his therapist discussed referring Ben to a group for adolescent boys who had been sexually abused as a way of helping Ben to feel less stigmatized and alone. Ben, who had been resistant at first to becoming involved in group treatment, agreed to give it a try.

Role-Play. Role-play and other forms of dramatic enactment provide adolescents with powerful tools for the safe exploration of issues, concerns, fears, and emotions (Gallo-Lopez, 2005). Role-play offers an opportunity to discover alternatives and experiment with solutions. Role-play is most conducive to group work and family therapy, but can be utilized successfully in individual therapy through the use of soliloquy and the empty chair technique. Several sets of cards can be created including feelings cards, theme cards, and conflict cards. Other card sets might include words identifying who, where, and when. Cards from one or more sets can be chosen blindly by participants, or assigned by the therapist in order to guide the enactment in a particular direction. Enactment can involve pure improvisation, where a scene is created on the spot without discussion, or can be planned by participants and then "performed" for the rest of the group. Role-play can also involve more spontaneous dramatic enactments with participants deciding on the theme, characters, etc., and then acting out the scene. Enactments with adolescents who have been sexually abused often involve themes such as court scenes, arrests, family conflicts, and violence. In a group in which fourteen-year-old Tina participated, members were angry that Tina's father had not been prosecuted for his abuse of Tina. They felt it was unfair that Tina was forced to live in foster care while her father remained at home. They decided to create a mock trial taking on the roles of prosecutor, judge, witnesses, and jury, with Tina's father as the defendant. He was, of course, convicted and forced to accept responsibility for his crimes.

IF THE WALLS COULD TALK

If The Walls Could Talk is a powerful intervention outlined by psychologist and psychodramatist Dayton (1994) in her book *The Drama Within.* This intervention allows clients to explore issues from the emotionally distanced perspective of the wall of a given room. Providing emotional distance from an issue which a client might find too difficult to address directly enables the client to safely explore issues that might otherwise remain repressed or unresolved.

Kelly, a fifteen-year-old, had been sexually abused by her stepfather from the time she was five years old, about a year after he married her mother. The abuse was disclosed when Kelly gave birth to her stepfather's baby. Kelly insisted she loved her stepfather and that they would be together when he was released from prison. She felt responsible for his incarceration and the fact that her baby would be growing up without her father. She refused to hold her stepfather responsible or accountable for the sexual abuse, insisting that she was a willing participant from the beginning. Kelly was quite resistant in therapy but enjoyed drawing and was usually willing to participate in art activities. Kelly was asked to close her eyes and envision the room that she slept in when she was five years old. She was then asked to draw her room on the paper provided. Kelly drew the pink flowered wallpaper, the sheets with cartoon characters, and the fluffy stuffed animals that lined her bed. Then she drew herself in the bed dressed in her Barbie nightie. Kelly was then asked to pretend that she was the walls of the room, witnessing the first incidence of sexual abuse of Kelly by her stepfather. Kelly refused at first to continue the activity. She was asked if she would prefer to write in the voice of the wall, rather then speak it and she agreed. Kelly hesitated, writing very slowly at first, and closing her eyes every so often. "The wall" described a little girl sleeping while cuddling her favorite stuffed toy. "The wall" told of the child being woken and touched by a man and of the child appearing frightened and confused and beginning to cry. As Kelly continued to write in the voice of her bedroom wall, she began to see herself as the vulnerable five-year-old who, in reality, could not and did not consent to the sexual abuse by her stepfather. She also connected with her child self from a new perspective, that of a mother. As she recognized her own child's innocence and vulnerability she began to see her stepfather's culpability and began to hold him responsible.

Telephone Call. Adolescents love telephones. This activity capitalizes on that love by asking adolescents to use the telephone to explore relationships and to feelings related to the people in their lives. Several real but nonworking phones are placed in the center of the room during a group session or on a table in front of the adolescent during an individual session. The therapist plays a tape recording of a ringing phone and the adolescent is asked to answer one of the phones. The adolescent can be asked to speak to someone with whom they have had no contact in some time, or to speak to their best friend about their day. The therapist can suggest who the person on the other end of the line might be or the adolescent can speak to someone of their own choosing. The telephone call can be used as a way to engage a resistant adolescent or to explore the dynamics of a given relationship.

Theresa, a fifteen-year-old living in a foster home, had been in sixteen different placements in her life. She was removed from her parent's custody as a toddler and had little memory of them. For six years, she was moved between various family members' homes until being placed in foster care at the age of nine when it was found that several of her uncles had been molesting her on a regular basis. Due to her difficulty trusting and forming relationships, Theresa had an especially difficult time in foster care. Her intense anger and continued acting-out behavior got her moved from foster home to foster home, validating her view of herself as unlovable. She was currently in a foster home with a family who wanted to adopt her, and Theresa was doing everything in her power to avoid bonding with them. During an individual therapy session, Theresa was asked to answer a "ringing" phone and to speak to someone with whom she'd had no contact in some time. Theresa then began a dialogue with her biological mother. She expressed love to her mother, told her how much she missed her and expressed a sense of loss and feeling abandoned by her mother at such a young age. She went on to express anger at her mother for not being able to take care of her and for not protecting her from her abusing uncles. Theresa wept as she continued to pour out her feelings to her mother. Theresa was later asked what message she would want to hear back from her mother if her mother could respond. Theresa indicated that she would want to hear her mother say "I love you and I'm sorry." Theresa "spoke" to her mother several more times, attempting to resolve some of her deep hurt and forge a sense of connectedness. Over time she was able to accept affection from her foster mother and to even entertain the idea of being adopted.

Self Identity Collage. Collages provide a creative alternative to drawing for adolescents who are resistant to drawing, and also provide a unique form of self expression for adolescents in general. The self identity collage utilizes a silhouette drawing of the client as the foundation for the collage. Using a flashlight to create a silhouette, the shadow of the client's face is traced onto a sheet of paper fastened to the wall. If the shadow created is clear and distinct, the silhouette will be a good likeness of the client. The adolescent is then instructed to use words, photographs, images from newspapers and magazines and any other objects or images to create a collage that represents who they are.

Sand Tray. Theresa Kestly (2005) advocates the use of sand tray therapy with adolescents, especially those who are survivors of sexual abuse. She maintains that the dimensions of the sand tray allow clients access to all areas of the tray, affording a sense of control over the space. Kestly asserts that the sand tray offers trauma survivors an opportunity to "reestablish their sense of control" (p. 24). As adolescents attempt to separate and individuate, many experience a loss of identity as they attempt to distance themselves from their pasts, without a clear and hopeful vision for the future. As adolescents play in the safety of the sand tray, they are able to explore and create a more positive vision of their future and of who and what they want to become. (Kestly, 2005).

The sand tray can be used in a variety of different ways and at different points in the therapy of adolescent sexual abuse survivors. Two themes that are especially appropriate for work with abuse survivors are creating a safe place and creating the future. The first theme provides adolescents with the opportunity to explore and identify the objects or people that will enable them to feel safe and to create that sense of safety in the sand tray. When adolescents are asked to build a scene depicting their life ten or fifteen years into the future, the hope is that they will be able to utilize the skills and the strengths gained in therapy to orient them toward a future where they feel safe, competent, and empowered.

CONCLUSION

The normal developmental tasks of adolescence are often severely compromised by the trauma of sexual abuse. Adolescents may find themselves unable to effectively move forward until trauma issues are resolved. The normal adolescent responses of rebellion and resistance complicate things even further. Playful and creative approaches to therapy enable adolescents to examine and work toward resolving significant issues in a supportive non-threatening environment and with the benefit of emotional distance and projection. This chapter presented an approach to treatment for adolescent survivors of sexual abuse that seeks to balance a respect for the adolescents developing sense of maturity and self identity while relying on the playfulness and childlike qualities inherent in most adolescents. A philosophy of treatment which allows adolescents to "behave as they actually feel" (Emunah, 2005, p. 111), supports this respectful approach and enhances the adolescent's ability to benefit from the therapeutic process.

REFERENCES

Browne, A., & Finkelhor, D. (1986). Initial and long-term effects: A review of the research. In D. Finkelhor, (Ed.), *A Sourcebook on Child Sexual Abuse.* Newbury Park, CA: SAGE Publications, Inc.
Cockle, S. (1994). The self-portrait technique. *International Journal of Play Therapy, 3*(1), 37–55.
Dayton, T. (1994). *The Drama Within.* Deerfield Beach, FL: Health Communications Inc.
Emunah, R. (2005). Drama therapy and adolescent resistance. In A. M. Weber & C. Haen, (Eds.), *Clinical applications of drama therapy in child and adolescent treatment.* New York: Brunner-Routledge.
Finkelhor, D., & Browne, A. (1986). Initial and long-term effects: A conceptual framework. In D. Finelhor, (Ed.), *A Sourcebook on Child Sexual Abuse.* Newbury Park, CA: SAGE Publications, Inc.
Gallo-Lopez, L. (2005). Drama therapy with adolescents. In L. Gallo-Lopez & C.E. Schaefer, (Eds.), *Play therapy with adolescents.* New York: Jason Aronson.
Gil, E. (1996). *Treating Abused Adolescents.* New York: The Guilford Press.
Kestly, T. (2005). Adolescent sandtray therapy. In L. Gallo-Lopez & C.E. Schaefer, (Eds.), *Play therapy with adolescents.* New York: Jason Aronson.
Merriam-Webster's Collegiate Dictionary, 10th Edition. (1995). Springfield, MA: Merriam-Webster, Inc.
Mills, J. (1999). *Reconnecting to the magic of life.* Kekaha, Kaua'I, HI: Imaginal Press.
Satir, V. (1988). *The new peoplemaking.* Palo Alto, CA: Science and Behavior Books.
Tysse Breen, D., & Dahlgren Daigneault, S. (1998). The use of play therapy with adolescents in high school. *International Journal of Play Therapy, 7*(1), 25–47.

BIOGRAPHICAL STATEMENT

Loretta Gallo-Lopez, MA, RPT-S, RDT-BCT, is a registered play therapist-supervisor and a board certified drama therapist and trainer, in private practice in Tampa, Florida. She has published several chapters on drama and play therapy and is co-editor of the book *Play Therapy with Adolescents.* She specializes in issues related to trauma, mood and behavioral disorders, and focuses her practice on therapy with children, adolescents and families.

Chapter 13

DANCE/MOVEMENT THERAPY WITH WOMEN SURVIVORS OF SEXUAL ABUSE

GRACE E. VALENTINE

INTRODUCTION

The violence of sexual abuse directly impacts the body in the most intimate way. It can create long lasting and devastating consequences for survivors. Their experience affects what they see when looking inward – often cited as "into a black hole of emptiness" – and affects how they relate to the outside world, hiding misplaced shame and guilt. Survivors must often separate, not only from their inner sensations, but also from their connection with others. Dance/movement therapy, a psychotherapy that focuses on the body, is uniquely qualified to address these consequences because it supports the creativity of clients, empowering them to find a more compassionate, integrated relationship with their bodies.

This chapter will define dance/movement therapy, especially as used with adults. It will outline the effects of trauma on survivors of sexual abuse, with reference to some of the new brain research. It will present the perspective and model of treatment used by this therapist in her work with women, focusing on examples of particular clients in individual and group sessions. It will outline the process of developing a trusting atmosphere and therapeutic relationship, taking gradual steps toward emotional expression, strengthening self-esteem, and working towards the emergence of healthy coping skills for dealing with the effects of abuse. The ultimate goal in this dance/movement therapy (DMT) work with survivors is a renewal of sensate connection and acceptance of the body. *(This and other phrases and terms particular to DMT and their specific usage herein are defined at the end of this chapter.)*

DEFINITIONS

Dance/movement therapy is a form of psychotherapy that uses the observation, analysis, and expression of *human* movement to bring about a change in overall functioning. Exploration and creative use of everyday movements and gestures, as well as verbal processing, help integrate the physical, emotional, and cognitive aspects of the Self. Dance/movement therapists (DMThs) have a vocabulary for describing movement and assessing the psychological needs of clients (Laban, 1971). DMT is based on the premises that: (1) one's history and current needs are observable in movement; (2) the therapist provides a trusting relationship that supports the client's movement process toward constructive change; (3) changes in movement behavior effect changes in total functioning.

TRAUMA AND THE BODY

Survivors of sexual abuse have a particular history of feelings concerning their bodies, including distrust, confusion, rejection, pleasure, helplessness, fear, shame, dislike extending to self-hatred and hostility. The most prevailing effect at the time of the event of the abuse is hyper-arousal. It overwhelms the rational ability to find meaning and contextualize what is happening and frequently leads to dissociation from any sensate connection with the body. This may further result in the somatization of emotional pain, eating disorders, distortion of body image and self-mutilation.

The research of van der Kolk (2002), Siegel (2002), and Schore (2003) has focused on the effects of trauma on areas of the brain, especially the brain stem, the area that takes in perceptions, and the limbic structures, having to do with the production of emotion and motivation. Their research has led to the opinion that the process of verbal, insight-focused therapy centered in the prefrontal lobe of the brain does not resolve traumatic issues. Experiential therapies, including those using movement, hold the promise of being successful, because they work with levels of the brain that verbal therapies do not reach. In addition, the creative arts therapies work toward integration of the experience through creativity. Siegel comments: "creativity is a natural outcome that further promotes the integrative process and deepens healing." (2002, p. 6). van der Kolk and Fisler discuss the problem that survivors have using words to express their traumatic experiences, a process that cannot be relied upon to resolve their issues (van der Kolk and Fisler, 1995). "It might be more valid to propose that performing the actions that would have overcome one's sense of helplessness at the time of the experience that became traumatic, and expressing the sensations associated with the memory of trauma effectively help people overcome their traumas" (van der Kolk, 2002, p. 6).

Embodying a concept such as empowerment that overcomes one's sense of helplessness is a basic procedure in a DMT session. A very simple structure emphasizes that clients can take control of what happens to them. In this structure, clients are asked to resist following the directive to stand up from sitting, at least one out of five times. They are encouraged to give feedback about their reactions during this activity – and at all other times during the incest survivors' group sessions. Their comments, such as, "I felt guilty about not obeying instructions," or, "My rebellious child loved it," may form the basis of issues to address later.

Another finding of this brain research is that a mediating factor that affects coping with the abuse has to do with the quality of attachment and early emotional regulation, which is developed between an infant and parenting figure on a nonverbal level (Siegel, 2002; Schore, 2003). The dance/movement therapist (DMTh), working on this level, is particularly equipped to support clients who have not been given this support at an early age. She does this through the sensitive body attunement that is provided in the DMT therapeutic relationship.

BACKGROUND FOR WORKING WITH SEXUAL ABUSE SURVIVORS

Until recently, educational programs in DMT did not include the treatment of sexual abuse survivors. Also, little has been written on the subject. The most extensive writing is in Bonnie Meekums' (2000) book, *Creative Group Therapy for Women Survivors of Sexual Abuse*. Other articles are noted in the "Further Reading" section below. Most of the instruction for working with survivors has come from the clients themselves. An incident illustrating this occurred with one of the first groups of incest survivors led by this therapist: (The names and identifying features of clients have been changed to protect their privacy.)

It was the third week of my first incest survivors' group. During the session, the group was very tense. I offered them an experience in Jacobson's Progressive Relaxation (Jacobson, 1929). They lay on mats on the studio floor and were invited to gently tense and then relax different parts of their body as I guided them, followed by a few minutes of lying quietly. Afterwards, I asked the participants what they had noticed about their bodies as they went through this process and what kind of reaction they had to this kind of relaxation technique. Their feedback was: "I feel good," "I think my muscles are relaxed," and "Yes, everything was fine." In the tenth week of the group, I repeated the same relaxation process again. Two minutes into the session there were cries of: "I'm scared," "This feels really creepy to me," and "I'm remembering some things I don't want to remember." I realized that in the earlier experience they had blocked out body sensations (dissociated) but that now they were grounded enough to allow some interior focus, even though it was too painful to continue for long.

So many lessons have been learned over the years! It is an inspiration and an honor to work with and learn from the courageous women that use DMT and the therapeutic relationship to work on healing from sexual abuse.

The general goals that DMT has in working with this population are:

- To work toward a connection/reconnection with the body
- To work toward compassion and nourishment for the body-self
- To find some pleasure and ease in moving
- To appreciate one's own creativity in movement
- To take in perceptions from the senses
- To expand movement repertoire in order to provide more options for coping with trauma issues
- To discover preferential movement patterning, qualities and other identifying characteristics of the self
- To be able to gain a sense of control over hyper-arousal
- To integrate physical, emotional, and cognitive expression, especially regarding the trauma and abuse from the past

INITIAL WORK WITH SURVIVORS

When beginning work with an individual or group of survivors, safety and trust are the primary issues. It is important to note that coping responses that were adaptive at the time of the abuse may hinder clients from further growth (Briere, 1989). However, it is essential to respect adaptive responses, especially those that armor the body. The amount of stability survivors possess is often dependent on preserving their defenses.

Dance/movement therapy with this population differs greatly from its practice with others. Survivors face special challenges doing this kind of therapy. For them, to move may recall the danger of being noticed by the perpetrator; to allow themselves to feel interior sensations may trigger flashbacks and/or very painful feelings; to express themselves authentically is the result of a long process of integrating the experience of the trauma into a rational, narrative history of their lives. Therefore, when introducing survivors to movement, it is essential to keep a constant check on their reactions. Also, more verbalization occurs in these DMT sessions as a safety outlet. However, DMT works with their creativity — often a great strength because they have had to use it to survive. This provides the foundation for work on self-esteem and the empowerment that allows them to work toward change.

The movement experience is prepared for carefully and gradually. Participants in groups are required to have had some individual therapy. Movement often brings up unexpected responses, and where there is stimulation from many sources, participants need to have developed some coping strategies. They also need to be in a fairly stable state.

Guidelines for both individual and group sessions include:

- Participants in sessions have control and choice over their participation.
- Clients suggest issues verbally or in movement, which form the themes of the session and give cues to the sequence of interventions.
- Boundaries of time and space are firm and personal space is respected.
- Nonjudgmental attitudes toward bodies and movement are encouraged.
- Defenses are respected.
- Therapists provide safety and containment for what happens in the session. (It is very important to have two facilitators for these groups – for observation, for individual help when needed, and to process the material and counter- transference issues afterward with the co-facilitator.)

An initial group session: In order to provide a safe container for initial feelings, a beginning group is usually fairly structured. Below is an example of an initial session:

We began sitting in a circle. After a brief introduction to DMT along with introductions of participants, we had a verbal check-in during which clients answered questions about what they wished to work on that evening (clients have already had an individual intake in which DMT is explained). A gentle stretching warm-up followed. One participant at a time was invited to initiate a movement that the rest of the group mirrored. (This structure is frequently used in DMT groups to let the identity of each person be shared and to build a sense of community.) Following the warm-up, we explored the theme of safety. (This is especially important early in a group's history.) The participants were invited to construct individual spaces that felt safe to them, choosing where in the room they wanted to be and building the structure with a variety of props such as scarves, mats, musical instruments, etc. The therapists tried to sense our clients' reactions to the above task and let that determine the next direction for the group. In this group, the participants built their safe spaces by constructing walls around themselves with mats. We honored this need to be enclosed, but also wanted to provide a comfortable way to bring the group members in touch with each other. We began a rhythm with a drum, inviting participants to join from behind their safe barriers by drumming on the floor with their hands. As the rhythm developed, the doors of the barriers slowly opened, participants began clapping, moving to the firmness of the beat. They circled each structure. Verbal processing followed. Some participants were able to express their apprehensions and other feelings about the activity.

Others were silent. Each client was respected for her own level of participation. The session ended with the whole group standing together in a circle. Participants were asked to press their feet into the floor, while feeling a sense of balance. This provided centering and grounding before leaving the room.

An Initial Individual Session. At the beginning of an individual session, the client may be very self-conscious in her movement. Therefore, the session usually begins sitting on the floor or in chairs, talking. Gentle stretching exercises, perhaps from some physical activity familiar to the client, may begin to mobilize us into movement. At this beginning stage, I usually move with the client. Later, the client may move alone unless she asks me to join her. No focus on inner body sensations would begin in this first session. We may get up to walk around the room with a scenario such as strolling together in the woods. After final verbal processing, some instruction in a grounding structure, such as using the image of the body as a tree, feet with roots that go down into the ground, may be provided. The session would end there. The steps of the process move slowly to build trust and familiarity. They proceed according to a particular client's needs and are designed to work toward more comfort with the movement process.

Other developments in that session, or future ones, may include touching features of the room (wall, chairs, etc.,) and/or observing and discussing how safe the client feels there. This might lead to exploring how the client feels in different places, finding images, postures, and narratives in movement. Alternatively, the client might use a prop that moves with the body, such as a scarf or paper streamer, and may start movement that focuses attention on a transitional object and distracts or ameliorates anxiety. Thus, the initial focus is on movement into space outside the body. Gradually, the client is encouraged to explore a focus initiating movement from different peripheral body parts and, eventually, to movement that is coming from the torso and involving the entire body. Any of these movement patterns may call forth scenes and feelings of the abuse or other memories. After grounding herself, the client may choose to do work further, verbally, or in movement. The above process is not in the form of a movement exercise but occurs within the context of an issue being pursued. For example, the expression of feelings about a relationship with a parent may develop from hesitant gestures into strong, pushing-away movements.

If she is feeling a great deal of fear, the client may want to make a nest or hiding place in the room. She is always given a choice as to the distance she may want to sit from the therapist. Body awareness questions may begin with: Where in your body are you feeling the sadness you mentioned earlier? What image does it look like? How would it express itself in gestures? What kind of music would support it? Where would it travel in the room?

The movement history of individual sessions with Martha illustrates how she prepared for in-depth work on issues. She discovered how she could find trust in the therapist that led to her desire to explore her memories of childhood and, eventually, the memories of abuse that surfaced:

> Martha, a thirty-three-year-old woman, wished to work on her issues of abuse and anger, which were interfering with her work. She was very self-directive and wanted to work from themes in an orderly sequence. This approach seemed to work well for her because it gave her the control necessary for her safety. After we had gone through some of her initial themes, she asked if I would role-play her grandmother. She wished to be an infant, making a bed with covers and requested that I sing to her "in another language." Her grandmother was the only adult in her past that she trusted and felt close to. We returned to this scene for our next three sessions together. She seemed to need this step to begin to solidify her trust with me. After this process she made another setting representing the crib in her bedroom at home and, in small increments from meeting to meeting, acted out several scenes from her sexual abuse that began in early childhood. She used suggestions from a few self-help books in this process and throughout our time together. Occasionally, during our months of therapy, a look or a remark I made broke this bond of trust, but we were able to reconnect and work through the stormy issues that surfaced. (She considered stopping therapy at one point.) Martha changed a great deal over our time together, becoming lighter and freer in her movements. In one of our last sessions she wanted to explore this new feeling of freedom and wanted me to dance with her, scarves moving in and out of each others' space and, sometimes separating, to move alone. It was a high point in reaching trust and resonance between us.

THEMES/ISSUES DEVELOPED OVER TIME

Some themes occur over and over again both in groups and individual sessions. Finding self identity is one of these themes.

> Nancy is a twenty-five-year old who grew up with a mother very critical of her looks, her relationships and her intelligence. Her mother used her children to gain status, including offering Nancy as a sexual partner (she was sexually abused from the age of three to eleven). One of the goals she stated early in therapy was, "I want to know who I am." She would note feeling "as if" she were at a younger age. Her view of herself was

constantly formed by the opinions of others. During the first two months of our weekly sessions, she wanted to pace around the outside of the room, constantly talking. This pattern was broken when a memory of herself at the age of nine surfaced. While walking around the studio in her stocking feet she could feel the dips and rises in our studio's wooden floor, which stimulated memories of play with her friends. She remembered chants and rhymes that she and friends used. This activated in her a new pattern of integrated movement, delighting as she was strutting "full of herself." This pleasure resonated in the relationship between her and the therapist. She was able to accept this happy child part of herself as a vital part of her identity and returned to it again during the course of our therapy together. After this turning point, she found herself social dancing without worrying about how others viewed her. And as she stated, "I took back my power," a comment that came up many times as she was able to connect with her inner self and to appreciate her looks, intelligence, and uniqueness.

Boundaries and limit setting are frequent issues presented by survivors. Because their boundaries have been so intensely invaded at a body level, many other aspects of their behavior have been affected. In DMT groups, many clients share that they cannot say "no," which affects them in many situations – from date sex, to care-giving requests, to parenting. In response to these issues, a structure was developed that is now used in many of my groups. Clients work in pairs with a length of paper streamer. One partner chooses the amount of personal space around her body by marking it with the circle of a paper streamer. She then stands in the center of the space and takes control by directing her partner to walk and/or run up to the streamer boundary from various angles. The client in the streamer space indicates where she wants her partner to stop by practicing strong gestures and words. After this activity, clients often find that they need more or less personal space and adjust the paper streamer, to make the circle larger or smaller. After the other partner has been in the center, they process how the activity made them feel, often adding events that it recalled:

> Carol placed the streamer very close to her body and could not say "stop" when approached at any angle. She retreated backwards in a shrinking movement, unable to make eye contact with the person who approached. She had a body memory of being frozen in fear. The group stopped and, with the support of others, Carol decided that she wanted to find the strength to say "stop" in a firm voice. In a later group, this became a role-play, as she repeated a gesture of pushing forward, pushing off her perpetrator. Over time, she started to feel strength in her

movements, pressing against things such as the floor, the walls, and then the hands of others. Her anger at what had happened to her was finally able to surface. Some of the group members supported her, mirroring her strong movements and voice. (This led to others wanting to work on their own expression of anger.)

The issue of reclaiming one's sexuality is one of the most difficult for survivors of sexual abuse. The client cited below worked with these issues for five years. She did not recover the memory of her abuse until a year after starting individual DMT. Up until that point it was unclear what was blocking her feelings.

Pat, a forty-five-year-old woman, began individual sessions in DMT, wanting to work on boundaries in family relationships, on connection with her body, and, especially, on enjoyment of her sexuality. She had had other therapy to work on issues of depression and an incident of date rape in her past, including a women's issues group with me. Thus, moving together previously, we had built a foundation of trust and attunement. She was able to be very active, purposeful and grounded in expressing many emotions with strong, integrated movements. About a year after she began this course of therapy, she brought a Christmas cactus plant to her session. It had belonged to her grandfather; she knew it had some meaning for her. At one point she stood, facing it, with her back to me and seemed to go "to another place," a technique she accessed from shamanic training. She saw her grandfather kissing her all over when she was four years old. In the months after this session, more memories of this incident surfaced in other settings. When intense issues arose and when she was sexually intimate, she frequently began to burp. It was a body reaction that seemed to be an attempt to get rid of the presence of her perpetrator inside of her, and of other bad memories and feelings. She put voice to this expression, saying, "get out of there," accompanying it with a variety of actions, such as graciously opening the studio door, or angrily throwing pillows across the room. In the setting of photos of herself before and after the abuse, she danced her feelings of anger and grief many times. She also continued her work on these issues in a verbal therapy group and in weekend intensive workshops. This and a weeklong intensive on sexuality with her husband were very rewarding for her. As she worked on her sexuality, her husband was quite supportive. It seemed to be that recovering the memory of her early abuse and expressing her feelings about it with the support of others allows her, most of the time, to release her previous numbness and dissociation during sexual intimacy. One of her latest comments was: "it can be quite wonderful."

BRAIN RESEARCH AND WORK IN
DANCE/MOVEMENT THERAPY

The work of people studying the effects of trauma on the workings of the brain validates the work DMTs have been doing with trauma survivors since the 1940s (Baum, 1991; Meekums, 2000; Sandel, Chaiklin, Lohn, 1993; see also "further reading" below). Interestingly, the foremost pioneer in DMT was Marian Chace (Sandel, Chaiklin, and Lohn, 1993), whose clients were traumatized veterans returning from WWII. She found that group movement helped these veterans connect to each other and work on many of the issues we now associate with PTSD.

Brain researchers have found that trauma survivors are left with emotion and thought fragments about the traumatic event, unable to integrate the experience. The trauma can be integrated by finding a way to allow clients to be as present as possible with perceptions, emotions, and thoughts experienced from the past. Within this process exists the possibility of repairing the damaged parts of the self and providing a foundation for creating, or re-creating, a core self (Siegel, 2002). This process is the very essence of what happens in the DMT session:

> As Bea (a pseudonym), developed trust with the therapist and the group members, she began to move using a wider range of movement parameters, indicating growth in her coping mechanisms. At first, she would freeze and go into a trance-like state when traumatic material was triggered, or she would move tentatively, struggling to remain present. Gradually, she was able to take risks by improvising movements that triggered painful memories. (Baum, 1991, p. 102)

Current brain research stresses a client's need to be connected to the present while exploring trauma memories. "As here and now consciousness builds a cohesive self in the moment, a past-present-future consciousness enables a coherent autobiographic self to emerge" (Siegel, 2002, p. 31). The implications of this research for treatment of trauma survivors shape the current focus of this therapist's work – directing a constant level of attention to present sensory and kinesthetic cues. The sensate experiences of the body give the most acute signals to being in the present. The following example illustrates how this is used in my sessions. Alice is a client who has been able to utilize body cues and sensory feedback that keep her in the present:

> After years of verbal therapy, Alice came to DMT to work on the body issues of her abuse. She was brutally abused by an older relative at the age of two and a half. We began our work by paying attention to the sensory

data that was perceived by her contact with the surfaces that supported her as she sat or walked – the wood floor under her stocking feet, the mats she sat on, the wall as she leaned against it, the arms and backs of chairs. This kind of grounding, plus using the body cue of pressing her hands together to remind herself of being in the present are techniques that were developed to prepare her for fearful experiences or to quiet herself afterwards, such as after having a bad dream. She practices them before air travel, therapy sessions and other anxiety-provoking events. They also help prepare her for the more intensive work of recalling the events of her abuse – work she is doing in her other therapy sessions and, with more active movement, in our sessions. She is trying to recover a more complete narrative of what happened to her, something very difficult, considering it occurred pre-verbally. Her comment about our work together is that "I didn't realize how much every aspect of my life has been affected by the abuse." Her ability to take in inner sensations has greatly improved; for example, in one session, noticing her tightening of her neck, shoulders and lower abdomen and, in another session, feeling the freedom of swinging her arms. We have danced a few times, always in a structured way, bouncing to the rhythms of the Beatles or twisting to The Twist. She seems to be finding more joy in her movement.

As with Alice in the example above, the process of DMT empowers the client to relive the trauma experience, utilizing sensory input to stay connected to the present. This connection allows the client to be "in charge," protecting and defending herself. She moves, where before she was frozen.

QUALITIES OF GROUP THERAPY

Although most of the focus in this chapter is on individuals in DMT with survivors, some mention must be made of the dynamics in group therapy sessions. In a group therapy session, experiences of the abuse can be shared and validated by others. Isolation and secrecy are ameliorated. Many changes in behaviors no longer useful occur because of the support of the group.

In the DMT group, the qualities of moving together are very empowering. Schmais (1985) outlined these qualities in an article on the process of healing in DMT groups (1985). With examples of the dynamics in some of the groups facilitated by this therapist over the years (and with great gratitude for the wisdom and support of her co-facilitator, Robyn Lending Halsten, in most of these groups) the following qualities are illustrated:

Cohesion, vitalization and education: "Feelings that were denied in a repressive atmosphere are resurrected in an atmosphere of acceptance" (Schmais, 1985, p. 21).

Susan wanted to work on the issue of her father's (her perpetrator) wish to contact her. One arm reached out to satisfy his wish while the other covered her face, protecting her. Two members suggested taking parts in different role plays. Susan felt both of these suggestions were too threatening because of their concreteness. She chose a third suggestion, putting a large ball in the center of the room, circling it while approaching and coming away from it. She asked the other group members to circle with her. She circled and stopped, sometimes gesturing toward the ball. She spent much time in silent contemplation. The ball became something or someone for the others in the group as well. At one point she exploded into a scream and wanted to use the ball to express her anger by throwing it against the wall and shouting "stay away." Others in the group were freed from their inhibitions and stood behind her, supporting her with their shouts as they also expressed their own anger at their perpetrators.

Expression: "Seemingly simple themes of work or play often shift into powerful emotional statements" (Schmais, 1985, p. 20.)

The group was dancing with a large blue cloth, holding on around the edge, much as one plays with a parachute. One of the group members, Pam, suddenly had a flashback, the cloth becoming sheets from the scene of her abuse. After stopping the play and asking all to press feet into the floor, then to sit and press hands into the floor – a common grounding structure to center members in the present – the therapist asked what Pam wished to do with this memory. With the help of the group, she decided she wanted to have them fold up the cloth very carefully and hide it behind a stack of mats. In this way they were able to support her desire to be in control and put her traumatic experience aside, at least for the time being, until she wished to bring it forward again and deal with its issues.

Synchrony, rhythm and integration: "People moving in the same rhythm with the same spatial configuration become identified with one another. Gradually they assume a common expression, moving with the same dynamic qualities in comparable areas of space . . . to the same rhythm. In this way the group achieves a sense of solidarity" (Schmais, 1985, p. 19).

At the end of many of the group sessions, the prop of a purple stretch cloth sewn into a circle is called for. Group members stand inside of it, swaying together as they lean backward into the cloth, into the support of each other as they all share in supporting the tension of the cloth. It is a way of being together without touching, which is often hard for survivors. Sometimes a sound may emerge, or a final thought shared. It marks an intense feeling of community that has been gained, often after many previous sessions of tentative reaching out to each other.

CONCLUSION

Dance/movement therapy is an important modality in the treatment of survivors because its methods focus on the body, the receptor of the abuse. It is essential to work gradually, building on the issues of the survivor through mind/body attunement with the therapist, and with peers in a group setting. Supporting the creativity of these clients builds a foundation of self-esteem. The experience of the body moving in space develops an awareness of kinesthetic sensations, an integration with emotional expression and a connection of inner states with the outer world of others. The process of grounding in the present can anchor the client in recovering traumatic memories. The studies of the brain and the effects of trauma are adding a scientific foundation for those working in body-focused therapies. Hopefully, this will lead to research investigating the congruence of work in these therapies with this new knowledge. And, finally, it will usher in a new age of healing for our clients.

APPENDIX – TERMS

The terms defined below are particular to DMT and the specific usage in this chapter.

acceptance of the body – the ability to recognize and own sensory data and the physical image of one's own body

body attunement – the nonverbal exchange between people that is especially strong between children and caregivers and includes eye contact, facial expressions, imitation and response to body movement, etc., sometimes referred to as kinesthetic empathy

body image – the picture of the body held in the brain

body memory – a bodily sensation that recalls a similar sensation at an earlier time

centering – connecting to the physical and imagined center of one's self

embodying – expressing an idea with the body in gestures and movement

grounding – finding secure balance and feeling one's energy extending downward toward the structures supporting one

hyperarousal – excessive emotional reaction that overwhelms rational thought

integrated movements – movements that appropriately express an idea and emotion and seem connected/related to each other, sometimes referred to as flowing from each other

kinesthetic cues – attaching an idea or practice to a muscle movement, for example, clasping the hands together to remind one to focus on the present moment

PTSD – post-traumatic stress syndrome, the set of characteristics that occur when a traumatic event is recalled on a cognitive, intuitive, and/or nonverbal level

personal space – the space around the body that one needs to feel safe

somatization – experiencing emotional sensations as bodily pain and/or disease

REFERENCES

American Dance Therapy Association (ADTA). (2005). *40th annual conference brochure*. 7.

Baum, E. Z. (1991). Movement therapy with multiple personality patients. *Dissociation, 4*(2), 99–104.

Jacobson, E. (1929). *Progressive relaxation*. Chicago: University of Chicago Press.

Laban, R. (1971). *The mastery of movement* (third edition, revised). Boston: Plays.

Meekums, B. (2000). *Creative group therapy for women survivors of child sexual abuse: Speaking the unspeakable*. London: Kingsley.

Sandel, S. A., Chaiklin, S., & Lohn, A. (Eds.). (1993). *Foundations of dance/movement therapy: The life and work of Marion Chace*. Columbia, MD: The Marion Chace Memorial Fund of the American Dance Therapy Association.

Schore, A. N. (2003). *Affect regulation and the repair of the self*. New York: W. W. Norton.

Schmais, C. (1985). Healing processes in group dance therapy. *American Journal of Dance Therapy, 8*, 17–36.

Siegel, D. J. (2002). An interpersonal neurobiology of psychotherapy: the developing mind and the resolution of trauma. *Healing trauma*. New York: W. W. Norton.

van der Kolk, B. A. (2002). Beyond the talking cure: somatic experience and subcortical imprints in the treatment of trauma. *EMDR, Promises for a paradigm shift*. F. Shapiro (Ed.). New York: APA Press.

van der Kolk, B. A & Fisler, R. E. (1995). Dissociation and the fragmentary nature of traumatic memories. Overview and exploratory study. *Journal of Traumatic Stress, 8*, 505–525.

FURTHER READING

Ambra, L. N. (1995). Approaches used in dance/movement therapy with adult incest survivors. *American Journal of Dance Therapy, 17*(1), 15–24.

Bernstein, B. (1995). Dancing beyond trauma: Women survivors of sexual abuse. In *Dance and Other Expressive Art Therapies*, Ed. Fran J. Levy, Judith Pines Fried, & Fern Leventhal. New York & London: Routledge.

Levy, F. (1995). Nameless: A Case of Multiplicity. In *Dance and other expressive art therapies*, Ed. Fran J. Levy, Judith Pines Fried, & Fern Leventhal. New York & London: Routledge.

Mills, L. J., & Daniluk, J. C. (2002). Her body speaks: The experience of dance therapy for women survivors of child sexual abuse. *Journal of Counseling and Development, 80*, 77–85.

Simonds, S. L. (1994). *Bridging the silence: nonverbal modalities in the treatment of adult survivors of childhood sexual abuse.* New York: Norton.

Wise, S. K. (1984). Uses of dance therapy with eating disorders. *The Journal of Obesity and Weight Regulation, 3*(2), 101–106.

BIOGRAPHICAL STATEMENT

Grace E. Valentine, Ph.D. (English), MA (Dance Therapy), ADTR (Academy of Dance Therapists, Registered), DTRL (Dance Therapist Registered and Licensed, State of WI), LPC (Licensed Professional Counselor, WI), works as the Senior Clinician at Hancock Center for Movement Arts and Therapies, Madison, WI. Her main teachers have been Constance Cook and Joanna Gewurtz, both ADTRs. She has worked with populations of older adults, the mentally ill, and children. For the past fifteen years, she has worked with women and, particularly, survivors of sexual abuse. She developed the women's programming at Hancock Center and facilitates individual sessions and groups. She has worked in community agencies with: clients with a combined history of trauma, mental illness and substance abuse; adult members of families affected by sexual abuse; and former prostitutes. She has lectured at the University of WI-Madison, taught and given presentations in the U.S. and abroad, including topics on intercultural issues. Her former publications have been on work with children and older adults. She has been President of the Northern CA and WI Chapters of the American Dance Therapy Assoc. and served on the Editorial Board of the *American Journal of Dance Therapy.*

Chapter 14

CLAIMING VOICE: MUSIC THERAPY FOR CHILDHOOD SEXUAL ABUSE SURVIVORS

Sandra L. Curtis

INTRODUCTION

There is an increasing awareness among therapists from all disciplines of the issue of childhood sexual abuse. Whatever the initial reason that brings our clients to us, we are seeing more than ever before lives that have been touched by such abuse (Chew, 1998; Curtis, 2000; Curtis & Harrison, 2006). The creative arts therapies in general, and music therapy in particular, are proving to be invaluable in helping women survivors to recover from the harm of this violence. The music therapy literature, however, is relatively recent and sparse. As well, little of what exists places this abuse directly and explicitly within the sociopolitical context of a patriarchal society, nor within the overarching issue of all male violence against women (Clendenon-Wallen, 1991; Curtis and Harrison, 2006; Rogers, 1993). This chapter presents a unique music therapy approach for women and teen survivors of childhood sexual abuse – an approach developed with its theory and techniques rooted explicitly in an understanding of this abuse within the context of male violence against women and children in our current culture. The nature of this violence is examined first, with a review of current explanatory models. The specifics of childhood sexual abuse are presented in light of these models. A music therapy program is described as it evolved to support women and adolescent girls on their journey to recover from the harm of this violence. Its effectiveness is reflected in the actual experiences of survivors as they reclaim their voices, their lives, and their true spirits.

VIOLENCE AGAINST WOMEN
AND CHILDREN

Until recently, the issue of violence against women and children has been neglected, unnamed, and unacknowledged (Burstow, 1992; Curtis, 1994, 2000; Marshall and Vaillancourt, 1993; Worell and Remer, 2003). It has now, however, been identified as pervasive, persistent, and serious in both nature and extent (Curtis, 2000). Once acknowledged, the attention of researchers and clinicians alike has been primarily focused on each of the many different types of violence as distinct and unrelated phenomena. From sexual assault, domestic violence, and childhood sexual abuse, to sexual exploitation and harassment, each has been examined independently in search of their own unique explanatory models and treatment techniques. This approach is now being challenged. Increasingly, all of these forms of violence are being seen as related, with each rooted in our patriarchal culture and in the harm experienced by both men and women within this culture as a result of gender-role socialization and unequal power distribution. In addition, the traditionally separate categories of physical, sexual, and emotional abuse are no longer being viewed hierarchically as one more serious than the other; they are now being seen as different manifestations of the same phenomenon (Curtis, 2000; Kelly, 1988). Underpinning each is an "inner abuse" – this is harm done to the core self. As a result of abuse at the individual and systemic levels, women and children may come to internalize the belief system of the predominant culture which dehumanizes and devalues them. This, in turn, serves to justify, perpetuate, deny, and minimalize violence against women and children. It results in acceptance of this violence, failure to see it as abuse, blaming of the victim for it, and eventually self-blame on the victims' part for their own experiences of violence (Curtis, 1994, 2000).

Traditional explanatory models for violence against women and children have identified it as a break down of social order in which a few aberrant individuals are out of control – whether for medical or psychosocial reasons. The increasingly accepted feminist explanatory model contradicts this view. Violence against women and children is seen instead as a logical extension of patriarchal culture and family. Control, rather than lack of control, is key to violence against women and children. It is control through the violence used by some which effectively results in social control of all. This is reflected in our culture's very definition of masculinity as the power to control; it has its roots in a patriarchal culture characterized by personal and systemic power inequality (Burstow, 1992; Curtis, 2000; Worell and Remer, 2003).

CHILDHOOD SEXUAL ABUSE

In light of this current view on violence against women and children, child-hood sexual abuse can be understood as one of the manifestations of patriarchal power imbalance and related to all other types of violence against women and children. It is a violation of power and control. Control is the central issue, with sex being the weapon, rather than the goal. It is the ultimate betrayal of a child by an authority figure. It can involve physical, sexual, and emotional components to the abuse, culminating in a combined harm to the core self (Curtis and Harrison, 2006; Palmer 1991).

As with all crimes of violence against women and children, an accurate incidence rate of childhood sexual abuse can be extremely difficult to ascertain. Any estimates are generally considered to be lower than reality, since research indicates that both children and adult survivors are reluctant to speak out for a myriad of reasons – fear, shame, self-blame, and fear of not being believed, to name just a few. Estimates range anywhere from 10% to 38% of the female population. In anecdotal terms, many therapists outside the field of childhood sexual abuse intervention are remarking on the number of survivors they encounter in their own practices (Brooke, 1997; Finkelhor, Gerald, and Smith, 1990; Schachter, Stalker, and Teram, 2001).

Childhood sexual abuse can have a profound, detrimental impact on its victims – both in the immediate and in the long term. I use the word *"victim"* here with careful deliberation. Women and children are harmed by their abusers and this must be documented. But they should not be defined by this victimization, for they are also strong survivors, seeking creative ways to recover and to rebuild their lives (Curtis, 2000). The impact of this abuse to the core sense of self cannot be overemphasized. It results in internalization of blame, an intense sense of shame, and long-lasting self-degradation. It can result in a pattern of relationship difficulties and re-victimization (Chew, 1998; Curtis and Harrison, 2006; Fedele and Harrington, 1990; Jacobs, 1994). It is important, however, to be careful not to pathologize survivors of this abuse and to be clear that ongoing problems do not arise from individual character-istics, but from the harm produced by the abuse.

Symptoms experienced by abuse survivors can be myriad and at times con-tradictory. They may exhibit unexplained feelings of rage on one hand or numbness on the other. They may be hypervigilant while denying the impact of the abuse in their lives (Curtis and Harrison, 2006; Palmer, 1991). The symptoms may appear immediately after the abuse or later as time elapses. Their thinking – in general terms, and about themselves and their abusers – may be confused. A pervasive sense of distrust in themselves and others is not uncommon (Finkelhor, Gerald, and Smith, 1990; Palmer, 1991). In light of the symptoms and the overall pervasive and profound impact of childhood sexual abuse, survivors may indeed benefit from creative therapeutic approaches to assist them in their journey of recovery. They are deserving of the best we can offer them, an approach informed by the latest understanding of violence against women and children, of childhood sexual abuse, and of effective intervention strategies.

MUSIC THERAPY FOR SURVIVORS OF CHILDHOOD SEXUAL ABUSE

Music therapy holds great potential for women and adolescent girl survivors of childhood sexual abuse. A unique approach to music therapy particularly well-suited to meet their needs is that of feminist music therapy. This approach developed out of the rise of feminist therapy seen in the disciplines of psychology, counseling, and social work in the 1970s (Curtis, 2000, in press).

Feminist music therapy represents an approach to intervention that is rooted in a feminist belief system with its sociopolitical understanding of men's and women's lives, as they are constructed within a patriarchal culture. It is unique among music therapy approaches with this understanding and in its twofold purpose – to accomplish personal transformation by individuals within their own lives and sociopolitical change within the community (Curtis, 2000, in press). Feminist music therapy recognizes that women's lives are constrained by the interaction of multiple oppressions such as sexism, racism, ageism, ableism, and heterosexism. As a result, feminist music therapists must support individuals in overcoming the harm of such oppression, as well as work actively towards eliminating that oppression and improving the situation in which women find themselves.

A number of specific therapeutic goals form the basis of feminist music therapy. These are:

1. to empower women, in personal, interpersonal, and social terms;
2. to permit a sociopolitical understanding of women's lives, their problems, and their experiences of oppression;
3. to facilitate recovery from the harm of this oppression and its resultant internalization;
4. to make it possible for women to achieve health and happiness as they define it; and,
5. to bring about necessary social change to eliminate oppression of women (Curtis, 2000, in press).

A small number of music therapy techniques are used to accomplish these important therapeutic goals. These techniques have been developed for practice with women in general and they have been implemented originally in work at battered women's shelters. These techniques include: (1) feminist analysis of gender-role socialization and power through lyric analysis, songwriting, performance, and CD recording; (2) women's empowerment and reclaiming of voice through songwriting and recording; and (3) valuing of women and fostering women's self-nurturance through music-centered relaxation and imagery (Curtis, 2000, in press)

Given that feminist music therapy is rooted in an explicit sociopolitical understanding of women's and girls' lives, given that it was first developed in practice with women survivors of male violence within intimate relationships, and given the strong link between childhood sexual abuse and all forms of male violence against women, feminist music therapy would appear to be well-suited for survivors of childhood sexual abuse. It meets the need for a creative therapeutic approach that incorporates for therapist and client alike an understanding of childhood sexual abuse and its sociopolitical context. The section which follows provides a closer examination of feminist music therapy and the shape it takes in clinical practice when used to support women and adolescent girls in their recovery from childhood sexual abuse.

WOMEN'S AND ADOLESCENT GIRLS' VOICES IN MUSIC THERAPY

Feminist Analysis

The music therapy technique of feminist analysis can be particularly effective in the process of recovery from childhood sexual abuse. It permits an understanding of men and women's gender-role socialization and differential power, and the role these play in childhood sexual abuse, in all women's lives, and in their own lives, experiences, and responses (Curtis and Harrison, 2006). This feminist analysis is not, however, limited to abuse, it also focuses on broader issues such as family, love, anger, power, romance, healing, resistance, recovery, and empowerment (Curtis, 2000).

Lyric analysis is a powerful vehicle for this feminist analysis. The music used is limited to songs written and performed by women. In listening to other women's voices and stories, music therapy participants can hear their own experiences validated. In listening to powerful women – women of fame and fortune – music therapy participants can break their isolation and see the abuse not as a personal problem, but as a sociopolitical one. Singing these songs is even more powerful – it evokes a combined physiological-cognitive-emotional response that permits internalization of the song's meaning. The music available for such lyric analysis is quite wide and varied. From mainstream pop, rock, and country to alternative and indie, women singer-songwriters are increasingly giving voice to women's lives and experiences (Curtis, 2000). The project as developed for women and teen survivors of childhood abuse makes use of approximately 150 songs, of which a sampling can be seen in Table 14.1. Music therapy participants can be provided with song-books/recordings from which to choose or they can bring in their own music. This opportunity to contribute music from their own collections can be very empowering.

Table 14.1. Thematic Song Listing: A Sampling		
Theme	*Song*	*Performer*
Violence	Don't Ever Touch Me [Again]	Dionne Farris (Farris and Harris, 1994)
	Kid Fears	Indigo Girls (1989)
	Run	Sweet Honey in the Rock (Casel, 1997)
Healing	Blackbird	Sarah McLachlan (Lennon & McCartney, 2002)
	Outside Myself	k. d. lang (1992)
Love	Torn	Natalie Ambruglia (Thornally, & Preven, 1999)
Men	Strong Enough	Sheryl Crow (Crow et al, 1993)
	No Scrubs	TLC (Briggs & Burrass, 1999)
	Any Man of Mine	Shania Twain (Twain & Lange, 1996)
Gender-Role Socialization	What It Feels Like for a Girl	Madonna (Madonna & Sigsworth, 2002)
	Not Bad for a Broad	Four Bitchin' Babes (Larkin, 1993)
Self Strength	Video	India Arie (2001)
	Bitch	Meredith Brooks (Brooks & Peiken, 1997)
	You Learn	Alanis Morisette (1995)

EMPOWERMENT AND RECLAIMING OF VOICE

Feminist analysis can be taken to a deeper, more personal level through writing, performing, and recording of music therapy participants' own songs. They can move beyond theoretical analysis to a true understanding of what it means in their own lives. They can move from hearing their own stories reflected in other women's songs, to singing and recording their own personal experiences, to claiming their own true voices. Given the fragile nature of the core self of many abuse survivors, the process of introducing songwriting must be approached carefully. To build confidence, music therapy participants are first asked to write only a few words of a song presented by the music therapist. They gradually proceed to the point where they compose the full lyrics to a completely original song. They can choose to work with the music therapist to write the music as well or to have the music therapist compose the music under specific direction from them in terms of mood, style, and instrumentation choice. At the conclusion of the therapeutic process, they can choose to record their song themselves or to have the music therapist record it for them. Both options are empowering for participants, with discussion led by the music therapist concerning different roles of professional songwriters and performing artists in the music industry. Ultimately, each participant leaves therapy with a CD of their own creation, including CD cover artwork, and a compilation CD of all of the participants' songs. The complete process can be incredibly effective in empowering women and teen survivors.

VALUING OF WOMEN AND WOMEN'S SELF NURTURANCE

The techniques of music-centered relaxation and imagery that are used to encourage valuing and self-nurturance are not unique in and of themselves. They are unique when used in the context of a feminist analysis of women's gender-role socialization. Women grow up in a culture which emphasizes the importance of selflessness for them. Selflessness in relationships can be important and indeed laudable, but only if it is not a one-way phenomenon (Curtis, 2000). With an understanding of the powerful societal messages to women around this, women and teen survivors of childhood sexual abuse can learn to value and nurture themselves through participating in music-centered relaxation and imagery. They can also learn to use these techniques independently, empowering them further.

JOSIE'S VOICE

The story of Josie that follows is a compilation of a number of clients I have seen in my music therapy practice. This compilation is used to best capture the essence of the therapeutic experience within the constraints of a brief chapter.

As I entered the therapy room, I spotted Josie sitting quietly in one of the big couches, with eyes downcast and with her legs curled up underneath her. I had learned that she was fifteen-years-old and had been sexually abused by her stepfather from the age of five. She and the other teenage girls in the group had been a challenge and it was hoped that music therapy might provide the means to connect.

As I pulled out my CD player and passed out the song books, the girls began to pore over the songs in an animated fashion. With the sounding of the first notes of Josie's selection, TLC's *No Scrubs* (Briggs and Burrass, 1999), the floodgates opened. The girls began tapping their toes, singing along, and talking. With a number of rapid song choices, the talk moved from the music and the performing artists to the more personal. Feminist analysis was underway. Upon the conclusion of Sheryl Crow's *Soak Up the Sun* (Trott and Crow, 2002), I pulled out my electric guitar and we made the transition from listening to performing. Re-writing the lyrics of this song provided a great vehicle for self-expression, confidence building, and a start to the process of original song writing.

At the end of the therapy journey, Josie met with me alone in the therapy room. She had decided that, after writing the song and creating the art work for her CD, she wanted to do her own recording. With a twelve track MIDI digital recorder, I had laid down the accompanimental tracks, leaving the vocal track for her. With hands trembling, she began to sing. In a clear voice, she sang a song of resistance, hope, and recovery.

While all of the women I saw for the complete fourteen weeks in feminist music therapy showed improvement in pencil and paper measurements (e.g., exit surveys, interviews, etc.), nothing spoke more strongly to the power of music than the expression on the women's faces as they listened to each other's CDs. Nothing spoke more eloquently of their empowerment than their own voices in song.

> You had no right! To have me carry your shame . . .
> You had no right! I give you back your shame
> You had no right! I survived
> You had no right! I now live for tomorrow
> I have the right! I have the right! (Curtis & Harrison, 2006)

APPENDIX – TERMS

Domestic Violence is just one of many terms used to identify male violence against women within intimate relationships. The naming of this particular type of violence is an important yet problematic issue, as it reflects and determines how this issue is understood. While the term domestic violence has become widely used, it is not one accepted by those with a feminist understanding of the issue, as it serves to effectively obscure the dimensions of gender and power. For feminists, the term woman abuse is preferred.

Oppression is a pervasive pattern of prejudice and discrimination at the individual and systemic levels, resulting in personal and societal barriers and power differentials for some and privilege for others. This oppression can be based on such characteristics as race (racism), on sex (sexism), on socioeconomic status (classism), on age (ageism), on sexual orientation (heterosexism), or ability (ableism). A feminist understanding of diversity acknowledges the complex interaction of multiple oppressions in men's and women's lives.

Woman Abuse is the preferred term to identify all forms of male violence against women. To reflect a clear understanding of the issue, I have adopted a definition of woman abuse which can accommodate all types of abuse (physical, sexual, psychological, etc.) and which does not mask dimensions of power or gender. It is a "pattern of coercive control over women that uses diverse methods and leaves women questioning their self-worth and perception of reality" (Yllö & Bograd, 1988, p. 14).

REFERENCES

Arie, I., Sanders, S., & Broady, C. (2001). Video [Recorded by India Arie]. On *Acoustic soul* [CD]. New York: Motown Recording Company.

Ballou, M. B., & Brown, L. S. (2002). *Rethinking mental health and disorder: feminist perspectives.* New York: Guilford Press.

Brooks, M., & Peiken, S. (1997). Bitch. On *Blurring the edges* [CD]. Capitol Records.

Briggs, K., & Burrass, Ki. (1999) No scrubs [Recorded by TLC]. On *Grammy nominees 2000.* RCA.

Brooke, S. L. (1997). *Healing through art: Art therapy with sexual abuse survivors.* Springfield, IL: Charles C Thomas Publisher, Ltd.

Burstow, B. (1992). *Radical feminist therapy: working in the context of violence.* Newbury Park, CA: Sage Publications.

Butler, S. (1985). *Conspiracy of silence: The trauma of incest.* Volcano, CA: Volcano Press.

Casel, N. B. (1997). Run [Recorded by Sweet Honey in the Rock]. On *Twenty-Five* [CD]. Ryko.

Chew, J. (1998). *Women survivors of childhood sexual abuse: Healing through group work: beyond survival.* Binghamton, NY: Haworth Press.

Clendenon-Wallen, J. (1991). Use of music therapy to influence the self-confidence and self-esteem of adolescents who are sexually abused. *Music Therapy Perspectives, 9,* 73–81.

Crow, S., Bottrell, B., Baerwald, D., Gilbert, K., Ricketts, D., & Macleod, B. (1993). Strong enough [Recorded by Sheryl Crow]. On *Tuesday Night Music Club* [CD]. Hollywood, CA: A & M Records.

Curtis, S. L. (1994). Killing us softly: Male inner violence against women. In Stanley G. French (Ed.), *Interpersonal violence, health, and gender politics,* (second edition), pp. 287–306. Dubuque, IA: W. C. Brown.

Curtis, S. L. (2000). Singing subversion, singing soul: Women's voices in feminist music therapy. (Doctoral dissertation, Concordia University, 1997). *Dissertation Abstracts International, 60*(12-A), 4240.

Curtis, S. L. (2003). *Empowering women through the healing arts: A manual for workers with survivors of violence.* Manuscript in preparation.

Curtis, S. L. (2004). *A diversity of voices: cultural competence for music therapists.* Manuscript submitted for publication.

Curtis, S. L., & Harrison, G. C. T. (2006). Empowering women survivors of childhood sexual abuse: A collaborative music therapy-social work approach. In Stephanie Brooke (Ed.), *Creative arts therapies manual.* (pp. 193–202). Springfield, IL: Charles C Thomas Publisher, Ltd.

Curtis, S. L. (in press). Feminist music therapy: Transforming theory, transforming lives. In Susan Hadley (Ed.), *Feminist perspectives in music therapy: empowering women's voices.* Philadelphia, PA: Barcelona Publishers.

Dolan, Y. (1991). *Resolving sexual abuse: Solution-focused therapy and Ericksonian hypnosis for adult survivors.* New York: W.W. Norton & Company.

Farris, D., & Harris, D. (1994). Don't ever touch me [again]. [Recorded by Dionne Farris]. On *Wild Seed – Wild Flower* [CD]. New York: Sony Music.

Fedele, N. M, & Harrington, E. A. (1990). *Women's groups: how connections heal. Work in progress no. 47.* Wellesley, MA: Stone Center.

Finkelhor, D., H., Gerald, L. I.A., & Smith, C. (1990). Sexual abuse in a national survey of adult men and women: Prevalence, characteristics, and risk factors. *Child Abuse & Neglect, 14*(1), 19–28.

Hammel-Gormley, A. (1995). Singing the songs: A qualitative study of music therapy with individuals having psychiatric illnesses as well as histories of childhood sexual abuse. (Doctoral dissertation, New York University, 1995). *Dissertation Abstracts International, 56*(10B), 5768.

Indigo Girls. (1989). Kid fears. On *Indigo Girls* [CD]. New York: CBS Records.

Jacobs, J. L. (1994). *Incest and the development of the female self.* NY: Routledge.

Kelly, L. (1988). How women define their experiences of violence. In Kersti Yllo & Michele Bograd (Eds.), *Feminist perspectives on wife abuse,* (pp. 114–132). Newbury Park, CA: Sage Publications.

Lang, K. D. (1992). Outside myself. On *Ingénue* [CD]. New York: Sire Records.

Larkin, P. (1993). Not bad for a broad. [Performed by Four Bitchin Babes]. On *Buy me – Bring Me* [CD]. Cambridge, MA: Rounder Records.

Lennon, J., & McCartney, P. (2002). Blackbird. [Recorded by Sarah McLachlan]. On *Women & Songs 6* [CD]. Scarborough, Ontario, Canada: Warner Music Canada.

Lindberg, K. A. (1995). Songs of healing: Songwriting with an abused adolescent. *Music Therapy, 13*(1), 93–108.

MacIntosh, H. B. (2003). Sounds of healing: Music in group work with survivors of sexual abuse. *Arts in Psychotherapy, 30*(1), 17–23.

Madonna & Sigsworth, G. (2002). What it feels like for a girl. On *Women & Songs 6* [CD]. Scarborough, Ontario, Canada: Warner Music Canada.

Marshall, P. F., & Vaillancourt, M. A. (1993). *Changing the landscape: Ending violence – achieving equality.* Final report of the Canadian Panel on Violence Against Women. Ottawa, Canada: Minister of Supply & Services Canada.

Morissette, A. (1995). You learn. On *Jagged little pill* [CD]. USA: Maverick Recording Company.

Palmer, N. (1991). Feminist practice with survivors of sexual trauma and incest. In Bricker-Jenkins, M., Hooyman, N., & Gottlieb, N. (Eds.), *Feminist social work practice in clinical settings* (pp. 63–82). Newbury Park, CA: Sage Publications.

Rogers, P. J. (1993). Research in music therapy with sexually abused clients. In Payne, H. (Ed.), *Handbook of inquiry in the arts therapies: One river, many currents* (pp. 197–217). Philadelphia, PA: Jessica Kingsley Publishers.

Rogers, P. J. (1994). Sexual abuse and eating disorders: A possible connection indicated through music therapy? In Dokter, D. (Ed.), *Arts therapies and clients with eating disorders: Fragile board* (pp. 262–278). Philadelphia, PA: Jessica Kingsley Publishers.

Rogers, P. J. (1995). Childhood sexual abuse: Dilemmas in therapeutic practice. *Music Therapy*

Perspectives. Special Issue. International Music Therapy, 13(1), 24–30.

Schachter, C., Stalker, C., & Teram, E. (2001). *Handbook on sensitive practice for health professionals: Lessons from women survivors of childhood sexual abuse.* Retrieved July 10, 2004 from Health Canada National Clearinghouse on Family Violence Web site: http://www.hc-sc.gc.ca/hppb/familyviolence/html/nfntsxsensi_e.html.

Thornalley, C. , & Preven. (1999). Torn. [Recorded by Natalie Ambruglia]. On *1999 Grammy Nominees* [CD]. Grammy Recordings Sony Music.

Trott, J., & Crow, S. (2002). Soak up the sun. [Recorded by Sheryl Crow]. On *Women & Songs 6* [CD]. Scarborough, Ontario, Canada: Warner Music Canada.

Twain, S., & Lange, R. (1996). Any man of mine. [Recorded by Shania Twain.] On *1996 Grammy Nominees* [CD]. Grammy Recordings Sony Music.

Whipple, J., & Lindsey, R. S. (1999). Music for the soul: A music therapy program for battered women. *Music Therapy Perspectives, 17*(2), 61–68.

Worell, J., & Remer, P. (2003). *Feminist perspectives in therapy: empowering diverse women.* New York: Wiley.

Yllö, K., & Bograd, M. (Eds.). (1988). *Feminist perspectives on wife abuse.* Newbury Park, CA: Sage.

BIOGRAPHICAL STATEMENT

Sandra L. Curtis, Ph.D., MT-BC, MTA, is Director of the School of Music and Coordinator of Music Therapy at the University of Windsor in Canada. She received a bachelor's degree in music from McGill University, Canada, a master's in music therapy from Florida State University, USA, and an interdisciplinary Ph.D. in music therapy and feminist therapy from Concordia University, Canada. Her published articles, chapters, and reviews appear in the *Journal of Music Therapy, Music Therapy Perspectives, Voices: A World Forum for Music Therapy*, the *Journal of Palliative Care, Feminist Perspectives in Music Therapy* (Barcelona Publishers, forthcoming), *Creative Modalities in Therapy for Children and Adults* (Charles C Thomas Publisher, Ltd., forthcoming), *Interpersonal Violence, Health, and Gender* (W.C. Brown, 1994), and *Research in Music Therapy: A Tradition of Excellence* (AMTA, 1994). She has been actively engaged in social justice work in Canada and the United States for more than fifteen years. Currently she serves as chair of the Commission on Education, Training, and Registration of the World Federation for Music Therapy.

Chapter 15

THE USE OF MUSIC IN THERAPY WITH CHILDREN WHO HAVE BEEN SEXUALLY ABUSED

E. MAGDALENA LAVERDIERE

INTRODUCTION

The use of music therapy in both individual and group therapy sessions provides an outlet for victims of sexual abuse to express their emotions, memories, and feelings related to their trauma. Sgroi (1982) cites that victims of sexual abuse often have no desire to think or talk about their victimization. Music therapy can provide a medium for victims to draw out communication in expressing their emotions and feelings regarding their traumatic experiences. Bonny and Savary (1990) explain that music can bring about feelings and emotions that were previously unspoken or unexplored. Bonny and Savary describe the use of music in therapy as a "healing force" (p. 19). Music, as used in therapy, whether performed or listened to, can provide many benefits for children who have been sexually abused.

Gil (1991) explains that children who have experienced abuse need a safe environment, as the abuse has often occurred in the home and feelings of insecurity are often prevalent. The therapy environment can present a safe environment for that child. Gil (1991) further cites that "because abused children are frequently forced or threatened to keep the abuse secretive, or somehow sense that the abuse cannot be disclosed, efforts must be made to invite and promote self-expression" (p. 66). Therefore, it is important that a child who has been sexually abused be presented with an environment in therapy that feels emotionally safe for that child. Furthermore, the child should be encouraged in the use of self-expression, as Gil (1991) explains that self-expression promotes the healing process for children who have been abused.

Music is identified by researchers (Bruscia, 1998; Sutton, 2002) as a valuable tool in therapy that promotes safe self-expression. Self-expression, which is helpful in promoting healing for victims of abuse (Gil, 1991) can come in the form of play or music within the therapy environment. Children who have expressed sexual abuse often have feelings of rage and anger (Sarnacki-Porter, Canfield-Blick, and Sgroi, 1982). Therefore, it is important that children who have experienced such trauma be presented with a method for expressing such emotions safely. The use of music therapy with children who have been sexually abused can provide a safe form of expression for clients who have been sexually abused.

This chapter discusses current trends in music therapy, as applicable to children who have been sexually abused. These trends are examined according to individual and group therapy techniques. Such trends discussed in this chapter include composition, improvisation, singing, listening to music, and lyric writing (see appendix for definition of these terms).

CURRENT TRENDS IN THERAPY

Music therapy, as implemented within a therapy plan, can assist clients who have been sexually abused to open lines of communication with their therapist. In working with victims of sexual abuse, there are specific issues that should be dealt with. Sarnacki-Porter and colleagues (1982) discuss the ten primary issues that are to be dealt with when treating a child for sexual assault or abuse. These crucial issues include the following (p. 109):

1. "Damaged Goods" syndrome
2. Guilt
3. Fear
4. Depression
5. Low self-esteem and poor social skills
6. Repressed anger and hostility
7. Impaired ability to trust
8. Blurred role boundaries
9. Pseudo-maturity coupled with failure to accomplish developmental tasks
10. Self-mastery and control

Attention to the processing and addressing of these issues is necessary in treating children who have been sexually abused. The integration of music therapy throughout the process of addressing each of these issues can assist in creating openness in therapy and can foster a working alliance between client and therapist (Bunt and Hoskyns, 2002). Furthermore, Gil (1991) explains that a safe form of self-expression, such as that of music, should be employed with children who have experienced abuse, as such a client is often apprehensive in talking and a creative forum is required for the expression of their emotions.

Music can be immensely helpful in the child's processing of their emotions regarding their traumatic experiences, according to researchers (Bannister, 2003; Gil, 1991). Bannister cites that when children are able to process their traumatic event and put meaning to the event, they are able to reach their potential. Reaching one's potential, in the case of children, translates into the child progressing into the next phase of emotional and cognitive development (Bannister, 2003). Music can be applied to Bannister's theory by having a child create lyrics (in writing by the child, or by the therapist if assistance is required). The child can be encouraged to process their emotions and feelings related to guilt, fear, and depression, as these are cited by Sgroi (1982) as issues that require addressing in order for the client to engage in the process of healing.

In applying music therapy with children who have been sexually abused, it could be proposed by a therapist, for example, that a portion of a specific therapy session be devoted to the client writing lyrics about their feelings of fear related to their sexual abuse. Feelings of low self-esteem, as associated with sexual abuse through feelings of being "damaged" or "spoiled," according to Sgroi (1982), can be addressed in lyric writing in therapy. Lyric or song writing is proposed by researchers (Wigram, Pedersen, and Bonde, 2002) as a beneficial technique to use in music therapy. Lyric writing or song writing is just one technique that can be applied when using music therapy with children who have been sexually abused. Another technique that can be used is that of song.

SINGING

Music, in the form of singing, can allow the child to voice their emotions, as Bannister (2003) explains that expression by voice and song is important to children in the therapeutic environment. Singing can help the therapeutic process by allowing the child to raise their voice and express previously unknown feelings of rage, anger, hate, guilt, or fear; as Gil (1991) explains that abused children are often unaware of their inner feelings regarding their abuse. The addressing and expression of such feelings is deemed by Sarnacki-Porter and colleagues (1982) as imperative in the healing process for individuals who have been sexually abused.

Song can also be used to help the child process specific emotions when a song with emotional undertones that parallel the child's emotions are sung in the therapy session. Gil (1991) explains that children must be provided a safe environment for the expression of potentially harmful emotions such as rage and anger. Gil asserts that the child should also be guided in the expression of such emotions in order to protect the child from harming himself/herself, or from harming others. Music provides a safe expression of such potentially harmful emotions. The therapist can therefore guide the child in employing the use of song in the expression of such emotions. The use of song and singing is just one example of how music can be utilized in group or individual therapy with children who have experienced sexual abuse.

ATTENTION SPAN

The attention span of children should also be taken into consideration in therapy (Gil, 1991). Music in therapy is of value, as it can provide entertainment for the child, thus engaging the child in therapy. Utilizing various techniques in the session in specific time blocks, for example, lyric writing: ten minutes, role play: ten minutes, expressing lyrics in a song verbally: ten minutes, etc. . . . can help progress the session while keeping the attention of the client.

Group therapy and individual therapy with children who have been sexually abused can employ the use of music therapy using a variety of current techniques. The techniques discussed below can be utilized in addressing the ten issues discussed previously.

GROUP THERAPY

Group therapy is recognized by researchers (e.g., De Luca, Hazen and Cutler, 1993) as an effective short-term treatment method for childhood victims of sexual abuse. Integrating the use of music therapy into group sessions can assist in creating trust and reciprocal interaction within the group, according to Hussey and Layman (2003). Wigram and colleagues (2002) explain that music can assist in motivating interaction by breaking feelings of isolation. Creating a feeling of group cohesion and absolving feelings of isolation are certainly important goals in group therapy. The sensitive nature of the topic of sexual abuse may make it even more difficult to overcome the feelings of isolation that a child may have in a group situation; therefore, the use of music is group therapy is beneficial as Wigram and colleagues (2002) suggest that it assists in breaking feelings of isolation. Wigram and colleagues explain that writing songs or melodies in therapy assists in the expression of emotions that may otherwise not be brought to fruition. In creating group cohesion in music therapy, group members can assist one another in such composition and such an activity may thereby enhance the atmosphere of group cohesiveness.

Davis, Gfeller, and Thaut (1992) explain how musical activities in therapy are beneficial for children in the preoperational stage of development (ages two through seven). See appendix for definition of this stage. Davis and colleagues (1992) explain that these benefits include language development and social cooperation. Furthermore, Webb (1999) cites that group therapy for children who have experienced sexual abuse often provides an environment where they are able to express their memories and feelings related to the abuse. Davis and colleagues also explain how children in the concrete operational stage of development (ages seven through eleven) can benefit from music therapy. See appendix for a definition of this stage. It is explained by Davis and colleagues (1992) that such children can utilize music therapy for the development of "motor functioning and for personal achievements and mastery of musical skills" (p. 43). Furthermore, children in the operational stage can benefit from the socialization and cooperative play that is provided in group sessions that use music therapy methods.

Music therapy can provide socialization for children, as Davis and colleagues (1992) explain that therapy sessions can include, for example, hello and goodbye songs that prompt hand shaking and interaction between group participants to encourage teamwork, cooperation, and "attending behavior" (p. 4). Utilizing songs in the beginning and closing of therapy with children who have been sexually victimized can encourage positive interaction between group members, thereby fostering a productive therapy progression with the group. Other music therapy methods that are appropriate to use with children who have been sexually abused include improvisation and composition (Bruscia, 1998).

Improvisation. A current technique employed by music therapists is improvisation. According to research by Bruscia (1998), musical improvisation (having the clients sing or play instruments) can establish a means of communication, fulfill self-expression, and can foster group skills and participation in therapy. In working with children who have been sexually abused, the emphasis on group interaction and cohesion is important for the long-range goal of participants openly sharing in the processing of their traumatic experiences. Music therapy, as used in the form of improvisation, can also assist in reducing group inhibitions and can thereby increase group participation and expression from clients, according to Bruscia. These skills are essential in working with victims of sexual abuse, as researchers (Sgroi, 1982) recognize that victims are often highly apprehensive in talking about their traumatic experiences.

Wigram and colleagues (2002) explain that the use of improvisation in music therapy can be used as a bridge between the inner and outer world of a child. For a child who is sexually abused, such a bridge may be essential in therapy, as children who have experienced a trauma are often, according to Sutton (2002), apprehensive in revealing inner thoughts and feelings related to the trauma. Wigram also explains that the use of improvisation can incorporate either free play with an instrument or can be implemented with rules attached. These "playing rules" according to Wigram and colleagues (1992) can be "for example, 'Let's play a beat each on the drum'" (p. 178). Improvisation can also be applied to vocal singing (Bruscia, 1998). Children in this situation can be encourage to hum or resonate sound in a manner that works together in harmony with the other group members or can simply be whatever a child feels to express. The expression of these musical interludes by the children can open the door for the therapist to engage the group in discussion regarding their inner emotions that are prompting each of their musical exchanges.

Composition. Another form of music therapy discussed by Bruscia (1998) is composition. Some techniques utilized in this form of music therapy include changing the words of a popular song to suit the client's own self-expression, lyric writing, instrumental composition, notational song writing, and musical collage or song fragmenting for purposes of self-expression (Bruscia, 1998). Song composition techniques, when employed with victims of sexual abuse, can encourage creative expression of the participants' emotions related to their trauma, thereby supporting the healthy and therapeutic processing of emotions and feelings related to the abuse. Furthermore, Bruscia states that lyric discussion also brings about a "springboard for discussion." Group discussion can be focused on popular music lyrics that are relevant. Lyrics written by each sexual abuse victim within the group can also be quite revealing. Although the work by children in lyric writing may appear simplistic on the surface, such work can bring about openness, participation, and, according to Bruscia, can help clients communicate inner experiences. However, the technical aspects of composing the lyrics into a musical framework can be complicated for children, and therefore, the work of a therapist as a musician may be required to varying degrees. For example, if a popular children's song melody is used with the integration of the participants' written lyrics, the level of musical expertise required from the clinician is of a lesser degree.

INDIVIDUAL THERAPY

Bunt and Hoskyns (2002) explain that music, when used in therapy, creates an empathetic environment for the client. Such empathy, according to Bunt and Hoskyns, can be achieved when the client's musical expressions or actual verbal statements are reciprocated by the therapist providing a musical response that appropriately reflects or reacts to the client's statement or musical projection. Therefore, the dynamic process of therapy can be initiated when music is appropriately employed, and a working relationship can be started between client and therapist through the mode of music.

Hussey and Layman (2003) state that music therapy can be used with children to assist in establishing "a meaningful relationship with an adult through musical play and interaction" (p. 38). The establishment of such a relationship will only help the therapeutic process that a therapist is attempting to achieve for the betterment of the client. Furthermore, Hussey and Layman (2003) recognize that music therapy is especially useful in instances where traumatized children are reluctant to communicate verbally. The trauma caused by a sexual assault may indeed create reluctance for a child to communicate verbally in therapy about the assault. Music as a mode of therapy can create an empathic therapy environment (Bunt and Hoskyns, 2002), as well as a venue of communication between client and therapist (Hussey and Layman, 2003).

Role-Play. Role-play, as integrated with song writing, can help a child client relate to their feelings toward their perpetrator. In this form of therapy, it is necessary for the therapist to be identified as the aggressor. According to Prior (1996), when a therapist is identified as the aggressor in role play, the child may be encouraged to openly engage in coping behaviors that may thereby transfer to reactions outside the therapy environment. However, Prior (1996) explains that the relationship between client and therapist should be progressed to a level where the child feels safe enough in the therapy environment for the therapist to role-play as the aggressor (through verbal exchange only). Music can be engaged in role-play activities by, for example, the child writing lyrics or verbally singing their expressions and feelings about the perpetrator (who is now being role-played by the therapist) is presently in the room. The child could also be encouraged to react with an instrument, such as a drum, cymbal, or piano, to statements made by the therapist (while playing the aggressor). The child will be allowed to release feelings of rage and anger in a safe environment using an emotionally and physically safe method. Engaging this role-play activity through song may heighten the therapy process, as researchers (Bannister, 2003; Bruscia, 1998) agree that music can increase spontaneity, creativity, and emotional expression in therapy.

Listening to Music. Listening to music in therapy can also be beneficial for children who have been sexually abused. Bunt and Hoskyns (2002) explain that listening to music can evoke emotional display for children who otherwise may repress such emotional display. The use of drums for example, may evoke excitement or anger (Bunt and Hoskyns, 2002). The display of such emotions while listening to music can open a door for the therapist to interact with the child. The therapist can pause the music and discuss what emotions and/or thoughts were being felt by the child while listening to a particular repertoire. Bunt and Hoskyns (2002) describe how some children may become more emotionally expressive when listening to particular instruments being played. For example, a child may express anger when hearing the sound of cymbals, sadness when hearing a bass or viola, or happiness when listening to the sound of a flute solo. The evoking of such emotions may bring to light the true source or causation of the inner feelings; the inner cause being sexual abuse for children who have experienced such a trauma. Listening to music can help the child express their emotions. Verbalization of these emotions can thereby be discussed with the therapist once such emotions are expressed by verbalization, body, and/or facial language.

CONCLUSION

The use of music therapy with children who have experienced a crisis such as sexual abuse has been proven beneficial in therapy according to researchers (Bannister, 2003; Webb, 1999). A myriad of benefits can be derived from the use of music therapy when used with children who have been sexually abused. Such therapeutic benefits include creating a pathway for self-expression of clients emotions (Bruscia, 1998), creating an empathetic therapy environment (Bunt and Hoskyns, 2002), and can assist in establishing trust between client and therapist (Hussey and Layman, 2003). Music therapy can also promote development and can assist in the development of self-worth and self-esteem (Wigram et al., 2002).

Music and other creative therapies can help clients progress developmentally, as Bannister (2003) states:

> Young children who have been repeatedly abused, by caregivers or close family members, suffer damage to their development which may have long-term effects. . . . Creative therapies can induce positive behavioral changes in abused children. It is likely that the positive effect of creative therapies results from their capacity to recreate developmental processes. Negative brain patterns caused by abuse may thus be reversed. (p. 22)

Children can derive from music therapy many benefits. In the group setting there are some specific advantages that music can present for children who have been sexually abused. Such advantages and benefits that music in group therapy can provide:

- Ability for children to openly communicate feelings with other children
- Greater understanding of feelings related to the trauma
- Courage to take new chances in self-expression
- Higher levels of social interaction achieved
- Greater empathy
- Enhanced sense of group cohesion and identity with group members

- Greater confidence in abilities related to self-expression
- Understanding and awareness of feelings
- Increased coping skills in regard to emotions related to the trauma
- Ability to give and receive feedback from peers
- Increased self-esteem and self-worth
- Validation of feelings and emotions
- Improved self-perception

Many of these benefits can also be derived in individual therapy sessions. The use of music therapy with children who have been sexually abused provides many advantages for the client. However, children who have experienced sexual abuse may require more than one method of therapy, as Sarnacki-Porter and colleagues (1982) state: "most child victims of sexual abuse will benefit from multiple treatment modalities carefully implemented as part of a comprehensive treatment plan" (p. 145).

APPENDIX – TERMS

Composition in Therapy – The client writes song lyrics or instrumental pieces by the direction of the clinician. The client can write the music using simple melodies from popular songs and adding their own lyrics into the melody. The goal is to help the client process their feelings through music writing. Composing also helps the client organize their thoughts and it also promotes self responsibility (Bruscia, 1998).

Improvisation in Therapy – Making music by playing an instrument or singing extemporarily. The client can make the music upon direction from the clinician. The music is made by the client as a means of self-expression using their own creativity and freedom. The clinician typically presents an idea (e.g., story, experience, image) by which the client can use musically to direct their feelings of self-expression (Bruscia, 1998).

Singing in Therapy – Singing can be done in therapy using improvisation, composition, or organized singing. Organized singing can be used, for example, in group therapy sessions using "hello" and "good-bye" songs (Davis and colleagues, 1992).

Listening to Music – The clinician plays specific music selections while prompting the client to visualize certain situations or environments. The goal is to help the client evoke emotions related to the situation or environment to help the client find insight, healing, and/or awareness (Bonny and Savary, 1990).

Lyric Writing – The clinician directs the client to write phrases or sentences that can be incorporated with musical melodies. The clinician will select the topic or idea upon which the client will write (Bruscia, 1998).

Concrete Operational Stage – The stage of development when children, ages seven through eleven, begin to think logically and are able to use reason (Santrock, 1999).

Preoperational Stage – The stage of development when children, ages two through seven, begin to form stable concepts and some use of mental reasoning emerges (Santrock, 1999).

REFERENCES

Bannister, A. (2003). *Creative therapies with traumatized children.* London, England: Jessica Kingsley Publishers.

Bonny, H.L., & Savary, L.M. (1990). *Music and your mind: Listening with a new consciousness.* New York: Station Hill Press.

Bruscia, K.E. (1998). *Defining music therapy: Second edition.* Gilsum, New Hampshire: Barcelona Publishers.

Bunt, L., & Hoskyns, S. (2002). *The handbook of music therapy.* New York: Brunner-Routledge.

Davis, W.B., Gfeller, K.E., & Thaut, M.H. (1992). *An introduction to music therapy: Theory and practice.* Iowa: Wm. C. Brown Publishers.

De Luca, R., Hazen, A., & Cutler, J. (1993). Evaluation of a group counseling program for preadolescent female victims of incest. *Elementary School Guidance Counseling, 28*, 104–114

Gil, E. (1991). *The healing power of play: Working with abused children.* New York and London: Guilford Press.

Hussey, D.L., & Layman, D. (2003). Music therapy with emotionally disturbed children. *Psychiatric Time, 20*(6), 37–41.

Prior, S. (1996). *Object relations is severe trauma: Psychotherapy of the sexually abused child.* New Jersey: Jason Aronson Inc.

Santrock, J.W. (1999). *Life-span development.* Boston: McGraw-Hill College.

Sarnacki-Porter, F., Canfield-Blick, L., & Sgroi, S.M. (1982). Treatment of the sexually abused child. In S.M. Sgroi (Ed.), *Handbook of clinical intervention in child sexual abuse* (pp. 109–145). New York: The Free Press.

Sgroi, S.M. (1982). *Handbook of clinical intervention in child sexual abuse.* New York: The Free Press.

Sutton, J.P. (2002). *Music, music therapy and trauma: International perspectives.* London: Jessica Kingsley Publishers.

Webb, N.B. (1999). *Play therapy with children in crisis.* New York: The Guilford Press.

Wigram, T., Pedersen, I.N., & Bonde, L.O. (2002). *A comprehensive guide to music therapy: Theory, clinical practice, research, and training.* London: Jessica Kingsley Publishers.

BIOGRAPHIC STATEMENT

E. Magdalena LaVerdiere earned her Ph.D. in Academic Psychology from Walden University in May 2005. Her dissertation research focused on misconceptions and myths that high school students accept about rape. In 2002, she earned her M.A. in Professional Counseling from Liberty University. Former work experiences include that of sexual assault counselor/advocate and domestic violence counselor/advocate. Her work as a sexual assault counselor/advocate included treatment of adults and children, in which she conducted both individual and group therapies for these victims. She maintains a keen interest in helping victims of sexual assault through research and writing on this significant topic.

E-Mail: mikeandmagdalena@hotmail.com

Chapter 16

MUSIC THERAPY AND SEXUAL VIOLENCE: RESTORING CONNECTION AND FINDING PERSONAL CAPACITIES FOR HEALING

To my mind, there is no single more destructive feeling in childhood than the icy horror of feeling isolated, inadequate, and totally alone. In that mute, alienated state you feel totally trapped, hopelessly vulnerable, and both frightened and angry. When a child has lost the ability to trust and communicate, he has lost his only means of getting the nurturing needed to counterbalance the fears and distortions in his small world.

Hammel-Zabin, 2003, p. 37

MEETING TISCHA

*I*arrived late to the gym class at the state child psychiatric facility where I was beginning my work as a therapist with children and adolescents who are labeled "severely emotionally disturbed." As I entered the gym, I saw a group of teens engaged in a game with two recreation therapists. On the top row of the gym's bleachers, one girl stood separate from her peers, pacing back and forth across the top bench and periodically slapping her open fist against the cement blocks on the wall. I immediately sensed that this patient was in crisis. I walked in her direction, unsure of my role but feeling compelled to let her know I was available.

"My name is Maria. I'm a new music therapist. I'm going to take a walk around gym. Would you like to join me?" I asked, wondering if a few laps around the gym would help her to release the energy I saw her expressing each time she fiercely slapped the wall.

"No. Leave me the fuck alone," Tischa responded briefly turning towards me to scowl.

218

"Okay. I'm going to do a few laps and if you decide you want to join me, feel free," I replied, wondering if I was crazy to assume there was any chance she'd acquiesce. I walked one complete lap around the gym, watching Tischa out of the corner of my eye as I did so. As I came around to the bleachers, I saw Tischa climb down to the gym floor.

"I want to walk," Tischa said.

I motioned to her that she should join me, smiling hesitantly, unsure of what might happen next. She moaned and stomped her feet as we walked. I listened.

After just one revolution around the gym's perimeter, Tischa explained the root of her current aggression. "My mother said she would be here today! She promised me, but she didn't come. And this is what she did last time! She hates me and I hate her!"

I continued to listen as she professed her hatred for her mother and all the times her mother had disappointed her in her thirteen years. Her steps became lighter and she began making eye contact with me as we walked. I noticed that she looked scared, and uncertain of whether or not she should be trusting me while she, paradoxically, flooded me with her hurt and anger. As her peers finished their game and were told to line up by the door, Tischa and I completed our final lap around the gym. She looked at me to say goodbye.

"I'm going to hang myself from the rafters up there," she said, pointing to the ceiling of the gym, "and no one will even care. I'll just die and it won't matter." Tischa's brow was furrowed and she whined, appearing, in that moment, half of her thirteen years.

My heart sank. "I know that I would care," I responded. "I just met you and it would matter to me if something happened to you. You have known other people a lot longer and I bet they would really care." I could sense that she was angry. Could she hear my words and experience them as empathic and genuine? Ultimately, her eyes softened and she partly smiled as she got in line with her peers to go back to her unit.

This was my introduction to Tischa who, two days later, asked for a music therapy session.

This chapter, which includes vignettes from a later music therapy session with Tischa, is adapted from a larger work, which explores music therapy in the healing of those who have experienced exposure to profound violence. Although consistently referred to as traumas or traumatic experiences, this chapter briefly explores trauma symptoms, therapy and treatment as they relate to sexual abuse or sexual violence specifically. This exploration is further shaped by the focus on an individual clinical music therapy session with Tischa, who experienced sexual abuse by a male family member and abandonment by her mother at a young age. This kind of trauma, to which I refer as a developmental trauma, caused a relentless fear within Tischa, beginning a spiral down into a distorted reality based on the fear she displayed in the gym on the day of our meeting. The music therapy vignettes included in this chapter provide an example of how music therapy can be used in the healing of trauma following sexual violence and the ways in which music therapy sessions can provide an important opportunity for re-engagement and inter-personal connectedness.

TRAUMA THERAPY AND TREATMENT

> Traumatic experiences present victims with the inescapable truth that reality can damage their sense of safety and trust. In order to sustain a sense of hope in the face of such an external onslaught, a person has to have a sufficiently enduring sense of identity and interpersonal connectedness. The ability to tolerate the truth of the traumatic experience involves a capacity to bear pain in the presence of another human being; this constitutes the core of mature intimacy. (Turner, McFarlane, and van der Kolk, 1996, p. 538)

The prevailing approach to trauma treatment endorses cathartic expression of the internalized trauma. This has historically involved the uncovering and retelling of the traumatic experience with the intent of integrating the traumatic experience and the various splits of self into the survivor's understanding of who she is. "Because the symptoms and emotions associated with trauma can be extreme, most of us . . . will recoil and attempt to repress these intense reactions" (Levine, 1997, p. 48). This suppression sometimes evokes denial, memory repression, or discussion avoidance of the traumatic experiences. "Unfortunately, this mutual denial can prevent us from healing" (Levine, 1997, p. 48). In this model of treatment, the therapist bears witness to the survivor's trauma as she remembers and relates the experiences. Drawing from a Gestalt perspective, the process of *integration* strives to make a whole out of the fragments of self that trauma survivors often experience (Powch, et al., 2004). The fragmentation that trauma evokes can lead to a split self that sometimes becomes a literal dissociation – a now more commonly acknowledged symptom of trauma (Powch, et al., 2004). According to Austin (2002), who developed and codified a series of techniques she describes as "vocal holding techniques," when unconscious experiences are "contacted and communicated with, these younger parts can be reunited with the ego . . . the vital energy they contain can be made available to the present day personality. Developmental arrests can be repaired and a more complete sense of self can be attained" (p. 236).

It can be argued, however, that this cathartic relaying of a traumatic experience or history is a form of "re-experiencing" that may not be appropriate in every context. Some argue that therapists can become seduced into evoking discussion of the trauma and must continually evaluate and re-evaluate the motivation for and relevance of bearing witness to the client's traumatic experience (Boothby and Crawford, 2004). Additionally, "some of the effects of trauma may mitigate against the use of therapy" (Smyth, 2002, p. 77). Some argue that the painful reliving of memories is simply not necessary in order to heal trauma (Levine, 1997, p. 39). In any form of therapy, music therapy being no exception, clinicians run the risk of re-traumatizing clients. Turry (2002) states that this is even possible through "spontaneous musical involvement" (p. 48).

Re-enactment initiated by survivors throughout the course of their lives is a common symptom prevalent in those who have experienced trauma. In re-enacting our traumas, we serve to retraumatize ourselves in a cyclical fashion, often unconsciously re-exposing ourselves to traumatizing experiences. These experiences typically resemble the initial trauma. Austin (2002) agrees that "the urge to resolve trauma through re-enactment is extremely compelling" (p. 244). As is the case with dissociation, re-enactment is the body and mind's ineffectual way of attempting to heal the inflicted trauma. van der Kolk (1996) states that self-destructiveness, re-victimization or harmful behaviors towards others can result from a person's failure to integrate a stressful incident.

Another possible explanation for the pull one might feel towards self-re-traumatization involves the bio-chemical components of heightened sensory experiences, which can relieve the suffocating symptom of emotional constriction. Austin (2002) refers to the compulsion to go back to the trauma repeatedly as an "addiction to trauma" (p. 244). Levine (1997) refers to this addiction as result of the trauma vortex. Austin (2002) refers to Levine and van der Kolk when she states:

> At some point in the re-traumatisation cycle, this pull toward the "vortex" appears to take on a life of its own. These highly activated emotional states have a biochemical component to them. The heightened arousal state can release a surge of energy that may feel exhilarating. . . . Some people who suffer from trauma symptoms have difficulty in accessing feelings, and intense or volatile emotional states may provide a relief from numbness and a sense of feeling alive. (pp. 244–245)

Related to the knowledge that biochemical changes are effected through trauma is the knowledge that traumatic experiences have the capacity to enact more enduring and formal changes in the brain's structure. "Excessive stimulation of the central nervous system (CNS) at the time of the trauma may result in permanent neuronal changes that have a negative effect on learning, habituation, and stimulus discrimination" (van der Kolk, 1996, p. 228). In children, an interruption in development can occur as a result which can result in cognitive deficits. Chronic affect dysregulation, learning disabilities, destructive behavior against self and others, and inhibited language development are cited by van der Kolk (1996) as some of the psychobiological effects of trauma on children at an early developmental stage.

Another general but important disturbance in the lives of many who have experienced trauma is the disruption of interpersonal relationships or the inability to develop, foster and sustain emotionally and psychologically healthy relationships. Certainly this is the case for children who experience disruptions in their primary relationships at an early age.

> Children who have not experienced fluid, reciprocal, intersubjective emotional relationships have a decreased capacity to develop a sense of valuing themselves or others. They may be unable to develop or sustain fluid, intersubjective emotional relationships with other human beings (Pavlicevic, 2002, p. 108).

Additional reactions often associated with sexual abuse include somatic problems, confusion about sexual identity, as well as the low self-image and internalized guilt and blame described by Pavlicevic. Hammel-Zabin (2003) describes the ways in which her childhood sexual abuse affected her inability to rid herself of guilt and its pervasive quality in her childhood existence. In her book on pedophilia, *Conversations with a Pedophile*, Hammel-Zabin (2003) describes a childhood memory of a hit-and-run accident of which she was the victim. She explains that, at the time, she did not want to draw attention to herself following the accident, witnessed by others. Instead, she hobbled home, hid the pieces of her bike, an additional casualty, and attempted to conceal her injuries from her mother. "I felt that I deserved what had happened to me and that only I was to blame. I was left feeling vulnerable and alone, and I suspected that I unconsciously broadcast my fragility to everyone in my sphere, no matter how hard I tried to appear strong and confident" (pp. 25–26).

Hammel-Zabin (2003) writes that sexually abused children suffer from an inability to communicate, further compounding this self-blame. "Feelings of self-disgust run so strong that the child is certain that any possible listener will share these same feelings of repulsion for him or her" (p. 27).

SOMATIC EXPERIENCING

Many trauma therapy models emphasize the recovery of feelings of efficacy and power (Turry, 2002). Increasing feelings of self-worth, safety and invulnerability are valuable goals. These goals are achieved through stabilization, the processing of the experience on the sensory/emotive levels, and re-engaging and reconnecting with others (Turry, 2002; van der Kolk, Turner and McFarlane, 1996). Restoring connections with other individuals, with family and within the community is, from my perspective, the single most important aspect of trauma therapy treatment.

One of these novel ways of approaching the process of treatment is based on Peter Levine's (1997) concept of the somatic and physiological processes that are engaged when one encounters a traumatic experience. His treatment philosophy is based on the premise that the mind and body work together as a unit and need to be treated as a unit for healing to occur. From this perspective, resolving traumatic symptoms through the traditional study of its effects solely on the mind is inadequate (Levine, 1997). This approach to healing trauma is rooted in individual, one-to-one work. "At the moment, the work of transforming trauma within groups of people is still in its infancy" (Levine, 1997, p. 7). However, exploration of psychosomatic philosophies, as I refer to them, and the methods that grow out of them are part of the process of discovery – the discovery of trauma treatment models for various survivors in various contexts.

Levine (1997) states that the body has a profound reaction to trauma, as the mind alters its state as a protective reaction. After the event, the mind often returns to normal. At this point, the body's response is also meant to normalize. "When the restorative process is thwarted, the effects of trauma become fixated and the person becomes traumatized" (1997, p. 6). Treating the victim solely through the process of verbal therapy, therefore, is inadequate. Creative methods of treatment that engage the body, inclusive of the creative arts therapies, are better able to access the trauma that is 'trapped in the body' rather than solely exploring the trauma that rests at the level of the psyche. As van der Kolk, Turner, and McFarlane (1996) suggest, the experiences are processed on the sensory/emotive levels. Protomusicality, as the "shared capacity for engaging in communication through sound and movement" (Stige, 2002, p. 87) allows us to process on these levels, as we engage with the world on a sensory level.

Levine (1997), in a description of theories which form the basis of his model of *Somatic Experiencing*, references the "freeze" or immobility response that mammals often enact when in danger. This altered state of consciousness is shared by all mammals and occurs when death appears imminent. This immobility response is, first, an attempt at playing possum and, second, an "an altered state in which no pain is experienced" (p. 16). This instinctive surrender has often been misjudged as cowardice, weakness or lack of aversion. However, movement into and out of this state of immobility is an adaptive response that is key to avoiding the debilitating effects of trauma.

Becomming psychologically stuck in the immobility response even after the danger has passed does not allow the release of the residual energy. Consequently, the victim is left in the traumatic maze with the experience of continual distress – trauma symptoms (Levine, 1997, p. 21) – or, as Austin (2002) puts it, stuck in the trauma vortex. Similarly, the first chapter of van der Kolk, McFarlane and Weisaeth's (1996) book is evocatively titled *The Black Hole of Trauma*. The frozen residue of energy that has not been resolved and discharged remains "trapped in the nervous system where it can wreak havoc on our bodies and spirits" (Levine, 1997, p. 19).

The treatment of trauma symptoms understood to be the result of the above processes demands focus on health rather than pathology. "What we need to do to be freed from our symptoms and fears is to arouse our deep physiological resources and consciously utilize them" (Levine, 1997, p. 31). Tapping into these deep physiological resources invites us to restore a sense of hope where lack of regularity, insecurity, and sense of helplessness has divorced us from our sense of optimistic hope. And this demands that we replace the focus on pathology with the focus on our inner resources.

Levine (1997) writes, "While trauma can be hell on earth, trauma resolved is a gift of the gods – a heroic journey that belongs to each of us" (p. 12). We can all claim ownership precisely because we all have innate capacity to heal our traumas (Levine 1997, p. 32). A discussion about that which constitutes the potentially ambiguous concepts of healing or resolution of a trauma might be fruitful. We can, however, imagine that it implies a reduction of symptoms, reduction of distress, and/or reduction of impairment in social, occupational, or other important areas of functioning (American Psychological Association, 2000). Ultimately, this resolution is an increase in survival skills and, most importantly, the re-experiencing of intimate connections to others, which is difficult to endure following traumatic experiences.

MUSIC THERAPY IN TRAUMA HEALING

"The healing of trauma is a natural process that can be accessed through an inner awareness of the body" (Levine, 1997, p. 34). This is especially important because traumatic experiences, as acts of violence, disturb our sense of "bodily connectedness" (Sutton, 2002, p. 35). Treatment, therefore, requires the restoration of wholeness to an organism that has been fragmented by trauma (p. 60). "Music offers experiences of ourselves as embodied and in sound and silence. . . . It follows that music therapy can be of use to those vulnerable to the effects of trauma because of these qualities of musical embodiment" (Sutton, 2002, p. 35). Moving through trauma requires "quietness, safety, and protection" (Levine, 1997, pp. 35–36).

> Internally resonating vibrations break up and release blockages of energy, allowing a natural flow of vitality and a state of equilibrium to return to the body. These benefits are particularly relevant to traumatised clients who have frozen, numbed off areas in the body that hold traumatic experience. (Austin, 2002, p. 235)

Additionally, music is a multi-dimensional alternative route to inner awareness. The use of music in music therapy may ask that the client take notice of his or her body as it relates to his or her emotions, memories, and present sensory experiences and use this information as a tool for healing.

In comparison to the traditional cathartic approach of retelling and re-experiencing, Levine's (1997) approach suggests that confronting the trauma head-on will allow for the continuation of that response which has enabled the traumatic response in the first place. It will "immobilize us in fear" when, instead, "the solution to vanquishing trauma comes not through confronting it directly, but by working with its reflection, mirrored in our instinctual responses" (Levine, 1997, p. 65). I believe that this reflection and these instinctual responses are available in the making of music.

"Could I trust in a process that seemed to involve reactivating people's trauma without a clear sense of how to contain it?" (Bosco, 2002, p. 72). Regardless of whether or not our goals as practitioners include reactivation, we must be trained and prepared for this circumstance and for the myriad emotions that may surface with it. While the esoteric and often seemingly strictly symbolic concept of containment is often mentioned in discussion of music therapy technique, a solid and tangible grasp on the concept is crucial when working with trauma victims who are at risk of being reactivated.

VIGNETTE: TISCHA

Tischa's History. I discovered that Tischa had been transferred to the state facility from another hospital. Prior to that admission she had been living in a group home. Tischa's history included physical and sexual abuse as well as parental neglect. Tischa felt much attached to her mother, who had a history of drug and alcohol abuse and who was then abusing alcohol. Tischa did not know that her father was deceased, having had little contact with him throughout her childhood. At the time, Tischa had three siblings in foster care and two siblings, aged twenty-four and twenty-two, who were no longer living at home. I later learned that Tischa felt especially close to one of these older siblings who had moved out of the city despite Tischa's appeals to her to stay. Tischa herself had been using alcohol, marijuana, and cigarettes since the age of nine. She had a history of running away from her group home, suicidal ideation, and command auditory hallucinations. Tischa was, in numerous assessments, described as impulsive, aggressive, argumentative, and disruptive.

At the time of our meeting, Tischa had been given Axis I diagnoses of Mood Disorder, not otherwise specified; Rule Out Bipolar Disorder; Rule Out ADHD; Rule Out Conduct Disorder. Also listed under Axis I were: Marijuana and Alcohol Abuse; Physical Abuse as a child; Sexual abuse as a child. Previous diagnoses had included Depressive Disorder, not otherwise specified; and Disruptive Behavior Disorder, not otherwise specified. Tischa's reported command auditory hallucinations, voices telling her to hurt herself, had not materialized into any diagnoses with psychotic features, as it was reported that she had not shown signs of psychoses while on the unit.

As mentioned previously, Tischa did request music therapy sessions and we began working together shortly after our meeting in the gym. The following vignette describes my third session with Tischa. While the two previous sessions had been composed exclusively of improvisations at the piano, an instrument that Tischa knew and on which she felt comfortable exploring, in this third session, she pushed herself into territory that appeared a little less safe for her.

Improvisation — The Little Girl and the Shark
"Play the drums and I'll do this," Tischa said, picking up the ocean drum and pointing to a conga. She began tipping the ocean drum slowly from side to side, listening intently as the beads between the drum moved in a circle around its circumference.

I allowed my fingertips to fall against the head of the conga drum in attempt to match the arrhythmic quality of her playing. She then let go of her monitored control and allowed the beads to fall violently from one rounded side of the ocean drum to the other.

"Play a little louder 'cause I'm kind of loud with this. Do you like it?" Tischa asked, continuing to play.

"I love it," I responded, increasing the power of my fingertapping on the drum head.

"Let's tell a story," Tischa suggested. "I start low and then when I go high, you go really high," she said referring to the levels of intensity of her playing.

"Okay," I responded, realizing that she was asking for musical storytelling. This made me wonder if Tischa's mother had read to her at bedtime while Tischa was a young girl. As I listened to Tischa play the ocean drum, I thought of my favorite childhood book which was about a girl who lived by the ocean. I decided to use these ideas to set a context for the story. "Once upon a time there was a little girl walking along the seashore collecting seashells. She also loved to collect sea glass," I began.

"What's that?" Tischa asked as she softly and carefully allowed the beads in the drum to roll across its surface.

"She collected sea glass made of old glass bottles that had been thrown into the ocean," I explained as Tischa went higher, abruptly turning the drum so that the beads fell across the drum loudly and swiftly. I responded by getting higher with her as she specified, using my open fingers to roll a rhythm across the conga head evocative of a more traditional drumming technique. "Pieces of them had been worn down by the waves and they now had smooth edges. She liked collecting them to bring home," I continued as I played.

"The girl met a shark named Bob who was very hungry," Tischa provoked, continuing to play loudly and aggressively.

"'I'm not very tasty,' the girl told him." I offered this to the story hoping to save the girl.

"'I know you only like junk food and I would taste like collard greens,' the little girl told him, but the shark said he wanted to eat her anyway," Tischa responded, continuing in the voice of the girl and expressing a futile hope that the girl might be spared. Tischa played softly when evoking the voice of the little girl. "'The seal would taste

*better,' she told the shark, 'and besides, the seal wants to die anyway,'" Tischa contin-
ued. Although my initial interaction with Tischa had been weeks prior, I immediately
thought of her reference to suicide in the gym on the day of our meeting when she referenced a wish for death in this story song.*

*I replied, "'I don't want the seal. I'd rather eat you. I like the taste of collard greens!'
the shark said." The roar of the ocean drum and conga together evoked an image of a
menacing shark. I experienced him as threatening the girl but allowing her to attempt
to persuade him as a crazy-making psychological tactic.*

*"I have to go to the bathroom. I'm sorry. When I come back, can we play the piano?"
Tischa asked, no longer in character.*

"Okay," I replied.

I hypothesize that this was Tischa's way of giving herself distance from the
intensity of the story we had just created and focusing on something new.
Time became an issue for her when she emerged, and this recurred throughout the remainder of the session. Although I heard Tischa's request for the
piano, I did not want to leave the story uncompleted because, symbolically, it
seemed that doing so would parallel Tischa's experience of abandonment and
feeling of being incomplete herself without a family member who can adequately care for her – especially in times of crisis. While, at this point, I additionally suspected that the story might be a metaphor for an experience of
sexual abuse, I only learned later that, indeed, it was a male family member
who had sexually abused her. Her mother did not protect her and this con-
tributed to Tischa's experience of abandonment.

*"Okay," Tischa said to herself as she emerged from the bathroom. "How much time
do we have?" I sensed that she was nervous about ending the session.*

"Five minutes," I replied. "Let's finish the story and then play the piano to end."

Tischa picked up a rainstick and smelled it. "Smell this," she commanded.

*I smelled the rainstick and immediately begun inviting us back into the story by ag-
gressively playing the conga. I wanted her to decide what might happen to the girl next,
so I began, "So . . . the little girl said . . ."*

*"I . . . WANT . . . TO . . . GO . . . HOME!!!" Tischa stated slowly, deliberately,
rhythmically, and emphatically in a demanding, childlike voice. She now shook the
rainstick up and down as I played a rhythmic pattern on the conga to reinforce the intensity of her words. I was not surprised that the little girl wanted to go home because
this was Tischa's consistent daily request. This statement confirmed for me that the little
girl in the story was Tischa.*

I offered, "And the shark said . . ."

*"'Well, too bad, I'm gonna eat you up!'" Tischa growled quickly, forcefully and quite
matter-of-factly. "Now you play this . . ." Tischa, then out of character, handed me the
rainstick and slid the conga into her reach.*

"And the little girl said . . . 'I don't really think I taste very good, I told you. You can eat the seal instead. He doesn't want to be alive. He wants to be eaten.'" I reflected a sentiment that Tischa had expressed earlier regarding the third actor in the story – the seal.

"'Too bad,' And the shark swallowed her up!" Tischa said while she played a very strict galloping rhythm on the conga. And she ended the story here, asking to play the piano.

The piano improvisation that followed this story's tragic ending was tender and comforting. Although I had started with something different, Tischa demanded that I stop and play the same rocking, arpeggiated pattern in ¾ time that I had played in our previous session. She played major second intervals on top of the arpeggios and listened attentively to my rubato, rocking back and forth with me. It felt like the kind of soothing crisis intervention that Tischa achieved when she sucked her thumb which was, at the time, one of her common signifiers of regressive behavior. Once we ended our piano improvisation, and Tischa knew it was time to officially end the session, she attempted to prolong it by exploring the instruments.

Tischa first shook the ocean drum softly and then began shaking it up and down with a lot of force. "This is my anger!" Tischa said and aggressively shook the ocean drum again. "This is my happiness," she said and allowed the beads to fall slowly from side to side slowly as she had done during the story song.
"What's your sadness?" I asked.
Tischa didn't hesitate. She gently allowed a few beads at a time to slide across the drum and then softly placed the ocean drum on the floor before her.

Tischa, in her telling of the story we created together previously, had explored the loud and angry quality which even the most "relaxing instrument" – the ocean drum – can take on when loud and angry emotion is present. She verbalized this in distinguishing between the two sounds for me outside the context of the story. And she chose to personalize these emotions by making them hers and relating them directly to her feeling states. "This is *my* anger . . . *my* happiness. . . ." I also knew that Tischa had more than two emotions and that much of her anger arises from her sadness. Therefore, I asked her how her sadness sounded next to her happiness and anger. She proceeded to explore these individual sentiments on a couple of other instruments before asking about future sessions together. Before we ended, I probed for more information about her perception of the story, hoping I'd gain additional insight into Tischa's processing of her abuse.

"That little girl in the story – was she sad that she got eaten?" I asked Tischa.
"Yeah," Tischa responds quietly. Then she brightened in affect, "But she was still alive in his belly."

"Oh, she was?" I asked. I was surprised to hear such an interesting turn of events.

"She used to eat the fish that he used to eat," Tischa explained matter-of-factly, being sure that I understood how she survived. I wondered if this was evocative of the abusive relationship with the family members who were also responsible for taking care of her basic needs – feeding her while simultaneously denying her safety.

"So once he swallowed her, when he would swallow fish later that day she would eat them inside his belly?" I asked, trying to be sure I understood her intention for the story.

"She'd eat it. Yeah, she'd share them inside with his guts and stuff." Tischa crinkled up her face.

"That's kinda gross, huh?" I asked, reflecting her facial expression.

"Yeah, that's really gross!" She responded.

"Was he really mean?" I asked. I was wondering if she could share more details about the shark's personality and intentions from her perspective.

Tischa responded as though she did not hear the question, appearing to avoid it and taking control of the session. "Next time I want to first play ten minutes of piano then you play this and I relax on the floor and then you relax," she responded. I acquiesced and walked her back to her unit.

DISCUSSION OF TISCHA

Tischa used the story song to tell her story. In the same way that Hammel-Zabin (2003) states that a pre-composed song "can serve not only as a vehicle for self-reflection but also as a way to address the unspeakable, particularly for a child" (p. 23), improvised songs can carry the same weight and provide valuable insight into the psyche of, in Tischa's case, a child who may not otherwise be able to reveal her trauma or share her experience of sexual abuse. It can be said that the story song she told was her opportunity to 'retell' her traumatic events and the history of her sexually violent experiences in metaphoric form, in a way that would not make her susceptible to retraumatization. The following section draws concepts from Peter Levine's *Somatic Experiencing* (S-E) model (Bosco, 2002) and Frank Bosco's (2002) application of this model to music therapy work with trauma victims.

Through the music, Tischa experienced what Bosco (2002) refers to as "primordial emotions and related bodily sensations" (p. 75) that were stirred up by the pressured conditions that the story song presented. The volume and intensity changes in her playing, used to evoke the girl and the shark, caused distinct "swells of pressure" and "tempo shifts" (Bosco, 2002, p. 75). These swells and shifts affected the activation or arousal (Levine, 1997) she experienced as a result of "telling her story." This activation refers to the movement in the nervous system that is the result of the anxiety surrounding the experience (Bosco, 2002, p. 74). But Tischa was able to draw on her *resources* (Bosco,

2002), signaling to me when she needed to stop and, in so doing, provided herself with "a sense of calm and control in the nervous system that can be readily revisited" (p. 74) and providing her with a greater sense of control and balance despite the potentially threatening story song. Bosco (2002) states that the resource properly contains the arousal. For instance, Tischa's bathroom break was the activation of her resource that served to contain the arousal she may have been experiencing.

Tischa's primary therapist had shared with me that in their sessions, repetitive play occurred in which themes or aspects of the trauma were expressed (DSM-IV-TR). Never before had Tischa allowed a tragic ending to occur. In essence, it was extremely significant that Tischa was able to recognize and express, in the story song, the tragic but ambiguous fate of the young girl, despite all attempts to evade it. Additionally, Tischa had a history of being provocative with men and boys, focusing more on seducing boys on her unit than on her relationships with her female peers. Tischa experienced taunting and was typically disliked by female peers. I considered this seeking out of sexualized relationships to be trauma-specific reenactment (DSM-IV-TR). Both of these symptoms are specific to the reexperiencing symptom of post traumatic stress disorder as experienced by children.

> Another concept in Levine's *Somatic Experiencing* model is that of *discharge.* Discharge refers to a releasing of the energy that is believed to have been trapped in the nervous system (remembered in the body/mind) at the time that a trauma occurred. This would be the energy normally stimulated in the sympathetic nervous system (fight or flight response) to mobilize towards survival in the face of a threatening situation, which then, due to overwhelming circumstances, is never utilized. (Bosco, 2002, p. 74)

The sometimes lingering effects of the "freeze" or immobility response (Levine, 1997) can be identified as trauma symptoms. The energy that was initially mobilized is not used, and the trauma victim never completes the fight-or-flight action (Bosco, 2002, p. 75). "It would seem that this kind of incompletion leaves us with a compromised feeling, lacking in the empowerment that comes from moving through a challenge and attaining a sense of victory or liberation" (Bosco, 2002, p. 75).

Tischa, through her story song, or musical storytelling, moved through her challenge. She was activated in the telling of the story and had control over the story's pace, pendulating back and forth throughout the session. Whenever she felt it necessary, Tischa was able to switch back to "a more calming experience . . . achieved with the support of a resource" (Poole Heller & Levine, as cited in Bosco, 2002, p. 74). This allowed for a deepened experience of "nervous energy discharge" (Bosco, 2002, p. 74). Most important for Tischa was that while she was, for the first time in her sessions, not able to save the little girl from being "eaten," she admitted her own resilience in her affirmation of the life of the girl following the abuse. Tischa did appear to have experienced the attainment of a sense of liberty or liberation following this story song.

CONCLUSION

Tischa, in her aggressive outbursts and over-sexualized behavior, presented unwanted information to her community. The key stress managers of socio-cultural roles, shared values, and historical continuity were not available to provide her assistance in the construction of relationships. Additionally, as stated earlier in the chapter, trauma victims already experience disruptions in their interpersonal relationships and struggle to sustain those that are emotionally and psychologically healthy. Therefore, the restoration of connection and building of social cohesion are essential components in the healing process of trauma survivors.

Music, in the context of our individual music therapy sessions, exposed its capacity for "stimulating and cementing social integration and personal relationships" (Swallow, 2002, p. 42). Being invested in shared music-making requires that two people are engaged in relationship. The act of shared music-making in music therapy offers the opportunity and confidence to rebuild relationships with themselves, with one another and ultimately, hopefully, within their communities (Sutton, 2002, p. 116).

Re-investing in oneself following exposure to profound violence is crucial, as every individual must learn how to access his/her personal capacity for healing. Tischa, a thirteen-year-old survivor of sexual abuse and abandonment, was astonished by the aesthetic of the music and story songs she created in her sessions. Additionally, she was able to give sound to her abuse and the feelings that accompanied it. As Sutton (2002) has noted of trauma victims with whom she has worked, Tischa's narrative, while metaphoric and sometimes even wordless, was clearly audible in the music.

> Music created through a process of interaction between people can take on a life of its own, and in turn transform those who create it. The transformation is temporary, but the experience of having been transformed, and the discovery of new possibilities, are more permanent. (Dixon, 2002, p. 128)

A "sense of self, other, and relationship is a central part of musical engagement. . ." (Dixon, 2002 p. 130). The potential for intimacy is "primarily an ability to tolerate one's inner world and the contradictions it presents. Withdrawal from intimacy in personal relationships is one of the most enduring effects of trauma. This makes it particularly important to understand the role of intimacy in the therapeutic relationship" (Turner, van der Kolk and McFarlane, 1996, p. 538). Tischa restored a connection through an intimacy generated in her active music-making. Because she was working within the context of individual therapy (as she was not yet ready to work within group music therapy), Tischa developed a single strong attachment to me as her music therapist.

While referencing communal rather than individual experiences of violence, I believe Dixon's (2002) statement is valid even in Tischa's case. He states that "the way music-making reaches and draws out the essential humanity of the most unreachable people places it in direct opposition to political violence, which denies the humanity and individuality of its victims" (p. 131). Musical interaction simultaneously reveals our uniqueness as individuals as well as the connections between us, constituting our common humanity (Dixon, 2002, p. 131). As Tischa demonstrates, creativity following exposure to sexual violence has the capacity to enable interpersonal connectedness. The little girl and the shark inform us that Tischa has found a way to admit and tolerate the truth of the sexual abuse and has explored this pain with all of her senses while "in" the music. She sought bodily connectedness as she explored an experience of herself embodied in sound and movement. With the help of the music experiences, Tischa discovered some mobility and, with this, a sense of safety and an ability to trust, revealing a restored ability to connect and revealing personal capacities for healing.

APPENDIX – TERMS

trauma vortex – a symbolic black hole initiated by a traumatic event which incites emotional chaos, pulls one towards re-experiences of the trauma, and inhibits resolution and healing
chronic affect dysregulation – consistent inability to regulate or tolerate negative or painful feelings, emotions or moods
arpeggiated pattern – a configuration of a chord whose pitches are sounded successively, usually from lowest to highest, rather than simultaneously.

REFERENCES

American Psychiatric Association. (2000). *Diagnostic and statistical manual of mental disorders* (4th ed., TR). Washington, D.C.: American Psychiatric Association.
Austin, D. (2002). In search of the self: the use of vocal holding techniques with adults traumatized as children. *Music Therapy Perspectives, 19*(1), 22–30.
Boothby, N., & Crawford, J. (2004, November). Former child soldiers in Mozambique: a life outcome study. In J. Ruzek & P. Watson (Eds.), *War as a universal trauma.* Symposium conducted at the meeting of The International Society for Traumatic Stress Studies, New Orleans, LA.
Bosco, F. (2002). Daring, dread, discharge, delight. In J. V. Loewy & A. F. Hara (Eds.), *Caring for*

the caregiver: the use of music and music therapy in grief and trauma (pp. 71–84). Silver Spring, MD: American Music Therapy Association, Inc.

Dixon, M. (2002). Representing musical time, *music and letters, 83*(7) p. 511.

Hammel-Zabin, A. (2003). *Conversations with a pedophile.* Fort Lee, NJ: Barricade Books.

Hara, A. F. (2002). Continuity through song. In J. V. Loewy & A. F. Hara (Eds.), *Caring for the caregiver: the use of music and music therapy in grief and trauma* (pp. 63–69). Silver Spring, MD: American Music Therapy Association, Inc.

Levine, P. A. (1997). *Waking the tiger: healing trauma.* Berkeley, CA: North Atlantic Books.

Pavlicevic, M. (1994). Between chaos and creativity: music therapy with "traumatised" children in South Africa. *Journal of British Music Therapy, 8*(2).

Pavlicevic, M. (2002). Fragile rhythms and uncertain listenings: perspectives from music therapy with South African children. In J. Sutton (Ed.), *Music, music therapy, and trauma.* London: Jessica Kingsley Publishers.

Powch, I., Scurfield, R., Daniels, L., Perkal, A., & Huwe, J. (2004, November). Gestalt and emotion-focused approaches to posttrauma therapy. In J. Ruzek & P. Watson (Eds.), *War as a universal trauma.* Symposium conducted at the meeting of The International Society for Traumatic Stress Studies, New Orleans, LA.

Smyth, M. (2002). The role of creativity in healing and recovering one's power after victimization. In J. P. Sutton (Ed.), *Music, music therapy and trauma: international perspectives* (pp. 57–81). London: Jessica Kingsley Publishers.

Sutton, J. P. (2002). Trauma in context. In J. P. Sutton (Ed.), *Music, music therapy and trauma: international perspectives* (pp. 21–40). London: Jessica Kingsley Publishers.

Swallow, M. (2002). The brain, its music and its emotion: the neurology of trauma. In J. P. Sutton (Ed.), *Music, music therapy and trauma: international perspectives* (pp. 41–56). London: Jessica Kingsley Publishers.

Turner, S. W., McFarlane, A. C. & van der Kolk, B. A. (1996). The therapeutic environment and new explorations in the treatment of post traumatic stress disorder. In B. A. Van Der Kolk, A. C. McFarlane & L. Weisaeth (Eds.), *Traumatic Stress: The Effects of Overwhelming Experience on Mind, Body and Society.* New York: Guilford Press.

Turry, A. (2002). Don't let the fear prevent the grief: Working with traumatic reactions through improvisation. In J. V. Loewy & A. F. Hara (Eds.), *Caring for the caregiver: The use of music and music therapy in grief and trauma* (pp. 44–53). Silver Spring, MD: American Music Therapy Association, Inc.

van der Kolk, B. A. (1996). The body keeps score: approaches to the psychobiology of posttraumatic stress disorder. In B. A. van der Kolk, A. C. & Weisaeth, L. W. (Eds.), (1996). *Traumatic stress: the effects of overwhelming experience on the mind, body, and society.* New York: The Guilford Press.

van der Kolk, B. A., McFarlane, A. C. & Weisaeth, L. W. (1996). *Traumatic stress: the effects of overwhelming experience on the mind, body, and society.* New York: The Guilford Press.

van der Kolk, B. A., Turner, S. W., & McFarlane, A. C. (1996). The therapeutic environment and new explorations in the treatment of posttraumatic stress disorder. In B. A. van der Kolk, A. C. McFarlane & L. W. Weisaeth (Eds.), *Traumatic stress: the effects of overwhelming experience on the mind, body, and society.* New York: The Guilford Press.

BIOGRAPHICAL STATEMENT

Maria C. Gonsalves received her undergraduate degrees in cultural anthropology from Johns Hopkins University and flute performance from Peabody Conservatory in Baltimore, MD. Maria holds a Master's degree in international studies from the University of Wyoming where she began her research in ethnomusicology, human security, as well as girl child soldiers. She holds a Master's degree in music therapy from New York University and completed an advanced clinical training degree in Analytical Music Therapy with Benedikte Scheiby. Maria works in New York City at St. Luke's and Roosevelt Hospitals' Comprehensive Adolescent Rehabilitation and Education Service day treatment program serving youth ages fourteen through twenty who struggle with severe emotional disturbance and chemical addictions. Maria's active engagement with the organization Music Therapists for Peace, Inc., her international work in Sierra Leone, West Africa, and her domestic work in New York focus on trauma and the effects of profound violence on adolescents.

Chapter 17

FEAR TO TREAD: PLAY AND DRAMA THERAPY IN THE TREATMENT OF BOYS WHO HAVE BEEN SEXUALLY ABUSED

CRAIG HAEN

One moment he's being kind, the next he's beating your mom. Then he almost kills her. You get scared and try to call the police, and he beats you. Then he sexually assaults you and does things to you. You don't like it, but you do it because you look up to him. He puts private parts all over [sic], and makes you do it to him. So, if this happens to you, tell the police or a doctor.

It feels sad when you tell people, or you feel angry or ready to cry. You might feel gay, but you're not. So tell someone if this happens. Some people might not believe you, but the police and therapists will.

Lennus, Age 11

INTRODUCTION

Boys who have been sexually abused present strong clinical challenges: guarded, evasive, tentative, angry, and terribly afraid to trust. Their presentation in the therapy space is often fraught with a multitude of conflicting feelings about power, intimacy, circumstances of their abuse, their own sexuality, relationships, and the future. The therapist working with this specialized population must have a number of effective tools for navigating the tenuousness of the relationship. The metaphoric and experiential components of the play and drama therapy processes can allow boys who have been sexually abused to explore the traumatic events safely while reclaiming empowerment, examining conflicting feelings, and re-learning self-protection (Cattanach, 1996; Gallo-Lopez, 2005; Haen, 2005; McGarvey and Haen, 2005).

235

Individual, group, and family therapy can all be effective modalities of treatment for boys who have been sexually abused, and often a multi-modal approach is recommended (Friedrich, 1995; Sheinberg and Fraenkel, 2000). Research on psychopharmacology for this population is still limited; however, medication, particularly SSRIs, may assist some clients with symptom management and may enhance the treatment process (Kreidler, Briscoe and Beech, 2002). This chapter will focus on the individual therapy component of the treatment framework. Individual treatment can be helpful in giving the child a space of his own, separate from the other family members (particularly when the abuse was interfamilial), so that he might begin to process his internal reactions and understanding of the trauma events. Individual therapy is an important forum for learning self-protective and problem-solving skills (Barrett, Cortese and Marzoff, 2000), and for practicing affect management and self-regulation (Friedrich, 1995).

In this chapter, I will advocate for the particular efficacy of play and drama therapy approaches to the treatment of sexual abuse. However, it must be noted that what is prime in this treatment process is a safe space and the development of trust between therapist and client. Sexual abuse often occurs within the context of a relationship of trust that is subsequently damaged. As such, the child's ability to work through the abuse with a clinician with whom he feels at ease is essential. The method a clinician utilizes for the work is secondary. I will discuss how this trust can be built in the drama therapy space and the role of the therapist in working with boys who have been sexually abused.

SEXUAL ABUSE AND THE MALE CHILD

Though much has been written on the topic of sexual abuse, there is still a significant amount to be learned. The vast majority of research on Post Traumatic Stress Disorder, for example, has focused on trauma resulting from public events such as terrorist attacks and natural disasters, and has not taken into account trauma derived from private events. Private trauma involves secrecy, which renders the child unable to organize his experience by recounting it to others (Siegel, 1999). In addition, the unique experiences of boys who have been sexually abused are still being examined and require further understanding.

Western epidemiological studies on child sexual abuse were first conducted in the 1920s (Bergevin, Bukowski and Karavasilis, 2003). However, the issue did not gain public attention until the 1970s when it was brought to light largely as a result of the advocacy efforts of the women's movement. This movement helped first to gain awareness, initially for the problem of rape, then of incest. The incest paradigm advanced a familial model in which girls were the victims of perpetrating fathers (Finkelhor, 1984). While this advocacy was vitally important in pushing the issue forward, the notion of boys as victims of sexual abuse remained obscured for some time.

It is estimated that approximately one in every six boys experiences direct sexual contact with an adult or older child by the age of sixteen (Gartner, 1999b). The sexual abuse of boys is largely underreported, underrecognized, and undertreated (Brooke, 1997; Friedrich, 1995; Gartner, 1999b; Holmes and Slapp, 1998). Researchers tend to attribute the underreporting to the following factors: the male ethic of self-reliance, which is contrary to admitting victimization; the stigma of homosexuality, which prevents boys from reporting abuse by a male perpetrator; a smaller age gap between male victims and their perpetrators that may influence the perception of the event as nonabusive; societal assumptions that minimize the impact of the abuse on boys or (particularly when the perpetrator is female) that fail to perceive the sexual interaction as abuse; the increased presence of shame in male victims; and the increased use of violence and threats by perpetrators of male sexual abuse to compel their victims not to tell anyone (Bergevin et al., 2003; Briere, 1996; Finkelhor, 1984; Froning and Mayman, 1990).

Though each individual processes his or her trauma uniquely and experiences different sequelae of symptoms, there are common patterns in children who have been sexually abused. Understanding reactions characteristic of boys can assist the clinician in formulating appropriate treatment goals. Boys are more likely to have their sexual abuse occur outside of the home and to experience a larger number of occurrences of the abuse. They are also more likely to be the victims of co-occurring physical abuse and other forms of violence either related or unrelated to the sexual abuse (Bergevin et al., 2003; Miedzian, 1995). One study (Garnefski and Diekstra, 1997) found that adolescent boys who had been sexually abused in childhood had far greater emotional problems, criminal and risk-taking behavior, and suicidal thoughts and gestures than adolescent girls with similar histories. This study, while highlighting the intensity of boys' reactions to sexual abuse, also supports the classic notion of males as tending to externalize their distress. This externalization is intimately tied to the way boys and men generally experience and express affect.

The western concept of masculinity is one that is largely incompatible with vulnerability and feelings other than anger. As a result, traumatized males are more likely to dissociate the affective components of their trauma experience (Gartner, 1999a) or to transform that affect into rage (Briere, 1996). When a boy has been sexually abused, it interferes with normal affective development, creating a challenging paradox. In Gartner's (1999a) words, ". . . at exactly the moment the boy is learning to control emotions in order to feel masculine, he is being flooded by the very emotional states that are considered nonmasculine by the culture" (p. 79). The result is that many sexually abused boys express their affect in the manner described in the aforementioned study. They might also externalize symptoms in the form of substance abuse (Brems, Johnson, Neal, and Freemon, 2004) or sexually reactive behaviors (Gallo-Lopez, 2005; Gartner, 1999a).

Because boys often learn to equate masculinity with autonomy and heroism, they struggle with being a victim. In particular, many boys who have been sexually abused hold themselves responsible for the abuse, thinking that they invited it or should have effectively fought back (Gartner, 1999a). These ideas, which manifest in feelings of shame, are often complicated by the male sexual response. As many boys experience overt physical reactions of arousal during the abuse, such as erection and ejaculation, they can become confused about whether the sexual acts constitute abuse and whether the arousal response means that they are homosexual. These questions are important to address in the therapy process, lest the feelings behind them be forced underground and become connected to further shame.

Finally, families find it particularly difficult to be supportive of their male children who have been sexually abused. Fathers, when still involved in the boys' lives, often face fears that their son will "turn out gay" and distance themselves due to homophobia. Mothers may find it difficult to connect with their sons who have been abused, particularly if the child becomes sexually reactive. Many boys who have been sexually abused have mothers who experienced similar abuse as children (Ambridge, 2001). While these mothers may have an easier time identifying with and supporting a daughter who has been abused, their victimized son may elicit more complex feelings, particularly if he is exhibiting sexually reactive behaviors. If their own perpetrator was male (as the majority of sexual abuse perpetrators are), they may transfer some of their feelings toward the perpetrator onto their son, or face a question of loyalties if the child's abuser is a family member or romantic partner. When the abuse has occurred within the home, the child experiences an intense dilemma in that the family system, which is supposed to serve as the secure base of comfort, is also the source of distress. This dilemma is one that has been aptly labeled "fear without solution" (Hesse and Main, 2000).

Briere (1996) recommends that therapists working with males who have been sexually abused make the following modifications to the treatment process: decrease the amount of time spent on emotionally activating verbal processing; limit the amount of contact with abuse-related memories; increase efforts to normalize shame, hurt, and fear; and maximize attention to defenses such as dissociation, denial, intellectualization, and precipitous action. He also recommends that therapists encourage clients to explore some of the more vulnerable feelings that exist beneath their anger.

TREATMENT OVERVIEW

Like many drama therapists who work with traumatized children (Cattanach, 1996, 1999; Gallo-Lopez, 2000, 2005; Grimshaw, 1998; Jennings, 1999; Weber, 2005), I am influenced by and incorporate techniques from play therapy. Both methods, through the use of metaphor and projection, provide safely distanced ways to address trauma that mitigate some of the client's ongoing avoidance and struggles with intense affect. Both allow the therapist to enter into the child's world through play and action, natural pathways of expression for boys. Likewise, both play and drama therapy allow for the child to simultaneously engage his experiencing and reflective selves, a position Rothschild (2000) calls dual awareness. In this way, he can step back from the material and begin to organize and metabolize the events so that they can be integrated into a wider sense of self and life story.

The most extensive research on treatment of child sexual abuse has been conducted on Cognitive Behavioral Therapy (CBT). CBT techniques are thought to be highly effective with sexually abused children in addressing faulty attributions and cognitive distortions about the abuse and in encouraging the acquisition of self-regulatory and coping skills (Rasmussen, 2001; Nader, 2004). However, many boys who have been sexually abused also require extensive work on internal affective patterns, ruptured relationships, and development of a cohesive narrative for the trauma experience (Woods, 2003). Some lack the cognitive development necessary for CBT work or are simply too internally fragmented.

When traumatized people become hyperaroused, they are often unable to respond to verbal and cognitive approaches (Perry, 1997). Thus, play and drama therapy can contribute much to creating safe pathways for expression and cognitive reprocessing, allowing for what James, Forrester and Kim (2005) identify as a cognitive developmental middle path between the extremes of re-experiencing and avoidance. Traumatized children often move between these two extremes or emerge through varying periods of numbness (Nader, 2004). These approaches represent a natural enhancement as role play is frequently utilized in CBT as a learning tool and can be effectively utilized for fostering empathy as well as a sense of mastery and personal agency (Hall, 1997). Drama therapy can help to challenge deeply imbedded schemas so that clients can incorporate new meanings (Bergman, 2001). The use of experiential approaches honors Briere's (1996) recommendation of not lingering on affectively charged verbal processing with male clients.

Finally, drama and play therapy involve kinesthetic action. As such, they provide opportunities to work with boys on issues of embodiment. As the body is the locus of invasion, the very act of being in one's body can be threatening (Young, 1992). Likewise, the body holds memories and affect related to the trauma (Levine, 1997; Rothschild, 2000). I often have treated boys around the age of eleven-years-old for the very reason that, as they enter puberty and their bodies begin to change (while their peer group simultaneously begins to express interest in sex), trauma memories and symptoms re-emerge or intensify.

Irwin (2005) identified the three general goals of drama therapy as: facilitating imaginative play at the highest possible level, strengthening self-control and affect regulation, and helping individuals to verbalize feelings and behaviors. These goals are in harmony with the therapeutic needs of traumatized boys.

THE POSITION OF THE THERAPIST

Each child brings to the therapy space his own patterns of relating to others, shaped by his attachment relationships and coping style (Wieland, 1997). Further, current research on attachment is demonstrating the importance of early life events in determining "what a particular individual appraises to be stressful, how he or she characteristically consciously and especially unconsciously responds to stressors, and how efficiently he or she psychobiologically copes with these stressors" (Schore, 2003, p. 231). Like the maturational process, the therapy process begins with a relationship. Though attachment to the therapist is not required, a trust must develop and the space itself must represent a safe haven (Gallo-Lopez, 2005). I have often worked with traumatized boys in chaotic hospital and residential settings in which the playroom must be especially protected and consistent (for a more complete description of creating a safe space and of the treatment model in these settings, see McGarvey and Haen, 2005).

Because boys who have been sexually abused often have significant difficulties with trust, the frame of the therapy is very important. Clear boundaries must be established, with a degree of familiarity and predictability to the process. I try to make the process visible to the client and to model a direct, open, and honest style of communication. Similarly, I make efforts to not be opaque during the process. I find that the boys I work with require a therapist who is active and tangible. The play materials help to ground the work and lessen the intensity of contact between therapist and child. The client must feel as though he has a voice, without being overwhelmed by too much choice.

It is important to reduce the power differential between therapist and client in order to differentiate the interaction from the abuse, in which the child's will was overpowered. However, it is also important for the child to know that he is working with an adult who remains in control and protective, and who can provide a safe anchor as they begin to venture into dark territory. In Cattanach's (1999) words: "The child needs to feel safe with the therapist, but must also feel confident that the therapist can enter the child's play world and help make sense of the confusion and misunderstandings which might be creating difficulties for the child" (p. 82).

Thus, we often begin slowly but directly through drawing. The drawing provides a warm-up that starts with a safe degree of engagement (Rasmussen, 2001; Weber, 2005). The client has a concrete task that is familiar and can make minimal eye contact if he needs. I will often give the client a choice of drawing a person or a tree, a house or a family. Or, I will engage him in Winnicott's (1971) Squiggle game. While drawing, I explain the ground rules of the space and give him some sense of the process, stating that things may feel worse for a little while but that we are aiming for a goal of him feeling better in the long-term.

I directly address transference, particularly if the child's perpetrator was male. I explain in a developmentally appropriate way that being alone in the room with me may evoke many feelings, including angry, fearful, and sexual feelings. I validate that all of these are acceptable and that we will learn to talk about them. I support the child's right to choose how much to talk about a particular subject and when to change topics, but let him know that I will also help him regulate the intensity of information. Finally, I explain that we are largely here to play about his worries connected to what has happened to him. It is important for the therapist to clearly articulate that the goal is to work on the sexual abuse and to honestly indicate that he already knows about some of what has happened to the child. It is also important to delineate the bounds of confidentiality, recognizing that the idea of confidentiality can be anxiety-provoking for some clients as they may associate it with the secret they were asked to keep regarding their abuse (Wheeler and Smith, 2001).

Within the first session, I typically introduce the idea of creating a story with the toys. I often use the language of "creating a movie," accessing terms endemic to film (freeze, rewind, pause, fast forward) for use in interventions and as a framing device. This language is readily accessible and engaging for today's technology-savvy kids. (Obviously, if the child's abuse involved pornography or him being filmed or photographed, this framework would not be appropriate). I explain that boys often use the toys to create a story very similar to events that have happened to them. However, this being pretend, the client can give the characters fantasy names and can make anything he wants happen in the story. The emphasis is on the client being the director and taking ownership of the story he would like to create. During the first session, I typically allow the client to create whatever story he chooses, though I may suggest possible themes if I get the sense that my involvement on that level is appropriate.

The story that the child creates in the first session often provides important diagnostic clues about the areas that require intervention, some of the meanings the boy ascribes to the abuse, and possible directions for future exploration. Some of my clients' stories are direct retellings of their trauma narrative or contain aspects of what happened, while others' stories are heavily metaphorical. In subsequent sessions, these stories are utilized to rework aspects of the trauma, to clarify feelings, or to sequence events into a coherent whole. Among the play themes common to children who have been sexually abused are classic battles of good versus evil, clashes of submission and dominance, highly sexualized interaction between characters, and the overwhelming of boundaries (Hall, 1997). I have also noted themes of invasion, bodily damage, monsters, and expansive rage in the boys I have treated.

WORKING THROUGH FANTASY

As Davies and Frawley (1994) have noted, many clients who have been sexually abused have a bifurcated relationship with fantasy. They might have a rich fantasy life regularly, but where the trauma material is concerned, their fantasies are either out-of-control and intrusive or avoided at all costs. Some severely abused and neglected children lack the ability to play and require stronger structuring and prompting from the therapist in order to engage in creating fantasy narratives (Irwin, 2005). Siegler (1994) wrote:

> Once the child has developed the capacity to create fantasy narratives, concepts of desire, intention, force, time, space and causality become integrated into a sense of self. Further, the capacity to create fantasies and to organize them into coherent narratives gives the child the possibility of constructing imaginary realms over which one may then have dominion. Within these imaginary realms is embedded both the child's conflicts and the child's solution to these conflicts, whether progressive or regressive. (p. 327)

Some boys resist engaging on even the fantasy level. In this case, the processing should be directed to talking about their fears. Many of these clients verbalize magical thinking, believing that even playing about their worries might cause the abuse to re-occur. It is important that after the client's fears are verbalized, the therapist seeks out an activity that feels safe to the client so that he might leave the session with a memory of being successful and responded to early in the treatment process. If the fears involve a perpetrator coming back to harm him, then we work together to develop a concrete safety plan and to communicate it to the family or, if in a residential setting, to the staff.

Many clients need to symbolically contain their perpetrator before they can feel safe enough diving into the treatment process. In this instance, we will often choose a toy to represent the perpetrator. Older children may be able to make the link that the metaphor relates to their perpetrator, while younger children may just need work on containing the monster, "bad guy," or whatever character resonates for them. We then build a jail/cage/fortress around the perpetrator using blocks or other toy barriers.

The scenes of containment often provide clues to the boy's relationship to the perpetrator and the type and degrees of affect they have toward him or her. For example, one boy chose a battalion of army and police officer figures to guard his perpetrator's jail cell and played out numerous escapes until he finally felt that the perpetrator was contained and the work could progress. Another boy placed a bed, a television, and furniture in the fort he built for his perpetrator. He expressed concerns that the "bad guy" might not be comfortable and might not get enough to eat. Each of these stories speaks to a different relationship. Determining the type of relationship is important in understanding the resulting feelings. A perpetrator who had minimal connection to the child and who used threats and violence provides for a different type of trauma than does a perpetrator who had an already-established relationship with the boy and used coercion and manipulation to achieve sexual gratification. Gartner (1999a) uses the term "sexual betrayal" to emphasize the pernicious violation of trust that occurs when the sexual abuse takes place in the context of an existing interpersonal relationship.

Gallo-Lopez (2000) describes another effective strategy for empowerment and containment of the perpetrator that I have used frequently. I have the boys use washable markers to draw their perpetrator (or the monster from their dreams) on a dry-erase board that hangs on the playroom wall. We then step away from the board to gain distance and will often sit side-by-side to talk about the feelings that arise when sitting in the room with the image. Together, we address the image and verbalize the feelings toward it as if the drawing were a character in the room with us. The boys are then given a spray bottle filled with water and are invited to eradicate the image. They are usually delighted to watch the image disappear and run down the wall when sprayed. Some of my clients spend several sessions with this process alone, building dramatic scenes around it. Their delight is palpable and speaks to their sense of empowerment.

PSYCHOEDUCATION

Early in the process, I allow my clients to read about the issue of sexual abuse of boys. Though there are some published books written for this purpose, I prefer to use stories created by past clients during their treatment. Near the end of our series of work, several of my clients have written stories designed to help other kids know they are not alone. The fact that the boy is reading a story written by another boy with whom I have worked enhances the sense of universality they receive and marks me as a therapist who has helped other children with similar problems. Lennus's story at the beginning of this article is one example.

I also educate boys on what symptom patterns and feelings they might experience. We work on concrete relaxation skills at the end of each session to assist them in achieving grounding after exposure to the trauma material. We strategize when and how they might transfer these skills to their life outside of session. A key to the acquisition of skills is the experiential nature of the delivery and practice.

An important piece of the work is sexual education. Younger boys are often confused or terrified about the physiological components of the abuse, not understanding the perpetrator's erection or ejaculation, and may need a context for what occurred. Older boys require normalization of their own physical responses to the abuse. I explain these in developmentally appropriate ways, providing analogies to how the body responds to other types of touch. For example, boys can readily tell me that if they are slugged on the arm, their arm might hurt and bruise. If they were poked in the eye, their eye might tear up. I explain that their sexual responses are similar bodily responses over which they have little control. Gil (1996) provides an effective visual when she peels an onion in front of a client. The client can see that she is crying, but also understands that it does not necessarily mean that she feels sad. Rather, it is her body's natural response.

COMPLEX NARRATIVES

The experience of sexual abuse is not a simple one. While therapists often seek to make it understandable for their young clients, it is important that we also appreciate the complexity of trauma. For many boys, their abuser is not just the person who hurt them, but also the person who took them for walks, played basketball with them, or paid attention to them in a way that others in their life had not. Sexual abuse is frightening, but it also might bring feelings of arousal and pleasure. Similarly, family members who abuse boys also often love them very much. Sheinberg and Fraenkel (2000) emphasize the importance of being able to hold and validate more than one truth and of asking about exceptions. For example, the therapist might inquire if there was ever a time that the perpetrator was nice to them, and a story might be played out in which this idea is expanded. To do so honors the confusion the boy faces.

One area in which drama therapy can be highly effective is in creating corrective reenactments in which the child gets to actively re-story his experience the way he wished it would have happened. Corrective reenactments counter the boy's sense of impotence in the face of having been overtaken by someone more powerful. It honors his body's need to mobilize in response to the abuse

(Levine, 1997). This is particularly significant for boys, who have an innate tendency to respond to affectively charged situations through action (Pollack, 1998).

Interestingly, my male clients rarely wish that the abuse had not occurred. Instead, many of their corrective reenactments involve being able to protect themselves, being saved by outside intervention, or seeing the perpetrator punished for his or her actions. In the playing-out, they often discharge large amounts of rage by beating and torturing the perpetrator. Reisner (2003) cites the working-through of retribution fantasies and revenge as one of the most important contributions the theater space can make to the healing of traumatized people. By using the toys to explore their rage, the boys need not face the real-world consequences of its expression.

Some clients prefer to metaphorize this process more heavily and it becomes reflected in epic battles between two opposing sides. In some instances, clients have engaged in full-body role play in which they cast me as a monster and we play out scenarios in which they conquer or immobilize me. This type of interaction requires the client's ability to understand the pretend nature of the action and their ability to distinguish when the therapist is in role and when he is not. It also requires assessment of the degree of embodiment with which the child is comfortable.

It is important that the choice to explore corrective reenactment is guided by the child. It becomes easy for a well-intentioned therapist to rush this intervention out of his own need to empower the client, or out of his own anger toward the perpetrator. A corrective reenactment that is ill-timed can ultimately lead to hopelessness, emphasizing the vast gulf between fantasy and reality.

One final exploration that might be valuable is that of the child's sense of self. I often ask older clients who they were before the abuse or what they imagine their life will be like in the future. These steps are important in putting the abuse in the proper life context. One eleven-year-old boy, at the end of the treatment process, created a drawing of his future. The drawing depicted a long road peppered with stop signs. He said that he would like to travel on throughout his life, stopping occasionally to remember his abuse and then continuing on again until the next stop sign. What he so eloquently metaphorizes is the ultimate goal of trauma treatment – to reach the point where the trauma event is filed away in memory as a significant life event, but not as one that defines the person.

CLOSING THOUGHTS

This chapter presents a brief exploration of the ways that play and drama therapy processes can contribute to the treatment of boys who have been sexually abused. The experiential nature of the process can assist clients with other aspects of the trauma experience including the management of nightmares, flashbacks, intrusive thoughts, dissociation, and sexually aggressive behaviors. Play and drama therapy have the potential for wider applications in the field of trauma treatment. Since they are creative by nature, they can easily be adapted or paired with other treatment approaches to enhance safety, depth of processing, and long-term efficacy.

An essential part of the play and drama therapy process is that of closure: stepping out of the dramatic space and the client's story and returning to self and to the playroom. As I close this chapter, I reflect on the many boys whose stories I have been privileged to witness. While each enters the space full of fear, and I meet them similarly afraid to step too quickly or hastily, somehow we find steady ground on which walking for a while together feels safe. Composer Charles Edward Ives' (1900) words capture the feeling well:

"today we do not choose to die or to dance,
but to live and walk"

APPENDIX – TERMS

Cognitive Behavioral Therapy – A type of psychotherapy that is aimed at targeting negatively biased and irrational thinking as a means of positively altering the client's mood and behavior.

SSRIs – Selective Serotonin Re-uptake Inhibitors; a class of antidepressant medication that is frequently used in the clinical treatment of anxiety disorders, obsessive compulsive disorder, and eating disorders.

REFERENCES

Ambridge, M. (2001). Using the reflective image within the mother-child relationship. In J. Murphy (Ed.), *Art therapy with young survivors of sexual abuse: Lost for words* (pp. 69–85). London: Routledge.

Barrett, Cortese, & Marzoff (2000). Treatment of the sexually abused child. In C. E. Bailey (Ed.), *Children in therapy: Using the family as a resource* (pp. 137–163). New York: Norton.

Bergevin, T. A., Bukowski, W. M., & Karavasilis, L. (2003). Childhood sexual abuse and pubertal timing: Implications for long-term psychosocial adjustment. In C. Hayward (Ed.), *Gender differences at puberty* (pp. 187–216). Cambridge: Cambridge University Press.

Bergman, J. (2001). Using drama therapy to uncover genuineness in civilly committed sexual offenders. In A. Schlank (Ed.), *The sexual predator: Vol. 2: Legal issues, clinical issues, special populations* (pp. 8-1–8-15). Kingston, NJ: Civic Research Institute.

Brems, C., Johnson, M. E., Neal, D., & Freemon, M. (2004). Childhood abuse history and substance use among men and women receiving detoxification services. *American Journal of Drug & Alcohol Abuse, 30*(4), 799–821.

Briere, J. (1996). *Therapy for adults molested as children.* New York: Springer.

Brooke, S.L. (1997). *Healing through art: Art therapy with sexual abuse survivors.* Springfield, IL: Charles C Thomas Publisher, Ltd.

Cattanach, A. (1996). The use of dramatherapy and play therapy to help de-brief children after the trauma of sexual abuse. In A. Gersie (Ed.), *Dramatic approaches to brief therapy* (pp. 177–187). London: Jessica Kingsley.

Cattanach, A. (1999). Co-construction in play therapy. In A. Cattanach (Ed.), *Process in the arts therapies* (pp. 78–102). London: Jessica Kingsley.

Davies, J. M., & Frawley, M. G. (1994). *Treating the adult survivor of childhood sexual abuse: A psychoanalytic perspective.* New York: Basic Books.

Finkelhor, D. (1984). *Child sexual abuse: New theory & research.* New York: The Free Press.

Friedrich, W. N. (1995). *Psychotherapy with sexually abused boys: An integrated approach.* Thousand Oaks, CA: SAGE.

Froning, M. L., & Mayman, S. B. (1990). Identification and treatment of child and adolescent male victims of sexual abuse. In M. Hunter (Ed.), *The sexually abused male: Application of treatment strategies, Vol. 2* (pp. 199–224). Lexington, MA: Lexington Books.

Gallo-Lopez, L. (2000). A creative play therapy approach to the group treatment of young sexually abused children. In H. Kaduson & C. E. Schaefer (Eds.), *Short-term play therapy for children* (pp. 269–295). New York: Guilford.

Gallo-Lopez, L. (2005). Drama therapy in the treatment of children with sexual behavior problems. In A. M. Weber & C. Haen (Eds.), *Clinical applications of drama therapy in child and adolescent treatment* (pp. 137–151). New York: Brunner-Routledge.

Garnefski, N., & Diekstra, R. F. W. (1997). Child sexual abuse and emotional and behavioral problems in adolescence: Gender differences. *Journal of the American Academy of Child & Adolescent Psychiatry, 36*(3), 323–329.

Gartner, R. B. (1999a). *Betrayed as boys: Psychodynamic treatment of sexually abused men.* New York: Guilford.

Gartner, R. B. (1999b). Relational aftereffects in manhood of boyhood sexual abuse. *Journal of Contemporary Psychotherapy, 29*(4), 319–353.

Gil, E. (1996). *Treating abused adolescents.* New York: Guilford.

Grimshaw, D. (1998). To all the flickering candles: Dramatherapy with sexually abused children. In A. Bannister (Ed.), *From hearing to healing: Working with the aftermath of child sexual abuse* (second edition), pp. 35–54. New York: Wiley.

Haen, C. (2005). Rebuilding security: Group therapy with children affected by September 11. *International Journal of Group Psychotherapy, 55*(3), 391–414.

Hall, P. E. (1997). Play therapy with sexually abused children. In H. G. Kaduson, D. Cangelosi & C. E. Schaefer (Eds.), *The playing cure: Individualized play therapy for specific childhood problems* (pp. 171–194). New York: Aronson.

Hesse, E., & Main, M. (2000). Disorganized infant, child, and adult attachment: Collapse in behavioral and attentional strategies. *Journal of the American Psychoanalytic Association, 48*(4), 1097–1127.

Holmes, W. C., & Slapp, G. B. (1998). Sexual abuse of boys: Definition, prevalence, correlates, sequelae, and management. *Journal of the American Medical Association, 280*(21), 1855–1862.

Irwin, E. (2005). Facilitating play with nonplayers: A developmental perspective. In A. M. Weber & C. Haen (Eds.), *Clinical applications of drama therapy in child and adolescent treatment* (pp. 3–23). New York: Brunner-Routledge.

Ives, C. (1900). Walking [Recorded by H. Boatwright, & J. Kirkpatrick]. On *American Masters – Songs of Charles Ives & Ernst Bacon* [CD]. New York: Composers Recordings, Inc. (1994).

James, M., Forrester, A. M., & Kim, K. C. (2005). Developmental transformations in the treatment of sexually abused children. In A. M. Weber & C. Haen (Eds.), *Clinical applications of drama therapy in child and adolescent treatment* (pp. 67–86). New York: Brunner-Routledge.

Jennings, S. (1999). *Introduction to developmental playtherapy: Playing and health.* London: Jessica Kingsley.

Kreidler, M. C., Briscoe, L. A., & Beech, R. R. (2002). Pharmacology for post-traumatic stress disorder related to childhood sexual abuse: A literature review. *Perspectives in Psychiatric Care, 38*(4), 135–145.

Levine, P. (1997). *Waking the tiger: Healing trauma.* Berkeley, CA: North Atlantic Books.

McGarvey, T. P., & Haen, C. (2005). Intervention strategies for treating traumatized siblings on a pediatric inpatient unit. *American Journal of Orthopsychiatry, 75*(3), 395–408.

Miedzian, M. (1995). Learning to be violent. In E. Pelad, P. G. Jaffe & J. L. Edleson (Eds.), *Ending the cycle of violence: Community responses to children of battered women* (pp. 10–24). Thousand Oaks, CA: SAGE.

Nader, K. (2004). Treating traumatized children and adolescents: Treatment issues, modalities, timing, and methods. In N. B. Webb (Ed.), *Mass trauma and violence: Helping families and children cope* (pp. 23–49). New York: Guilford.

Perry, B. (1997). Incubated in terror: Neurodevelopmental factors in the "cycle of violence." In J. D. Osofsky (Ed.), *Children in a violent society* (pp. 124–149). New York: Guilford.

Pollack, W. (1998). *Real boys: Rescuing our sons from the myths of boyhood.* New York: Random House.

Rasmussen, L. A. (2001). Integrating cognitive-behavioral and expressive therapy interventions: Applying the Trauma Outcome Process in treating children with sexually abusive behavior problems. *Journal of Child Sexual Abuse, 10*(4), 1–29.

Reisner, S. (2003). Private trauma/public drama: Theater as a response to international political trauma. *The Scholar & Feminist Online, 2*(1). Retrieved March 29, 2005, from http://www.barnard.edu/sfonline/ps/reisner.htm

Rothschild, B. (2000). *The body remembers: The psychophysiology of trauma and trauma treatment.* New York: Norton.

Schore, A. N. (2003). *Affect dysregulation & disorders of the self.* New York: Norton.

Sheinberg, M., & Fraenkel, P. (2000). *The relational trauma of incest: A family-based approach to treatment.* New York: Guilford.

Siegel, D. J. (1999). *The developing mind: Toward a neurobiology of interpersonal experience.* New York: Guilford.

Siegler, A. L. (1994). The boy with two kingdoms: Ontogeny of a narrative. *Psychoanalytic Psychology, 11*(3), 309–328.

Weber, A. M. (2005). "Don't hurt my mommy": Drama therapy for children who have witnessed severe domestic violence. In A. M. Weber & C. Haen (Eds.), *Clinical applications of drama therapy in child and adolescent treatment* (pp. 24–43). New York: Brunner-Routledge.

Wheeler, M., & Smith, B. (2001). Male therapist countertransference and the importance of the family context. In J. Murphy (Ed.), *Art therapy with young survivors of sexual abuse: Lost for words* (pp. 36–49). London: Routledge.

Wieland, S. (1997). *Hearing the internal trauma: Working with children and adolescents who have been sexually abused.* Thousand Oaks, CA: SAGE.

Winnicott, D. W. (1971). *Therapeutic consultations in child psychiatry.* New York: Basic Books.

Woods, J. (2003). *Boys who have abused: Psychoanalytic psychotherapy with victim/perpetrators of sexual abuse.* London: Jessica Kingsley.

Young, L. (1992). Sexual abuse and the problem of embodiment. *Child Abuse and Neglect, 16*(1), 89–100.

BIOGRAPHICAL STATEMENT

Craig Haen, MA, RDT, CGP is the Clinical Director of Adolescent Services for Kids in Crisis, in Greenwich, CT. He worked for five years on the child psychiatric inpatient unit of New York Presbyterian Hospital – Cornell Medical Center, where he coordinated the group therapy program and conducted individual, trauma-specific sessions with the severe sexual and physical abuse cases. He is the co-editor of *Clinical Applications of Drama Therapy in Child and Adolescent Treatment* (Brunner-Routledge, 2005). He has presented trainings nationally, and has worked with youth in shelters, community centers, hospitals, schools, residential programs, and on Native American reservations.

Chapter 18

DRAMA THERAPY WITH ADOLESCENT SURVIVORS OF SEXUAL ABUSE: THE USE OF MYTH, METAPHOR, AND FAIRYTALE

Yehudit Silverman

INTRODUCTION

Society has few priorities greater than its children, and yet, in so many countries, our children are in trouble. Abuse and neglect are rampant, and despite the seriousness and danger of this situation, very little progress has been made. Only a small proportion of abused children and adolescents seek help; most remain isolated, at risk, and without treatment. One form of abuse, sexual, is particularly devastating in terms of its long-term effects on normal psychological, sexual, and interpersonal development. Tragically, although often the most damaging, sexual abuse is also the least reported. Indeed, most sexual abuse is unreported because children and adolescents are not believed, and because the truth of the situation is so appalling and frightening (Buchwald et al., 1993). Even when legal measures are pursued, less than 10% of all abusers go to jail (Ledray, 1994). Not only does the victim of the abuse feel shame, but society confirms and perpetuates the victim's shame by not seriously confronting the perpetrators. Since children and adolescents are difficult to reach and often unable or unwilling to verbalize their distress, there is a very real need to find innovative and effective avenues for prevention and treatment. The problem of child sexual abuse can no longer be ignored. It is essential that society understand both the nature and potential solution to this crisis afflicting it.

The effect of sexual abuse on children is psychologically devastating. Sexual abuse is a traumatic assault on the fundamental integrity of a person. A basic sense of self has been destroyed. According to Elliott, Davis, and Slatick (1998) after experiencing a trauma, a person then divides her world into three parts:

250

before, during, and after the trauma. Each of these parts becomes a whole world. Before the trauma there is a sense of wholeness, personal integrity, and safety. During the trauma this safety is lost, and an overpowering force threatens the person's very existence. This leads to feelings of helplessness, terror, and vulnerability; yet self-blame and shame prevent the person from reaching out for help. After the trauma has occurred, there is an expectation of further abuse, a mistrust of others, and an avoidance of meaningful relationships and experiences (Elliott, Davis, and Slatick, 1998 pp. 249–271). In most cases of sexual abuse, the perpetrators are male and known to the victim. Often they are family members, and prey on girls ages four through seven or twelve through fifteen. Unfortunately, incidents of sexual abuse usually continue for more than six months (Trocme and Wolfe, 2001). When the abuse happens in childhood, the child is powerless, and often has a dependent relationship with the abuser. The very person who is supposed to offer love, protection, and safety, instead is violent, threatening, and causes physical and emotional harm. Adding to the trauma, the abuser often uses the exchange of sexual favors for affection or uses sexual abuse as a punishment. This perpetuates the dependent relationship, isolation, and self-blame that so many victims feel (Grimshaw, 1995, 1998).

To survive the appalling experience of sexual abuse, a child must develop coping strategies or defense mechanisms such as repression, denial, detachment, or disassociation (Grimshaw, 1998). From the onset of the abuse, the child's self-narrative is interrupted, the personal story line stops, and the child no longer feels whole, or integrated with her own feelings. She often internalizes a damaged self-scheme, which persists long after the abuse has ceased. It is important to recognize that sexual abuse is a crime of violence, control, degradation, and humiliation (Backos and Pagon, 1999). The child or adolescent, although powerless at the time of the abuse, sustains feelings of shame, responsibility, and self-loathing. As the child matures, these feelings can manifest in anxiety, depression, eating disorders, self-mutilation, sexual dysfunction, promiscuity, alienation, and/or suicidal ideation. Briere (1996) referred to these symptoms as PSAT (Post Sexual Abuse Trauma).

Although serious, these symptoms are typically not identified as such, as adolescents suffering from PSAT are reticent to seek therapeutic help. Adolescents in general are not easy to reach, and an adolescent who has been sexually abused carries a legacy of shame and secrecy. They are often suspicious of adults, and the medical system. This failure of adolescents who have been sexually abused to seek help only worsens an already distressful situation, but it is to be expected, given the nature of adolescence. Adolescence, usually defined as the period of life between the ages of thirteen through eighteen, is not an easy time. As Erik Erikson points out it is ". . . a turning point, a crucial period of increased vulnerability and heightened potential" (1968, p. 96). This increased vulnerability can lead to important discoveries about the self and identity, or it can lead to extremely self-destructive behaviours. Hormonal upheaval, mood swings, and peer pressure are all normal adolescent challenges. Adolescents must contend with the ambiguity of letting go of the past and developing a new image of the self. One is neither a child, nor fully an adult, and therefore constant experimentation with new social roles takes place. For some adolescents, this period becomes a transitional crises (Kidwell, Dunham, Bacho, Pastorino, and Portes, 1995). They feel the pressure from society and their peers to conform to certain roles and expectations, yet are conflicted as to what they themselves believe or want. Subsequently, adolescence becomes a turbulent time, yet the adolescent is often unable to verbalize these feelings (Arieti, 1976). The challenge is how to engage them when they often will not or cannot communicate. Although they have a great need to express and communicate their internal world, they have not yet acquired the capacity, trust, or willingness to verbally articulate what has happened to them. A form of expression is desperately needed, one which matches the intensity and complexity of their experience. The creative arts can provide a powerful means of expressing this inner turbulence, while at the same time, engaging the adolescent's strengths, idealism, and healthy inner resources (Arieti, 1976).

Specifically, Drama Therapy is an effective creative arts therapy method for engaging resistant adolescents (Emunah, 1990, 1994, 2005) and adolescents who are survivors of sexual abuse (Cattanach, 1993; Grimshaw, 1998). Drama Therapy is a form of psychotherapy that brings role-play, improvisation, and dramatic projection, into the therapeutic process. In dramatic projection, the adolescent can express herself through a dramatic form such as a role, mask, puppet, artwork, or story, thereby fostering the development of a profound relationship between the adolescent's inner emotional world and her dramatic form. At the same time, dramatic projection provides safety when working through difficult material and the ability to discover new perspectives about the problem (Jones, 1996). It offers the adolescent an opportunity to project hidden and shameful secrets onto a dramatic form, such that the adolescent is not required to verbally articulate her problems but is free express difficult feelings through creative media. This use of projection is very different from its use in traditional psychology, which views projection as a defense mechanism, a way for clients to deny their own feelings by putting them outside themselves. Winnicott's notion of the transitional object provides the crucial link to dramatic projection. For the young child, a blanket or teddy bear is a transitional object imbued with a subjective personal significance that includes both "me" and "not me" (Winnicott, 1971). Similarly, dramatic projection is an activity that is at once separate from and related to the client's personal problem. The projection of difficult feelings onto an unthreatening object or role provides a safe way for adolescents to gain perspective, and its symbolic expression becomes a powerful means of communication between the therapist and the adolescent. Drama Therapy has proven effective with children and adolescents who have emotional problems (Dequine and Pearson, 1983; Irwin, 2005), and Muriel Gold and Barbara Mackay (1987) found that after participation in an eight week Drama Therapy group, adolescent girls who had been sexually abused reported less hostility, depression, and psychotic symptoms.

In the initial stages of therapy with an adolescent who has been sexually abused, the issue of control is very present. As victims of abuse, they were coerced and physically forced to do behaviours against their will. Thus, any effective therapy must recognize and respect the adolescent's direction; the content and progression of therapy cannot seem to be forced upon her. In Drama Therapy, the therapist follows the client's lead, and, therefore, the adolescent has a sense of control over the course of the treatment. She recognizes she will not be coerced into an activity but will engage when and if she is ready. Once the medium is chosen and the creative dramatic projection is underway, the therapist monitors the adolescent's emotional engagement with her personal material. Drama Therapy offers a unique opportunity to simultaneously establish a strong emotional empathy and a safe emotional distance. This balanced state can be attained in a variety of ways: the adolescent may enter deeply into the role as an actor, or stand outside it as a director, or witness; the adolescent may use her body as the dramatic medium, or choose an object outside herself. These dramatic possibilities permit the therapist and adolescent to shift easily between the cognitive and the emotional. One session might intensify the emotional engagement by an improvisational role-play, while another might encourage emotional distance by placing the adolescent outside the role as director (Jones, 1996). Reliving trauma can lead to a flood of anxiety, and instead of integrating the experience, the adolescent will just be re-traumatized. Avoidance does not work either, as the adolescent will be unable to deal with other life traumas (Naar, 1998). Drama Therapy allows for a middle ground, addressing trauma without the accompanying overwhelming anxiety. Since the adolescent has a sense of control through manipulation of symbolic materials and role-play, she can prevent emotional flooding or re-traumatization. Through the techniques of Drama Therapy, the adolescent can maintain a balance between emotional engagement and distance to be able to access and eventually integrate disassociated parts of him or herself.

As opposed to verbal therapies, experiential psychotherapy, such as Drama Therapy, targets interventions directly at the somatic, perceptual, cognitive, affective, adaptive, and behavioural, processes that are critical in the healing (Courtois, 1998). In Drama Therapy, the experiential is central and multifaceted. It provides an arena where all kinds of behaviors, emotions, and attitudes can be expressed within a controlled and structured setting. For adolescents who have been sexually abused, the opportunity to express anger, rebelliousness, and autonomy is essential for healing. Adolescents can act as themselves and take their anger and strong feelings into the drama, and as their rebelliousness becomes part of the therapy, the need to resist treatment loses its power. Through Drama Therapy, the adolescent's age-appropriate and healthy rebelliousness can be engaged within the context of dramatic activity, thereby bypassing or minimizing the resistance to treatment (Emunah, 2005 p. 119). Since it is not uncommon for survivors of sexual abuse to regard therapy as another form of abuse (Haugaard, 1992), the therapist must be attentive in her comments and actions not to replay abuse and to continually reinforce a positive working alliance.

Not only does Drama Therapy allow for effective expression, integration, and participation, it also provides access to the adolescents own subjective narrative, something not easily accomplished with conventional therapies. Every child that has been sexually abused has a story, a unique set of circumstances that led to this drastic act. Understanding this story is key for healing and addressing phenomena in the context of a story is ageless. Ancient myths and tales helped early societies make sense of the world; stories and fairytales help young children acquire language and deal with their fears even today. Bettelheim (1976) described the use of fairytales as a way to confront and give form to children's archaic fears, anxieties, and longings. Stories meet the emotional and cognitive need to belong, to feel a part of something both familiar and yet safely separated from our everyday reality. In Drama Therapy, myth and fairytale are used by several therapists. Gersie (1993) selects stories from myths or fairy tales to work with themes emerging from her groups; Jennings (1990) asks her clients to create masks based on myths or fairy tales she judges to be appropriate; and Lahad (1992) uses a mythic structure to help clients deal with stress. My approach, called *The Story Within – myth and fairytale in therapy* (Silverman, 2004) differs from other uses of myth and fairytale in Drama Therapy in several respects. Firstly, the myth/fairytale, character, and the specific dramatic situation or tension within the story to be worked on is selected by the client, not the therapist, and each client works on his or her own personal story instead of working as a part of a group on a collective story. Furthermore, unlike much of Drama Therapy, in which many roles are assumed, here the client takes on and moves deeply into one role for many weeks or months, and in order to intensify identification with the story, clients are required to identify *one specific moment* in the chosen story that has special significance, even if the reason for its significance remains obscure. Also, clients move through different stages of creative process, which frequently involve artistic media, such as mask-making, artwork, movement, writing, and scene work. Finally, unlike in alternate approaches, to establish a sense of distance and perspective, the client directs other people (therapist, other members of a group) in dramatizations of his or her character (Silverman, 2004, 2006).

Throughout this process the client interprets the metaphors and symbols in the story within his or her own personal experience rather than within a Jungian, or other established, framework. It is the client's personal and unique relationship to the story that is emphasized and explored.

> Clients begin this process by carefully selecting a myth or fairytale that evokes a personal, although still not understood, sense of relevance to their central psychological issue. The process of discovering why this story is interesting and important represents the central activity of this therapeutic method (Silverman, 2004, p. 3).

The process of finding and working with the right story, character, and dramatic moment provides a safe container within which to connect the challenge in the story with the client's own personal problem. Clearly, the effective use of story can be both healing and psychologically revealing.

The survivor of a trauma, such as sexual abuse, is often conflicted between wanting to return to the pre-traumatic world before the sexual abuse, and an unconscious tendency to re-experience the abuse through nightmares or destructive relationships. This inner conflict plays out as a need to avoid pain, and yet at the same time, a need to resolve the painful experience (Johnson, 1987). Thus, it is not uncommon for an adolescent survivor to vacillate between engagement and resistant to treatment. In Drama Therapy, the therapist can recognize and work with this internal conflict through the dramatic medium. The variety of creative mediums used in Drama Therapy opens the door to many adolescents who would never engage in more traditional verbal therapies. These adolescents who are so wounded by previous trauma believe that the world is unsafe, people are dangerous, no one can or will help them, and it is inevitable that they will be attacked again (Elliott, Davis, and Slatick, 1998). Rather than continuing to disassociate with their traumatic memories, through Drama Therapy, adolescents can learn to express experiences, which are beyond words. They can break the taboo of secrecy through fictional re-enactment. In a safe and controlled way, they can acknowledge and re-examine their trauma so that they become empowered and can move on to a normal adulthood.

Most children and adults who are abused become numb to their inner life. The seriousness of this internal disconnection depends on the age, violence, coercion, secrecy, family structure, and the subsequent process after revealing the abuse (Hartman and Burgess, 1988). The goal in treatment is to integrate the trauma into a comprehensive self-narrative that allows for a healthy re-connection with the adolescent's internal world. An abused child learns that their value is to meet adult sexual needs. Through role-play, improvisation, and scene-work adolescents can undo this distorted sense of self-worth and begin to explore their value in healthy and constructive ways.

In my work as a drama therapist, I have often had to contend with the poignant problems of adolescents who have been sexually abused. Through the use of myth and fairytale these adolescents were able to reveal and work with, often for the first time, the trauma of their abuse. The story that was hidden, shameful, and buried was gradually revealed. As the adolescents become immersed in creating masks, artwork, costumes, dramatic scenes, dramatic sculptures, and movement, they enjoyed the identification with their character. The therapeutic process involved an evolving relationship between the adolescent and the therapist, the adolescent and the chosen character, the adolescent and the artistic creations, and ultimately the adolescent and her own personal story.

CASE EXAMPLE: TARA

Tara was a fifteen-year-old girl who lived on the street. She was highly intelligent, very attractive, and extremely evasive. The emergency room doctors knew her well. At least once every couple of months, she would be rushed in by ambulance after being found unconscious on the street, in the metro station, or in a stranger's apartment. Once stabilized, she would refuse further treatment and go back to the streets. She abused drugs and alcohol and was sexually promiscuous to the point of consistently waking up in strange beds, naked, and sometimes bruised, with no memory of how she got there. After a particularly dangerous sexual and substance abuse encounter, she agreed to see a therapist. It was suspected that there was early trauma and possible sexual abuse, due to scars in the genital area.

My first impression of Tara was of her slouching on a chair outside my office reading a book. The book was water-stained and torn, but she was engrossed. To the surprise of my colleagues, I was encouraged. I figured if she could engage with a story, any story, then perhaps there was a way to reach her. When she entered my office she was suspicious, hostile, and silent. I asked her about her book, reluctantly she told me about it. I asked if I could borrow the book when she finished. She laughed and asked me if I was just trying to get her to come back. I laughed and said "yes, but I promise to read the book." She did come back, brought the book, which I subsequently read, and we began our journey together into the world of story.

We formed an alliance based on whatever novel she was reading. Somehow this girl, despite living on the street, abusing drugs and alcohol, and waking up in strange beds, always had a book. She said she found them in the trash. One day I asked her about myths and fairytales. I showed her my books and we looked through them together. While looking through the titles in the Complete Fairy Tales of the Brothers Grimm (Zipes, 1987), she was immediately drawn to one story: *The Handless Maiden.* I read the story out loud.

Synopsis: Once upon a time, the devil deceived a poor miller into trading his beautiful daughter for all the wealth in the world. Three years later the devil came and tried to take the girl away, but because of her purity he could not approach her. Furious, the devil demanded that the father chop off the girl's hands. Then, as she laid her hands over a hardened tree stump, the razor-sharp, iron-lipped ax fell on her wrists, severing her hands and changing her life forever. Her tears washed away the blood and still the devil could not come near. He went off in a rage cursing the miller and his family. With her arms bound in gauze, the handless maiden left her family and wandered into the forest. Years passed and she learned to survive without hands. Eventually after hardships, adventures, and true love, her hands grew back.

After I read the story, she sat in silence, visibly moved. She asked if I had paper and pen and when I gave her some, she furiously started to draw hands. Thus, began a six-month process of her obsession with hands. She came every week and as soon as she entered my office began to work creatively on the subject of hands. Big hands, little hands, sculpted three-dimensional hands, talking hands, dancing hands, angry hands, and beautiful hands. She never discussed what she was doing and she never missed an appointment. Once again my colleagues were surprised. This was a girl who never came to appointments, and would end up bruised and unconscious in the emergency room. Now there were no more emergency room visits, and she would arrive early, often with art supplies (torn and broken, which she found in the trash). My approach was to trust the metaphor, to trust that the image of the hands in the fairytale had touched her deeply. I knew that she was still extremely fragile and that one wrong move on my part would send her away. I never asked her for self-reflection or answers, and I never interpreted what she did. We stayed in the metaphor, in the character of the hands, and within that structure she thrived. She discovered a universe within a narrowly confined theme.

After six months with me, bringing different props and art supplies, I happened to bring in some rope. She took one look at the rope, started breathing rapidly, and frantically tied the rope tighter and tighter around one of the hand sculptures she had made. Then she stood in front of it, frozen, her body started to shake. I realized she was reliving a trauma and was paralyzed with fear. She literally could not move. I guided her to a chair where she started to sob uncontrollably. When she could speak, she told me her story. At age three, her father had tied her hands to the bed and raped her; this went on for four years. At age seven, he left the house and never returned. She had never told anyone. Her mother was an alcoholic and blamed her daughter for the father leaving. All this time she had forgotten, blocked out the abuse, yet was filled with shame and self-loathing. When she heard the story of the handless maiden, something deep inside of her was touched, and now, seeing the rope, she remembered.

Over the next six months, she worked with her own hands, the rope, sounds, movement, and improvisation. She fought back, she freed her hands, she killed her father, she mourned her lost childhood, and she began, slowly, to heal. When she finished therapy, she had found a job, was off the streets, off of strange sexual encounters, and was attending school part time. During the last session she showed me a pair of bright colored gloves she had bought. Each finger was a different color. As she wiggled her fingers she told me "Finally my hands are my own."

The story itself had led her to where she was almost ready to go. Through the use of fiction, she could discover her truth. According to Jennings (1990), metaphor helps children make sense of their experience. It allows insight into the experience while maintaining a safe distance from the trauma. It was essential that Tara work at her own pace, and I needed to convey the message that I trusted her process. I knew that adolescents who have been sexually abused have negative expectations of intimate relationships and that I treaded a fine line to gain her trust. Tara was frightened and angry, as well as lost. Over the course of treatment, I was a witness, a voice of encouragement, a presence of hope, and a belief in her and her process. Eventually, I was the voice that validated her truth and her pain. As Margaret Mary Kelly (1995) proposes, a course of therapy for survivors of sexual abuse repeatedly returns to three core processes: testing the therapeutic relationship, addressing traumatic experiences, and undoing denial. The techniques of Drama Therapy allow for theses core processes to occur in an organic and effective manner.

Within the context of Drama Therapy, the adolescent can experience and express many different roles, emotions, and interactions. She can gradually and safely explore her trauma without becoming re-traumatized. Through metaphor and story, she can symbolize the trauma – giving it a voice, while at the same time keeping it at a distance. And finally, when she is ready, she can tell her own story out loud and undo the legacy of shame and secrecy, and move on with her life.

APPENDIX – TERMS

Defense Mechanism – in psychoanalysis, any of a variety of unconscious personality reactions, which the ego uses to protect the conscious mind from threatening feelings or perceptions.

Repression – in psychiatry, the classical defense mechanism that protects one from impulses or ideas that would cause anxiety, by preventing them from becoming conscious.

Denial – in psychology, an ego defense mechanism that operates unconsciously to resolve emotional conflict, and to allay anxiety by refusing to perceive the more unpleasant aspects of external reality.

Dissociation – in psychology, a state or condition in which certain thoughts, emotions, sensations, or memories are separated from the rest of the psyche.

Post Sexual Abuse Trauma – Briere (1996) questions the use of psychiatric labels for victims of sexual abuse. He suggests instead that the psychological disturbances experienced by survivors of sexual abuse be considered as *Post Sexual Abuse Trauma*. This term refers to symptomatic behaviors that were initially adaptive, but that over time became contextually inappropriate components of the victim's adult personality.

REFERENCES

Arieti, S. (1976). *Creativity: The magic synthesis.* New York: Basic Books.

Backos, A., & Pagon, B. (1999). Finding a voice: art therapy with female adolescent sexual abuse survivors. *Journal of the American Art Therapy Association 16,* 93, 126–132, Chichester: John Wiley and Sons.

Bettelheim, B. (1976). *The uses of enchantment.* New York: Knopf.

Briere, J. (1996). Psychometric review of the Trauma Symptom Checklist - 40. In B. H. Slam (Ed.), *Measurement of stress, trauma, and adaptation.* Lutherville, MD: Sidran Press.

Buchwald, E., Fletcher, P., & Roth, M. (1993). Are we really living in a rape culture? In Buchwald, E., Fletcher, P., & Roth, M. (Eds.), *Transforming a rape culture.* Minneapolis: Milkweed Editions.

Cattanach, A. (1993). *Play therapy with abused children.* London: Jessica Kingsley.

Courtois, C. (1998). Issues and challenges in assessing trauma. *Centering Newsletter, 3*(3).

Dequine, E.R., & Pearson-Davis, S. (1983). Videotaped improvisation with emotionally disturbed adolescents. *The Arts in Psychotherapy, 10,* 15–21.

Elliott, R., Davis, K. L., & Slatick, E. (1998). Process-experiential therapy for post-traumatic stress difficulties. In Greenberg, L. S., Watson, J. C., & Lietaer G. (Eds.), *Handbook of experiential psychotherapy* (pp. 249–271). New York: The Guilford Press.

Emunah, R. (1990). Expression and expansion in adolescence. *The Arts in Psychotherapy, 17,* 2, 101–107.

Emunah, R. (1994). *Acting for real drama therapy process, technique, and performance.* New York: Brunner Mazel.

Emunah, R. (2005). Drama therapy and adolescent resistance. In A. M. Weber & C. Haen (Eds.), *Clinical applications of drama therapy in child and adolescent treatment.* NY: Brunner- Routledge.

Erikson, E. (1968). *Identity: Youth and crises.* New York: W. W. Norton.

Gersie, A. (1993). On being both author and actor: Reflections on therapeutic storymaking. *Dramatherapy, 15.*

Gersie, A., & King, N. (1990). *Storymaking in education and therapy.* London: Jessica Kingsley.

Gold, M., & Mackay, B. (1987). A pilot study in drama therapy with adolescent girls who have been sexually abused. *The Arts in Psychotherapy, 14,* 77–84.

Grimshaw, D. (1995). Shall I be a mother? The development of the role of the dramatherapist and reflections on transference and counter transference. In S. Jennings (Ed.), *Dramatherapy with Children and Adolescents.* London: Routledge.

Grimshaw, D. (1998). To all the flickering candles: dramatherapy with sexually abused children. In A, Bannister (Ed.) *From hearing to healing: working with the aftermath of child sexual abuse.* Chichester: John Wiley and Sons.

Hartman, C., & Burgess A.W. (1988). Information processing of trauma. *Journal of Interpersonal Violence, 3*(4), 443–457.

Haugaard, J. (1992). Sexually abused children's opposition to psychotherapy. *Journal of Sexual Abuse 1*(2), 1–16.

Irwin, E.C. (2005). Facilitating play with nonplayers: a developmental perspective. In A. M. Weber & C. Haen (Eds.), *Clinical applications of drama therapy in child and adolescent treatment.* NY: Brunner-Routledge.

Johnson, D. R. (1987). The role of creative arts therapies in the diagnosis and treatment of psychological trauma. *The Arts in Psychotherapy, 14,* 7–13.

Jennings, S. (1990). Masking and unmasking: The interface of dramatherapy. In S. Jennings (Ed.), *Dramatherapy with families, groups, and individuals.* (pp. 108–128). London: Jessica Kingsley.

Jones, P. (1996). *Drama as therapy: Theatre as living.* London: Routledge.

Kelly, M. M. (1995). Play therapy with sexually traumatized children: Factors that Promote healing. *Journal of Child Sexual Abuse, 4*(3), 1-11.

Kidwell, J. S., Dunham, R. M., Bacho, R. A., Pastorino, E., & Portes, P. R. (1995). Adolescent identity exploration: a test of Erikson's theory of transitional crises. *Adolescence. 30,* 120, 785–793.

Lahad, M. (1992). *Dramatherapy theory and practice 2.* London: Tavistock/Routledge.

Ledray, L. (1994). *Recovering from rape.* New York: Henry Holt & Company.

Kelly, M., (1995). Play therapy with sexually traumatized children: Factors that promote healing. *Journal of Sexual Abuse, 4*(3), 1–11.

Naar, R. (1998). Short term psychodrama with victims of sexual abuse. *International Journal of Action Methods, 51*(2), 75–84.

Silverman, Y. (2004). The story within – Myth and fairy tale in therapy. *The Arts in Psychotherapy, 31*(3), 27–135.

Silverman, Y. (2006). Drama therapy: Theoretical approaches. In S. Brooke (Ed), *Creative arts therapies manual: A guide to the history, theoretical approaches, assessment, and work with special populations of art, play, dance, music, drama, and poetry therapies.* New York: Charles C Thomas Publisher, Ltd.

Trocme, N., & Wolfe, D. (2001). *Child maltreatment in Canada: selected results from the Canadian incidence study of reported child abuse and neglect.* Ottawa, Ontario: Minister Of Public Works and Government Services, Canada.

Winnicott, D. W. (1971). *Playing and reality.* New York: Penguin Books.

Zipes, J. (1987). *Complete fairy tales of the brothers Grimm.* New York: Bantam Classics.

BIOGRAPHICAL STATEMENT

Yehudit Silverman, M.A., DTR, RDT is a registered Dance Movement Therapist and a registered Drama Therapist who is an assistant professor in the Creative Arts Therapies Graduate Program at Concordia University in Montreal, Quebec. She developed an original approach to using myth and fairy tale in therapy based on her twenty years of clinical experience working in hospitals with adults, adolescents, and children suffering from psychiatric disorders, eating disorders, delinquency, and abuse. She has written about this approach in an article, two textbook chapters, and produced and directed an original documentary film, *The Story Within – Myth and fairy tale in therapy.* Professor Silverman has presented her work and her film internationally, and as a performer, director, and choreographer. Her film is distributed by Insight Media see http://www.insight_media.com and the category ("therapeutic approaches"). Information about her approach and film are available at http://www.thestorywithin.ca.

Contact: yehudit@vax2.concordia.ca.

Chapter 19

DRAMA THERAPY WITH SEXUAL ABUSE SURVIVORS WITH SUBSTANCE ABUSE ISSUES

Linda M. Dunne

Very early in my work as a therapist, I discovered that simply listening to my client, very attentively, was an important way of being helpful. So when I was in doubt as to what I should do in some active way, I listened. It seemed surprising to me that such a passive kind of interaction could be so useful.

Carl R. Rogers (1980, p. 137)

INTRODUCTION

This chapter looks at the use of drama therapy in the treatment of childhood sexual abuse with a client population in clinical treatment primarily for substance abuse addiction. A clinical account of drama therapy with a group is shared to illustrate the spontaneous implementation of drama therapeutic tools in the treatment process of sexual abuse. Names have been changed to protect the identity of the clients. Emphasis is placed on the clients' acceptance and acknowledgement of the sexual abuse, in some cases in relation to their addiction, as it intermittently arises during drama therapy sessions.

In addition, I include excerpts from my personal processing notes which I use after each session to reflect on what has taken place. This serves as a valuable exercise in acknowledging anything that may have arisen for my own 'internal patient' (Jennings, 1990) needing further consideration during weekly supervision. I feel this to be of utmost importance here, as I, in the role of drama therapist, bring the additional role of survivor to the session. While I am not suggesting that it is necessary for the drama therapist to have experienced the trauma of her clients to better treat or understand their therapeutic

261

needs, my personal journey through the pain of sexual abuse grants me the opportunity to connect with these women not only in the capacity of therapist-client but also that of survivor-survivor.

Finally, I feel the role of addiction is only important in this discussion if, from the clients' perspective, there is a direct link between the sexual abuse and the substance abuse. For many clients, separating the incidents of sexual abuse and their relationship with their addiction is, at this point, an impossible task. For some, the sexual abuse occurred in combination with the substance abuse, resulting in a complicated web of psychological and emotional pain. This work remains a challenging process of witnessing and attempting to ease the clients' fear of the unbearable encounter with the past and the desperate struggle to heal.

My work as a drama therapist is largely influenced by Carl Rogers' person-centred approach (1980), Renee Emunah's five phase model in drama therapy (1994), the concept of "flow"as described by Mihaly Csikszentmihalyi (1990) and Winnicott's (1971) "potential space." Every drama therapy session is a unique discovery, and includes not only drama but a mixture of art, music, movement, and creative writing.

Some of the clients I describe in the cases below are still in treatment while others have moved on to another stage of their healing. It is my hope that their experiences within the group provide them with a renewed strength as they move further along their path. This chapter is a compilation of all that I have learned and continue to learn. With every client-therapist interaction, I recognize new ways of welcoming them into the healing space of drama therapy and maintaining the safety while they are present.

MEETING THE PLAYERS – FIRST IMPRESSIONS

The group consists of women between the ages of twenty through fifty-five. Attendance fluctuates between six and twelve members and the group meets weekly for two one-hour sessions. While all group members speak fluent Dutch, it is for some members and for the drama therapist a second language. The drama therapy group is a mandatory module in the clinic's general treatment program and must be attended by every one on the unit. Treatment at this clinic, for some women, is an in-between step to a more permanent living arrangement or to another treatment program. Therefore, regular attendance can last for as little as two weeks or as long as six months. Obviously, this plays a significant role in the development and maintenance of cohesion within the group, a discussion that would extend beyond the scope of this chapter. I will say, however, that when there is a change in membership within the group this is dealt with openly and group members are given the opportunity to express concerns and share feelings. As group therapists, we know that , "group membership, acceptance and approval are of the utmost importance in the individual's developmental sequence" (Yalom, 1985, p. 51). Since personal tragedies are often discussed in the group and trust remains a fragile factor, confidentiality is a frequent concern when membership changes.

Within the group, there is a history of prostitution, extensive substance abuse, sexual abuse, and in some cases, rape and physical abuse, emotional and psychological degradation, and an absence of identity. Several women have additional diagnoses including personality and anxiety disorders. Defined by the DSM-IV (APA, 1994), "A personality disorder is an enduring pattern of inner experience and behaviour that deviates markedly from the expectations of the individual's culture, is pervasive and inflexible, has an onset in adolescence or early adulthood, is stable over time, and leads to distress or impairment" (p. 629). In the client group discussed here, one individual has a diagnosis of borderline, two with antisocial, and one of narcissistic personality disorder. Post-traumatic stress disorder (PTSD), is the most prevalent anxiety disorder in this group, for which the group receives a special group session to learn safe and effective coping methods. "Post-traumatic stress disorder is characterized by the re-experiencing of an extremely traumatic event, accompanied by symptoms of increased arousal and by avoidance of stimuli associated with the trauma" (APA, 1994, p. 393). Almost every group member suffers from PTSD and many have great difficulty accepting this, as they feel it is in some way a character defect and a sign of weakness. This can further complicate the client's ability and attempts in maintaining abstinence, as well as confronting and processing past traumas.

Some clients openly admit that though their substance abuse problems have taken a back seat in their current treatment program, it remains a comforting "option" when the past becomes too much to handle. Occasionally, group members know one another from prior admissions at other clinics or from life on the street in the drug and prostitution scene. It is not uncommon for unresolved conflicts from the past to find their way into the drama therapy room. In working with these courageous women, it is my belief that successful treatment may mean a collective approach to both the substance and sexual abuse problems simultaneously. Philip Flores (1997) writes that:

> In the last few years more and more evidence has been accumulated that suggests that the incidence of untreated sexual abuse is alarmingly high for female addicts and alcoholics (p. 309). For many of these women, getting past the hurdle of substance abuse is just the tip of the iceberg. The "real" problems are housed beneath the surface occupying a vast and dark place, out of sight and mind.

PERSONAL REFLECTIONS

I have had four sessions with the group. It seems there are ongoing attempts, continually vying for one's position within the group. It stirs something in me — what? Dominant members of the group overwhelm those quietly present with loud voices, incessant chattering, "confrontational" style of dress, and occupation of the space. I recall Yalom's (1985) description of "The Monopolist" (p. 375). In a group of ten, can there really be three monopolists? How accurate is this assertive, tough, street-wise bravado I see before me? Is this the hardened shell housing the wounded child? My own wounded child feels threatened; I have to be patient.

WHAT'S IN A NAME? – MAKING SENSE OF DRAMA THERAPY

The clients with whom I work were initially exceedingly resistant to drama therapy and, in some cases, to *any* form of therapy. Many of my clients have never heard of drama therapy or have experienced it during a prior admission with little or no enthusiasm, and most often a great deal of criticism. They have been in and out of treatment facilities for many years and repeatedly assure me that there is no therapy they have not seen or experienced. Essentially, there is nothing new to learn and no further insights to be gained.

"I'm not going to dance around this room until you tell me to be a tree," quips a client during her first session. Furthermore, they are under no circumstances about to revisit the past to explore or dramatize old traumas. I clearly understand this skepticism when I listen to some of their previous experiences. These include, among others, being tied at the wrist to another client until a conflict was resolved and confronting oneself in a mirror until self-hatred was replaced by self-love.

I assure the clients that these are not among my practices as a drama therapist and that every one works differently. I choose to accept these opinions as the clients' way of communicating their uncertainty and to let me know they need time to get used to working this way.

To assist the clients in gaining a clearer understanding of what drama therapy is and how I, as a drama therapist, work, I set several boxes and baskets filled with an assortment of objects throughout the room. These boxes contain musical instruments, puppets, masks, art supplies, hats, and a collection of postcards and pictures. I explain that under the vast "umbrella" of drama therapy — which I literally draw on newsprint and tape to the wall — there are many possibilities for treatment. What we as a group choose as our method of working depends largely on who we are, where we are going (clients' therapeutic goals), and how we plan on getting there. This brings enormous relief, as does my weekly reassurance that I have no hidden agenda to secretly analyze them or haul out past wounds. I suggest in the first several sessions of coming together in this new way that we move through the space as a group. After we meander around the room together, occasionally moving to music, it appears a mutual understanding takes place. An innocent playfulness replaces suspicion and I announce that this is how we will proceed in our drama therapy sessions, *together* and with a tempo comfortable for everyone. We "move" forward *together*, no one goes it alone, and there is no pushing or pulling.

SETTING THE SCENE

My drama therapy room is a wonderfully bright room with large windows lending itself to sun-drenched walls and ample physical space. Storage cabinets occupy a separate area, and mats, cushions, and large spongy couches offer a variety of seating arrangements. A tall, free standing easel is in one corner and serves as an outlet in the absence of verbal expression. Here, a client can sketch or paint that which she wishes to convey without the pressure of having to articulate the thought or emotion with words. Natalie Rogers (1993) reminds us that, "The visual arts offer an opportunity for images to come forth when words are not yet formed" (p. 141). In the case of sexual abuse trauma, it is not unusual for the emotions to overwhelm any possibility for verbal articulation.

Lastly, the circle formation is maintained in the space at the beginning and end of every session, sometimes amongst mats or cushions on the floor and other times next to another on the couches. It is one of the components in providing a group with structure that I routinely "enforce." Emunah (1994) writes of the circle:

> The circle connotes the cyclical. In drama therapy, the dramatic rituals, beginning and ending in a circle, celebrate the cycles and stages within the group process. The circle formation contributes to the sense of containment and continuity provided by the ritual; it *holds* the group – with all its intricacies – in simplicity. More significantly, the circle embodies and intensifies the sense of unity and interconnection within the group. (p. 23)

On days when it seems like all else has "failed" or that nothing "worked," it is this one event that group members can always count on. These women crave an atmosphere of harmony, peace, safety, warmth, and colour for which they routinely ask. Coloured scarves draped randomly throughout the room serve as the backdrop and oversized puppets take up residence on window sills. A recent and favorite addition are faceless, sexless forms filled with soft beads that can be stretched, pinched, and twisted in every direction always popping easily back to its original form – a prized object for expressing anger, confusion, and sadness.

FURTHER REFLECTIONS

A few weeks have passed now and if I am completely honest, it is rather overwhelming. We meet twice a week for one-hour sessions and the group energy is heavy and dense. The monopolists have lost their steam and one has moved on. There is not an ounce of enthusiasm or pleasure in sight. What do I expect? Too much? I have sifted my way through the files of these women; where to begin? The list is endless: substance abuse, childhood sexual abuse, rape, unspeakable acts of physical abuse, emotional and psychological degradation, years of sibling incest, rape, life on the street, history of prostitution, loss of parental rights, loss of innocence, splintered identities, and remnants of the self. Where do I begin? What is my entry point? My own experiences of sexual abuse and rape bubble to the surfaced, discussed further with supervisor. What did I need then? Someone to listen, to accept me and my shame? Carl Rogers comes to mind!

SESSION PROGRESSION-COMBINED INGREDIENTS

While Emunah's integrative five phase model of drama therapy (1994) serves as the basis of how I structure each session and group, choices along the therapeutic passage are largely influenced by the uniqueness of the group as a whole, and of the individuals within the group. I abide religiously to Rogers' (1980) three conditions for a growth-promoting environment: "realness, acceptance, or unconditional positive regard" and empathic understanding (p. 116). Every session is organized around the basic format of a check-in, warm-up, introduction to the theme (or, as is most often the case, an acceptance of the theme that emerges in the here and now), putting the theme into action, review and reflection, and finally, closure of the session that includes taking a positive "piece" of the action with you. While the principles of drama therapy are always front and centre, during the sessions I also incorporate the magic and beauty of music, movement, art, and creative writing into the healing process.

STRENGTH IN NUMBERS

Before any emotions or thoughts associated with sexual abuse become apparent in the group, sessions are geared more towards general themes directly associated with substance abuse rehabilitation. When there is significant turnover in the group, we "repeat" the pattern of spending several weeks in phase one of Emunah's (1994) five phase model, focusing on the healthy components of the individual (p. 35). In addition, we introduce, develop, and practice social skills, learning to say no, and creating and maintaining personal boundaries. As every drama therapist knows, groups are rarely predictable, and spontaneity and improvisational abilities of the drama therapist are central to the group's safety. While I begin each group with a session plan, I must admit that plan is rarely carried out as outlined. I meet the clients where they are in the moment, and the mood of the group always gets more respect and attention than my neatly organized bullet points on paper. This is vital in working with such a challenging group where the group members have been so heavily traumatized. Outlined below is a moving account of how this group of surviving women deal with the issue of sexual abuse when it rises unexpectedly during a drama therapy session. This session takes place after two months of participation in the drama therapy group.

Monday afternoons are sometimes an automatic indicator that the group atmosphere will be slightly dark, and often group members are highly sensitive to even the slightest prickle from one another. Mondays are mentally and physically demanding for the group. They follow a mandatory module, learning new skills in coping with PTSD, led by the unit's psychologist, and after lunch drama therapy, followed by recreational activities. Since these women are accustomed to very little daily structure, many find the program extremely tiresome and *too* intensive.

A rainy Monday afternoon brings with it an absence of emotion; slow shuffling feet and a heavy air of fatigue guide the women into the drama therapy room. Some sling themselves over the backs of couches like wounded rabbits and others spread themselves immediately across mats on the floor as if to declare a strong opposition to ever moving again. Not a word pierces the air, and I take up my customary position quietly bouncing on an oversized, red stability ball trying to get a sense of what is happening. Amidst the stillness, some reddened puffy eyes stare in my direction with a peculiar but patient anticipation of what will unfold. A few of the women reach for their favourite puppets and clutch them tightly to their chests burying their faces. Another group member gently pulls a green scarf across her face and softly announces "I am here and I am not here." Others use their puppets as pillows stuffing them under their heads and close their eyes. This is the first time in over two months the group enters in such an air of defeat. I glance at the session plan I had prepared and my mind empties as my body fills with the uncertainty and fear of the group before me.

In the last several weeks, the group has been taking great pleasure in naming the group mood at the start of every session and the women have become very adept at listening to their bodies and deciphering the group mood. Today, it needs no prompting. Out of these clouds of sadness, falling crisply like raindrops, the words spill into the empty quiet. "Heavy" (silence) . . . "And black, very black," "Prickly" . . . "Nervous, yes, nervous and bumpy" (more silence). I ask the group what did this "mood" look like, and as heads begin to rise up and the women come out of their self-made cocoons, a detailed description ensues and I begin to assemble supplies in an attempt to "build" this mood that apparently invades us. Without discussion we begin building a makeshift tent between the couches. Soft mats provide us with a floor, two massive rain sticks frame the entry way, and black cloth stretches over our heads.

Therapist: Do we need music?

I have no idea where this is headed. There is a vibrating energy and my instinct and logic tell me to keep the group moving. A newcomer in the group, Mary, chooses an African drum CD and it begins to play. At this point, I am not sure what will emerge and I possess an odd mixture of creative contentment and genuine uncertainty. Stay in the moment, I tell myself. We move in an undirected but cooperative scene as if we have done this a thousand times. We stop and stare at our constructed hut.

Sue: Do we go in?
Therapist: I don't know, what do you all think?

Silence. I dare to suggest to the group that it may be interesting to see what it looks like from the other side of this heavy dark mood. Heads nod, scarves and puppets are collected, possible provisions, as we scurry inside. A nervous giggling begins but is quickly intercepted by falling tears. One woman begins to speak.

Alice: I am a grown woman and I still have to hide from him.

Alice is a woman who attended the drama therapy group consistently for the past two months and until today, has consistently possessed a "bubbly," vivacious energy, always enthusiastic, rarely showing any signs of pain or torment. The drums mumble on outside our fort. I glance at the faces of the women and my instinct assures me I do not need to ask what this is about. My inner survivor wakes up, recognizes the familiar anxiety of being "found out" as she senses their alarm.

Sue: Yes, you're right, we are all in here hiding, and they are out there free, and everyone thinks we are the crazy ones.

I contemplate that maybe what I am witnessing is "leftover" emotional residue from another group or from a discussion that began at lunch and is not quite finished yet. Then, I snap back to the anger rising inside the hut and realize that it does not matter, this is where they are.

Sandra: There are no crazy people here.

I offer my hands to the women seated on either side of me and they do the same until our circle is fully connected. There are some heavy sighs as I look around the circle.

Therapist: What is it like here on the inside of all this emotion, this heavy dark mood?
Anna: I'm scared.
Sandra: I feel safe.
Tessa: I feel like I am in the womb.
Alice: I've never been on the inside before. This is the hole I usually fill up with drugs. I never even knew this was empty until I got clean.
Sue: I feel like I am in a cave, a haunted cave, a cave where the crazy people go.

The group is taking care of itself and I continue to hold the space allowing further expression.

Alice: Something came loose in me today and all I can think of is to call my dealer.
Therapist: Maybe that's because that's what you have always done until now, all you knew to do.

I offer this as a suggestion, an attempt – and a feeble one at that, I thought – to reassure her in the moment, and to gently suggest that now other possibilities exist. To keep the group grounded in the here and now I ask what other options are available at 2:06 pm on this Monday afternoon. There is a quiet contemplation.

Alice: My own mother needed "proof" to believe that what I said my grandfather had done was true, but she needed no proof that I was using.

I fear that multiple wounds are beginning to open too quickly, since the topic at hand is one with which every group member, including myself, could identify. My brain filters through all the potential risks of such a moment re-calling, "The risk of a client's becoming overwhelmed, decompensating, having anxiety and panic attacks, flashbacks or worse, retraumatization, always lingers" (Rothschild, 2000, p. 78). Are these concerns for my clients of for myself? As I glance around our makeshift hut, I can see that the group is all right, and this little cloth structure is playing an important role. Deep breaths draw inwards and heavy sighs push out. We not only reach a therapeutic threshold, but move over it into a safe healing place. Tears slowly dry making room for smiles, and through the stillness, a petite woman whispers.

Sue: I'm getting out. Who's coming?
Alice: I'm coming, I'm getting the hell of this fucking prison.

With a delightful sneakiness, we all join hands and Sue begins the counting. On three we charge to the outside with a renewed sense of confidence, pushing the heavy dark mood far away. Mats slide across the floor and the air erupts with giddiness and laughter.

We collapse in a heap on the floor. There are lots of "wows" and a peaceful moment enjoying what we have accomplished.

Sue: Well, now that the drama is over, we can get on with the therapy.

Everyone laughs. This experience needs little verbal processing as knowing looks of satisfaction are exchanged around the room. I offer the group the opportunity for reflection and comments. The reactions come in the form of full body sculpts accompanied by wonderfully funny faces but no words. It appears to be more of a victory than a "this is what I learned" moment. I feel it unnecessary on my part to inquire about the origins of this powerful energy that overtook the group. I would later discover that this is the result of the women hearing for the first time they had a "sickness" called PTSD. The group see this as their punishment for a crime they did not commit.

One of the women comments that if this should happen again that she would not be "running away or hiding" again. This sparks an intense discussion and several candid confessions of how and why the years of substance abuse proved so "comforting." I know in this moment that before the group leaves the room on this rainy afternoon we have to find a safe, yet effective way of receiving these emotions, and then give them a safe place. I ask the group for suggestions. The decision is unanimous. Once the emotions are identified, the simple option of throwing them away (thankfully my space contains an oversized trash can) will suffice. Agreed. As the session draws to a close, we stand and pass a gentle hand squeeze around the circle to symbolize the giving and receiving of strength and support in what we have shared this afternoon.

CLOSING REFLECTIONS

I look at back at what happened that afternoon. It is only in this moment that my body truly feels the extent of what the group faced. I am excited at the healing possibilities that drama therapy can offer these women in the paralysing moments of upset. Many of these women have never had treatment for the sexual abuse, outside their personal attempts at numbing the pain and shame through years of substance abuse. And with only a short period of drug-free living, I see them slowly beginning to truly feel the past pain. Today, at the coffee machine, a member from the group casually shared in passing that the pain and confusion she feels as a result of the sexual abuse can be so powerful that she would rather have a blade slicing through her flesh.

Clients respond to drama therapy as witnessing another part of themselves they did not know existed, a healthy part, a strong and courageous part. It is an experience they never thought possible, but feel they needed to have to keep moving forward in treatment and in their lives. Being truly present in drama alters how these women see themselves, and after having the experience they place greater value on themselves as unique individuals resulting in a recognition similar to that described by Sue Jennings (1990): "Since drama is intrinsic to the human experience, and is part of our essential development and evolution as people, drama itself is the means whereby inner change, and therefore outer change, can be brought about" (p. 29).

CONCLUSION

Since the initial writing of this chapter, there have been other incidents where potent and perplexing emotions associated with sexual abuse have resurfaced in the group. In both situations, a time-out was called and the group came together to offer their support to one another. They stand in silence interlocking their arms followed by a ritual "sweeping" of what they call "poison to the soul" and together they place it in the trash can.

As I look back over my session notes, I see some cues I missed. Moments when maybe they were trying to tell me that something more important than drugs was on their mind. During a "group visit" to the "magic shop," a psychodramatic technique where human qualities can be purchased (Emunah, 1994, p. 220), one member of the group became very angry when it was time to "pay" for the respect and self-confidence she wished to purchase. She snapped that her whole life all she ever had was taken from her by people who used her for her their own pleasure without permission and she had nothing left to give. Her anger was indeed an "an emotion of self-protection" (Rothschild, 2000, p. 61).

Though the symptoms of unprocessed traumas associated with sexual abuse are arising here as somewhat of a "secondary" treatment concern, I feel it is our responsibility to put on the brakes and give it the attention it needs. For this group, that means respecting and accepting the pain as well as the confusion. Now that we have broken through this wall of what first was unspeakable shame, I, as the drama therapist, am more alert to the subtle cues from the group, and in turn, the group has permission to stop and process the moment. Recognition and acknowledgement of the sexual abuse suffered in childhood has now positively prompted these women to examine other areas of their lives where they have been abused, manipulated, and taken advantage of. By bravely facing the secrets of sexual abuse, we unlock numerous other possibilities that can now be reintegrated into the group's treatment, forming valuable links between behaviours such as saying no, standing up for yourself, and establishing personal boundaries.

As members move out of this drama therapy group onto the next stage of their lives, my wish is that they continue to value their uniqueness, beauty, and strength, and nurture the fragile child within. While the substance abuse has done its share of damage on the minds and bodies of these women, the sexual abuse has left a seemingly indelible mark on their souls. One woman describes herself often as "an empty shell with nothing inside, no treasures, nothing new to discover, simply lying lifeless on the shore hoping to be washed out to sea." While there is still a great deal of work and healing to be done, these women no longer fear their personal, creative processes. They can appreciate the spontaneity of others, and are less suspicious of playful interactions with one another. Every day I am surprised at the spontaneity, trust, and insight that remains in motion and at the end of every session I tell these courageous women, "Lieve dames het is altijd een eer" – Literally: "Sweet ladies, it is always an honour."

APPENDIX I – TERMS

Substance Abuse – in dealing with this client population, substance abuse is referring to a highly destructive pattern of excessive drug and alcohol use. The extended and increased use, as well as a worsening of the behavioural patterns, such as a decomposition of psychological and physiological faculties, moves the individual into a controlling state of addiction and dependency. Abused substances include: amphetamines, alcohol, cannabis, hallucinogens, opioids, and cocaine. It is not uncommon, especially in the beginning stages of treatment, for individuals to turn to other substances in an attempt to reach a high or to dull strong emotions that often arise with the onset of sobriety. This can take the form of excessive use of cough medications and sport or energy drinks.

Internal Patient – Extremely important for every Creative Arts Therapist, and described by Sue Jennings (1990) as, "The internal patient brings together those aspects of ourselves that have made similar journeys to those of our clients and patients" (p. 48). Since pain, suffering and loss is an unavoidable factor of our humanness, it is crucial that this component of who we are is continually nurtured and monitored as we journey further with our clients.

Person Centered Approach – I begin every interaction with clients, groups, or individuals, with the three elements of Carl Rogers' person centered approach (1980) as the basis for our initial contact with one another. Working in the field of addictions makes the first element of this approach, "genuineness and realness" (p. 115), quite simple. Recovering addicts are very real, and often their own anxiety of being sober and experiencing emotions and thoughts in a sober state makes them highly demanding as clients. They have, for example, seen it all and done it all and are very anxious and impatient. They prefer honest and direct interaction with others and if they sense that you are not being real and authentic, they will immediately challenge you on this point. It is for me, as the therapist, a comfortable place to be and establishes the nature of each unique client-therapist relationship. Secondly, "unconditional positive regard" (p. 116) is often a matter of trust, and trust that is accrued over several weeks. I tell the client that the only thing they *have* to be to come to drama therapy is on time. In relation to their feelings, I tell them up front that anger, confusion, fear, and uncertainty are warmly welcomed in the drama therapy room. This gives some relief, but as recovery addicts are often weary of their own feelings, which are frequently *new*, they are seldom enthusiastic and worry that others will see them as weak and vulnerable. It is also vital that I prepare myself for what I may hear or witness, and that I give permission to myself to experience my own internal reactions. Often clients will test if their true emotions will indeed be accepted by dramatically expressing frustration or impatience, only to say later that it was a joke. When they are applauded for taking the first step towards emotional expression they gain a sense of relief and safety, and we are able to move forward. Finally, "empathic understanding" (p. 116) is often what a client desperately seeks; yet once they have it, they experience difficulty in accepting it. For example, that you are so attuned to what they say and how they feel gives them a sense that they are respected and treated other than an addict or junkie; however, such honest interaction is a new experience for many and needs a period of adjustment. Once the client can accept this, it becomes a powerful instrument for change.

Five Phase Model – Emunah's five phase model (1994) is an integrative framework for drama therapy, and greatly influences how I structure my drama therapy sessions with a client population of recovering addicts. It includes: (I) Dramatic Play; (II) Scenework; (III) Role Play; (IV) Culminating Enactment; (V) Dramatic Ritual (p. 34). The advantage of such an approach is that it simultaneously provides both structure and flexibility, and clients can quickly adjust to the session formation, enjoying the safety of knowing what happens next.

Flow – Mihaly Csikszentmihalyi (1990) writes, "Flow is the way people describe their state of mind when consciousness is harmoniously ordered, and they want to pursue whatever they are doing for its own sake" (p. 6). For the average individual, flow can be simply equivalent to that of a state of happiness, but for my clients it gives them a sense of hope, hope for a better future, and the possibility of healing. Maintaining a therapeutic space where clients have the possibility of achieving flow serves as a potent tool in building self confidence and trust and acceptance of oneself and others. When clients are engaged in a process such as a drama therapy session, and they feel emotionally safe and enjoy the process, they can easily stay focused and present in the moment. As a result, they learn to trust the process and themselves, and eventually can endure longer periods in such a contented state with greater emotional control. This in turn generates movement towards healing and understanding, and the awareness of endless possibilities.

Potential Space – Winnicott (1971) "The potential space between baby and mother, between child and family, between individual and society or the world, depends on experience which leads to trust. It can be looked upon as sacred to the individual, in that it is here that the individual experiences creative living" (p. 103).

Monopolist – The role of the monopolist is a common and highly active role in a group of recovering addicts. A great deal of tension resulting from honest interaction between members can create unbearable anxiety for the monopolist. It is crucial to be aware of the monopolist(s), since they can very quickly take on the "leading role" and your session may run the risk of being a one person show. Yalom (1985) describes the monopolist as, ". . . a person who seems compelled to chatter on incessantly. These patients are anxious if they are silent; if others get the floor, the monopolists reinsert themselves with a variety of techniques. . ." (p. 375).

APPENDIX II – SESSION PLANS

Since new admissions and duration of stay fluctuate frequently, sessions are planned in three week blocks to ensure needs and goals of the group members are adequately and appropriately accommodated. In this way, session goals and activities can be rapidly adjusted for new members should there be changes in group needs. The length of admissions at this stage of treatment can sometimes be quite brief, lasting for as little as three to four weeks. As a result, the intention of the drama therapy sessions is not *intensive*, long-term therapy. Given that these clients *are* heavily traumatized, it is not uncommon for the past to unexpectedly creep into the drama therapy session. In such circumstances, we, as a group, welcome and respect the client and her emotions, emphasize the present moment, and bring the group to emotional safety with appropriate containment.

In this program, drama therapy provides first an opportunity to practice staying in the present moment, and in addition addresses the following: an assessment of one's self image and manageable goals for desired behavioural changes, building and encouraging play and spontaneity, a brief examination of the current role repertoire, a toleration and acceptance of the "sober self," and a discovery and appreciation for one's unique creative process and self expression. Below are session plans for a three week block with a theme of "Me Now!" designed for clients who have already experienced drama therapy during their treatment.

Theme (Three Week Block). "Me, Now!"- While staying focused in the here and now clients will briefly examine who they are as unique individuals aside from their past history. There is an emphasis on accepting all sides of the self while learning to appreciate and celebrate who they are today and slowly and safely emerge from the often comforting role of victim.

Methods Used: Drama, music, art and creative writing

Week One

Goal: exploration of a personal qualities/talents
Check-in: (Varies greatly, depending on general group mood at the start of the session)
   Object Identification: I simply fill the floor with an assortment of items including hats, scarves, puppets, small musical instruments, various clay shapes and forms, trinket boxes, and cushions. I ask clients to choose an item with which they most identify at this time. They have the option of explaining their choice, but it is not mandatory. Many are unable to explain this clearly, and can only say that it is a feeling. At the end of the session, many come back to this activity and then wish to elaborate on the reason for their choice.
Warm-up:
   What can you expect?: Consider educational backgrounds here, as some clients have limited reading and writing skills, and exposure can cause shame and embarrassment. If an activity involves reading or writing, I always give the added option of using drawn or painted images as a means of communication. This activity encourages the group members to imagine that they have the opportunity to be in the shoes of another person for one day, and that someone else will come into their shoes. They are to write a letter to the unknown visitor as to what can be expected in their shoes.

Clients are asked to think about such factors as what is so great about being you? What can the visitor look forward to? The focus is on positive aspects of the self, special talents and skills, and strengths. This provides a non-threatening and creative way for each member to share with the group their positive qualities, which can otherwise be an uncomfortable process and one to which many are unaccustomed. Members leave their letters scattered throughout the room so that everyone has the chance to read them. This activity is discussed during the reflection and feedback portion of the session.

Main Activity:

Making it Real: Clients can use the space as they wish, many choose to set up their own personal play-space, to *show* the rest of the group what their unique talent, skill or quality is. The possibilities are endless and give clients a great deal of creative expression and freedom while providing substantial structure for safety. Clients have made therapists' offices (to show their listening and caring skills), art galleries (to display their much guarded artistic abilities) and settings in nature (to celebrate their concern for the environment).

Reflection and Feedback:

Discussion of "What can you expect?"

Closing:

Take it or leave it: Clients have the option of "taking" something positive away from the session. This can include something they saw in another group member that they admire or a behaviour or quality that they themselves expressed and are proud of. Often members take "a piece of the atmosphere" generated by the whole group and in so doing see the uniqueness of everyone involved. If there is no desire to "take something" there is always the possibility of "leaving" something behind. This can be an attribute that someone can "afford" to share with or give to another.

Week Two

Goal: acknowledgement and implementation of skill

Check-in: (Varies greatly depending on general group mood at the start of the session)

What's the weather? Clients have the option of physically showing the group what for weather they are or simply naming it. For instance, you may get "Snowstorm" or an active pounding rendition of thunder. If the group energy is low, descriptions are one word responses are common, if there is a energetic buzz in the air rain dances and blowing gales may sweep in. Often clients see how they truly feel at that moment in the demonstrations and weather reports of other group members.

Warm-up:
   Follow the movement: Every group member takes a turn leading the group with her own choice of movement with the rest of the group following.
Main Activity:
   Knock-knock: This activity involves a great deal of imagination and the ability to sustain a playful participation in a state of "What if"; therefore, use caution and ensure that clients safely de-role and are appropriately grounded in the here and now. I have a huge door drawn on newsprint, magically decorated and taped to the wall. Now that clients have discovered a new aspect of " Me now!" from session one, they have the option of going through the door and exploring new possibilities on the other side. I ask another member to be the door keeper and she "opens" the door for the client who wishes to embark on such a journey. This is exciting for the entire group, as a great deal of spontaneous improvisation usually takes place. I always accompany the client on the journey and encourage the exploration of new possibilities through a series of questions. It is important that you constantly monitor the journeying client, as well as the rest of your group. In addition, do not "lead" your client into territory that is *too* unrealistic where achieving such a goal in her current situation is too unimaginable. This can lead to a sense of hopelessness and despair and defeat the purpose of the activity. Clients may take turns, and are usually enthusiastically ready to do so.
Reflection and Feedback:
   Exchange experiences and observations from Knock-Knock. Ensure that both "travellers" and observers have the opportunity to share.
Closing:
   Take it or leave it: (Same as Week One)

Week Three

Goal: acceptance and celebration of "Me, Now!"
Check-in: (Varies greatly depending on general group mood at the start of the session)
   Nonverbal emotional expression: Using only facial expressions and movement, moods and feelings are shared with the rest of the group. The nonverbal communication is rarely difficult to understand; however, it is always good to "double check" through a short discussion to ensure that everyone was clearly understood.
Warm-up:
   Group Movement: In a circle, the entire group moves and dances to music chosen by the group. (A popular warm-up with this group, usually becoming quite theatrical with hats and scarves.)

Main Activity:
    Wall of Fame: Each group member makes her own "wall of fame," which is essentially a celebration of the individual. Each client receives her own area of the wall to be covered with newsprint, which the client then decorates to include aspects of the present self (previously discussed and explored in weeks one and two) that the client wishes to share, celebrate, and further develop. There is also the option of role playing a situation (past or future) where the specific quality or skill was or would be used.

Reflection and Feedback:
    Clients are encouraged to view each others' work and give feedback to one another. (I am always amazed at the surprising depth with which clients express appreciation for one another's creative process.)

Closing:
    What will you take with you and what will you do with it?: Clients share with the group what they will "take" from the experience of the last three weeks. Most common are new insight, hope, and self love and appreciation. They then give an example of how, such as in a concrete situation, they will use this. A frequent favourite is, "The next time I screw up I won't be so hard on myself, everybody makes mistakes."

REFERENCES

American Psychiatric Association. (1994). *Diagnostic and Statistic manual of Mental Disorders* (fourth edition). Washington, DC: American Psychiatric Association.

Csikszentmihalyi, M. (1990). *Flow: The psychology of optimal experience.* New York: Harper & Row Inc.

Emunah, R. (1994). *Acting for real-drama therapy process, technique and performance.* New York: Brunner/Mazel Publishers.

Flores, P. J. (1997). *Group psychotherapy with addicted populations: An integration of twelve-step and psychodynamic theory.* New York: The Haworth Press, Inc.

Jennings, S. (1990) *Dramatherapy with families, groups and individuals. Waiting in the wings.* London: Routledge.

Rogers, C. R., (1980). *A way of being.* New York: Houghton Mifflin Company.

Rogers, N. (1993). *The creative connection: Expressive arts as healing.* California: Science & Behavior Books, Inc.

Rothschild, B. (2000). *The body remembers: The psychophysiology of trauma and trauma treatment.* New York: W.W. Norton & Company, Inc.

Winnicott, D.W. (1971). *Playing and reality.* New York: Tavistock Publications Ltd.

Yalom, I. D. (1985). *The theory and practice of group psychotherapy.* New York: Basic Books.

BIOGRAPHICAL STATEMENT

Linda M. Dunne, M.A., is a drama therapist originally from Canada, who now makes her home in The Netherlands. She is a member of the National Association for Drama Therapy, the Nederlandse Vereniging voor Creatieve Therapie (NVCT) and the Stichting Register Creatief Therapeuten (SRCT). She holds a Bachelor of Arts degree from Memorial University of Newfoundland and a Master of Arts from Kansas State University. She has developed and runs a Drama Therapy Program for groups and individuals recovering from substance abuse. In addition, she offers individual therapy to children with autism and maintains a small private practice working with a multi-cultural group of expatriates living in The Netherlands.

Chapter 20

BUILDING A CONTAINER WITH THE CREATIVE ARTS: THE THERAPEUTIC SPIRAL MODEL™ TO HEAL POST-TRAUMATIC STRESS IN THE GLOBAL COMMUNITY

KATE HUDGINS

INTRODUCTION

For many years, creative arts and drama therapists, psychodramatists, Gestalt therapists, and other practitioners of experiential therapies alike have known that action methods provide hope for people who experienced trauma in their lives (Johnson, 2000). In many cases, we have seen people's lives literally saved, as they have found a way to safely "tell their story" of rape, homelessness, addiction, eating disorders, earthquakes, and fires through art, movement, dance, drama, music, literature, poetry or psychodrama when words were not enough. Today, neuroscience and psychotherapy research come together to demonstrate that experiential methods of change are the treatment of choice for people with Post-Traumatic Stress Disorder (PTSD) (van der Kolk et al., 1996). This new partnership calls for a paradigm shift from talk therapy alone to experiential methods that include the nonverbal, emotional symptoms that are the hallmark of PTSD. Creative arts therapists can lead the way in the treatment of trauma.

As originally conceived by J. L. and Zerka Moreno (1969), classical psychodrama was a model of healing for people who suffered traumatic experiences, such as refugee resettlement. It is the seminal method of experiential therapy, most often a group therapy method. Research on Gestalt therapy traces the effectiveness of experiential interventions in psychotherapy research. The psychologist's bible, *The Handbook of Psychotherapy and Behavior Change* (Bergin and Garfield, 1994; Lambert, Bergin and Garfield, 2003), demonstrates that experiential therapy interventions are equally effective as psychodynamic and cognitive behavioral therapy for general psychiatric populations. Research suggests experiential methods are more effective than talk therapy with people with PTSD (Elliott, Greenberg and Lietaer, 2002). Action methods do work.

While individual action interventions have been tested, there has not been a clinical system of experiential therapy to treat PTSD that can be replicated for research and training until now (Johnson, 2000). The Therapeutic Spiral Model™ is such a clinical system (Hudgins, 2002). The Therapeutic Spiral Model, or TSM as it is colloquially called, is a step-by-step, clinical system of experiential therapy that modifies classical psychodrama interventions for containment and safety when working with survivors of traumatic experiences (Hudgins, in press a, b, 2002, 2000, 1998, 1989; Hudgins and Kellermann, 2000). The creative arts have always been a core thread of this experiential method to treat PTSD.

TSM has been used with survivors of human-made violence and natural catastrophe for more than twenty years. TSM was originally designed for people with Dissociative Identity Disorder with the goal of making psychodrama clinically safe for even the most severely traumatized people. Subsequently, TSM has been used to treat survivors of war, acts of terror, political and religious persecution, cult and clergy abuse, torture, kidnapping, forced resettlement, poverty, racism, sexual and physical abuse, domestic violence, addiction, eating disorders, earthquakes, floods, fires, illness, and accidents. It has been used with families (Chimera, 2002), adolescents (Cossa, 2002), and children. As you will see, TSM is also finding success in the research and validation of its treatment effectiveness with PTSD.

This chapter briefly presents an overview of the Therapeutic Spiral Model with a clinical example of how the creative arts are an integral part of building spontaneity and providing containment for clients who have a history of trauma. Client examples are used to make the theory come alive. Applications to the community are also briefly discussed.

OVERVIEW OF THE THERAPEUTIC SPIRAL MODEL™

The Therapeutic Spiral Model™ has been taught to hundreds of clinicians over the past fifteen years in over a dozen countries. It has brought deep healing to thousands of survivors of violence, natural catastrophes, and traumatic losses through our *Surviving Spirits*™ and other TSM workshops. We have worked to repair the effects of traumatic stress on individuals, families, groups, organizations, and communities for more than twenty years (Hudgins, 2002).

Like many of our Action Trauma Team members, I carry images of dancing and singing with native women, sharing the hope of stopping violence in their communities in South Africa. Of quietly crying in a circle of Chinese men and women in Taiwan as we each role reversed and heard a new family legacy spoken by our ancestors, healed of intergenerational patterns of violence. The joy of seeing men and women who had long been enemies, Protestants and Catholics alike, come together in Northern Ireland as they created a Group Metaphor of shared strengths, experiences, and hope for their future. The privilege of witnessing many a young woman reclaim her innocence and beauty following decades of physical and sexual abuse. That is the spirit of the Therapeutic Spiral Model.

As a clinical system of experiential psychotherapy, the Therapeutic Spiral Model provides an integrated theoretical base, clinical principles of change, and fourteen experiential intervention modules (Hudgins, 2002, in press b). TSM has a clinical map to guide the development of Prescriptive, Trauma-based, and Transformative roles for full developmental repair. TSM seeks to be a safe and effective treatment for PTSD by balancing left and right brain action interventions. The creative arts are an important part of the psychological, and at times, physical container that TSM builds to hold the cognitive, nonverbal, emotional and defensive symptoms of PTSD in conscious awareness for change. All TSM experiential interventions are designed to increase the spontaneity and creativity needed for survivors to reclaim their lives following traumatic stress.

TSM THEORETICAL ORIENTATIONS

During the last decade, we have seen graphic evidence of how the brain changes as a result of overwhelming stress. The scientific facts strongly suggest a paradigm shift is needed in the psychological treatment of PTSD from cognitive talk therapy to experiential methods that involve body, mind, emotion, and spirit (van der Kolk, 2003; van der Kolk et al., 1996). Here is a brief overview of the theoretical foundations of TSM that create a safe and creative method of healing the effects of trauma in the global community.

The Neurobiology of Trauma: Body – Bessel van der Kolk is a Harvard neuroscientist who proclaims that *only* experiential methods can access the traumatic images stored in the limbic system where they are inaccessible to words (van der Kolk et al., 1996). Hug (in press a, b) details how the brain's response to traumatic stress creates splits between the cognitive centers of the left brain and the emotional centers of the right brain, making experiential methods a logical choice. Johnson (1987) discusses the use of creative arts to access traumatic images in safe and effective ways, as he calls for a system of experiential therapy to treat trauma. The Therapeutic Spiral Model presents a systematic, clinical map that promotes a balance between right-brain and left-brain action interventions to safely provide full developmental repair for survivors of trauma. TSM utilizes experiential interventions for containment to prevent the brain from being overwhelmed once again by intense affects and dissociated trauma material.

The Containing Double is one of the fourteen core intervention modules developed to safely treat people with PTSD using experiential methods of change using the Therapeutic Spiral Model. The Containing Double (CD) is a role of internal self-support that balances thinking and feeling, as you will see in the clinical example. Research using a single-case design showed decreases in body memories, dissociation and general trauma symptoms over three individual therapy sessions using the CD (Hudgins and Drucker, 1998; Hudgins, Drucker and Metcalf, 2000).

Attachment Theory: Body/Mind/Heart/Spirit – Attachment is a physical, mental, emotional, and spiritual process. Research into family therapy and social systems shows the neurophysiological attachment bond to self and others is damaged when someone experiences traumatic stress, especially when it is human-caused violence (Schore, 2003; Siegel, 1999). As a clinical modification of psychodrama for people with PTSD, The Therapeutic Spiral Model builds intrapsychic strengths in order to create interpersonal connections. TSM is both experiential and group-centered, meaning that opportunities to experience new and healthy attachments is a natural part of any session.

The creative arts, especially body-based movement and dance, have brought many moments of healing to people participating in TSM workshops. Witnessing people share a timeline of life before and after trauma – expressed in movement without words – is a powerful and connecting experience for all. Dressing up as the Wizard of the Magic Shop, and bargaining with folks about what they need to change increases spontaneity and creativity with others in a fun, playful way.

Cognitive Behavioral Therapy: Mind – The theories of mind in CBT explain the role of cognitive schemas, negative introjects, and maladaptive coping strategies that are internalized by traumatic experiences. Many CBT and classical psychodrama interventions are remarkably similar. TSM places an equal emphasis on cognitive and expressive interventions, aiming at all times to maintain a state of conscious awareness where new roles can be created for psychological change. TSM defines the state of spontaneity as a balance between thinking and feeling, and has a set of Prescriptive Roles to achieve that. In this way, TSM reduces the risk of experiential methods once again overwhelming the brain with intense affect and creating re-traumatization.

The first experiential intervention module of any TSM session is always to concretize a role of the Observing Ego or Witness to the Work. This role, called the "OE," can be developed in many ways. The easiest and most adaptable action structure we have found in TSM is to bring decks of inspirational cards as a standard creative prop – cards with words and images. Left-brain and right-brain input. Put the cards out on the floor around a pile of brightly colored scarves. As people come in, they pick one or more cards with symbols or words that remind them of the qualities they need to be able to observe and witness themselves with compassion. People share in dyads or small groups, interacting with more than one partner. Then the cards are taped somewhere in the room and a cognitive container is immediately established for all participants. People can then role reverse with characters, symbols, words, and other representations of this cognitive role, if needed to increase spontaneity and creativity.

Object Relations Theory: Mind/Heart – The psychodynamic view of self-development has long shown the importance of early childhood experiences on stable self-organization and development (Stern, 1985, 1990). Object relations theory describes the normal intrapsychic internalization of representative templates of "self and object/other" in psychodrama and other action methods (Holmes, 1992). During traumatic experiences, people internalize the TSM trauma-based roles of victim, perpetrator, and abandoning authority (Hudgins, 2002). To counteract those internalized roles, TSM concretizes Prescriptive Roles of observation, restoration, and containment for healthy personality development. The Observing Ego and Containing Double roles already mentioned are examples of the TSM Prescriptive roles. More roles will be listed in the clinical example to come.

Spontaneity and Creativity Theory: Spirit – Drawing on the essence of classical psychodrama, TSM views psychological health as the development of spontaneity and creativity (Moreno, 1953; Moreno, Blomkvist, and Rutzel, 2000; Moreno, in press). For people who have experienced the true helplessness of traumatic experiences, this view of Self as spontaneous and creative is a pure antidote to years of despair and hopelessness. TSM defines spontaneity as the active experiencing of the Prescriptive Roles to maintain stable self-organization in the here and now. Then when the self is spontaneous, new creation can happen and life can change.

Scene 1 in all TSM Dramas is always to pick people to play roles that increase spontaneity and creativity prior to increasing experiencing of trauma-based roles. Each person's story has different characters, different roles. Everyone starts with the Observing Ego role. Often the next TSM role prescribed is the Body Double (Burden and Ciotola, 2003; Ciotola, 2004). The clinical goal of the Body Double (BD) is to provide nonverbal and verbal soothing of trauma memories as they are held safely in here and now awareness.

It helps people stay in their body in a good way. I have seen people dress their BD up as a Tai Chi Master, a yoga teacher, or a well-trained marathon runner, combining movement and drama to increase spontaneity and creativity. Often, the Body Double relies on meditational breathing, a steady physical presence, and possibly humming a favored song quietly at times during the drama.

Role Theory: Integrating Body, Mind, Emotion and Spirit — Role theory, another core component of classical psychodrama (Blatner, 1991), helps normalize the clinical symptoms many people experience as a result of the right-brained, nonverbal, emotional, limbic system symptoms of PTSD: body memories, flashbacks, ego state shifts, intense emotions, and dissociation. Instead of psychiatric labels, TSM uses the Trauma Survivor's Intrapsychic Role Atom, or the TSIRA (Hudgins, 2002) to assess personality functioning and pinpoint where there are decreases in spontaneity. The TSIRA is a clinical map of Prescriptive, Trauma-Based, and Transformative Roles that guide clinical action interventions at all times in TSM. The TSIRA details the minimum number of internal roles needed for stable personality functioning following traumatic stress (Hudgins, Cho, Chen, Lai, and Ou, 2005). A role atom is developed in the clinical example below.

TSM AND THE CREATIVE ARTS

As Blatner (1991) states, the creative arts have a long history of promoting change through theatre, dance, literature, music, art, and other creative ways of dealing with trauma. TSM personal growth workshops have always included an art project as a container for unconscious trauma memories and a guide for meaning-making. In this way, many of the most disruptive symptoms of PTSD following traumatic stress – body memories, flashbacks, ego state changes, mood changes, and defenses such as dissociation – are given a place for containment and an avenue for expression. TSM workshops have included art, dance, movement, and music as a focal point for healing throughout the past twenty years. We have used poetry and writing to reach out to the larger global community. You see how role playing is a core TSM intervention in all its dramatic forms. This chapter gives a brief clinical example of how integral the creative arts are to the theoretical and experiential foundation of the Therapeutic Spiral Model.

RESEARCH ON TSM

Therapists and clients alike report 92% satisfaction following TSM three-day experiential workshops over the past decade (Hudgins, in press, a). The

Containing Double, a core TSM intervention module was shown to effectively decrease dissociation and body memories over three individual therapy sessions (Hudgins and Drucker, 1998; Hudgins, Drucker and Metcalf, 2000). A recent one-year clinical research pilot study showed improvement in dissociation, anxiety, depression, and PTSD symptoms from the three-day intensive intervention with clients in Taiwan and Mainland China (Hudgins, Cho, Chen, Lai, and Ou, 2005). Additional evaluation studies show treatment effectiveness with dual diagnosis patients with addictions and PTSD (Forst, 2001). Significant moments of emotional healing in mother-daughter bonding are reported in a change process study of a TSM drama completed in Australia (McVea, in press). A study funded by the University of Virginia showed reduction in PTSD symptoms for community leaders following the terrorist attacks on the Pentagon in 2001 (Hudgins, in press a). A clinical comparison of TSM treatment effectiveness across cultures and language is currently being completed on groups in the following six countries: Canada, China, England, South Africa, Taiwan and the U.S.A.

A CLINICAL EXAMPLE OF CREATIVE ART PROJECTS IN TSM

Over the past twenty years of clinical practice of TSM, we have used a wide variety of art projects – collages, sandtrays, clay models, handprints, soulmaps, medicine wheels, songwriting, movement, and other creative arts as part of our experiential process of change. While different mediums are used, the creative art projects always follow a TSM clinical action structure to provide containment and expression of nonverbal emotional trauma material, so that it can be brought to words by the end of the three-day workshop. The art projects always follow the three strands of the therapeutic spiral: Energy, Experiencing, and Meaning-Making (Hudgins, 2002). This TSM clinical action structure allows clients to integrate the right-brain experience of traumatic stress into their left-brain structures for here and now cognitive processing. Here is a clinical example during a TSM workshop:

On the first night of any TSM personal growth workshop, participants show their strengths through the creative project chosen to build safety and increase energy prior to working directly on trauma material. On day two, when we are consciously increasing the active experience of trauma memories, clients are asked to express their trauma and the defenses they have formed against through the creative medium. On the final day of the workshop, everyone finds words to connect the combined expression of strengths and trauma material as it results in new narrative labeling of their past experiences.

MAKING A MEDICINE SHIELD: WEAVING TOGETHER BODY, MIND, HEART, AND SPIRIT IN TSM

In my many years as a therapist, supervisor, and trainer using experiential methods with men and women who were sexually abused as children, I have seen a number of clients who were diagnosed with Dissociative Identity Disorder when the abuse was particularly extreme. In fact, the Therapeutic Spiral Model was originally designed to modify classical psychodrama to be safe for this often fragile and easily triggered population of clients. Today, many of these same clients would be diagnosed with Complex PTSD instead to avoid the stigmatizing effects of a DID diagnosis. But the clinical question remains, how to work safely with severely traumatized clients when we use experiential methods? Building a container with the creative arts is one of the answers in TSM.

One of my most heart-warming moments was when a woman who had been diagnosed with DID used the creativity of the TSM art project to express the fragmentation and integration of twelve parts of self. "Jennifer" – a composite client – expresses both the fragility and the resiliency of many people who are survivors of childhood and adult traumas. The art project was to make a "TSM Medicine Shield" during a *Surviving Spirits: Healing Sexual Abuse* three-day workshop.

As clients entered the room on Friday night, our safety and energy building session, they found several large tables covered with a wide and colorful array of materials of various textures, shapes, and uses. There were ribbons, stickers, feathers, bells, seashells, sea glass, magazines, and materials such as felt, velvet, silk, and others. People came in and spontaneously touched the beauty of the many art materials the team had collected over years. At the end of the evening of actively experiencing the Six Safety Structures of TSM (Cox, 2000), group members were asked to spend the last half hour of the workshop putting their strengths on wreaths made out of grapevines. From simple circles of nature, wonders emerged. One woman covered her wreath in purple feathers. Another wove golden thread through the strands of vine. A third hung tiny seashells and miniature bells from the bottom of the wreath. The team joined together to create our own medicine shield, each of us adding an expression of our strengths to a single wreath.

The evening ended with people sharing their strengths in dyads, putting words to their magnificent expressions. We joined together to sing a song I had learned from my Mohawk teacher. A simple song that expresses the idea of the spiral in a musical and creative way. The words are:

> Spiraling into the center, the center of the shield.
> Spiraling into the center, the center of the shield.

> I am the weaver.
> I am the woven one.
>
> I am the dreamer.
> I am the dream.

We repeated the song several times, different members singing different parts until the room was filled with aliveness and vitality. Thanks to the creative arts, the first night of the workshop ended with everyone connecting to their strengths to face their traumas with new spontaneity and creativity the next day.

After an initial check in and experiential warm up on Day Two, the clients were asked to return to their TSM medicine shields, this time to add their experience of sexual abuse to the contained circle of grapevines. The energy in the room immediately changed as people became more silent, more caught in their internal process, emotions, and defenses. The team encouraged each person to move to the art materials and let their traumas speak to them and be expressed in the safety of the creative project.

Jennifer added a background of black felt to cover the open space of the circle. Scissors slashed into the material creating gaps and tears. Red paint made tears of pain. Another woman cried quietly, a team member sitting next to her, as she added acorns brought in from trees outside the venue. Two other women sat side by side, looking at each other's shields, seeing similarities as they added crossed and knotted strands of black ribbon from one side of the shield to the other. Others added heavy rocks dragging down the bottom of the shield. All the while, the team moved from one client to another, providing containment with a few words or the use of the Body or Containing Doubles to keep people in their bodies, and balance thinking and feeling.

Seeing a client caught in her emotions, overwhelmed by trauma memories, a trained auxiliary took the role of the Containing Double (CD). She sat next to the woman crying, starting to regress into trauma memories as she added acorns to her medicine shield. The CD said:

CD: I am shedding tears to honor the pain of sexual abuse. A pain that has been locked inside me for many years, like these acorns.
Client: Yes, I have felt like these acorns. Memories, feelings, urges to destroy myself . . . locked inside me, making me unable to grow into a tree. Dead . . . dead inside.
CD: And now, today I have a chance to open myself in the safety of this TSM workshop. I can let the memories, the feelings, the deadness out of that locked place inside me . . . out by choice. They can come out slowly and safely. I can see that today I have a chance to grow and to become a sapling . . . a chance to grow into a big sturdy oak . . . a tree that has withstood many storms.

Client (looking surprised): Yes . . . yes, maybe I can do that. Maybe I can let out some of the pain inside of me. Maybe, just maybe, there is a chance for me to become a tree . . . a tree that has stayed rooted against the lightning, the thunder . . . all that could destroy, but maybe it hasn't.

After a half hour, the clients were asked to join the big group and we used the shields as a warm up for the protagonist selection in a TSM drama to heal memories of sexual abuse. Once again, the art project served as a bridge between nonverbal, emotional images and feelings and the words needed to express them safely in the here and now.

It is the final day that truly touches my heart. After three TSM dramas, we moved to the final session of the *Surviving Spirits* workshop, the day to make new meanings to guide the future. The team asked clients to return to their medicine shields to put transformation on them. People struggle to concretize their changes.

Jennifer has struggled to stay present and not split off or regress into child parts without conscious choice all weekend. She works quietly on her shield. She has twelve photos of herself in childhood. She ties each one onto the black background in the center of her shield. Each picture of herself is decorated with a ribbon, a bow, or a small shell. When asked about her shield by a team member, she says: "Now, I can accept all these child parts of myself. I know they are real. They happened from the ongoing and sadistic sexual abuse in my family. Today, I have hope they can join together, and I can become whole." There is a moment of silence as everyone hears her truth and takes a deep breath.

The final TSM session is always group work, the group working together on a single theme rather than doing an individual psychodrama. That day, I directed a TSM action structure "Creating a New Family Legacy." Each person was told that today they could create a new family legacy. They brought their Observing Ego cards off the walls and sat with them inside the larger TSM Circle of Safety. They were asked to close their eyes and get in touch with an ancestor who could give them a new message. As they were ready, each person role reversed with this ancestor to give the new family legacy to be carried forward into the future.

Jennifer steps up last, holding her medicine shield. She is quaking with emotion. She says she is her great grandmother, a woman she has never met, but someone she was told about as a child – a woman of spirit. In role reversal, she cries as she says:

> I know I did not stop the legacy of sexual abuse in our family. I looked the other way when my husband abused our daughter, your grandmother. I am so sorry I closed my eyes. I now see the cost, the burden you have carried. I am glad to be here today to change the future of our family. Let each part of you hear what

I have to say today. You can heal. You don't have to keep living in the horror of the past. Accept the help around you. Tell the family secrets. Set yourself free.

Another client, Helen, in the final stages of recovery and integration from DID, spontaneously steps into the great grandmother role and repeats the message to Jennifer as she hears it from her adult self, holding the medicine shield showing all of her parts. They stand, holding each other, crying deeply, a cry of release and hope. The group looks around and all are a part of this moment of healing. It is a sacred circle. Each person holds the creativity of their medicine shield close to his or her hearts.

FUTURE PROJECTIONS:
CREATIVITY IN THE COMMUNITY

It has been a joy to write this chapter on the use of the creative arts in the Therapeutic Spiral Model. As you can see, the creative arts are an integral part of TSM as a clinical system of experiential therapy to treat PTSD. From the theoretical foundations of clinical theory to the aliveness of the creative arts, TSM embraces the wounds of traumatic stress and offers healing through spontaneity and creativity. Consistent with research on other experiential interventions with PTSD, research on the treatment effectiveness of TSM clinical action structures shows promise. Adding creativity also adds hope.

Writing this article, I see more clearly the many paths the creative arts bring to TSM for the psychological, and often physical, containment of trauma memories. I have long known the arts as an avenue of expression for the nonverbal, emotional, limbic system symptoms of PTSD. I have a lot to learn about integrating the creative arts even more into the Therapeutic Spiral Model to treat PTSD. I believe the creative arts will be the springboard of spontaneity for TSM as it moves from a clinical system of experiential therapy to treat PTSD with psychiatric diagnoses to an experiential method of change in the global community.

The Therapeutic Spiral Model is proving itself as a solid clinical model of experiential psychotherapy to treat PTSD with research evaluation and validation beginning to come in. There are many people both trained and training in TSM to build Action Trauma Teams in local communities of mental health professionals. Now, as the left-brain work is done, I can turn once again to the creative right-brain. I hear the call of inspirational speaking and community applications of TSM.

Writing this chapter has brought back the whispers of my muses – the lingering body memory of twenty-five years as a ballet dancer, the ever-changing moods of music, the aliveness of creating a representation of life from random art materials. I am reminded why I fell in love with psychodrama almost thirty years ago. The true healing agent in psychodrama is to increase spontaneity and creativity. It is the perfect antidote for people who have experienced the helplessness, hopelessness, and despair of traumatic stress. I have thoroughly enjoyed this dance as it has grown into more of a creative arts focus than I usually take. I am left with images of people, people of all kinds, coming together for healing. They are surrounded by the energy of spontaneity and creativity. Anything is possible.

APPENDIX – TERMS

Therapeutic Spiral Model™ Terms

Post-Traumatic Stress Disorder (PTSD) – The definition of Post-traumatic Stress Disorder from the DSM-IV-R (APA, 2001) is used to describe the impact of overwhelming stress on psychological functioning from a wide variety of natural catastrophes and human-made violence.

TSM The acronym that is used to refer to the Therapeutic Spiral Model as a clinical system of modified psychodrama to treat PTSD. This is a trademarked model of experiential change for trauma survivors with clearly defined post-graduate accreditation levels of training. TSM has three stages of treatment, six clinical principles of change, six safety structures, and fourteen experiential intervention modules.

TSI – The acronym that is used to refer to Therapeutic Spiral International, LLC, a business organizing events using the Therapeutic Spiral Model. This is the Training Institute that provides post-graduation accreditation in the Therapeutic Spiral Model to treat Post-Traumatic Stress Disorder (PTSD) in the global community. TSI provides training, education, motivational seminars, and direct services for people who have experienced overwhelming stress and/or violence in their families and communities.

Therapeutic spiral image – A graphic image that visually presents the three strands of the Therapeutic Spiral Model: Energy, Experiencing, and Meaning. It shows all three strands working together in a therapeutic direction where awareness can flow up or down the spiral consciously as needed to balance thinking and feeling in the here and now.

Trauma spiral – A second graphic image that visually presents the impact of trauma on the three strands of TSM. It shows the explosions of energy, constriction of experience, and blocked cognitive processing demonstrating the chaotic, nonverbal and intense feelings many people with PTSD report. A shorthand many survivors find useful when they become bombarded by PTSD symptoms – "help, I'm going down the trauma spiral."

- *Energy* – The first strand of the spiral is named Energy. Following the theory of classical psychodrama, TSM defines Energy as a spontaneous state of learning that leads to creative actions. Spontaneity is further defined into seven clinically defined Prescriptive roles that provide the psychological functions of observation, restoration and containment for healthy self-organization. Spontaneity is the antidote for the helplessness and hopelessness of the experience of overwhelming stress, natural catastrophes, and violence for individual, families, groups, organizations and cultures.
- *Experiencing* – This is the second strand of the therapeutic spiral image. All TSM action interventions have the goal of increasing active experiencing as a principle of change. In this way, TSM interventions directly access the in-the-moment experience of the nonverbal, emotional, right-brained symptoms of PTSD that include body memories, flashbacks, dissociation, and intense affects from the past. TSM allows clients to consciously re-experience and integrate unprocessed trauma memories in safe and contained steps following a clinical map that uses role theory to guide client and therapist alike.
- *Meaning* – This is the third strand of TSM and represents the need to bring unprocessed trauma material into the cognitive processing centers of the left brain, so that new meanings can be made that integrate the fragmented information from the past. Meaning-making guides all experiential interventions in TSM. As a clinical model of change, TSM always seeks to maintain a balance between cognitive and expressive interventions so that all experiential work is contained in conscious awareness for safety.

TSIRA – TSIRA is the acronym that is used to refer to the *Trauma Survivor's Intrapsychic Role Atom.* This is a clinical assessment tool that is unique to the Therapeutic Spiral Model. It is the clinical map that guides all action interventions in TSM. The TSIRA uses role terms to identify ego states or parts of personality and self-organization in user-friendly terms that clients can easily understand. It provides a way to look at self-organization without pathologizing survival skills such as dissociation, splitting, and multiple states of consciousness.

Prescriptive roles – TSM has developed a set of eight clinical roles that are prescribed for healthy self-organization for people with PTSD. Together, these eight roles create a state of spontaneous learning by providing the psychological functions of observation, restoration, and containment as needed to maintain conscious awareness. The Prescriptive Roles include: the Observing Ego, the client role, personal, interpersonal, and transpersonal strengths, the Body Double, the Containing Double, and the manager of defenses.

- *OE* – Acronym that is used to refer to the TSM *Observing Ego intervention module*. This is a prescriptive role from the TSIRA that is used to concretize a role where clients can neutrally observe and cognitively label their behaviors. It also marks a physical space that notes cognitive processing. If anyone starts to become overwhelmed with affect, they can walk over to the OE spot to let someone know they are being triggered. The OE is always the first role to be concretized in a TSM session, regardless of setting.
- *BD* – Acronym that is used to refer to the TSM Body Double intervention module. This is a prescriptive role from the TSIRA that is used to decrease dissociation and help people experience their bodies in a healthy state. The Body Double is an experiential intervention where an inner, nonverbal voice is concretized by having an auxiliary sit next to a client and take on their posture and movements. The BD speaks in the first person and makes reflections to help anchor the client into a sense of healthy body awareness, such as "I can feel my feet on the floor."
- *CD* – Acronym that is used to refer to the TSM *Containing Double intervention module*. This is a prescriptive role from the TSIRA that is used to increase cognitive processing and narrative labeling, as unprocessed trauma material is held in conscious awareness for identification, exploration, expression, and release from the past. The CD speaks in the first person and makes statements that balance thinking and feeling so right-brained trauma memories can be held in conscious awareness for left-brain cognitive interventions.
- *MD* – Acronym that is used to refer to the manager of defenses intervention module. This is a prescriptive role from the TSIRA that is used to manage survival defenses, such as dissociation, denial, projective identification, etc. This technique increases the safe experiencing of trauma material without triggering clients into unconscious defenses or the acting out of trauma patterns.

Trauma-based Roles – After the prescriptive roles are concretized in TSM, it is safe to move onto the trauma-based roles, which are the internalization of overwhelming stress. They include: victim, perpetrator and abandoning authority.

- *Victim Role* – This role holds all the memories and pain of the traumatic experience. It is often held in a childlike ego state. In TSM, we re-label the victim role "the wounded child," so that clients can bond with this role for developmental repair.
- *Perpetrator Role* – This role is the internalization of violence, and can be acted out toward the self in self-blame, self-harm and suicide, or toward others with criticism, violence, and even murder.

- *Abandoning Authority* – This role is unique to the trauma triangle of TSM. It is about abandoning self in terms of self-care, recovery, or other roles needed to maintain healthy self-organization. It is the internalization of the abandonment and neglect that occurs during overwhelming stress when no amount of spontaneity or creativity can save the person from catastrophe or violence.

Transformative Roles – Transformative roles develop out of the interaction of the prescriptive and trauma-based roles. They are unique roles for each individual, but always include: a change agent, the sleeping/awakening child, good enough parents, and good enough spirituality.

Action Trauma Team – Therapeutic Spiral International builds teams in local communities to use the Therapeutic Spiral Model to treat trauma in settings from individual therapy to large groups of hundreds of people in the community. TSI teams are called Action Trauma Teams, because they use experiential methods to facilitate change for people with PTSD. While TSM can be, and often is, done without a team, having a team provides the most safety for the deepest level of developmental repair in self-organization.

- *Team Leader/TL* – The Team Leader role is Level Three Accreditation in the Therapeutic Spiral Model post-graduate training program. The TL role certifies a basic set of competencies that can be found in the Training section on our website. On a TSI team, the TL is the clinician who has overall responsibility for directing the TSM workshop. Most often, the TL directs the majority of TSM dramas and clinical action structures that are used for interventions and leads the team in doing so.
- *Assistant Leader/AL* – The Assistant Leader role is Level Two Accreditation in TSM. Professional standards can be found on our website. The AL is a team role that is unique to the Therapeutic Spiral Model. It was created to help manage the integration of group members into a TSM drama when they are triggered by experiential methods. The AL and TL work in shared leadership to manage a balance of cognitive and expressive interventions so that all group members are safely held and contained in conscious awareness as they work with right-brained PTSD symptoms.
- *Trained auxiliary ego/TAE* – The trained auxiliary ego is Level One Accreditation in TSM. This is the team role that provides support for the team, the director and TSM dramas. TAEs are trained to concretize the containing roles of BD, CD, and MD so they can facilitate healthy self-organization for the protagonist and group. TAEs also enact projective identifications and the trauma-based roles of victim, perpetrator, and abandoning authority so group members do not have to do this for safety

and containment. In TSM, TAEs most often play internalized parts of self, but can also play interpersonal roles as needed.

Six Safety Action Structures – This is a set of six clinical action structures that define the first session of any three-day intervention that uses the Therapeutic Spiral Model™ as originally designed and as used in research testing. They include: The Observing Ego, the Circle of Safety, Spectragrams, Action Sociograms, Circle Similarities and a Creative Arts Project.

- *Circle of Safety* – After the OE is concretized, the next clinical action structure to start a TSM workshop is the Circle of Safety. Clients pick one or more scarves to represent their personal, interpersonal, and transpersonal strengths. They share them with the group and create a physical circle that marks the experiencing space for dramas.
- *Spectragrams* – This action structure is a classical psychodrama assessment tool. Mark an imaginary line with two points on the floor and have people place themselves on the spectrogram to symbolize where they are on a certain criteria, i.e., anxiety vs. safety, self-care vs. self-harm, etc. Usually four to seven spectragrams are used in the first TSM session of a weekend workshop.
- *Action Sociograms* – This action tool is also a classical psychodrama intervention designed to show interpersonal connections among group members. In TSM, it is used to see who is connected to whom, as well as a projective tool to show transference and projections between group members.
- *Circle Similarities* – In classical psychodrama, action structure is called circle Sociometry and is used to show how people share similar experiences. In TSM, people are asked to step into the circle if they share a traumatic experience such as sexual abuse, addiction, domestic violence, etc. TSM mixes in positive shared experiences, so that people do not become triggered during this exercise, such as "Who has found some help along the way to recovery?"

TSM Drama – A TSM drama consists of a minimum of three scenes. The first concretizes prescriptive roles. The second moves to defenses or the trauma-based roles. Scene three is always developmental repair.

Surviving Spirits: Healing Sexual Abuse – This is the original three-day workshop using the Therapeutic Spiral Model. It follows a basic structure each time. Friday night the six safety action structures are used to build up safety and containment through boundaries, connections, narrative labeling and self-disclosure. Saturday, there are two TSM dramas. On Sunday, there is one more TSM drama and the final session is group work with the whole group. This is the structure that has been researched and shown to decrease dissociation, anxiety, and general trauma symptoms over three days.

Clinical and Psychological Terms

Trauma – TSM defines trauma as any stress that overwhelms the normal coping mechanisms and threatens psychological and/or physical survival. In this way, the cause of overwhelming stress is not as important as the effect on the individual, family, group, organization, or culture. Trauma can be caused by natural catastrophes and/or human-made violence.

Dissociative Identity Disorder – This is a DSM-IV-R diagnosis that is given when clients have ego states that are completely dissociated from each other. It is usually caused by severe and ongoing abuse and represents the mind's way of protecting the self against a sense of annihilation.

Neurobiology – In the past decade, the brain has become one of the most studied organs of the body with the advent of MRI's and CAT scans – pictures of the brain while it is in action – thinking, feeling, and creating movement and behavior. Due to the information from brain scans, we now know that unprocessed traumatic memories are stored in the nonverbal, emotional centers of the brain, which are then cut off from the cognitive processing centers, because they are flooded by stress hormones such as Cortisol. Research scientists are calling for experiential treatment as the treatment of choice for people with PTSD and other stress related disorders.

Self-organization – The term self-organization is a term from experiential psychotherapy that defines an ongoing, ever changing, active experience of self as the core of personality functioning. In TSM, healthy self-organization is a state of spontaneous learning as defined by the concretization of the eight prescriptive roles of the TSIRA to provide observation, restoration, and containment as needed to maintain conscious awareness.

- *Observation* – Two of the prescriptive roles, the OE and the Client Role facilitate the development of cognitive processing of information from a neutral, nonjudgmental perspective. This psychological function demonstrates the ability to self-reflect on the process of actively experiencing the self, others, and the world in the here and now.
- *Restoration* – The personal, interpersonal, and transpersonal strengths are concretized as part of the prescriptive roles in the TSIRA. These strengths help restore self-organization to a sense of spontaneity and creativity as an antidote for the learned helplessness and resulting hopelessness of PTSD.
- *Containment* – Containment is a primary focus of all TSM experiential interventions. Containment is a balance of thinking and feeling that allows conscious awareness to increase into unprocessed trauma memories without triggering survival defenses or overwhelming affect. The containing roles in the TSIRA are the Body Double, the Containing Double, and the

Manager of Defenses, which have all been described above. The Six Safety Action Structures were all developed to provide containment through narrative labeling and group cohesion prior to enacting TSM dramas focused on trauma-based roles.

Experiential Psychotherapy – As defined by Greenberg (1996, 2003) in *The Handbook of Psychotherapy and Behavior Change*, experiential therapy is any system that focuses on the active experiencing of self, others, and the world in the here and now. It is a process-oriented model of psychotherapy that focuses on the bodily felt, ever-present flow of information that is available through internal awareness. This is a general category that includes such systems as Gestalt therapy, classical psychodrama and the Therapeutic Spiral Model. Experiential psychotherapy has been shown to be equally effective as cognitive behavioral therapy for over a decade and is being called the treatment of choice for stress related disorders.

Classical Psychodrama Terms

Psychodrama – The seminal method of experiential psychotherapy to treat trauma developed by J.L. and Zerka Moreno (1969). Classical psychodrama, as it has come to be called today, has a basic set of experiential interventions such as the soliloquy, double, mirror, role reversal, and role training that have been used in many subsequent methods of experiential, expressive, and cognitive of behavior change. Psychodrama concretizes internal reality through dramatic and creative methods of expression.

Spontaneity/Creativity Theory – As defined by Moreno (1953), spontaneity was an abstract concept that proposed an ever-renewable source of energy held inside each person that was fueled by a spiritual source called the "godhead," a non-denominational image of a god within. In TSM, spontaneity remains the curative agent of change, but it operationalized as the eight prescriptive roles as needed to stabilize self-organization in the here and now.

Concretization – This is an action process of taking words, concepts, metaphors, or other left-brain ways of communication into hands-on, tangible actualities, such as asking the protagonist to pick an animal that represents courage, rather than just having a TAE play the abstract role of courage when asked for a strength to restore the self-organization. Many forms of creative arts can be used to concretize abstract ideas and right-brained symptoms of PTSD such as art, dance, movement, music, and other forms of nonverbal expression.

Double – The role of the classical psychodrama double is to facilitate the portrayal of psychological reality to its fullest expression by the protagonist. A TAE or group member becomes the double and concretizes thoughts, feelings, and behaviors that are out of awareness, expanding unconscious awareness by speaking in the first person. TSM has modified the classical double to perform the clinical function of containment rather than expansion through the Body and Containing Doubles.

Enactment – The portrayal of life situations in dramatic form and the physical externalization of roles that have only existed in the protagonist's internal reality. Enactments can be past, present, or future.

Protagonist – The person playing the principal role in the enactment. The client whose story is being enacted by team and group members.

Role Reversal – This is a classical psychodrama intervention where two people exchange roles so the protagonist can see another perspective of his or her internal reality. Role reversal also provides a chance to demonstrate a role to a TAE for accurate enactment or correction when a statement is wrong.

REFERENCES

Bergin, A. E., & Garfield, S. L. (Eds.). (1994). *Handbook of psychotherapy and behavior change*, (fourth edition). New York: John Wiley and Sons, Inc.

Blatner, A. (1991). Role dynamics. In R. J. Corsini & D. Wedding (Eds.), *Journal of Group Psychotherapy, Psychodrama and Sociometry, 44*(1), 33–40.

Burden, K., & Ciotola, L. (2003). *Report from a Body Double: An advanced clinical action intervention module in the therapeutic spiral model.* Workshop handout. Charlottesville, VA: Therapeutic Spiral International, LLC. www.therapeuticspiral.org

Ciotola, L. (2004). *The body dialogue.* Workshop handout. Charlottesville, VA: Therapeutic Spiral International, LLC. www.therapeuticspiral.org

Chimera, C. (2002). The yellow brick road: Helping children and adolescents to recover a coherent story following abusive family experiences. In A. Bannister & A. Huntington, (Eds.), *Communicating with children and adolescents: Action for change.* London: Jessica Kingsley Publications.

Cossa, M. (2002). Drago-drama. Archetypal sociodrama with adolescents. In A. Bannister & A. Huntington, (Eds.), *Communicating with children and adolescents: Action for change.* London: Jessica Kingsley Publications.

Cox, M. A. (2000). The six safety structures in the Therapeutic Spiral Model™. Workshop handout. Charlottesville, VA: Therapeutic Spiral International, LLC. www.therpeuticspiral.org

Elliott, R., Davis, K. L., & Slatick, E. (1998). Process-experiential therapy for post-traumatic stress difficulties. In L. S. Greenberg, J. C. Watson, & G. Lietaer, (Eds.), *Handbook of experiential psychotherapy*, (pp. 249–271). New York: Guilford Press.

Elliott, R., Greenberg, L. S., & Lietaer, G. (2002). Research on experiential therapies. In M. Lambert, A. Bergin, & S. Garfield (Eds.), *Handbook of psychotherapy and behavior change* (5th Edition). New York: John Wiley & Sons, Inc.

Forst, M. (2001). *The therapeutic spiral model: A qualitative enquiry of its effectiveness in the treatment of trauma and addiction.* Unpublished master's thesis. University of Ottawa.

Holmes, P. (1992). *The inner world outside: Ojbect relations theory and psychodrama.* London: Routelege.

Hoy, J. M. (2005). Personal communication. Using the therapeutic spiral model with children.

Hudgins, M. K. (1989). Experiencing the self through psychodrama and gestalt therapy in anorexia nervosa. In L. Hornyak and E. Baker (Eds.), *Experiential therapy for eating disorders.* New York: Guilford Press.

Hudgins, M. K. (1998). Experiential psychodrama with sexual trauma. In L. S. Greenberg, J. C. Watson, & G. Lietaer (Eds.), *Handbook of experiential psychotherapy.* (pp. 328–348). New York: Guilford Press.

Hudgins, M. K. (2000). The therapeutic spiral model: Treating PTSD in action. In P. F. Kellermann & M. K. Hudgins (Eds.), *Psychodrama with trauma survivors: Acting out your pain.* London: Jessica Kingsley Publishers.

Hudgins, M. K. (2002). *Experiential treatment of PTSD: The therapeutic spiral model.* New York: Springer Publishing Company.

Hudgins, M. K. (In press, a). *Action against trauma: A trainers manual for community leaders following traumatic stress.* Charlottesville: University of Virginia, Virginia Foundation for the Humanities, Institute on Violence and Culture.

Hudgins, M. K. (In Press, b). Clinical foundations of the therapeutic spiral model: Theoretical orientations and principles of change. In M. Marciano, J. Burgmesiter & C. Baim (Eds.) *Advanced theories of psychodrama.* New York: Routeledge.

Hudgins, M. K. & Drucker, K. (1998). The Containing Double as part of the Therapeutic Spiral Model for treating trauma. *The International Journal of Action Methods, 51*(2), 63–74.

Hudgins, M. K., Drucker, K. & Metcalf, K. (2000). The containing double: A clinically effective psychodrama intervention for PTSD. *The British Journal of Psychodrama and Sociodrama, 15*(1), 58–77.

Hudgins, M. K., & Kellermann, P. F. (Eds.). (2000). *Psychodrama with trauma survivors: Acting out your pain.* London: Jessica Kingsley Publishers.

Hudgins, M. K., Cho, W, Chen, J, Lai, N. W, & Ou, G. T. (2005). *Therapeutic spiral model in Asia: Theory, research & practice 2000–2005.* Paper presented at the Pacific Rim conference of the International Association on Trauma.

Hug, E. (in press, a). The neurobiology of violence. In Hudgins, M. K. *Action Against Trauma: A Trainers Manual for Community Leaders Following Traumatic Stress.* Charlottesville: University of Virginia.

Hug, E. (in press, b). A neuroscience perspective on psychodrama. In M. Marciano, J. Burgmesiter & C. Baim (Eds.), *Advanced theories of psychodrama.* New York: Routeledge.

Johnson, D. R. (1987). The role of the creative arts therapies in the diagnosis and treatment of Psychological trauma. *Arts in Psychotherapy, 14,* 7–14.

Johnson, D. R. (2000). Creative therapies. In E. B. Foa, T. M. Keane, & M. J. Friedman, (Eds.), *Effective treatments for PTSD.* New York: Guilford Press.

Lambert, M., Bergin, A., & Garfield, S. (Eds.). (2003). *Handbook of psychotherapy and behavior change* (5th Edition). New York: John Wiley & Sons, Inc.

McVea, C. (in press). Mother-child bonding as a moment of healing in the Therapeutic Spiral Model. *Journal of Group Psychotherapy, Psychodrama & Sociometry.*

Moreno, J. L. (1953). *Who shall survive?* New York: Beacon House. Copyright now with NJ: American Society of Group Psychotherapy and Psychodrama.

Moreno, J. L., & Moreno, Z. T. (1969). *Psychodrama: Volume III.* New York: Beacon House. Copyright now with NJ: American Society of Group Psychotherapy and Psychodrama.

Moreno, Z. T. (in press). *The Quintessential Zerka.* London: Routledge.

Moreno, Z. T., Blomkvist, L.D., & Rutzel, T. (2000). *Psychodrama, surplus reality and the art of healing.* London: Routeledge.

Schore, A. (2003). *Affect regulation and the repair of the self.* New York: Norton.

Siegel, D. J. (1999). *The developing mind: How relationships and the brain interact to shape who we are.* London: Guilford Press.

Stern, D. N. (1985). *The interpersonal world of the infant: A view from psychoanalysis and developmental psychology.* New York: Basic Books.

Stern, D. N. (1990) *Diary of a baby.* New York: Basic Books.

van der Kolk, B. (2003). In terror's grip. *Connections,* Feb/March. Washington, DC: International Association of Eating Disorders Professionals.

van der Kolk, B., McFarlane, A. C., & Weisaeth, L. (Eds.). (1996). *Traumatic stress: The effects of overwhelming experience on mind, body, and society.* New York: Guilford Press.

BIOGRAPHICAL STATEMENT

Dr. Kate Hudgins is a clinical psychologist, board certified trainer, educator, and practitioner of psychodrama, Sociometry, and group psychotherapy, international expert on experiential methods with PTSD, and an inspirational speaker in the global community. Dr. Kate is the developer of the Therapeutic Spiral Model™ and founder of Therapeutic Spiral International, LLC – A training institute to accredit practitioners and trainers. She is a publisher author and currently builds Action Trauma Teams in over a dozen countries. The Therapeutic Spiral Model is the personal and professional weaving of her training as a psychologist and a psychodramatist and her personal experience as a survivor of childhood sexual abuse and family alcoholism. Please visit her website at www.therapeuticspiral.org for additional articles and information on the Therapeutic Spiral Model in your local area.

Contact: DrKateTSI@aol.com

Chapter 21

CLINICAL SUPERVISION AND THE TRAUMA THERAPIST

GISÈLE C.T. HARRISON

INTRODUCTION

Within the four walls of my office, on the phone or in a group treatment room, I have listened to and witnessed the re-telling of molestation by fathers, brothers, teachers, priests, doctors, police officers, and uncles. The impact of hearing these stories in the privacy of my office, isolated from the rest of the world, has transformed me, and I am no longer the person I was before I started working with survivors of sexual violence.

Since childhood sexual abuse occurs in the context of a trusted relationship, the same issues of trust, safety, power, and control can find their way into the therapy relationship, which can become both complicated and compelling (Baker Miller and Pierce Stiver, 1997; Courtois, 1988; Dolan, 1991). Clinical supervision facilitates an examination of the process of therapy, allowing the trauma therapist to share thoughts, feelings, struggles, and fantasies with the expressed purpose of creating healing connections for survivors (Courtois, 1988; Pearlman and Saakvitne, 1995; Saakvitne and Pearlman, 1996).

Despite its potential benefits, the reality is that most trauma therapists do not receive regular clinical supervision, mainly due to a lack of understanding in the process combined with reluctance, on the part of designated supervisors, to obtain adequate training. Additionally, some trauma therapists may be resistant if a previous attempt with supervision was ineffective (Hewson, 2001). Other complications with safety and trust might include a supervisor who holds multiple roles in relation to the trauma therapist or a lack of choice in supervisors, which is a reality in most hierarchical organizations (Hewson, 2001).

The mental health profession itself holds the unrealistic notion that competent trauma therapist never allow themselves to be impacted by their work, and that they are always aware of what is occurring within the therapy relationship (Pearlman and Saakvitne, 1995). The profession's denial of the humanity of the therapist does a disservice by confusing "not knowing," being moved, and feeling with a client, with ignorance and incompetence, thus equating clinical supervision with weakness (Herman, 1997; Pearlman and Saakvitne, 1995).

As funding becomes increasingly tied to hours of service to clients, it becomes easy for staff and agency administration to focus solely on the provision of service, as opposed to providing clinical supervision to its staff (Richardson, 2001). Similarly, therapists in private practice and/or trauma therapists who are not provided supervision in their workplace would have to choose to spend their own time and money on private clinical supervision, a choice that might not be feasible given other financial, family, and personal commitments.

The purpose of this chapter is to highlight the myriad benefits of clinical supervision for the trauma therapist, and the trauma client, by discussing (a) the nature and purpose of supervision, (b) common issues in trauma therapy supervision, (c) popular models of supervision, and (d) characteristics of effective supervisors and supervisees, and (e) finding the right supervisor.

THE NATURE AND PURPOSE OF SUPERVISION

Thankfully, my first experience with clinical supervision was a positive one. It began in the second semester of my master of social work internship at a local women's shelter. Like most shelters there was little funding to provide residents with "on-the-spot" immediate and/or long-term therapy. To help meet the needs of the residents, the university I attended agreed to provide a clinical social work intern (me), and a faculty member who would provide me with 1.5 hours of weekly clinical supervision.

I was worried and confused, and had no idea what clinical supervision entailed, until my supervisor provided me with an article explaining the process. I was relieved to discover that rather then a weekly evaluation of my work, the relationship was intended as more of a mentorship. Throughout the duration of our meetings, my supervisor showed increasing curiosity about my interest in working with women; my beliefs about power and control; how I planned to take care of myself; how I felt before, during, and after each meeting with a client; and how my view of the world might be changing as I listened to the women's stories of abuse, poverty, and racism.

My clinical supervisor was respectful and encouraging of my choice to pursue my own personal therapy. When I felt I had made a "mistake" with a client, she helped me to process it and to see how I might use this new learning in my next therapy session. She created an interpersonal container where it was safe for me to discuss transference, counter-transference, and vicarious trauma (see appendix for definitions). The relationship that emerged was based on mutual respect and empowerment, curiosity, education, personal growth, support and confrontation. We were both willing to be challenged and transformed. Through this first supervisory relationship, my love for learning and reading evolved into a passion for therapy.

Unfortunately, this type of growth-fostering supervisory relationship is not the norm. I have worked in environments that have ranged from no supervision at all or, worse yet, bad supervision, to environments where training, education, and quality supervision were embraced and encouraged. The inconsistencies with how support, education, and training are viewed in the field of trauma work seem to point to a general lack of understanding of clinical supervision by both supervisees and supervisors (Mathews, 1995; Richardson, 2001).

To begin with, clinical supervision is not, nor should it ever be, linked to performance management, whereby the supervisee might fear the content of supervision making its way into a performance review (Richardson, 2001). The purpose of clinical supervision is to provide a safe space for supervisees to debrief, share difficult experiences, relax, promote self-care, be affirmed, and have energy restored (Richardson, 2001). More like an apprenticeship than counseling, the supervisor must still use therapy skills to create the trust and safety necessary for the supervisee to feel free enough to explore difficult feelings and experiences, while creating a process that is both "stretching and fluid" (Hewson, 2001).

COMMON ISSUES FOR TRAUMA THERAPY SUPERVISION

Ideally, the space of supervision serves as a refuge between sessions with clients, and is used for education, consultation, analysis, personal growth, and introspection. Over the lifetime of the therapist, regular ongoing clinical supervision can help ward off boredom and mediocrity, by encouraging the creation of a new therapy with each new client (Baker Miller and Pierce Stiver, 1997; Hewson, 2001; Pearlman and Saakvitne, 1995; Yalom, 2002). The following section will explore the various issues for trauma supervision.

Mastery of Theory and Skill. Pearlman and Saakvitne (1995) claim that the supervisor has the task of holding a theoretical container to provide the therapist with a sense of context and meaning. The theoretical container would include knowledge about normal responses to childhood sexual abuse, child development, feminist theory, and self-care, as well as various approaches to therapy.

Expressive Arts Applications and Repertoire. An art-centered approach to supervision ensures a central role for art-making, and helps the expressive arts therapist remain connected to their creative community (Baratta, et al., 2001). Ensuring that the required competencies are met, the supervision process would include making art and bringing in the artwork of clients to ensure that art is the primary form of clinical analysis and expression (Knill, Levine, and Levine, 2005). Finding an expressive arts supervisor who also specializes in trauma therapy might not be possible, and may necessitate having two supervisors, one who specializes in trauma work and another who can offer in-depth, analytically-oriented expressive arts supervision (Austin and Dvorkin, 2001).

The Therapy Relationship. Since childhood sexual abuse normally occurs within the context of an interpersonal relationship with a trusted person, the therapeutic relationship can, as previously stated, become complicated and compelling (Courtois, 1988; Pearlman and Saakvitne, 1995). The goal of therapy is to model a healthy, nonexploitative relationship through therapist authenticity, empathy, and openness, adding the spark of humanity that was missing in the survivor's perpetrator (Courtois, 1988; Wosket and Page, 2001). Despite good intentions, navigating through the needs and emotions of both client and therapist can trigger certain aspects of the other's personhood or behavior that can derail the healing connection (Courtois, 1988; Wosket and Page, 2001). Given the potential stressful working conditions, and the possible harm to both client and therapist, clinical supervision that focuses on improving the therapy relationship is essential to the success of therapy (Pearlman and Saakvitne, 1995).

Boundaries. Sexual abuse is a violation of the child's physical and emotional space, leaving the adult survivor with a potentially distorted idea of healthy and unhealthy boundaries (Dolan, 1991). Balancing empathic engagement with the negotiation of clear and safe boundaries between therapist and survivor communicates safety, care, and respect. At times, this might be difficult faced with the intense emotions that often emerge during the re-telling of abuse (Herman, 1997; Kottler, 2003; Mathews, 1995; Saakvitne and Pearlman, 1996). Clinical supervision can provide the necessary container to examine the motives of the therapist in negotiating the conflicting requirements between flexible and rigid boundaries (Herman, 1997; Kottler, 2003).

Transference. Survivors, who report having felt confused, betrayed, humiliated, helpless, and abandoned at the time of their abuse, often report similar feelings toward people in positions of authority over them, including therapists (Herman, 1997). The dynamics this can introduce into the therapeutic process can alternate between periods of conflict, attachment, idealization, withdrawal, and hostility (Courtois, 1988). Clinical supervision can help therapists, depersonalize transference responses by examining how past relational images might be showing up in the present and finding ways to work towards reconnection and healing (Baker Miller and Pierce Stiver, 1997).

Counter-Transference. Experienced at various levels of awareness, counter-transference responses can be confusing, personal, and often embarrassing for the therapist. Trust and safety within the supervisory relationship can provide the space to differentiate between the personal issues of the therapist versus the issues that can be addressed in the therapy relationship (Pearlman and Saakvitne, 1995). Shining light on the impact therapist and client have on one another can provide an opportunity for insight, transformation, and healing.

Vicarious Trauma. The natural consequence of empathic connections with survivors can result in vicarious trauma, which is the inevitable and cumulative effect on the therapist of hearing repeated stories of childhood sexual abuse (Dolan, 1991; Saakvitne, Gamble, Pearlman, and Tabor, 2000). Vicarious trauma can impact the trauma therapist's view of herself and the world around her and, if left unchecked, can leave her feeling battered, helpless, guilty and confused (Saakvitne and Pearlman, 1996). Ultimately, clinical supervision would educate and offer suggestions for self-care, while drawing attention to the signs of vicarious trauma (Dolan, 1991; Herman, 1997, Saakvitne and Pearlman, 1996; Yalom, 2002). The latter can parallel the symptoms of traumatic stress including: anxiety, disconnection, guilt, emotional flooding, numbing, social withdrawal, hopelessness, avoidance, rage, helplessness, hypervigilence, difficulty in relationships and with sexuality, and social withdrawal (Herman, 1997; Saakvitne and Pearlman, 1996).

Self-Care. Saakvitne et al. (2000) claim that if *the self* of a therapist is the *tool of the trade,* self-care is the regular maintenance required to combat the occupational hazards of trauma work. Therapists can demonstrate a serious commitment to physical, emotional, and spiritual well-being through self-care (Kottler, 2003). Sound clinical supervision, which is part of self-care, can ensure that therapists strive toward maintaining balance between work and leisure, action and reflection, and giving and receiving (Saakvitne and Pearlman, 1996). Practical self-care in the workplace would include (a) monitoring caseload, (b) limiting the number of clients seen each day, (c) taking breaks, and (d) making time to nurture colleagueship (Kottler, 2003; Saakvitne and Pearlman, 1996).

Community Work. Herman (1997) argues that working with survivors requires a strong committed moral stance from the therapist. This would include a well-developed critical analysis of the fundamental injustice of various forms of oppression – and how they intersect with childhood sexual abuse. Ideally, clinical supervision can help keep trauma workers grounded in the knowledge that individual acts of sexual abuse are connected to a much larger notion of the political domination of one group over another. Exploring or re-connecting with a wider feminist consciousness and joining with others to address abuse on a macro level through activism, can help trauma therapists feel connected to something larger then themselves, thus leading to transformational conversations between therapist and client (Mann, 2005).

Survivor Therapists. Despite the fact that 26% to 43% of trauma therapists are also survivors (Elliott and Guy's study as cited in Pearlman and Saakvitne, 1995), the acknowledgment of the value and presence of survivor therapists is almost nonexistent in the literature and in the workplace (Pearlman and Saakvitne, 1995). Ideally, clinical supervision would acknowledge, recognize, understand, and openly address the possible advantages and disadvantages survivor therapists can bring to their work with trauma clients (Pearlman and Saakvitne, 1995).

MODELS OF CLINICAL SUPERVISION

Current literature advocates a combination of individual, peer, and group supervision as the ideal when considering the well-being of trauma therapists and the clients they work with (Herman, 1997; Richardson, 2001). Individual supervision consists of a formal contract between a supervisee and a supervisor, who would meet on a weekly or bi-weekly basis to explore identified issues in a reflective manner (Wosket and Page, 2001). These meetings would provide a bridge between sessions with survivors, providing the supervisee with an opportunity to review the work of therapy (Wosket and Page, 2001).

Group supervision normally takes place with an internal or an external facilitator. The purpose is threefold: (a) to debrief, problem-solve, and discuss painful emotions resulting from trauma work, (b) promote organizational and individual self-care, and (c) to identify the specific effects of trauma work on the self of the therapist (Richardson, 2001; Saakvitne and Pearlman, 1996). Connecting with colleagues in group supervision can provide the usual transformational powers of a group through cohesion, intimacy, validation, reality testing, and problem solving (Kottler, 2003; Saakvitne and Pearlman, 1996). More importantly, regularly scheduled group supervision can counteract the isolation, boredom, and despair that can be experienced when therapists lack opportunities for real connection with colleagues (Kottler, 2003).

Peer supervision occurs when at least two clinicians consult with one another (Pearlman and Saakvitne, 1995). Meetings can range from informal debriefing to a more formal structure where each person is allotted a set amount of time to present and discuss their clinical work (Pearlman and Saakvitne, 1995). This type of meeting can help revitalize one another by focusing on encouraging each other to be more creative and innovative, while providing a special source of comfort and energy (Kottler, 2003).

Working with the issue of sexual abuse can be draining, and even with regular personal therapy, individual, group, and peer supervision, trauma therapists should also have access to a supervisor to debrief or consult with throughout the workday to ensure proper mental and emotional functioning (Kottler, 2003; Richardson, 2001). When a therapist finds herself working alone in private practice or in a workplace that does not offer effective quality supervision, she might consider creating a peer support network as well as paying for regular private clinical supervision.

CHARACTERISTICS OF EFFECTIVE SUPERVISORS AND SUPERVISEES

Supervisors. In my experience, the best clinical supervisors are the ones that display a deep sense of respectful curiosity within a safe yet "stretching" environment. They facilitate growth through their own commitment to ongoing training and development, as well as obtaining personal consultation for their role as supervisor. They are confident enough to be open to being changed and taught by the supervisee. Effective supervisors share a sense of reciprocal responsibility within the relationship, thus being open to evaluating the supervisory process, including any unspoken feelings between supervisor and supervisee, and subsequently taking due responsibility (Hewson, 2001).

Committed to the idea of "not knowing," effective supervision is more of an exploration of the unknown, through which the supervisor encourages the therapist to develop the courage and the willingness to face the unknown within themselves and in the relationships they have with their clients (Wosket and Page, 2001). By modeling this type of exploration, supervisors are empowering the supervisee to do the same with their clients, thus working towards creating a healing process based on mutual empathy, intuition, instincts, and, of course, "not knowing" (Wosket and Page, 2001).

With a compassionate eye, the clinical supervisor helps the supervisee to pick out details that may be out of her sight during actual therapy with clients with the purpose of trying to make sense of patterns and outcomes (Hewson, 2001; Wosket and Page, 2001). As mentors, supervisors must be willing and able to abandon particular styles of supervision in order to create a new supervision with each new supervisee (Wosket and Page, 2001; Yalom, 2002).

Supervisees. Clinical supervision is most effective when it is a collaborative process. It is essential that the supervisee become an active participant in developing and monitoring the supervision process (Orlans and Edwards, 2001). Characteristics of an effective supervisee would include a commitment to learning and mentorship, as well as a willingness to be stretched and transformed. Throughout this lifelong process, an effective supervisee would be able to identify and communicate priorities and areas for growth, as well as the parts of their practice that might require attention (Wosket and Page, 2001).

A major task in therapy is to pay attention to one's immediate feelings, which can be discussed or processed in supervision, with the purpose of moving the therapist toward a greater knowledge of self (Yalom, 2002). With increased self-knowledge, the therapist works toward eliminating, or at least noticing, the counter-transference responses that can lead to disconnection in the therapeutic process (Yalom, 2002). The supervisee's willingness to risk exploring these unconscious responses can further increase the chances of successful connections in therapy (Baker Miller and Pierce Stiver, 1997).

An effective therapist/supervisee would feel comfortable engaging in personal therapy, a process Yalom (2002) says should be as prolonged and as deep as possible. Yalom argues that the best way for therapists to learn a particular therapeutic approach is to enter into it as a client. This provides a threefold opportunity to (a) resolve personal issues, (b) develop an awareness of inner strengths, and (c) gain a firsthand appreciation for the strengths and weaknesses of a specific approach (Yalom, 2002).

Finding the Right Supervisor. The qualities listed above can assist both supervisors and supervisees develop expectations, roles, tasks, and the required training to ensure a process that is both fluid and stretching. When internal supervision is not available or is ineffective, therapists have the right and the ethical responsibility to obtain private supervision outside of the workplace. Finding the right match involves conducting a search of local therapists or faculty who provide private clinical supervision, asking for referrals from valued colleagues and past mentors, and conducting interviews. Interview questions can be developed using this chapter as a guide. At times, finding the right match might necessitate long distance clinical supervision, which can be done over the telephone and/or by email.

CONCLUSION

Working with survivors of sexual abuse regularly offers therapists opportunities to experience hope, sisterhood, and connection. The work is intense, powerful, and rewarding, and carries with it the inevitability of vicarious trauma. Effective clinical supervision is a safeguard against injury to clients, boundary violations, and therapist burnout. Quality clinical supervision is one of the most significant factors in the success or failure of therapy, and is an essential part of both personal and professional accountability (Courtois, 1988; Dolan, 1991; Herman, 1997; Mann, 2005; Mathews, 1995; Orlans and Edwards, 2001; Saakvitne et al., 2000; Wosket and Page, 2001). Complications in the supervisory relationship can be minimized when there is a clear understanding of the purpose and process of supervision, a choice of supervisors, and a desire to achieve the qualities of effective supervisors and supervisees.

APPENDIX – TERMS

Counter-transference – Refers to the therapist's conscious and unconscious feelings about the client. It may be, in part, an expression of the personal issues that the therapist brings into the therapy relationship, and it may be, in part, a response to the client's transference reactions (Baker Miller and Pierce Stiver, 1997, p. 142).

Transference – Refers to the client's conscious and unconscious feelings about the therapist. It may be, in part, an expression of past experiences and relational images from the original trauma that are brought into the therapy relationship, and it may be, in part, a response to the therapist's counter-transference reactions (Baker Miller and Pierce Stiver, 1997).

Vicarious Trauma – The inescapable transformation of the therapist's inner experience as a result of empathic engagement with survivor clients and their stories of devastation or betrayal that challenge our cherished values and beliefs (Saakvitne and Pearlman, 1996, p. 25). In the role of witness to atrocity, the therapist will at times become emotionally overwhelmed and may experience, to a lesser degree, the same terror, rage, and despair as the client (Herman, 1997, p. 140).

REFERENCES

Austin, D., & Dvorkin, J. (2001). Peer supervision in music therapy. In M. Forinash (Ed.), *Music therapy supervision.* (219–229). Gilsum, NH: Barcelona Publishers.

Baker Miller, J., & Pierce Stiver, I. (1997). *The healing connection, how women form felationships in therapy and in life.* Boston, MA: Beacon Press.

Baratta, E., Bertolami, M., Hubbard, A., MacDonald, M., & Spragg, D. (2001). Peer supervision in the development of the new music and expressive therapist. In M. Forinash (Ed.), *Music therapy supervision.* (181–194). Gilsum, NH: Barcelona Publishers.

Courtois, C. A. (1988). *Healing the incest wound: Adult survivors in therapy.* New York: W.W. Norton.

Dolan, Y. M. (1991). *Resolving sexual abuse, solution-focused therapy and Ericksonian hypnosis for adult survivors.* New York:W.W. Norton.

Herman, J. (1997). *Trauma and recovery, The aftermath of violence – from domestic abuse to political terror*, (2nd Ed.). New York: Basic Books.

Hewson, J., (2001). Integrative supervision, art and science. In M. Carroll, & M. Tholstrup (Eds.), *Integrative Approaches to Supervision.* (pp. 42–49). London, England: Jessica Kingsley Publishers.

Knill, P., Levine, E, & Levine, S. (2005). *Principles and practice of expressive arts therapy.* London, England: Jessica Kingsley Publishers.

Kottler, J. A. (2003). *On being a therapist.* (3rd Ed.). San Francisco, CA: Jossey-Bass.

Mann, S. (2005). "How can you do this work?" Responding to questions about the experience of working with women who were subjected to child sexual abuse. *The International Journal of Narrative Therapy and Community Work, 2,* 11–22.

Mathews, F. (1995). *Combining voices, supporting paths of healing in adult female and male survivors of sexual abuse.* Ottawa, ON: National Clearinghouse on Family Violence, Health Canada.

Orlans, V., & Edwards, D. (2001). A collaborative model of supervision. In M. Carroll, & M. Tholstrup (Eds.), *Integrative Approaches to Supervision.* (42–49). London, England: Jessica Kingsley Publishers.

Pearlman, L. A., & Saakvitne, K. W. (1995). *Trauma and the therapist: Countertransference and vicarious traumatization in psychotherapy with incest survivors.* New York: W.W. Norton.

Richardson, J. I. (2001). *Guidebook on vicarious trauma: Recommended solutions for anti-violence Workers.* Ottawa, ON: Health Canada.

Saakvitne, K. W., Gamble, S., Pearlman, L. A., & Tabor, B. (2000). *Risking connection, a training curriculum for working with survivors of childhood abuse.* Baltimore, MD: The Sidran Press.

Saakvitne, K. W., & Pearlman, L. A. (1996). *Transforming the pain: A workbook on vicarious traumatization for helping professionals who work with traumatized clients.* New York: W.W. Norton.

Wosket, V., & Page, S. (2001). In M. Carroll, & M. Tholstrup (Eds.), *Integrative approaches to supervision.* (13–31). London, England: Jessica Kingsley Publishers.

Yalom, I. D. (2002). *The gift of therapy: An open letter to a new generation of therapists and their patients.* New York: Perennial.

BIOGRAPHICAL STATEMENT

Gisèle Harrison is a registered social worker with a part-time private practice and a full-time public practice at a rape crisis center. She provides individual, couple, and group therapy, as well as Eye Movement Desensitization and Reprocessing. Gisèle also has over fifteen years of practical experience facilitating psycho-educational groups and anti-oppression workshops across Canada, in New York, and in East Africa. Much of her work and formal training has focused on learning how gender, race, sexual orientation, class, and other forms of oppression can impact individuals and communities. She is passionate about women's issues and is always honored to be part of the healing journey of survivors of sexual violence. As a sessional instructor with the University of Windsor, she has taught courses on diversity, crisis intervention, and gender. Gisèle received her master in social work from Wilfrid Laurier University and is a member of the Ontario Association of Social Workers.

Chapter 22

ETHICAL GUIDELINES FOR CREATIVE THERAPISTS IN THE TREATMENT OF SEXUAL ABUSE SURVIVORS

KRISTIN LARSON

INTRODUCTION

The use of creative therapies in the treatment of sexual abuse can bring gentle awareness and provide deep healing for some of the most profound wounds brought to the therapeutic arena. Art, play, dance, music, drama, and poetry therapists have a humbling opportunity to share in a journey of healing, but also have an awesome responsibility to protect the well-being, freedom of choice, and dignity of their clients (Levick, 1995; Miller, 2003). The examination and discussion of these ethical responsibilities is a vital part of professional development, yet such a discussion inevitably raises as many questions as it answers. The purpose of this chapter will be to emphasize knowledge and practice of ethical standards in the unique circumstance of treating sexual abuse and encourage therapists to wrestle with the "gray areas" where standards are less clear.

ETHICAL GUIDELINES

Professionals who provide creative therapies can turn to ethical codes for guidance in ethical treatment. General guidelines for the provision of psychological or counseling services are described in the current American Psychological Association's *Ethical Principles of Psychologists and Code of Conduct* (2002) and the American Counseling Association's *Code of Ethics and Standards of Practice* (1995). There are also guidelines specific to each creative discipline, including the American Art Therapy Association (2003), American Dance Therapy

Association (1966), American Music Therapy Association (2003), Association for Play Therapy (2000), National Association for Music Therapy (1987), and National Association for Poetry Therapy (National Fair Access Coalition on Testing, 2000). While these guidelines do not specifically mention the treatment of sexual abuse in their codes, each generally addresses the issues raised in this chapter.

COMPETENCE

Therapist competence is the foundation for ethical practice (Bruscia, 1988; Hammond and Gantt, 1998; Maranto, 1987; Maranto and Ventre, 1985; Wilson, 1987) especially when using creative techniques that require expert skills. In addition, a population with specific needs such as survivors of sexual abuse requires specific training (ACA, 1995; APA, 2002; Courtois, 1997; Daniluk and Haverkamp, 1996). Therefore, the creative therapist who treats survivors of sexual abuse must be competent in both the technique and the population.

Creative therapies have the potential to generate more intimacy than traditional therapies. Strong feelings on the part of the therapist can be created by using touch during dance, movement, or drama therapy, or by seeing the depth of the client's pain through art, poetry, or play therapy. The therapist must guard their professionalism and objectivity from being swept into the emotional moment. Simon and Gutheil (1997) add that the disclosure of recovered memories can result in countertransference characterized by the therapist's need to rescue or feelings of helplessness. When a therapist questions their own objectivity, it is best practice to seek out colleagues for consultation or supervision (ACA, 1995; APA, 2002).

In addition, some of the most effective creative therapists have been forged out of traumatic childhoods of their own. While personal experience can increase understanding and connection, it can also bias the therapist's judgment. Therefore, those professionals who have experienced trauma themselves must be particularly cautious of projection of their own feelings and experiences onto the client.

INFORMED CONSENT

For the client who has been sexually abused, being informed of the methods and consequences of therapy and being allowed to consent prior to starting the therapeutic relationship is vital. It is especially important with this population, whose physical and psychological boundaries have been violated

(Daniluk and Haverkamp, 1996). In addition, informed consent needs to be handled carefully and thoroughly to ensure that the survivor of sexual abuse is aware of their choices and rights during the creative therapeutic process (ACA, 1995; APA, 2002; Willis, 1987). Although it is not required by any ethical standards, consent with a written signature provides protection for the therapist and the client.

When working with minors, informed consent is given by the child's or adolescent's parents (ACA, 1995). Guidelines suggest obtaining the child's assent, given in language the child can understand, in addition to parental consent (APA, 2002). Providing information regarding confidentiality and the laws related to mandated reporting is particularly important with this population.

Informed consent also includes agreeing on the focus of therapy. It is possible that, in the process of a creative therapy, an adult client will report childhood sexual abuse but deny any negative impact. For example, a client participating in poetry therapy may allude to a childhood incestual relationship with an adult relative in a neutral or even positive tone. Does the therapist have a right to treat an issue that the client does not present for therapy (see O'Neill, 1998 for a discussion)? While some researchers believe that victimization has occurred regardless of the client's denial (Finkelhor, 1979), ethical guidelines require the therapist to inform the client of their choice and obtain consent prior to including this experience as a focus of their treatment. Nichols (1992) contributes by saying that our ethical responsibility requires us to question and explore the issue with the client in order to determine if there is any related emotional or psychological damage.

Informed consent does not always end with a signed paper during the first session. As new techniques or new directions in therapy are introduced the therapist should obtain consent before proceeding. In addition, adult survivors of sexual abuse may display a dependence on the therapist that results from boundary violations in their past. They may be overly compliant in agreeing to participate in alternative therapies or in suggestions from the therapist. A commitment to continued informed consent protects the client's autonomy and avoids recreating the client's early loss of control (Daniluk and Haverkamp, 1996).

CONFIDENTIALITY

Confidentiality refers to the client's right to have all aspects of their therapy kept private. This includes information revealed during therapy, products of the creative therapy, and the fact that they are even attending therapy. There are many challenging questions a creative therapist faces regarding confidentiality when a client has revealed or indicated a history of sexual abuse.

How do I maintain the confidentiality of the art or poetry produced in the treatment of sexual abuse? Do I talk with the parents of a child whose art indicates sexual abuse? How do I respond to a teenager who reveals sexual abuse during drama therapy, but does not want their parents informed? Should a spouse be told when body issues are uncovered during dance therapy?

Children often create dramatic representations of their experiences and emotions when participating in creative therapies to treat their sexual abuse trauma. There may even be opportunities to anonymously display their art or play therapy products to raise public awareness, promote a treatment center, or to decorate the office. Even with the assent of the child and consent of the parent, it is important that the therapist discuss all the ramifications of public exposure, including unintentional identification of the artist/client. Art therapists must have a secure space to keep the products of therapy confidential (Larson, 2006). Intentional or unintentional display of a client's creative product without consent is a breach of confidentiality (ACA, 1995; APA, 2002; Larson, 2006).

Confidentiality must also be maintained between spouses. When an adult client is married, the treatment or revelation of childhood sexual abuse is bound to impact the marital relationship. Even so, it is ultimately the client's choice whether, when, and how he or she informs his or her spouse. Therefore, the therapist must exercise caution in sessions involving the spouse not to share art, poetry, or other products of creative therapy that might reveal this issue before the client is ready.

Maintaining confidentiality can be even more complex when treating children. When a creative therapeutic process reveals indications of sexual abuse in a minor, it is important to exercise caution and be aware of the relevant laws. While it is agreed upon in the informed consent that this kind of information will not necessarily be held confidential, a therapist must use their judgment to determine if the evidence is strong enough to reveal to parents or report to protective services. Ethical codes and laws provide guidelines, but are purposely vague in their instructions, for they are unable to account for all of the possible circumstances for reporting (Larson, 2006). A therapist must also consider the child's safety first when deciding to inform parents or guardians. Again, therapists must use their professional judgment. Yet, every therapist belongs to a larger community of professionals that, collectively, are an endless source of wisdom and experience. Consultation and/or supervision should be the industry standard when faced with this kind of ethical dilemma.

MANDATORY REPORTING

There are times that creative therapists may encounter an ethical dilemma when faced with a revelation of sexual abuse or a suspicion based on evidence that qualifies for mandatory reporting (Daly, Jogerst, and Brinig, 2003; Hammond and Gantt, 1998; Serrano and Gunzburger, 1983; Maranto and Ventre, 1985; Wilson, 1987). Therapists in this situation grapple with maintaining confidentiality in order to protect the client or involving a protective services agency and law enforcement. There can be a very real risk to the client of retaliation from the abuser or ostracism by family members who do not believe the abuse occurred (Daniluk and Haverkamp, 1993; 1996). This can be especially detrimental in the case of a child victim (Serrano and Gunzberger, 1983). Ethical guidelines encourage therapists to consider the best interest of the client in addition to obeying the local laws (ACA, 1995; APA, 2002). In most cases, the laws and guidelines are intentionally vague; therefore therapist would be wise to consult with experienced colleagues and/or contact their state's ethics board for guidance. Therapists must recognize that if they choose to protect the abuse survivor's confidentiality, they may be breaking the law.

It is imperative that the therapist be familiar with their individual state's laws regarding mandatory reporting. In addition, therapists can educate themselves regarding the potential consequences of reporting by talking with professionals who have made reports and by becoming familiar with the staff of the local protective services agency. Lastly, ethical practice calls for supervision when a therapist is inexperienced in this aspect of client treatment (ACA, 1995; APA, 2002).

REPRESSED MEMORIES

Additional complexity arises when the creative therapy unearths the details of sexual abuse not previously known (Applebaum, Uyehara, and Elin, 1997; Courtois, 1997; Pettifor, Crozier, and Chew, 2001). In the last twenty years there have been more than 800 cases filed in the United States by accusers against their alleged perpetrators (Lipton, in press). This number has decreased in recent years, which may have been influenced by the court's increased standard for scientific evidence (Leif, 1999).

In an actual case (with details altered to protect anonymity), an art therapist employed at an inpatient treatment center entered the weekly staffing and stretched out a drawing created by a newly admitted female. It depicted her home including the young woman, her mother, and her uncle by a picnic table. Drawn in crayon, her uncle faced the young woman with "a chain saw to cut wood" extending from his belt line. A debate regarding her treatment plan ensued; some of the staff believed it was evidence of a repressed memory of sexual abuse, while others did not believe that memories of trauma could be repressed (see Loftus, 1993).

In spite of this disagreement, many see the safe and expressive nature of creative therapies as providing a fertile atmosphere for memories to surface. Creative therapists who turn to the growing boding of literature related to repressed memories for guidance may find a maze of political, emotional, and contradictory findings (Pettifor, Crozier, and Chew, 2001; Brooke, 1997). In addition, those familiar with the media coverage of the false memory syndrome law suits in the 1990s may find themselves hesitating to act on a client's claim of recovered memories. While there is considerable controversy related to the accuracy and meaning of repressed memories, clear guidelines exist that focus on the welfare of the client and best practice for the therapist. The American Medical Association (1994), The Australian Psychological Society Limited (1994), and the British Psychological Society (1995) all offer guidelines for the therapeutic response to recovered memories. In addition, Crozier and Pettifor (1996) have also provided the *Guidelines for Psychologists Addressing Recovered Memories* based on the *Canadian Code of Ethics for Psychologists* (CPA, 1991). Most agree that it is possible that some recovered memories may be accurate and some may be inaccurate, but that the client is best served by focusing on their needs rather than determining the veracity of their claim (Pettifor, Crozier, and Chew, 2001).

It is rare to find a therapist who, from personal and professional experience, has not formed an opinion regarding repressed memories. And yet, each therapist must strive to avoid bias in his or her response to the client. The duty of neutrality (Simon, 1992) is a guiding principle that limits the therapist's expression of a strong belief or disbelief in the authenticity of a client's recovered memory (Simon and Gutheil, 1997; Pettifor, Crozier, and Chew, 2001).

In addition, creative therapists must guard against prompting what they might believe is a repressed memory (Daniluk and Haverkamp, 1996). While this ethical principle might seem to be common knowledge, Loftus and Ketcham (1994) found that it is not uncommon for clients to be told during their first therapy session that, based on their symptoms, they had likely been sexually abuse in childhood. Courtois (1997) states, "When a specific memory is absent, it is crucially important that the therapist not 'fill-in' or 'confirm' reported suspicions of a non-remembered abuse history – the patient needs to come to his or her own understanding and may need to tolerate considerable uncertainty, especially when corroboration is lacking" (p. 350). It is ultimately the responsibility of the client to determine the accuracy and meaning of any memory (Daniluk and Haverkamp, 1996).

CONCLUSION

The quote, "To make a goal of comfort or happiness has never appealed to me; a system of ethics built on this basis would be sufficient only for a herd of cattle" commonly attributed to Albert Einstein, is a good description of the challenge of treating sexual abuse survivors and maintaining the highest ethical standards. It is not a comfortable or easy task. Yet, witnessing the healing process facilitated by creative therapies and knowing that the client's well-being and dignity has been protected is worth the investment.

APPENDIX – TERMS

Competence – A professional standard of training and/or experience established by appropriate organizations or ethical guidelines that indicate the therapist has developed sound professional judgment and can provide services independently and effectively.

Confidentiality – The client's right to have no information regarding their therapy revealed, including the fact that they are attending therapy.

Countertransference – An emotional reaction on the part of the therapist in response to the client's story, emotions, or behavior, often characterized by strong positive feelings (such as attraction or desire to rescue) or strong negative feelings (such as dislike or anger).

Ethical Guidelines – Codes of conduct that describe, in general terms, the highest standard of professionalism, emphasizing the client's welfare.

Informed Consent – A written or verbal agreement for any therapeutic focus, method, or activities based on the client's full understanding of the procedures, limitations and consequences of participation. This agreement must also include the limitations of confidentiality and client's right to refuse any activity or withdraw from therapy at anytime.

Mandated Reporting – The legal requirements, that vary from state to state, of certain professionals in the helping fields to notify local law enforcement or agencies for the protection of vulnerable populations (children or the elderly) when any form of abuse or neglect is determined or suspected.

Supervision – Guidance, consultation, and review by a professional with more experience or training than the supervisee in order to increase the supervisee's therapeutic skills or effectiveness in responding to an unfamiliar therapeutic focus, skill, population or ethical dilemma.

REFERENCES

American Art Therapy Association. (2003). *Ethical principles for art therapists.* Retrieved Sept. 10, 2004. http://www.arttherapy.org/aboutarttherapy/ethicsfinal2003.pdf

American Counseling Association. (1995). *Code of ethics and standards of practice.* Alexandria, VA: Author.

American Dance Therapy Association. (1966). *ADTA code of ethical practice.* Columbia, MD: Author.

American Medical Association. (1994). *Report of the council on scientific affairs, CSA Report* 5–A–94.

American Music Therapy Association. (2003). *AMTA code of ethics.* Retrieved August 30, 2004. http://www.musictherapy.org/ethics.html

American Psychological Association. (2002). Ethical principles of psychologists and code of conduct. *American Psychologist, 57*(12), 1060–1073.

Applebaum, P. S., Uyehara, L. A., & Elin, M. R. (1997). *Trauma and Memory: Clinical and Legal Controversies.* New York: Oxford Press.

Association for Play Therapy. (2000). *Recommended play therapy practice guidelines.* Retrieved September 7th, 2004. http://www.a4pt.org/forms/guidelines.pdf

Australian Psychological Society Limited. (1994). *Guidelines relating to the reporting of recovered memories.* APS Board of Directors, October, 1994.

British Psychological Society. (1995). *The report of the working party of the British Psychological Society: Recovered memories.* Leicester, UK: Author.

Bruscia, (1988). Standards for clinical assessment in the arts therapies. *Arts in Psychotherapy; Special Issue: Assessment in the creative arts therapies, 15*(1) 5–10.

Canadian Psychological Association. (1991). *Canadian code of ethics for psychologists.* Ottawa: Author.

Courtois, C. (1997). Informed clinical practice and the standard of care: Proposed guidelines for the treatment of adults who report delayed memories of childhood trauma. In J. Don Read & D. Stephan Lindsay (Eds.). *Recollections of trauma: Scientific evidence and clinical practice.* New York: Plenum Press.

Crozier, S., & Pettifor, J. (1996). *Guidelines for psychologists addressing recovered memories.* Ottawa: Canadian Psychological Association. Retrieved July 1, 2005 from http://www.cpa.ca/memory.html

Daly, J., Jogerst, G., & Brinig, M. F. (2003). Mandatory reporting: Relationship of APS statute language on state reported elder abuse. *Journal of Elder Abuse and Neglect, 15*(2), 1–21.

Daniluk, J. C., & Haverkamp, B. E. (1993). Ethical issues in counseling adult survivors of incest. *Journal of Counseling and Development, 72,* 16–22.

Daniluk, J. C., & Haverkamp, B. E. (1996). Ethical considerations in working with survivors of sexual abuse. In Joya Lonsdale (Ed.), *Hatherleigh guide to issues in modern therapy.* New York, NY: Hatherleigh Press.

Finkelhor, D. (1979). What's wrong with sex between adults and children? Ethics and the problem of sexual abuse. *American Journal of Orthopsychiatry, 49*(4), 692–697.

Hammond, L. C., & Gantt, L. (1998). Using art in counseling: Ethical considerations. *Journal of Counseling & Development, 76*(3) 271–276.

Larson, K. (2006). Ethical delivery of creative therapeutic approaches. In: Stephanie L. Brooke (Ed.) *Creative arts therapies manual: A guide to the history, theoretical approaches, assessment, and work with special populations of art, play, dance, music, drama, and poetry therapies.* Springfield, IL: Charles C Thomas Publisher, Ltd.

Leif, H. (1999). Patients versus therapists: Legal actions over recovered memory therapy. *Psychiatric Times, 16*(11). Retrieved January 1, 2006 http://www.psychiatrictimes.com/p991136.html

Levick, M. F. (1995). The identity of the creative arts therapist: Guided by ethics. *Arts in Psychotherapy, 22*(4) 283–295.

Lipton, A. (in press). Recovered memories in the courts: Report of the FMSF Legal Survey. In: S. Taub (Ed.) *Recovered memories of abuse, psychological, social and legal perspectives on a contemporary mental health controversy.* New York: Charles C Thomas.

Loftus, E. (1993). The reality of repressed memories. *American Psychologist, 48,* 518–537.

Loftus, E., & Ketcham, K. (1994). *The myth of the repressed memory.* New York, NY: St. Martin's Press.

Maranto, C. D. (1987). Continuing concerns in music therapy ethics. *Music Therapy, 6*(2) 59–63.

Maranto, C. D. & Ventre, M. (1985). Confidentiality and the music therapist: Ethical considerations. *Music Therapy, 5*(1) 61–65.

Miller, C. (2003). Ethical guidelines in research. In J. C. Thomas & H. Hersen (Eds.) *Understanding research in clinical and counseling psychology.* (pp. 271–293). Mahwah, NJ: Lawrence Erlbaum Associates Publishers.

The National Association for Music Therapy. (1987). *Code of Ethics.* Silver Spring, MD: Author.

National Fair Access Coalition on Testing. (2000). *NAPT code of ethics.* Retrieved July 1, 2004 http://www.fairaccess.org/naptE.htm

Nichols, W. C. (1992). *Treating adult survivors of childhood sexual abuse.* Sarasota, FL: Professional Resource Press.

O'Neill, P. l. (1998). *Negotiating consent in psychotherapy.* New York: New York University Press.

Pettifor, H., Crozier, S., & Chew, J. (2001). Recovered memories: Ethical guidelines to support professionals. *Journal of Child Sexual Abuse, 10,* 1–15.

Serrano, A., & Gunzberger, D. W. (1983). An historical perspective of incest. *International Journal of Family Therapy, 5,* 70–80.

Simon, R. I. (1992). Treatment boundary violations: Clinical, ethical, and legal considerations. *Bulletin of the American Academy of Psychiatric Law, 20,* 269–288.

Simon, R. I., & Gutheil, T. (1997). Ethical and clinical risk management principles in recovered memory cases: Maintaining therapist neutrality. In Paul S. Applebaum, Lisa Uyehara, & Mark R. Elin (Eds.), *Trauma and Memory: Clinical and Legal Controversies.* (pp. 477–495). New York: Oxford Press.

Willis, C. (1987). Legal and ethical issues of touch in dance/movement therapy. *American Journal of Dance Therapy, 10,* 41–53.

Wilson, L. (1987). Confidentiality in art therapy: An ethical dilemma. *American Journal of Art Therapy, 25*(3) 75–80.

BIOGRAPHICAL STATEMENT

Kristen Larson, Ph.D., LPC is an Assistant Professor at Monmouth College, in Monmouth, Illinois, and a Licensed Clinical Psychologist. Her doctorate is in Counseling Psychology, and she has been teaching for ten years. In addition, she has been in clinical practice for ten years, and her research interests are in the area of ethical research and practice.

AUTHOR INDEX

A

Addison, D., 46, 56, 57
Agaibi, C. E., 3, 12
Allan, J., 125, 127, 128, 131, 134, 141, 147
Allen, F., 125, 134
Allers, C. T., 122, 132, 137
Ambra, L. N., 194
Ambridge, M., 238, 246
Ammen, S., 151, 157, 159, 160, 168
Anderson, H., 156
Andersen, S., 88, 92
Applebaum, P. S., 315, 318
Arieti, S., 252, 259
Ater, M. K., 124, 129, 132, 133, 13
Austin, D., 220, 221, 224, 232, 304, 309
Axline, V., 125, 127, 134

B

Bach, H., 87, 99
Backos, A., 251, 25
Bacho, R. A., 252, 260
Bagley, C., 128, 134
Bailey, S., 59–72
Baker Miller, J., 301, 303, 305, 308, 309
Balint, M., 108, 119
Bannister, A., 209, 213, 214, 216
Baratta, E., 304, 309
Barnes, M. M., 45, 57
Barrett, 236, 246
Bass, E., 65, 71
Baum, E. Z., 190, 194
Beech, R. R., 236, 248
Beezley, P., 122, 136
Bergevin, T. A., 236, 237, 246
Bergin, A. E., 280, 298, 299
Berger, J., 87, 99
Bergman, J., 239, 246
Berkliner, L., 123, 134, 139, 147
Berman, P., 33, 41

Bernstein, B., 194
Bethel, B. L., 138–148
Bettelheim, B., 254, 259
Bilodeau, L., 65, 71
Blatner, A., 285, 298
Blomkvist, L. D., 284
Bograd, M., 206
Bollerud, K., 89, 99
Bolkovatz, M. A., 129, 137
Bonde, L. O., 209, 216
Borkin, J., 34, 41
Bonny, H. L., 207, 215, 216
Booth, P. B., 123, 135, 158, 168
Boothby, N., 220, 232
Bosco, F., 225, 229, 230, 233
Bottoms, B., 121, 134
Bowers, J., 37, 41
Brems, C., 238, 246
Briere, J., 93, 99, 237, 238, 247, 251, 259
Briggs, F., 5, 12
Brinig, M. F., 315, 318
Briscoe, L. A., 236, 248
Brittain, W. L., 11, 14, 33, 42
Brooke, S. L., 3, 4, 5, 7, 9, 10, 11, 12, 15, 16,
   33, 41. 44, 45, 47, 57, 123, 134, 139,
   147, 198, 204, 237, 247, 316
Broughton, D., 123, 135
Brown, D., 24, 27, 28, 29
Browne, A., 124, 134, 171, 180
Brunnello, B., 28, 29
Bruscia, K. E., 208, 210, 212, 213, 214, 215,
   216, 318
Buckland, R., 36, 41
Buchwald, E., 250, 259
Bukowski, W. M., 236, 246
Bunt, L., 208, 212, 213, 214, 216
Burden, K., 284, 298
Burgess, E. J., 3, 5, 6, 10
Burgess, A. W., 4, 9, 11, 12, 13, 255, 259
Burns, R. C., 13
Burstow, B., 197, 204

321

F

Faller, K., 5, 13
Farrell-Kirk, R., 48, 57
Fedele, N. M., 198, 205
Finklehor, D., 32, 42, 122, 123, 124, 134, 171, 180, 198, 205, 237, 247, 318
Fisher, J., 123, 135
Fisler, R., 45, 58, 182, 194
Flores, P. J., 263, 278
Forrester, A. M., 239
Frank, L., 34, 41
Fraenkel, P., 236, 244, 248
Frawley, M. G., 242, 247
Freemon, M., 238, 246
Freud, A., 125, 134
Friedrich, W. N., 123, 135, 236, 237, 247
Froning, M. L., 237, 247
Fryrear, J. L., 86, 87, 95, 99, 100

G

Gallo-Lopcz, L., 121, 129, 135, 170–180, 235, 238, 239, 240, 243, 247
Gamble, S., 305
Gantt, L., 86, 99, 100, 312, 315, 318
Garfield, S. L., 280, 298, 299
Gardner, H., 11, 13
Garnefski, N., 237, 247
Garrett, C., 6, 13,
Gartner, R. B., 237, 238, 243, 247,
Gerald, L. I. A., 198, 205,
German, D., 7, 13
Gersie, A., 254, 259
Gfeller, K. E., 210, 216
Gil, E., 123, 128, 132, 133, 135, 139, 140, 141, 142, 147, 150, 168, 171, 180, 207, 208, 209, 210, 216, 244, 247
Ginott, H., 124, 127, 135
Giorgi, A.,151, 168
Glover, G., 140
Glover-Graf, N., 86–101
Gold, M., 253, 259
Gomez-Schwartz, B., 34, 42
Gonsalves, M. C., 218–234
Goodwin, J., 8, 13
Goolishian, M. A., 156
Gordy, P. L., 89, 90, 100
Green, A., 36, 42

Griffith, M., 134, 135
Grimshaw, D., 239, 247, 251, 252, 259
Guerncy B. G., 142, 147
Gunzberger, D. W., 315, 319
Gutheil, T., 312, 316, 319

H

Hackbarth, S. G., 7, 8, 11, 13
Hagood, M. M., 5, 6, 8, 13, 44, 45, 51, 57
Haen, C., 235–249
Haizlip, T., 34, 37, 42
Hall, P. E., 122, 123, 124, 128, 129, 130, 134, 135, 139, 140, 141, 142, 147, 242, 247
Hall-Marley, S. E., 122, 135
Hammer, E., 6, 13
Hammond, D. C., 24, 29
Hammond, L. C., 86, 99, 100, 312, 315, 318
Hammel-Zabin, A., 218, 222, 229, 233
Harrington, E. A., 198
Harrison, G. C. T., 196, 198, 200, 203, 205, 301–310
Hartman, C. R., 4, 5, 6, 10, 13, 255, 259
Harvey, S., 132, 135
Haugaard, J., 254, 259
Haverkamp, B. E., 312, 313, 315, 316, 318
Hazen, A., 210, 216
Hedges, R. E., 88, 91, 100
Heflin, A., 139, 147
Heirsteiner, C. L., 3, 5, 10, 13, 33, 41
Herman, J., 25, 28, 30, 44, 51, 57, 60, 65, 71, 89, 100, 302, 304, 305, 306, 309, 310
Hesse, E., 238, 247
Hewson, J., 301, 303, 307, 310
Hibbard, R. A., 5, 6, 13
Ho, G., 104, 119
Hogan, S., 45, 57, 100
Holmes, P., 284, 298
Holmes, W. C., 237, 247
Holmstrom, L. L., 6
Homeyer, L. E., 125, 126, 129, 130, 133, 135, 136, 140, 147
Horovitz, E., 8, 13
Hoskyns, S., 208, 212, 213, 214, 216
Houston, M., 123, 135
Howard, M. C., 5, 6, 13
Hoy, J. M., 281, 298

SUBJECT INDEX

A

Addiction,65-66, 280
Adolescence, 170–180, 251–258
AIDS, 87
Alcohol/Substance Use, 61–62, 81, 90, 261–278
American Counseling Association, 311
American Music Therapy Association, 311
American Psychiatric Association, 278
American Psychological Association, APA, 224, 263, 311
Anger, 22, 35, 65, 78, 83, 89, 90, 93, 122, 132, 139, 143, 144–145, 150, 178, 187, 219, 228, 235, 254, 257, 258, 265, 268
Anxiety, 19, 48, 49, 90, 110, 122, 123, 129, 131, 140, 142, 143, 165, 175, 186, 191, 253
Anorexia/Eating Disorders, 49, 90, 96, 280
Arpeggiated pattern, 232
Art Therapy, 3–120
Association for Play Therapy, 311
Attachment theory, 283

B

Boys/Males, 6, 235–249
Boundaries, 304,
Broca's area, 60

C

Center, 193
Chronic affect dyregulation, 232
Clay, 37
Cognitive Behavior Therapy (CBT) 239, 246, 283–284
Collage, 49, 179, 212, 286
Competence, 312, 317
Composition, 212, 215
Concrete Operational Stage, 216

Concretization, 297
Confidentiality, 313–314, 317
Conflict resolution, 17–30
Counter-transference, 305, 309, 317

D

Dance/movement therapy, 180–195
Defense mechanism, 258
Denial, 258
Dissociation, 63, 132, 259, 285
Dissociative Identity Disorder, DID, 296
Divorce, 73–85
Domestic violence, 203–204
Drama therapy, 63, 66, 172, 235–279

E

Ecosystemic Play Therapy, 150–168
Embodying, 193
Ethics, 94, 98–99, 311–319

F

Family, 116
Feminist theory, 44–58, 199–202
Five phase model, 273
Flashbacks, 50, 52, 53, 55, 184, 192, 285
Flow, 274

G

Graphic Indicators, 4–11, 32
Group therapy, 210–212, 261–278, 289
Grounding, 193
Guilt, 18, 93, 145, 171, 208

H

Hyperarousal, 193

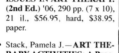
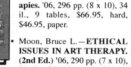
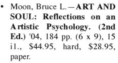
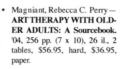
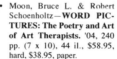
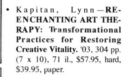
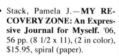
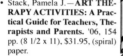
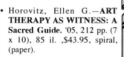
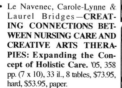

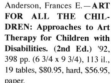